GONZO

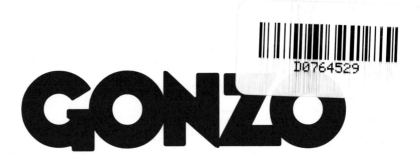

GONZO

A Graphic Biography of Hunter S. Thompson

BY WILL BINGLEY & ANTHONY HOPE-SMITH
FOREWORD BY ALAN RINZLER

Abrams ComicArts
New York

Written by: Will Bingley
Illustrated by: Anthony Hope-Smith
Original Cover Design: Anthony Hope-Smith and Andy Huckle
Cover Design, U.S. Edition: Neil Egan
Page Layout and Lettering by: Andy Huckle
Editorial Assistant: Lizzie Kaye
Marketing Director, SelfMadeHero: Doug Wallace
Publishing Director, SelfMadeHero: Emma Hayley
With thanks to: Casy Barrett, Jane Laporte, and Nick de Somogyi

Cataloging-in-Publication Data has been applied for and may be obtained from the Library of Congress.

ISBN: 978-1-4197-0242-6

Originally published in 2010 by SelfMadeHero, London, U.K.

Printed and bound in China
10 9 8 7 6 5 4 3 2 1

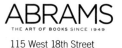

ABRAMS
THE ART OF BOOKS SINCE 1949
115 West 18th Street
New York, NY 10011
www.abramsbooks.com

Why isn't Hunter S. Thompson taken more seriously? As his editor and literary goad for 35 years over four of his best books, I'm sorry to see that the public spectacle of Hunter as the King of Gonzo – a brain-addled, angry, deeply depressed, self-destructive lout – has prevailed in the popular consciousness while the real story of this ground-breaking prose artist and investigative journalist has all but disappeared.

If you've only been aware of Hunter as Uncle Duke, the cartoon character in the Doonesbury comic strip; if you've seen him in person or on a video throwing up and falling down drunk during an alleged public lecture (for a high fee); or read his puerile middle-age fantasies about working in a porno film studio or any of the repetitious, mediocre, regurgitated articles and books and collections he allowed to be issued and reissued over the last 30 years of his life, or bought the largely inaccurate and pandering biographies written since his tragic suicide, you'd never know Hunter in his prime had been in fact a very serious, hard-working writer who cared deeply about every carefully chosen word, labouring over each sentence and its content, the layers of meaning, the rhythm, the inimitable voice, the humour and ferocious impact.

Hunter could have been the heavyweight champion of American letters. In the words of Marlon Brando as Terry Malloy in Budd Schulberg's script for the film *On the Waterfront*: "I coulda had class. I coulda been a contender. I coulda been somebody, instead of a bum, which is what I am, let's face it." That's a harsh judgement but Hunter heard it about himself frequently, and probably agreed.

Hunter was an alcoholic, drug-gobbling addict all his life, in the tradition of his idols F. Scott Fitzgerald and Ernest Hemingway. Hunter told me that during his starving and rejected writer period (which lasted more than ten years, by the way) he had typed out the entire *Great Gatsby* by F. Scott Fitzgerald. "I wanted to get the feel of what it was like to actually write like that, the mechanical effort, the choice of words, the voice and rhythm of being a genius at work." Those two, however, somehow managed to produce a lot more good books, despite their self-destructive habits.

A year before his death, he phoned me in the middle of the night and said "Rinzler, you Jewish swine. Come to Owl Farm and help me write this damn piece of shit I owe Simon & Schuster. I need the rest of their advance and what I've done so far is awful crap. We lashed together those other books, you're a credit to your race, and I need you now…" (Hunter liked to sound anti-Semitic with me, since he knew it pushed my buttons.) A week later, he sent me the manuscript, a lame incoherent recitation of all his old stories about growing up in Louisville, Kentucky. But he shot himself in the head before we could do any work on it. Nevertheless, Simon & Schuster published the same manuscript he'd sent me, unchanged, with the title *Kingdom of Fear*, and it was on the *New York Times* best-seller list for weeks, an embarrassing testament to his loyal readers.

Hunter and I weren't big buddies. We never hung out socially for fun, or reminisced about our war stories we'd experienced together in our joint past, like a

12-step meeting. I was his editor. We had a strictly professional relationship. I usually wore a tie when we'd work together head to head. I tried to remain calm and sober at all times and largely, though not completely, succeeded.

Hunter hated editors and was the most difficult writer I ever worked with. He avoided me at first, threatened me with physical harm, insulted my personality and ethnicity, and generally gave me a terrible time. Nevertheless, I gradually persisted in breaking into his motel rooms, invading his home for weeks at a time, and hammering out a successful working relationship.

In order to make the deadline for *Fear and Loathing on the Campaign Trail,* for example, we set up an old Nagra reel-to-reel tape recorder in his room at the Seal Rock Inn, and I'd pepper him with questions, which he'd answer profusely. Then we'd have it transcribed, edit me out, and polish up the remaining text for the book itself. It took three days and nights but turned out pretty well in my opinion. After that we did *Amerika,* *The Great Shark Hunt,* and *The Curse of Lono* using better hardware, smaller machines, ending up in 1981 with a tiny hand-held table-top micro-recorder.

Following up on these projects we had many late-night phone conversations that were also recorded. Hunter was always loaded, of course, but still fairly creative and funny as we brainstormed new books. *Gutsball* and *The Man with the Blue Arm* were two of our favourite titles, parts of which made their way into *The Curse of Lono.*

Lono was the last good thing we worked on together. It took several visits to Owl Farm where we spent days in his kitchen ranting and taping. Things weren't going smoothly by that point. Hunter's substance abuse, writer's block and brief attention span were increasing exponentially. He'd slip out to see his dealer and come back so tanked he couldn't think straight. Ultimately I had to wait for him to pass out, then gathered up all the tapes and scribbled notes on scraps of paper he'd left all over the house. I tiptoed out and took them on the plane back to New York where I tried to iron out a final manuscript to meet Bantam Book's deadline. *Lono* wound up a bit scattershot but had some of his greatest writing in it, plus Ralph Steadman's fabulous art. A lavish, large-format colour edition that really does it credit was published by Taschen 30 years later.

Two Hollywood feature films have been made from Hunter's work, both of which inflate the myth and greatly distort the reality. The first, *Where the Buffalo Roam*, features a dead-on impersonation of Hunter by Bill Murray. It was originally based solely on the *Banshee Screams for Buffalo Meat*, an obituary Hunter wrote in *Rolling Stone* for Oscar Acosta, his real-life sidekick during the Las Vegas caper, and co-starred Peter Boyle, notably non-Hispanic, playing Oscar. Later, Johnny Depp starred as Hunter in a far more lavish production with the great Puerto Rican actor Benicio de Toro, as Oscar. Based entirely on *Fear and Loathing in Las Vegas*, this film was a flop artistically and financially. Depp, moreover, became so immersed in his role that he began to live with Hunter and shepherd him around the country to promote the film. Depp recently announced that he intended to film *The Curse of Lono* as well, and who knows, with his star power, he might pull it off.

In any case, it's sad and ironical that Hunter's tremendous power as a writer and journalist has been largely forgotten and what primarily remains is the adolescent Gonzo mythology. Yes, Hunter was a nasty, selfish, obsessive drug and alcohol addict who behaved horridly in private and public, but he was also a highly sensitive, acutely intelligent observer and critic of society, government, politics and journalism. Not only that, he could be very charming in a kind and courtly southern way.

Oscar Acosta deeply resented Hunter's fame and felt that his friend had betrayed him by stealing his style and language for his version of their Las Vegas trip together. Subsequently I published two of Oscar's books on *Rolling Stone*'s Straight Arrow Books list. The first was *The Autobiography of a Brown Buffalo* and very well written. The second was about Oscar's run for mayor of Los Angeles (he got 60,000 votes, not bad) but had to be largely ghost written since by that time Oscar had succumbed to a nasty cocaine habit and become progressively incoherent. Oscar is still a famous Chicano hero, and the subject of classes in Hispanic studies, but the truth is he couldn't speak Spanish and grew up with a mother who sought safety in assimilation.

Oscar was a complex and troubled guy, a practising attorney who died tragically during a drug deal gone sour off the coast of Yelapa, south of Puerto

Vallarta. I was with Hunter at Owl Farm when he got the phone call from a private detective in Mexico he'd hired to find out what had happened. "Shot and thrown off the boat..." he told me, hanging up.

Meanwhile, I can't escape Hunter. After he died there were several memorial services here in San Francisco and also a *Rolling Stone* employees reunion for those still alive from the early years. (Hunter wasn't the only one to die prematurely.) I've chewed over all of my contradictory and ambivalent feelings *ad nauseam*. But even now, whenever I speak at a writers' conference or blog on my website, I get dozens of emails asking, "What was it like to work with Hunter Thompson? Was he really so wild and crazy? Were you ever straight? Can you remember it?"

As an editor, moreover, I've had so many terrible imitations and derivative memoir, fiction and nonfiction submitted to me for publication by young men who are trying to be "gonzo". Most of them seem to think it's easy, that writing gonzo is a licence to knock off any silly, intoxicated, first draft prose. Awful stuff arrives daily, no kidding.

I've gone back and forth about Hunter in the five years since his death, from disappointment and sorrow to resentment and anger. "Damn, Hunter, why couldn't you have straightened out and been more productive? You were so good!" But who am I or anyone else to say what he should have done? That was him. His life. I hope this is my last word on the subject, but doubt it, since I'm still getting over it.

I believe Hunter will be remembered by those who appreciate his work as well as those who know him now only as the Gonzo myth. The reason is that his art and persona both represent the essence of a young man's iconoclastic humour and rebellious inner rage against the perception of adult authority. Like J. D. Salinger's Holden Caulfield, Hunter was the romantic, self-aggrandizing bad boy in so many guys, especially those who are just turning 14 and reading for the first time:

"We were somewhere around Barstow, on the edge of the desert, when the drugs began to take hold. I remember saying something like 'I feel a bit lightheaded; maybe you should drive…' And suddenly there was a terrible roar all around us and the sky was full of what looked like huge bats, all swooping and screeching and diving around the car, which was going about a hundred miles an hour… And a voice was screaming: 'Holy Jesus! What are these goddamn animals?' "

– *Alan Rinzler*

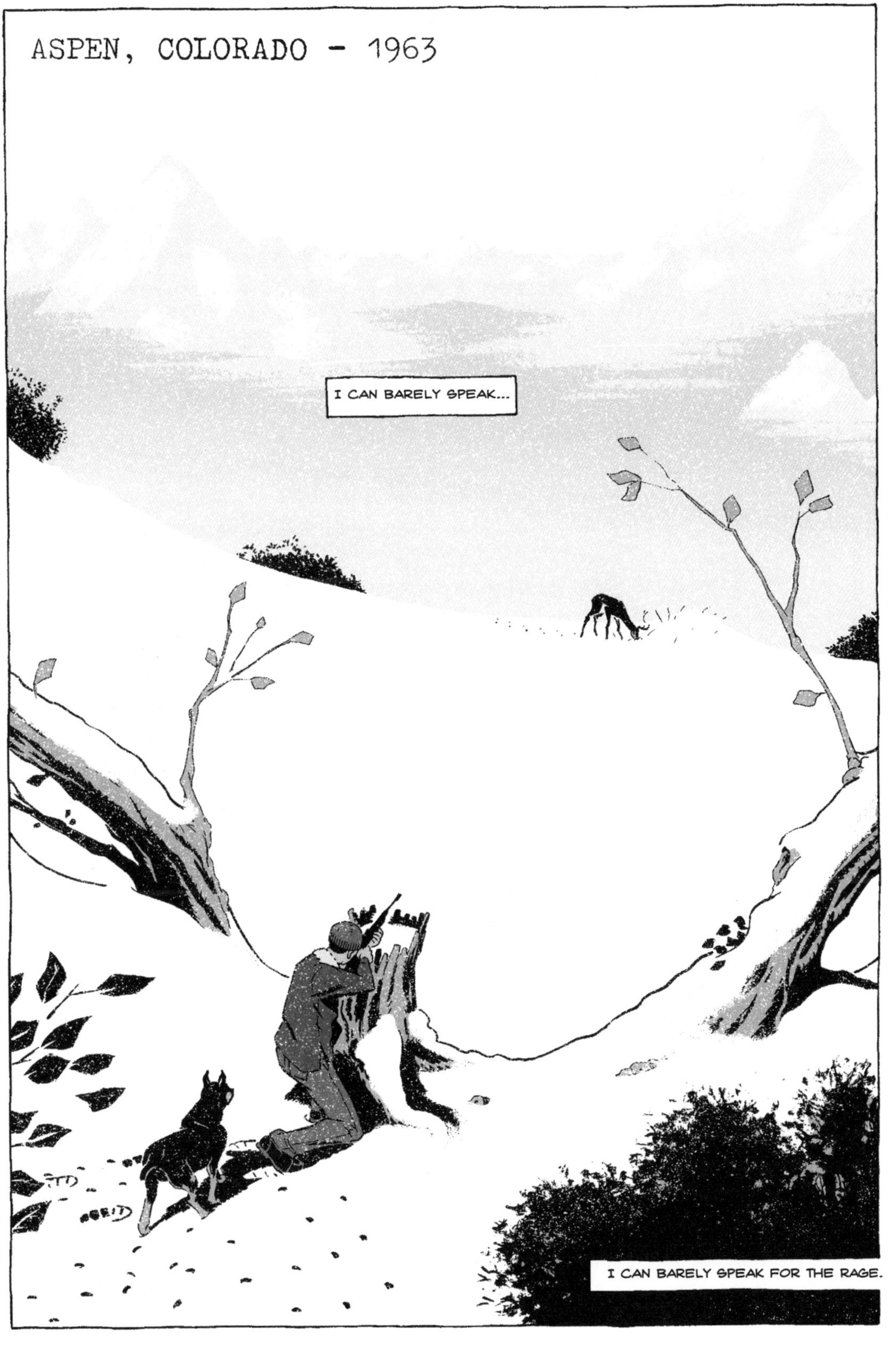
ASPEN, COLORADO - 1963
I CAN BARELY SPEAK...
I CAN BARELY SPEAK FOR THE RAGE.

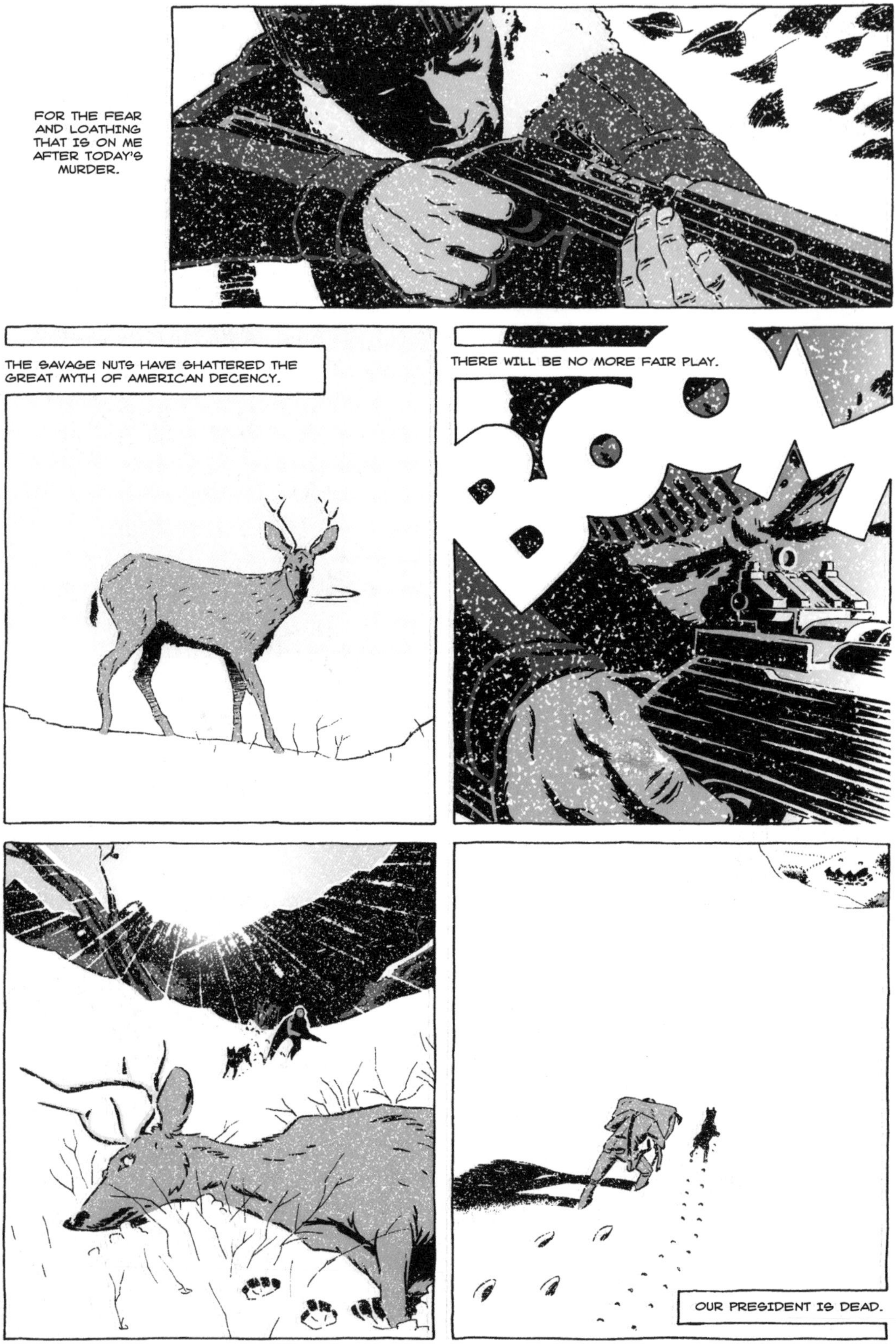
FOR THE FEAR AND LOATHING THAT IS ON ME AFTER TODAY'S MURDER.
THE SAVAGE NUTS HAVE SHATTERED THE GREAT MYTH OF AMERICAN DECENCY.
THERE WILL BE NO MORE FAIR PLAY.
OUR PRESIDENT IS DEAD.

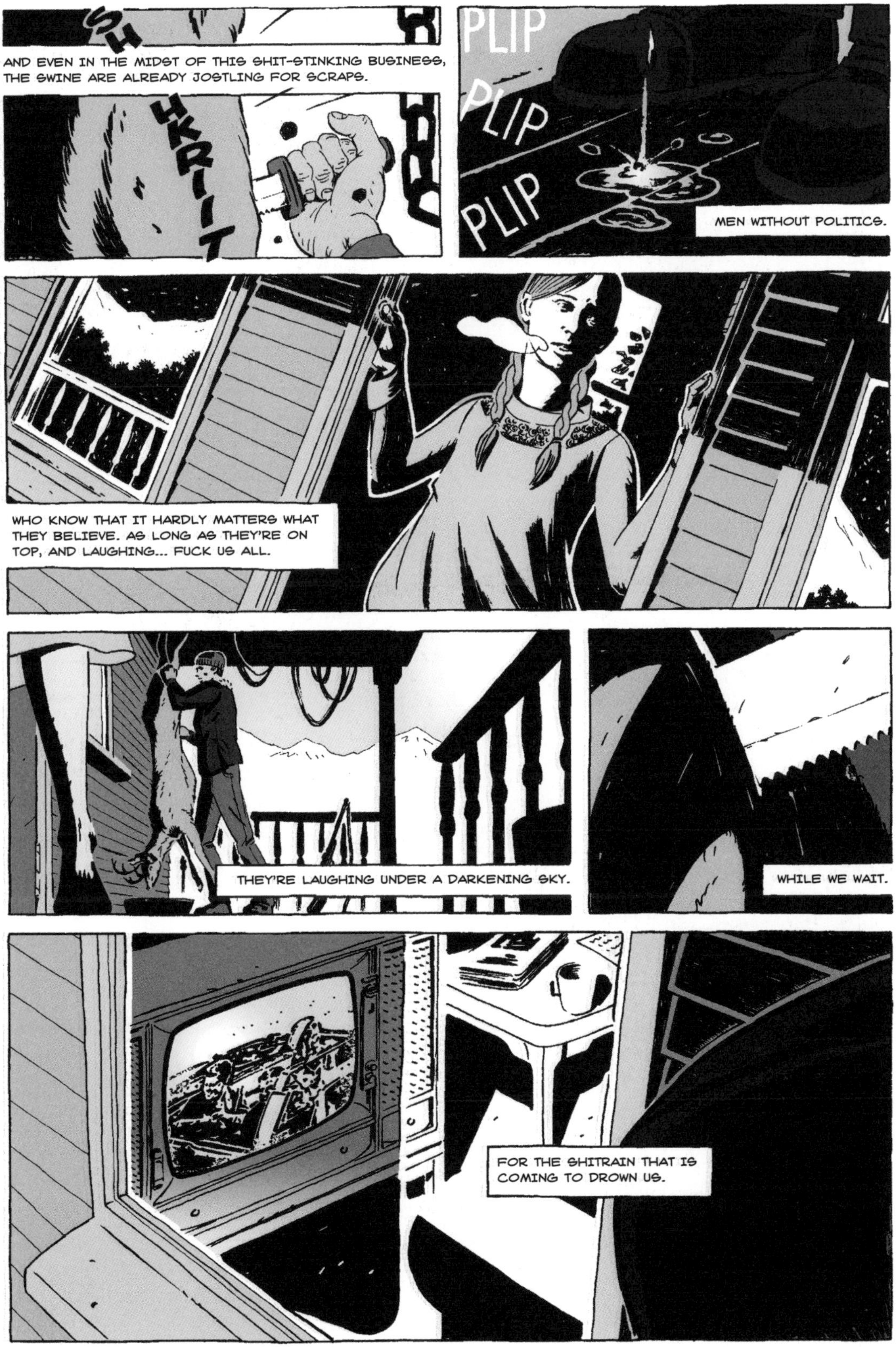
SH
AND EVEN IN THE MIDST OF THIS SHIT-STINKING BUSINESS, THE SWINE ARE ALREADY JOSTLING FOR SCRAPS.
UKRIIT
PLIP
PLIP
PLIP
MEN WITHOUT POLITICS.
WHO KNOW THAT IT HARDLY MATTERS WHAT THEY BELIEVE. AS LONG AS THEY'RE ON TOP, AND LAUGHING... FUCK US ALL.
THEY'RE LAUGHING UNDER A DARKENING SKY.
WHILE WE WAIT.
FOR THE SHITRAIN THAT IS COMING TO DROWN US.

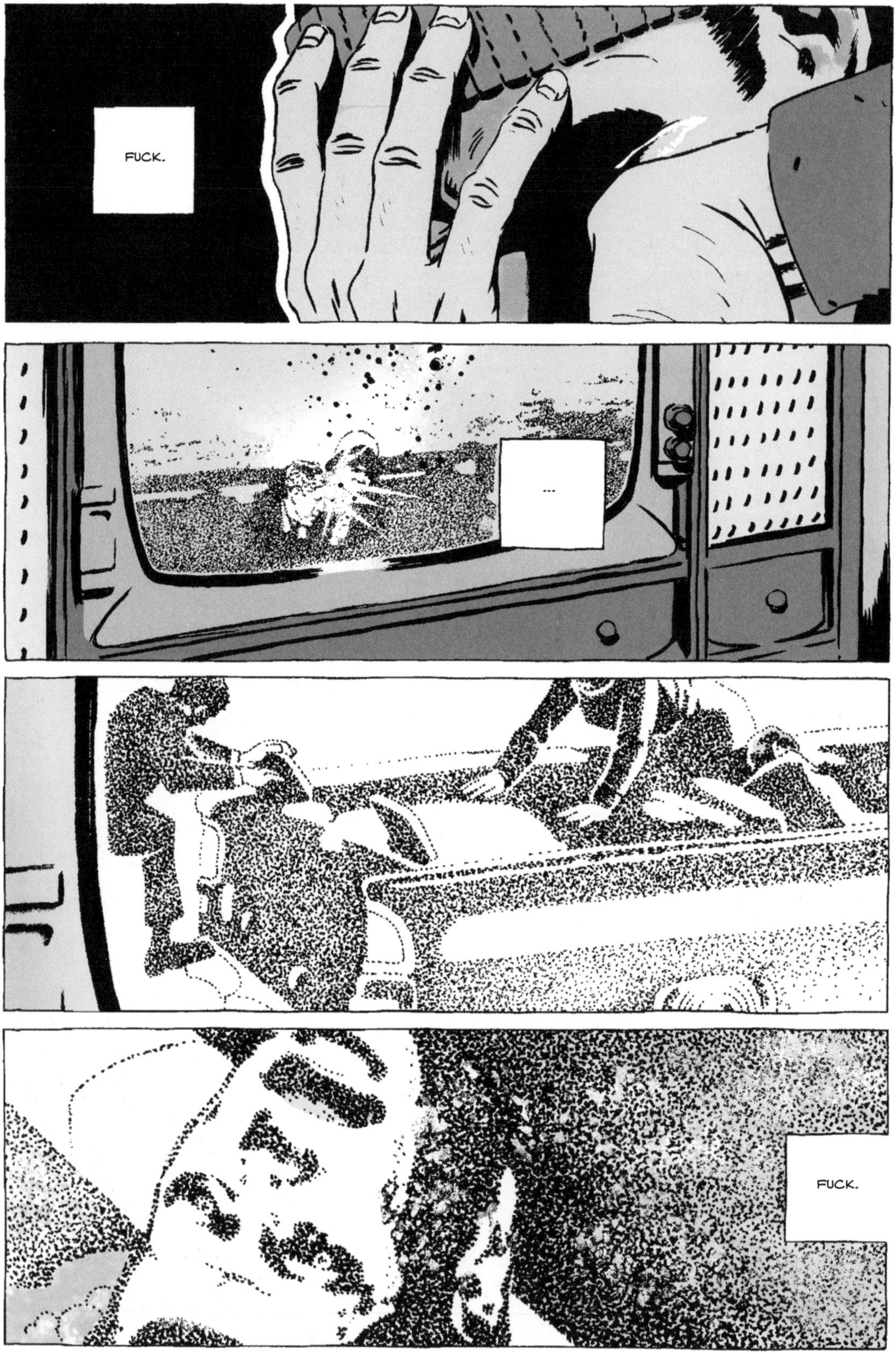
FUCK.
...
FUCK.

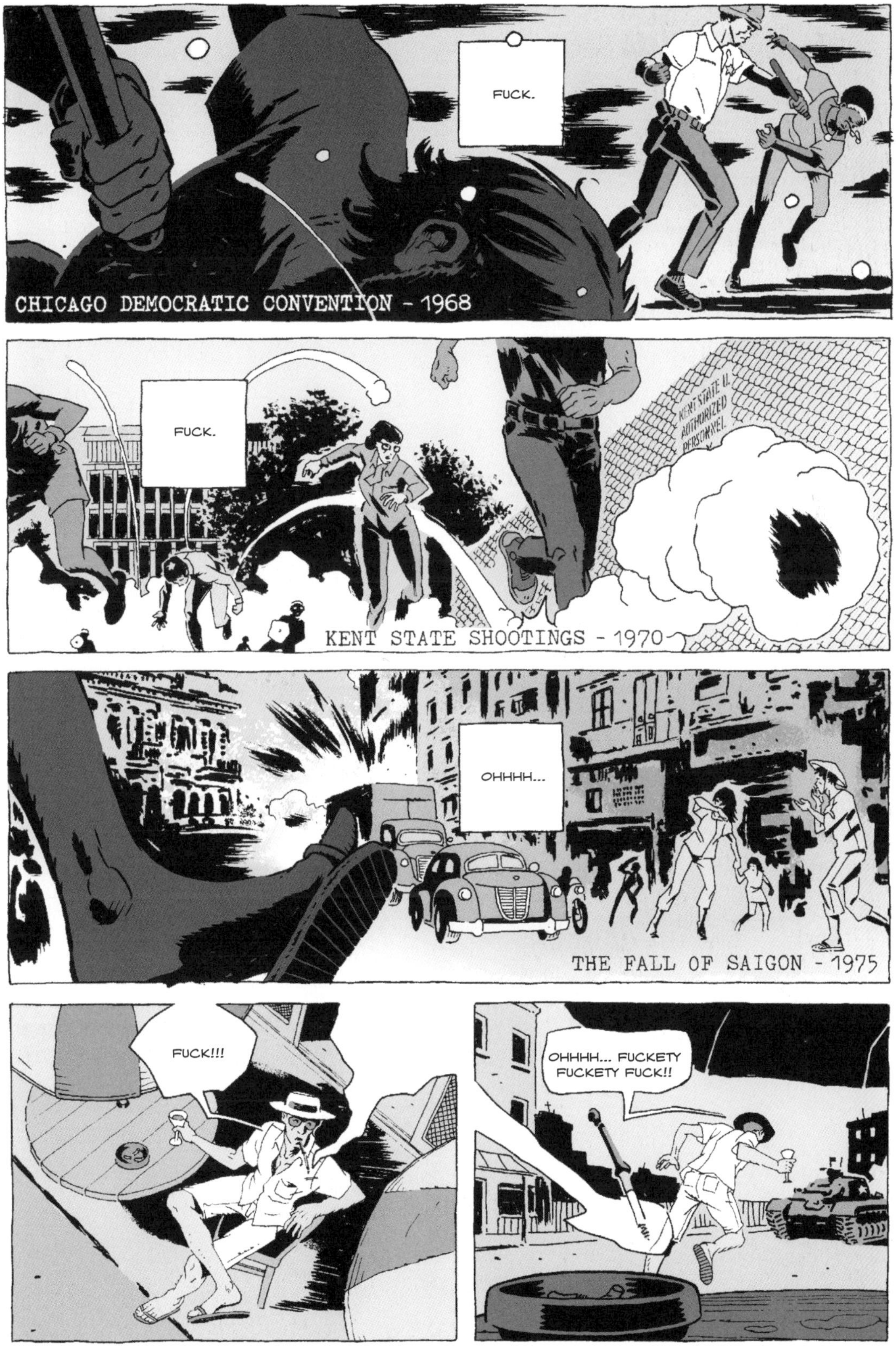
FUCK.
CHICAGO DEMOCRATIC CONVENTION - 1968
FUCK.
KENT STATE U.
AUTHORIZED
KENT STATE SHOOTINGS - 1970
OHHHH...
THE FALL OF SAIGON - 1975
FUCK!!!
OHHHH... FUCKETY FUCKETY FUCK!!

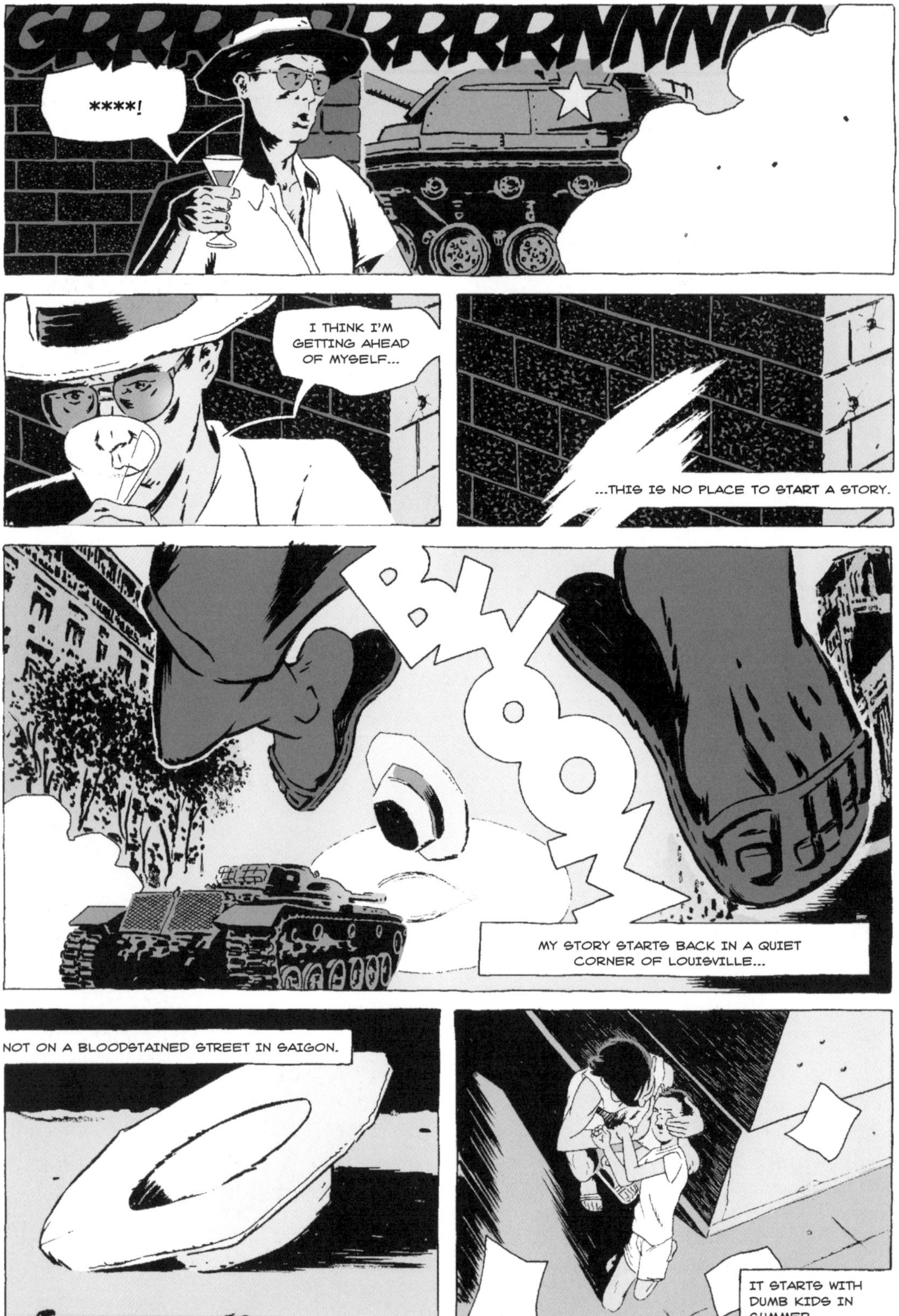
GRRRRRRRRRRRRNNNN
****!
I THINK I'M GETTING AHEAD OF MYSELF...
...THIS IS NO PLACE TO START A STORY.
MY STORY STARTS BACK IN A QUIET CORNER OF LOUISVILLE...
NOT ON A BLOODSTAINED STREET IN SAIGON.
IT STARTS WITH DUMB KIDS IN SUMMER.

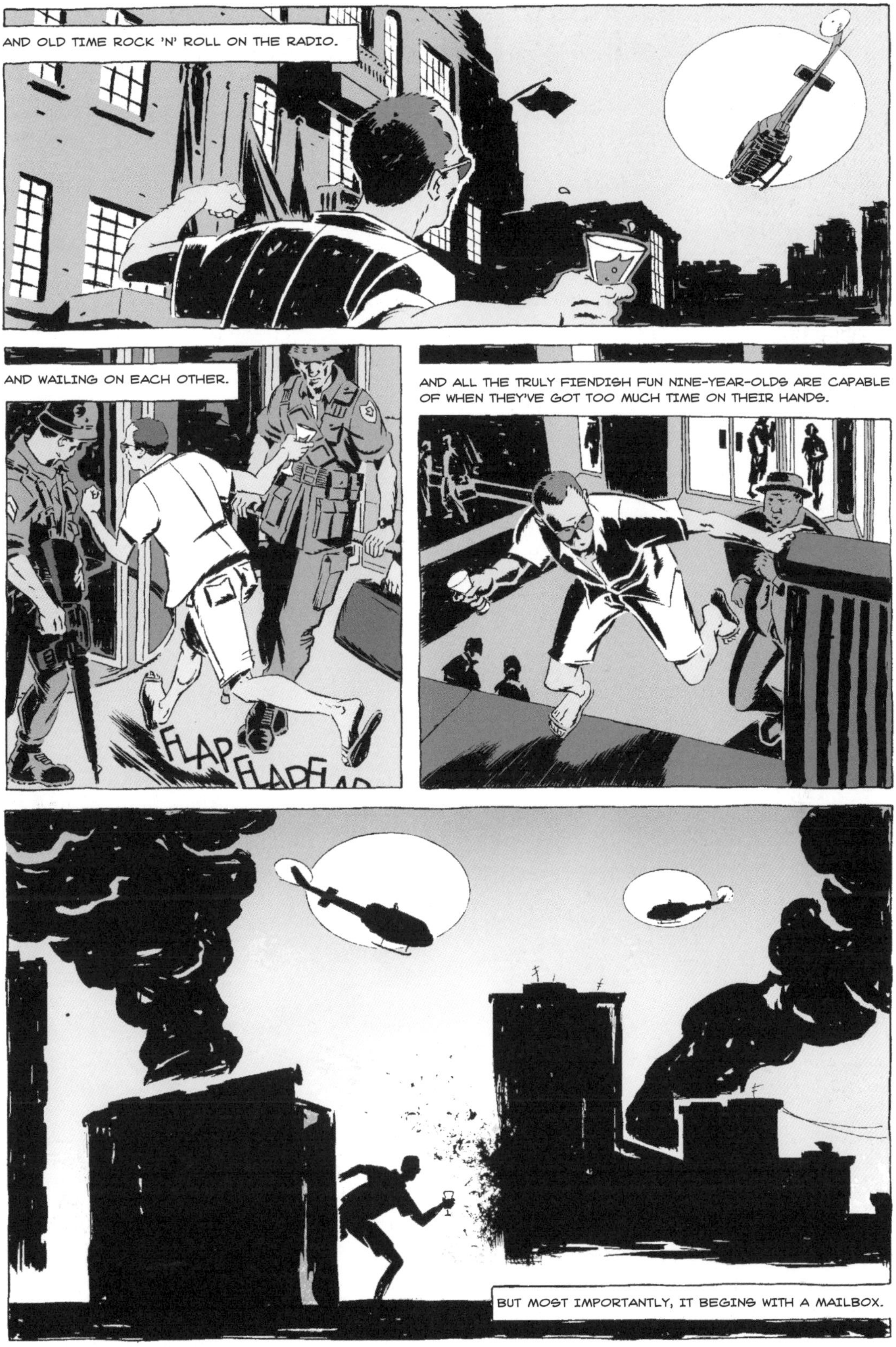
AND OLD TIME ROCK 'N' ROLL ON THE RADIO.
AND WAILING ON EACH OTHER.
FLAP
AND ALL THE TRULY FIENDISH FUN NINE-YEAR-OLDS ARE CAPABLE OF WHEN THEY'VE GOT TOO MUCH TIME ON THEIR HANDS.
BUT MOST IMPORTANTLY, IT BEGINS WITH A MAILBOX.

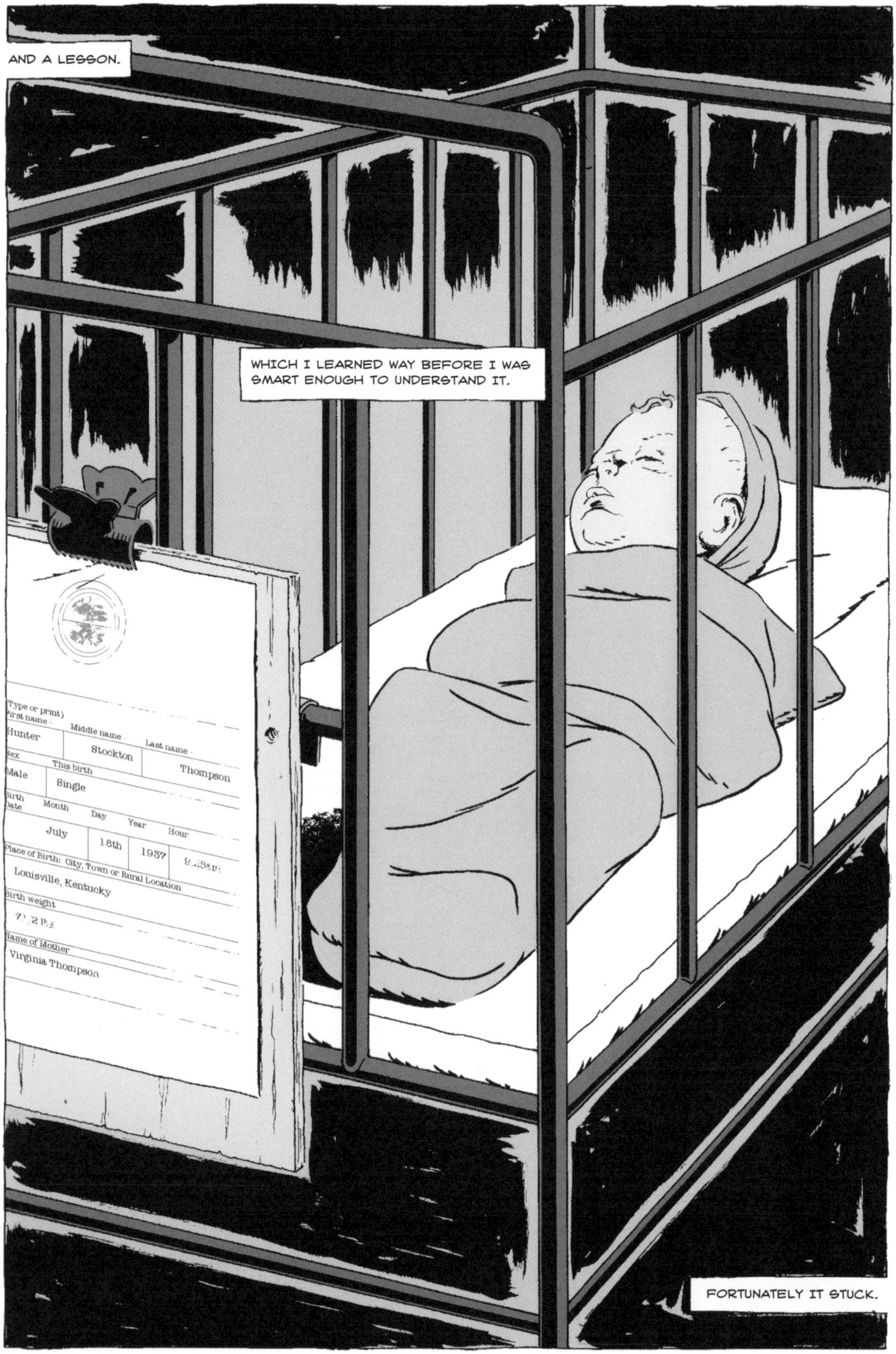
AND A LESSON.
WHICH I LEARNED WAY BEFORE I WAS SMART ENOUGH TO UNDERSTAND IT.
(Type or print)
First name
Middle name
Last name
Hunter
Stockton
Thompson
Sex
This birth
Male
Single
Birth Date
Month
Day
Year
Hour
July
18th
1937
Place of Birth: City, Town or Rural Location
Louisville, Kentucky
Birth weight
Name of Mother
Virginia Thompson
FORTUNATELY IT STUCK.

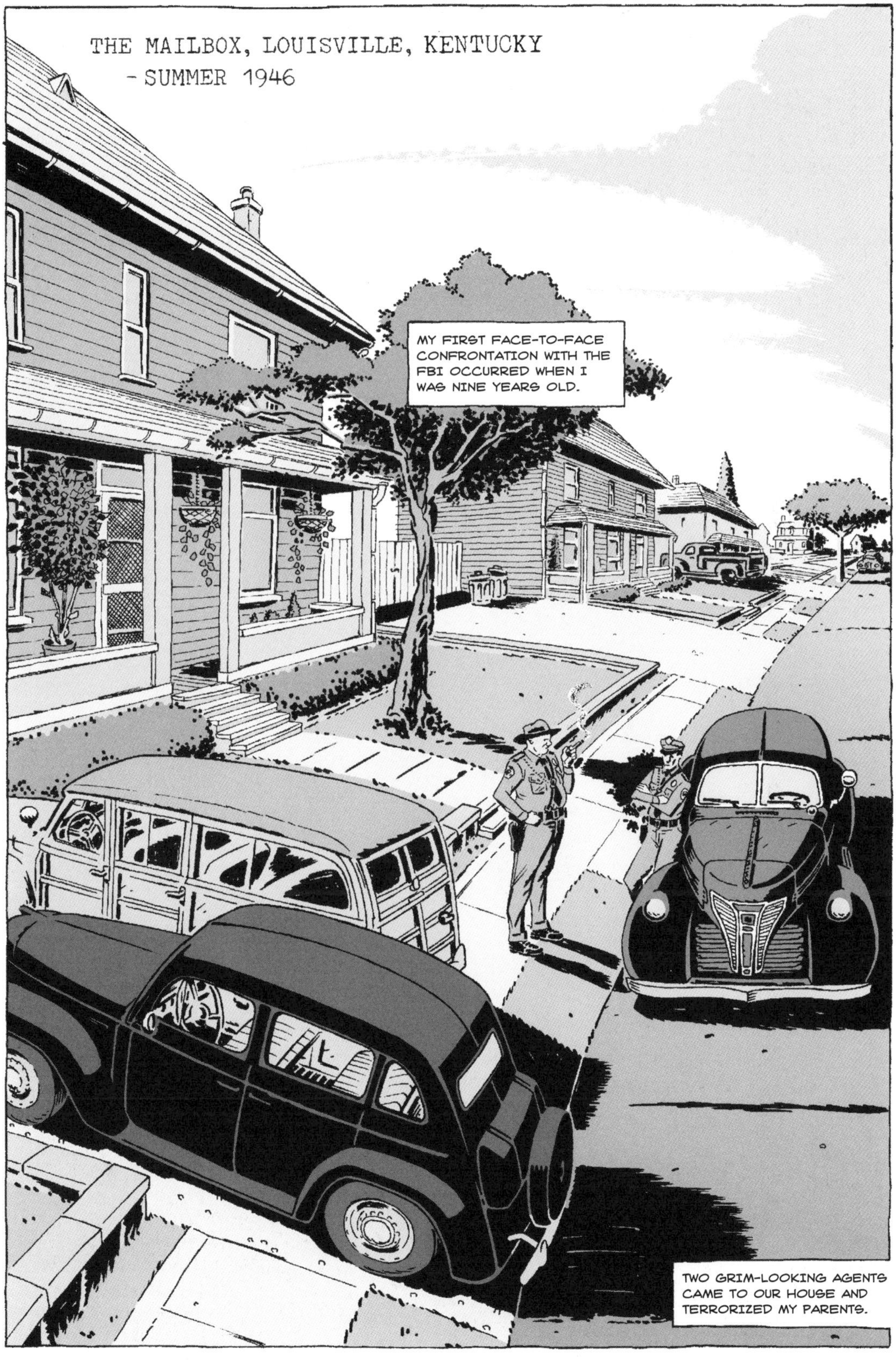
THE MAILBOX, LOUISVILLE, KENTUCKY
- SUMMER 1946
MY FIRST FACE-TO-FACE CONFRONTATION WITH THE FBI OCCURRED WHEN I WAS NINE YEARS OLD.
TWO GRIM-LOOKING AGENTS CAME TO OUR HOUSE AND TERRORIZED MY PARENTS.

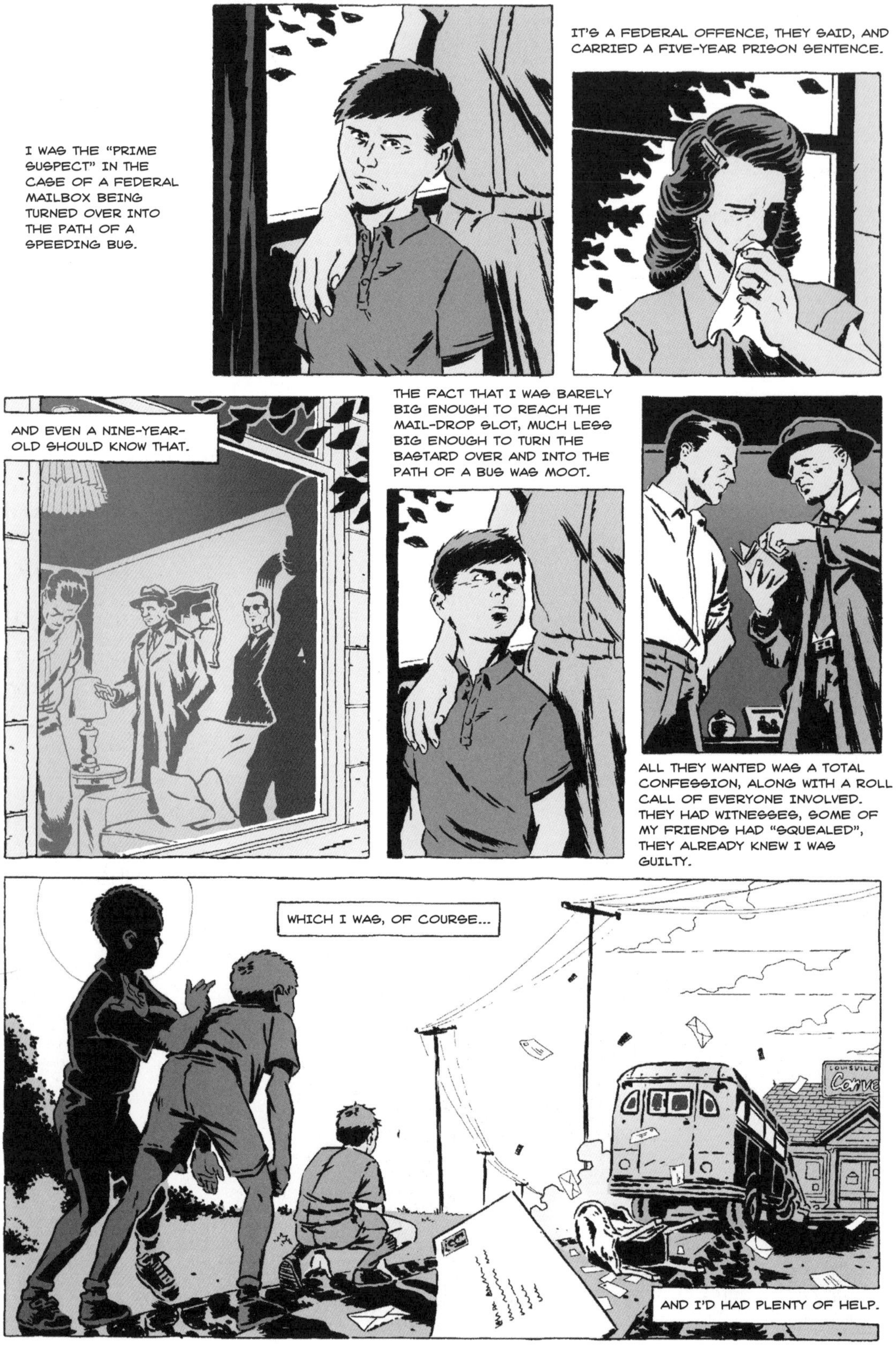
I WAS THE "PRIME SUSPECT" IN THE CASE OF A FEDERAL MAILBOX BEING TURNED OVER INTO THE PATH OF A SPEEDING BUS.
IT'S A FEDERAL OFFENCE, THEY SAID, AND CARRIED A FIVE-YEAR PRISON SENTENCE.
AND EVEN A NINE-YEAR-OLD SHOULD KNOW THAT.
THE FACT THAT I WAS BARELY BIG ENOUGH TO REACH THE MAIL-DROP SLOT, MUCH LESS BIG ENOUGH TO TURN THE BASTARD OVER AND INTO THE PATH OF A BUS WAS MOOT.
ALL THEY WANTED WAS A TOTAL CONFESSION, ALONG WITH A ROLL CALL OF EVERYONE INVOLVED. THEY HAD WITNESSES, SOME OF MY FRIENDS HAD "SQUEALED", THEY ALREADY KNEW I WAS GUILTY.
WHICH I WAS, OF COURSE...
AND I'D HAD PLENTY OF HELP.

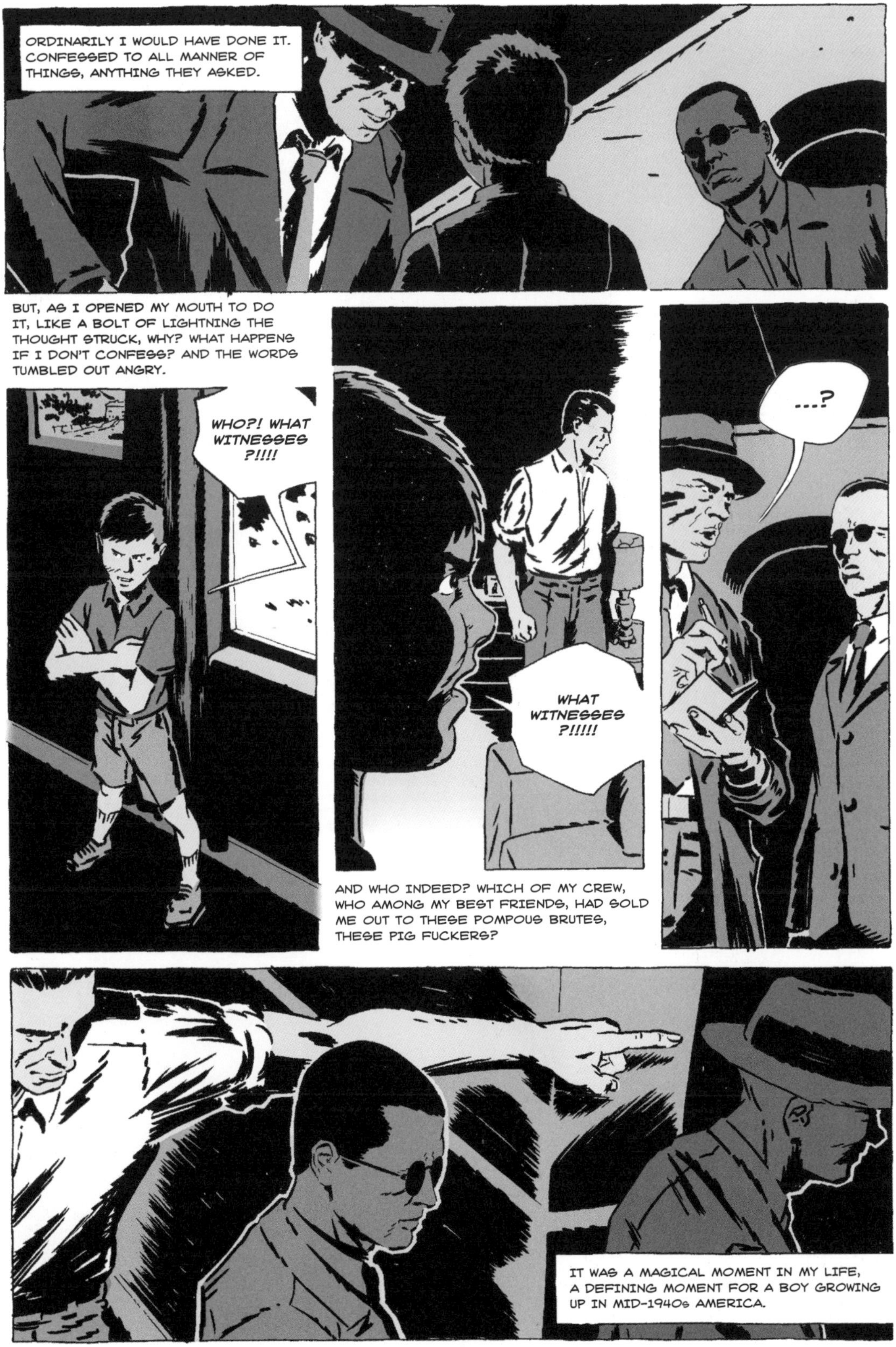
ORDINARILY I WOULD HAVE DONE IT. CONFESSED TO ALL MANNER OF THINGS, ANYTHING THEY ASKED.
BUT, AS I OPENED MY MOUTH TO DO IT, LIKE A BOLT OF LIGHTNING THE THOUGHT STRUCK, WHY? WHAT HAPPENS IF I DON'T CONFESS? AND THE WORDS TUMBLED OUT ANGRY.
WHO?! WHAT WITNESSES ?!!!!
WHAT WITNESSES ?!!!!!
...?
AND WHO INDEED? WHICH OF MY CREW, WHO AMONG MY BEST FRIENDS, HAD SOLD ME OUT TO THESE POMPOUS BRUTES, THESE PIG FUCKERS?
IT WAS A MAGICAL MOMENT IN MY LIFE, A DEFINING MOMENT FOR A BOY GROWING UP IN MID-1940s AMERICA.

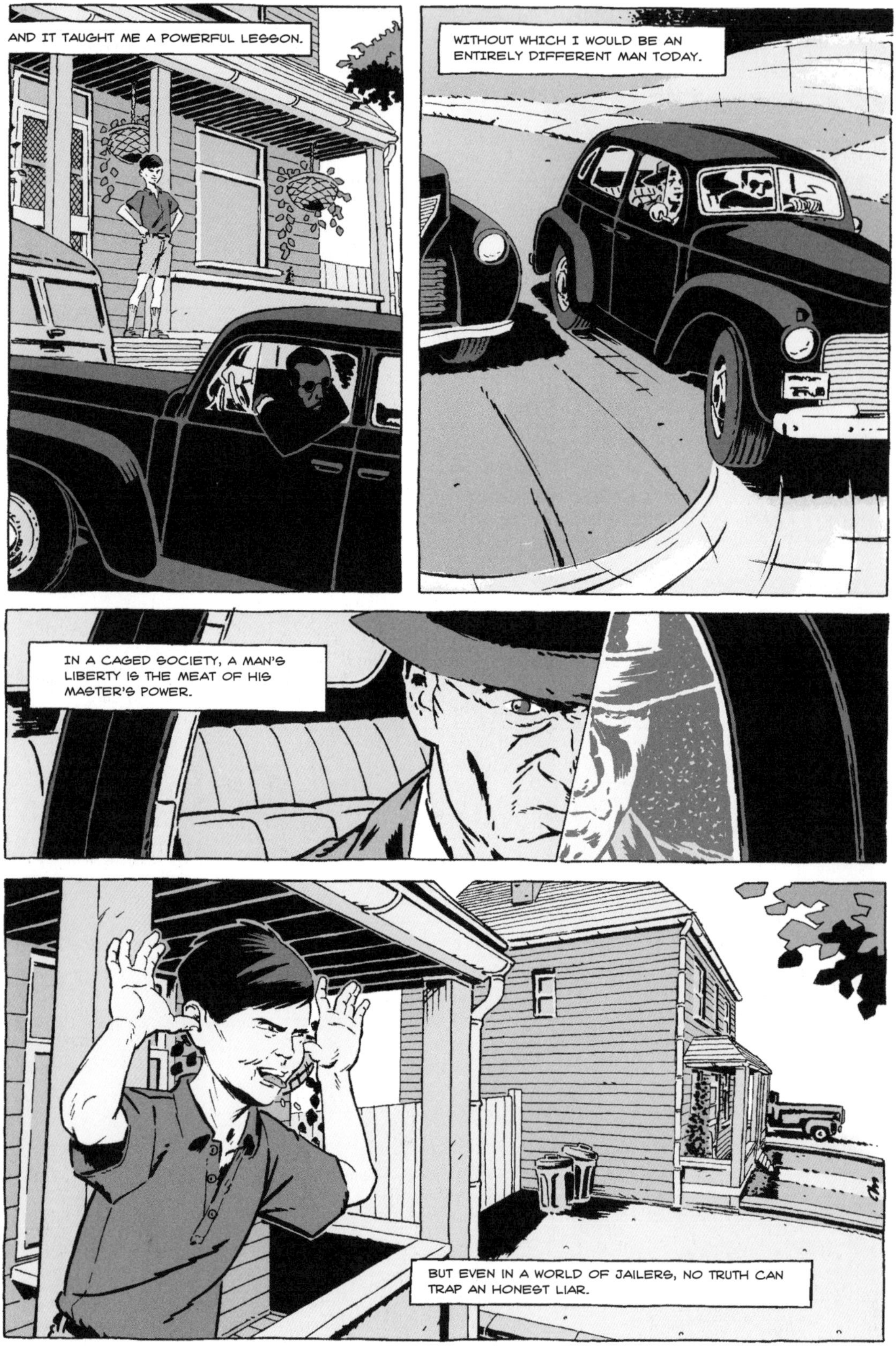
AND IT TAUGHT ME A POWERFUL LESSON.
WITHOUT WHICH I WOULD BE AN ENTIRELY DIFFERENT MAN TODAY.
IN A CAGED SOCIETY, A MAN'S LIBERTY IS THE MEAT OF HIS MASTER'S POWER.
BUT EVEN IN A WORLD OF JAILERS, NO TRUTH CAN TRAP AN HONEST LIAR.

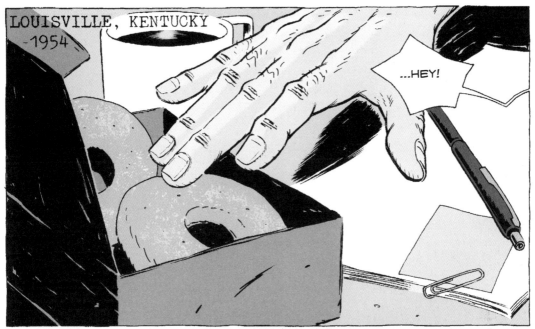

LOUISVILLE, KENTUCKY
-1954

...HEY!

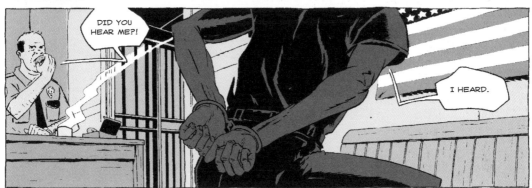

DID YOU HEAR ME?!

I HEARD.

TIME TO GO, KID.

I'M COMIN', BUBBA.

SAY THAT AGAIN BOY...

DO I LOOK... DO I LOOK THAT STUPID?

WELL...

NOW I PROBABLY DO.

MOST OF US WOULD IN THIS SITUATION.

I CAUGHT A BEATING ON MY FIRST NIGHT IN JAIL.

. THE FACT THAT I DESERVED IT DIDN'T HELP ANY.

THIS IS WHAT I WAS DOING THE NIGHT I GRADUATED FROM HIGH SCHOOL.

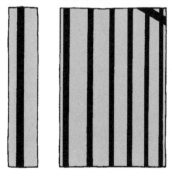

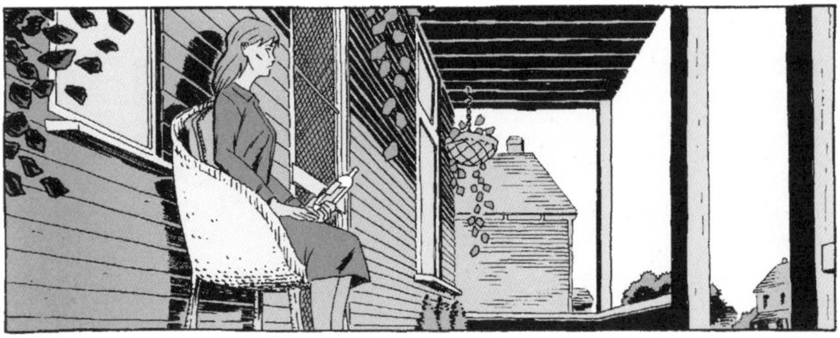

AND THIS
IS WHAT MY
MOTHER DID.

WELL I'D IMAGINE THAT'S WHAT SHE WAS DOING.

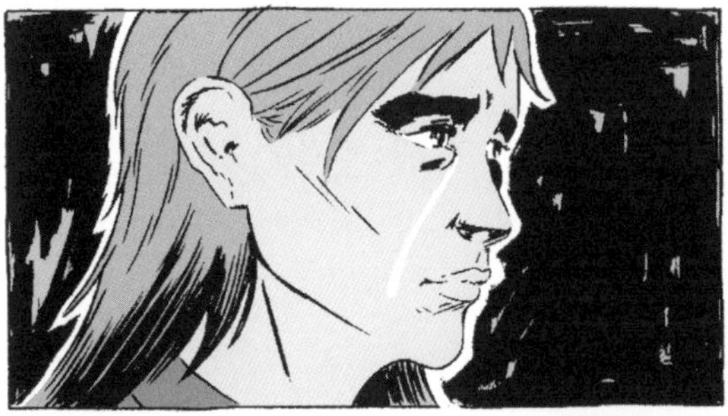

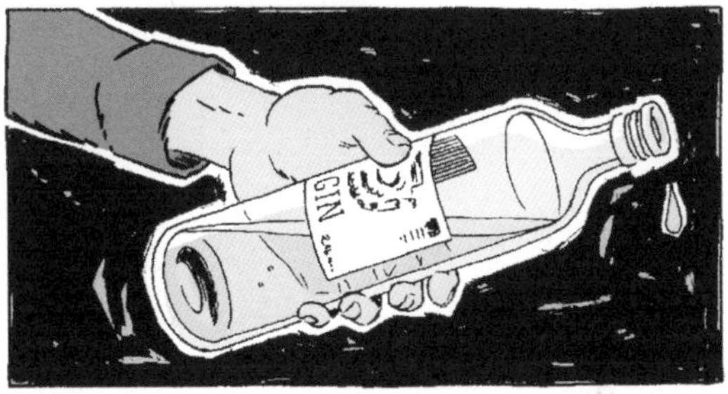
GIN

MY FATHER DIED TWO WEEKS BEFORE
MY FIFTEENTH BIRTHDAY.

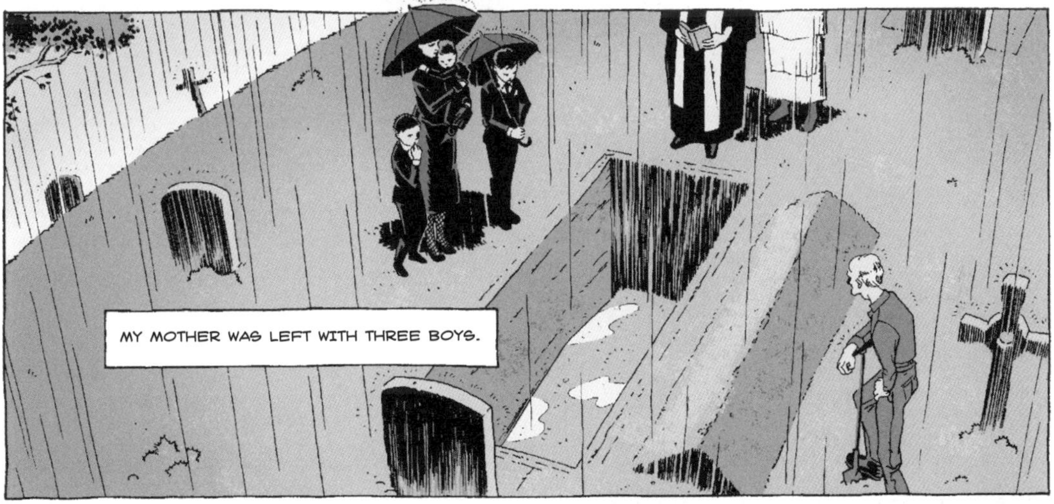
MY MOTHER WAS LEFT WITH THREE BOYS.

I CANNOT IMAGINE HER LONELINESS, NOR THE DIFFICULTIES
SHE MUST HAVE FACED DAILY.

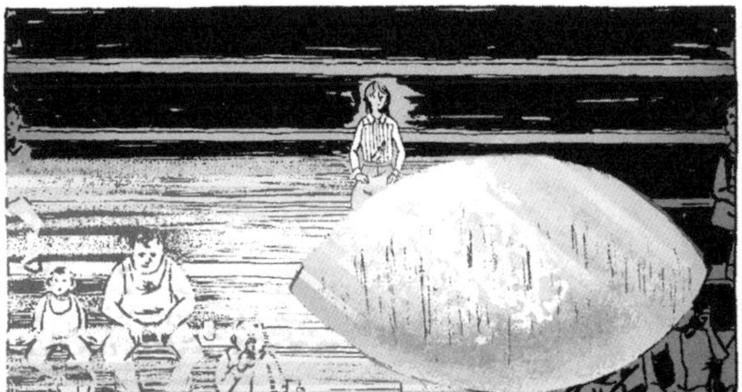

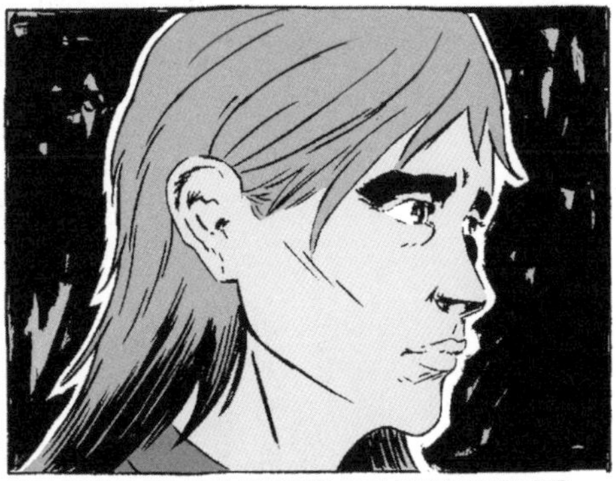

THE SIGHT OF HER ELDEST SON INCARCERATED
MUST HAVE BEEN HARD TO BEAR.

FOR ALL MY SINS, I SERVED 30 DAYS IN PRISON, FOR ACCOMPLICE TO ROBBERY.

IT WAS A BULLSHIT CHARGE. I CAN ONLY GUESS THE JUDGE KNEW IT TOO. WHICH IS WHY HE LET ME OUT EARLY.

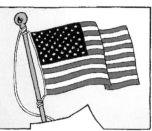

TENNNNN HUTTTTTTT!

EGLIN AIRBASE, FLORIDA - 1956

BUT WHY HE FORCED ME INTO THE ARMY, I HAVE NO IDEA. MAYBE HE WAS A SADIST. WHY ELSE WOULD YOU BECOME A JUDGE?

ANYWAY, I SERVED FOR ANOTHER 18 MONTHS.

IN THAT TIME I GOT MY FIRST BREAK, WRITING FOR THE BASE NEWSPAPER. MY FIRST TASTE OF PROFESSIONAL JOURNALISM.

BY THE TIME I GOT OUT, I'D DECIDED THAT THERE WASN'T ANYTHING ELSE I'D RATHER DO.

KRSHHH!

I'D MADE A CHOICE THAT SET ME ON A LONG, LONG...

YEAH, A LONG ROAD.

16

WHICH WENT SOMETHING LIKE THIS.

MY FIRST JOB WAS AS A SPORTSWRITER IN NEW JERSEY IN 1957.

DEAR MR. JOHNSON,

IT IS WITH NO REGRET WHATSOEVER THAT I TERMINATE
MY EMPLOYMENT AT THE JERSEY SHORE HERALD AS OF
THIS AFTERNOON. THOUGH IT IS A FINE PAPER AND
INGENIOUSLY TAILORED TO THE TASTES OF THE CRETINS,
SAILORS AND WHORES WHO COMPRISE ITS CORE READERSHIP,
I FIND IT AN UNSUITABLE BANNER FOR A MAN OF MY
TALENTS TO CARRY.

YOURS GRACIOUSLY,

HUNTER.

IT DIDN'T LAST TOO LONG.

17

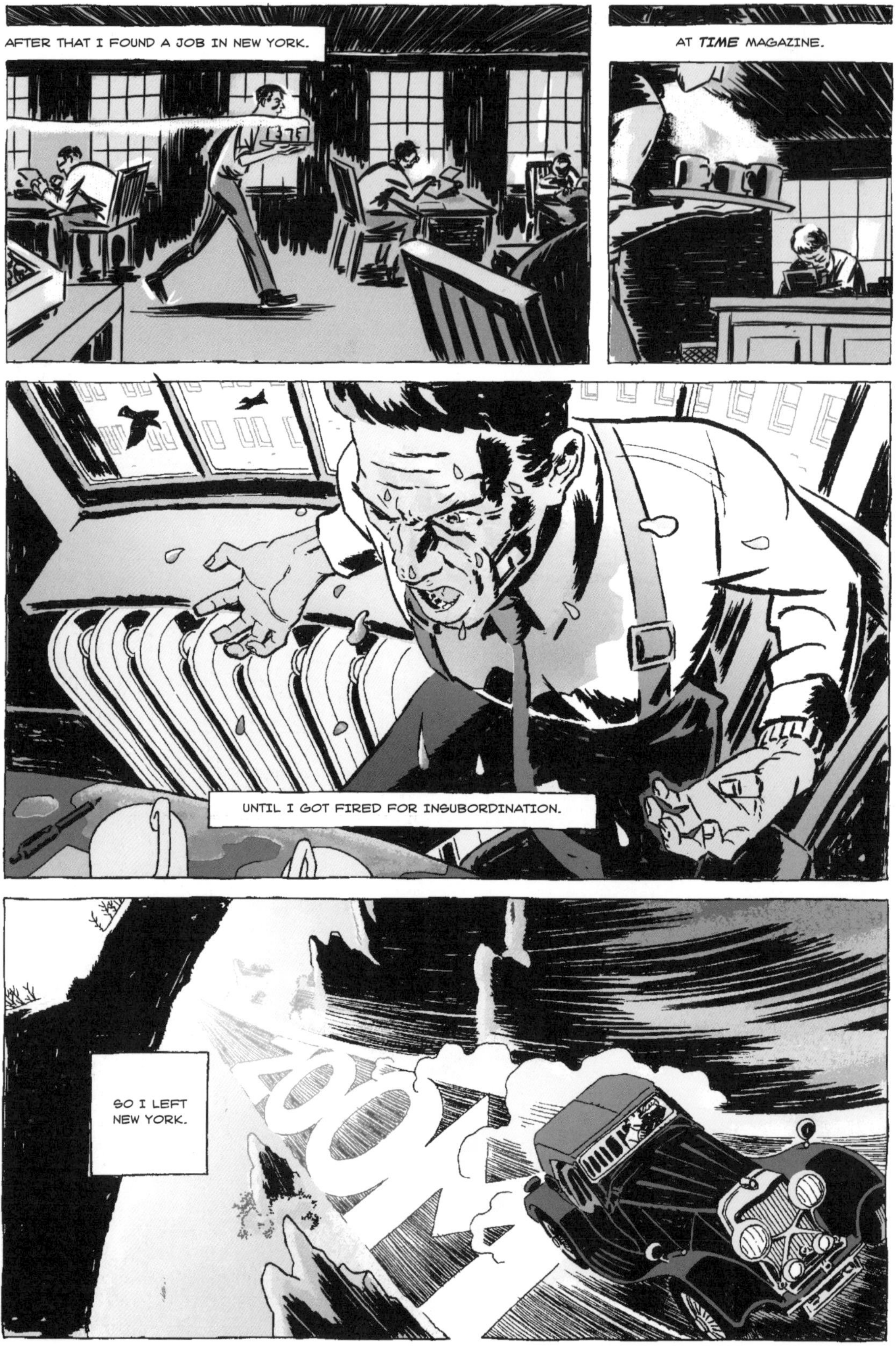
AFTER THAT I FOUND A JOB IN NEW YORK.
AT *TIME* MAGAZINE.
UNTIL I GOT FIRED FOR INSUBORDINATION.
SO I LEFT NEW YORK.

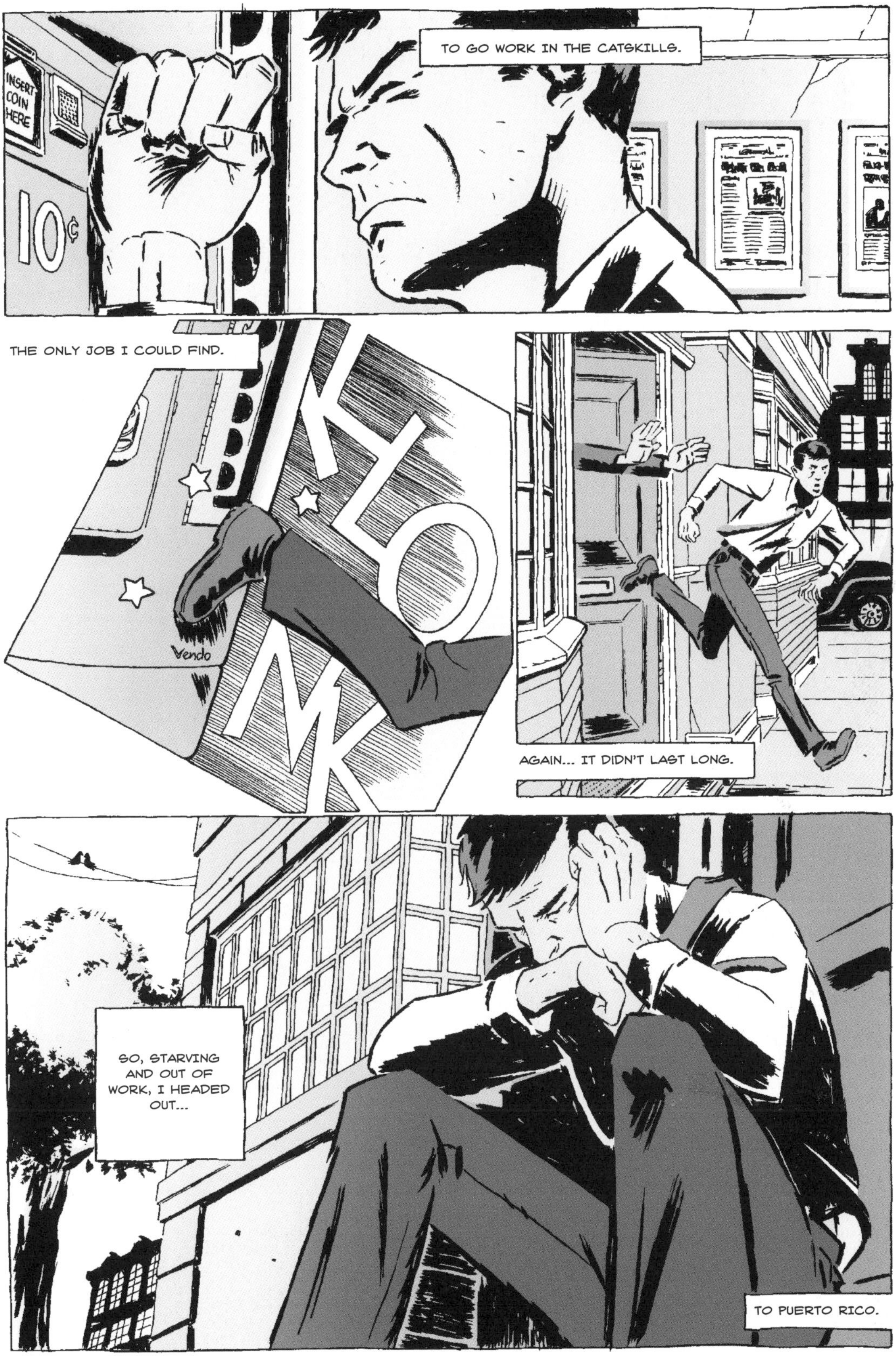
INSERT COIN HERE
10¢
TO GO WORK IN THE CATSKILLS.
THE ONLY JOB I COULD FIND.
KLONK
Vendo
AGAIN... IT DIDN'T LAST LONG.
SO, STARVING AND OUT OF WORK, I HEADED OUT...
TO PUERTO RICO.

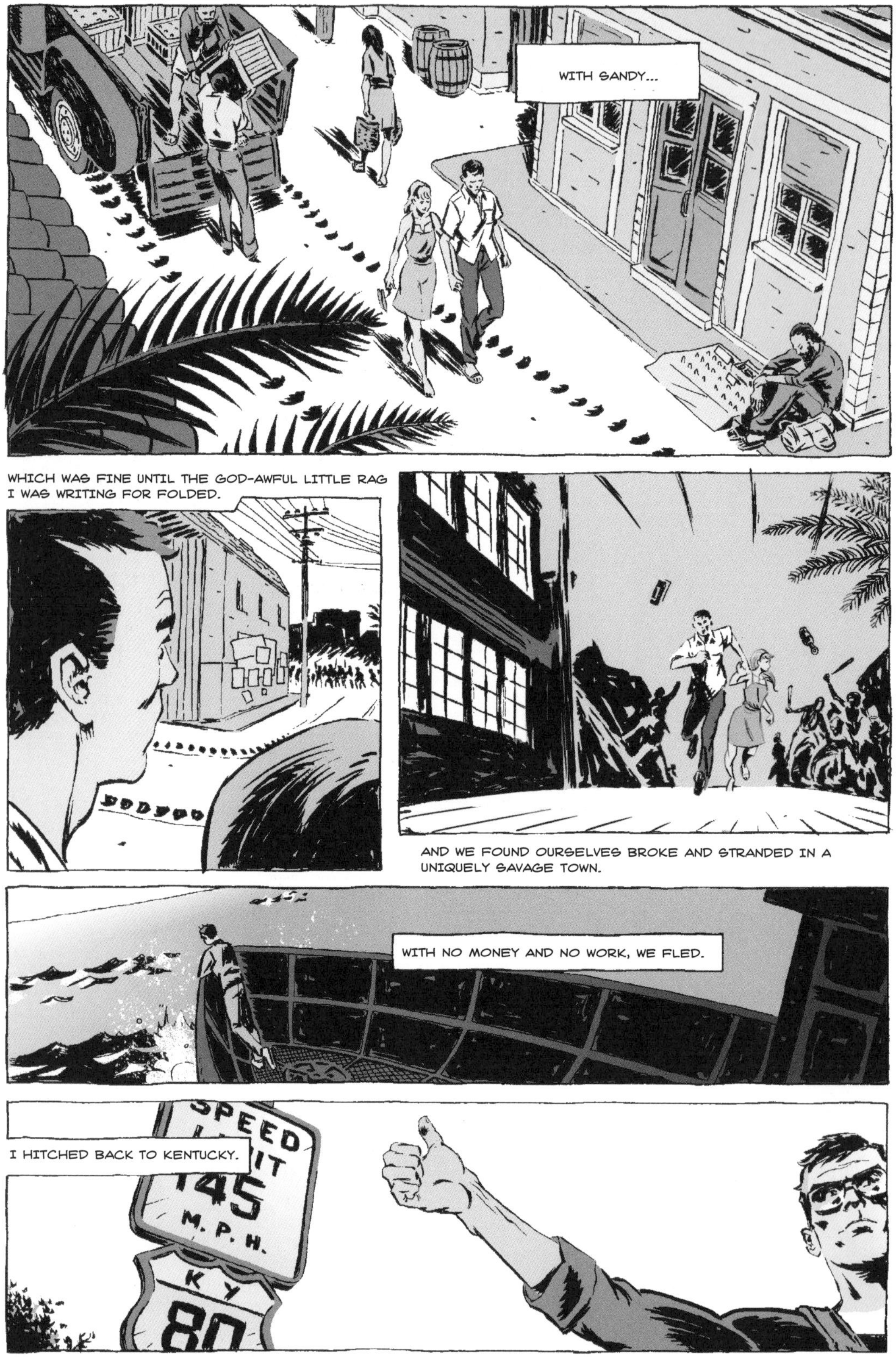
WITH SANDY...
WHICH WAS FINE UNTIL THE GOD-AWFUL LITTLE RAG I WAS WRITING FOR FOLDED.
AND WE FOUND OURSELVES BROKE AND STRANDED IN A UNIQUELY SAVAGE TOWN.
WITH NO MONEY AND NO WORK, WE FLED.
I HITCHED BACK TO KENTUCKY.
SPEED
145
M. P. H.
K Y
80

ON TO SAN FRANCISCO.

CALIFORNIA AND BIG SUR, I GUESS 1961.

WHERE WE GOT BY FOR A WHILE.

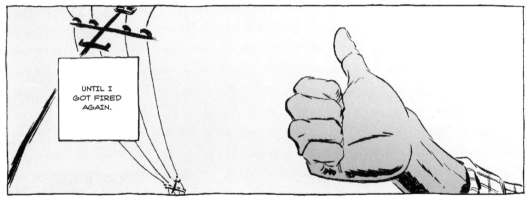

UNTIL I GOT FIRED AGAIN.

SO BACK... BACK TO NEW YORK.

GOD I HATE NEW YORK, THERE IS NEVER WORK IN NEW YORK.

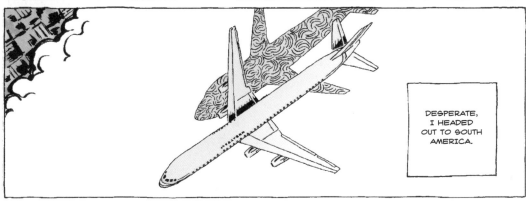

DESPERATE, I HEADED OUT TO SOUTH AMERICA.

AND LANDED ON MY FEET.

IN RIO.

ASPEN – 1963

I CAME HOME A WORKING JOURNALIST.

MY INCOME WAS SMALL, NOT REALLY ENOUGH TO SUPPORT A WIFE.

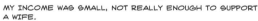

BUT SANDY AND I MARRIED ANYWAY IN 1963.

SANDY FELL PREGNANT.

KENNEDY WAS ASSASSINATED.

AND I KEPT ON WORKING.

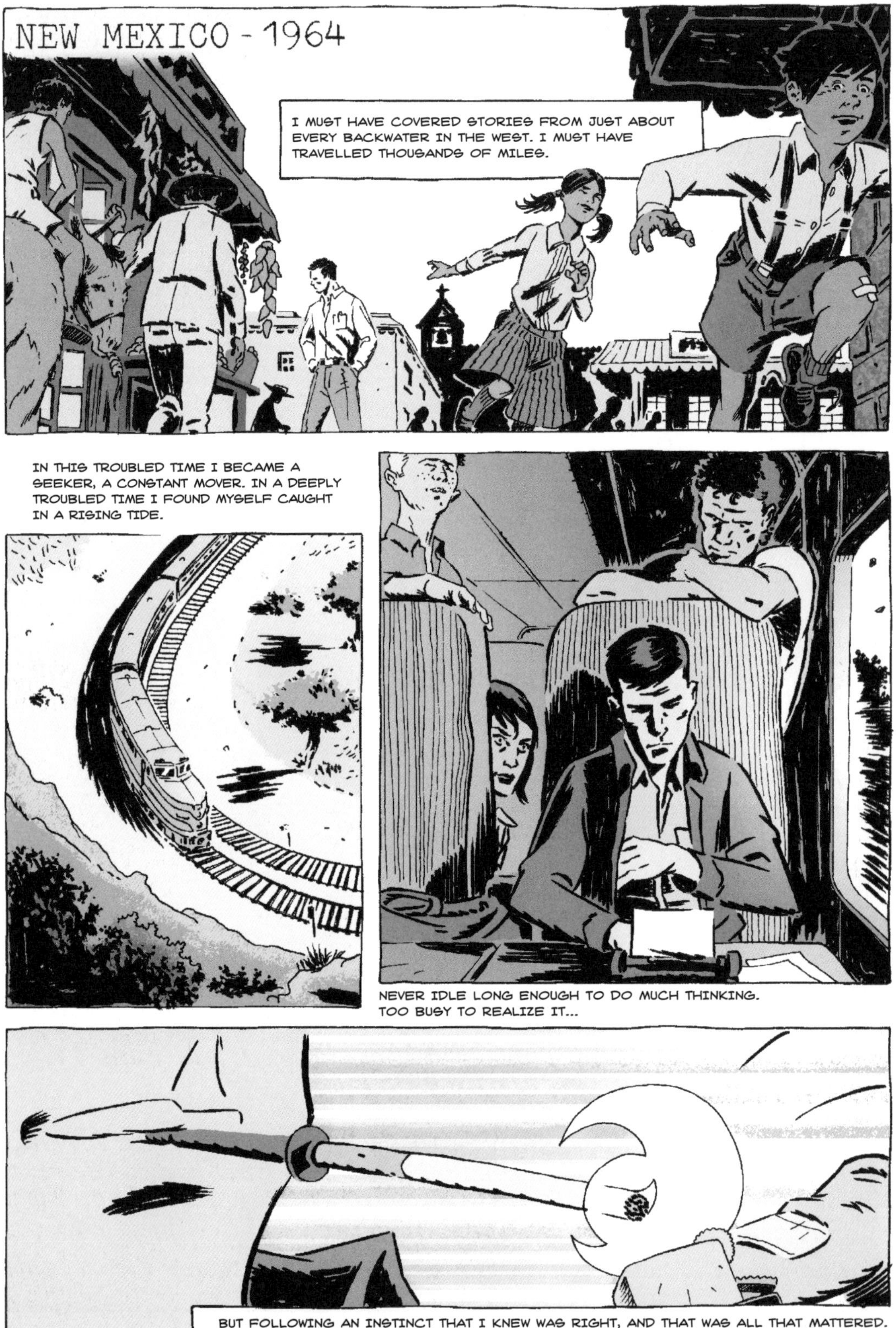
NEW MEXICO - 1964
I MUST HAVE COVERED STORIES FROM JUST ABOUT EVERY BACKWATER IN THE WEST. I MUST HAVE TRAVELLED THOUSANDS OF MILES.
IN THIS TROUBLED TIME I BECAME A SEEKER, A CONSTANT MOVER. IN A DEEPLY TROUBLED TIME I FOUND MYSELF CAUGHT IN A RISING TIDE.
NEVER IDLE LONG ENOUGH TO DO MUCH THINKING. TOO BUSY TO REALIZE IT...
BUT FOLLOWING AN INSTINCT THAT I KNEW WAS RIGHT, AND THAT WAS ALL THAT MATTERED.

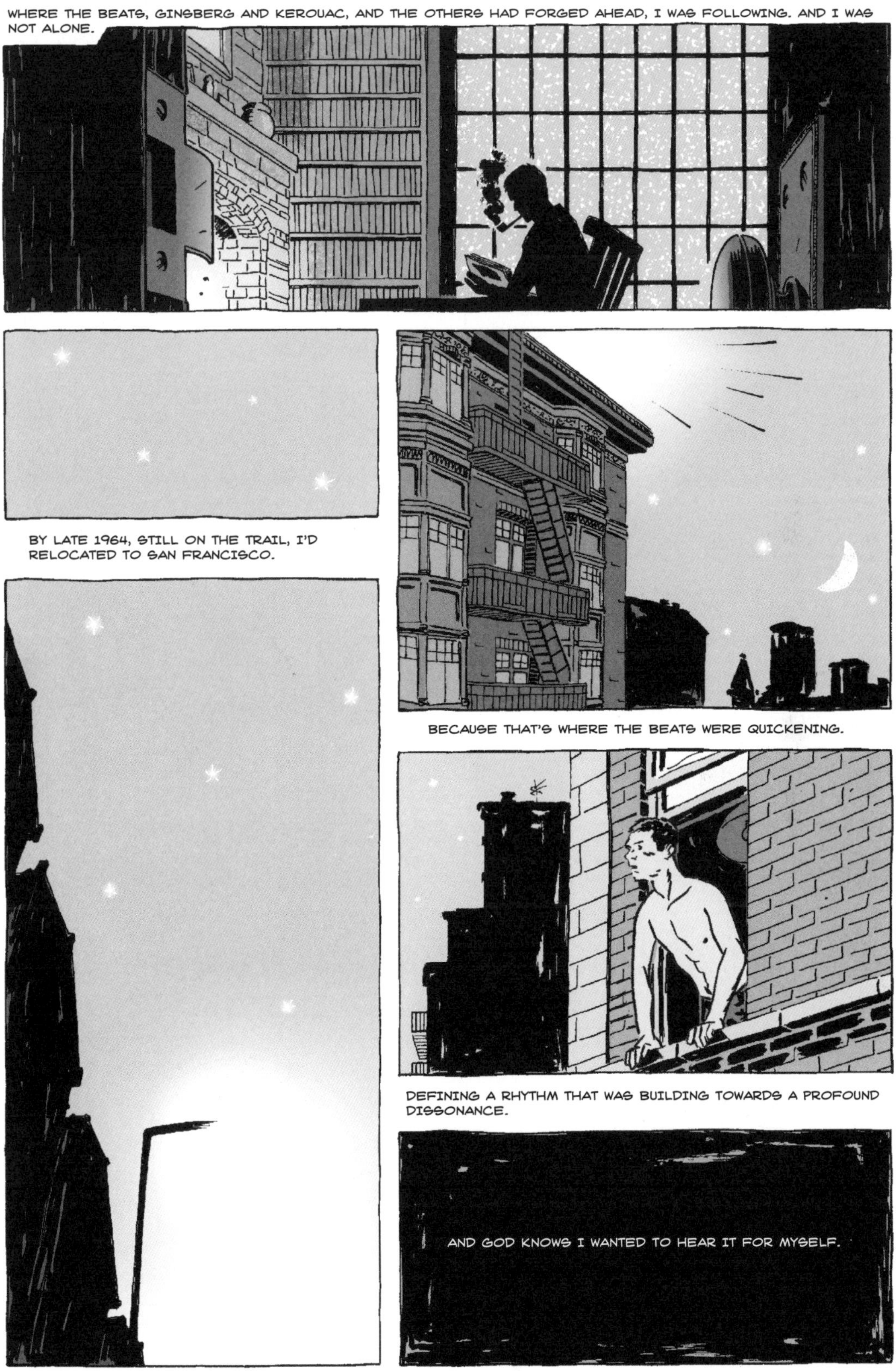
WHERE THE BEATS, GINSBERG AND KEROUAC, AND THE OTHERS HAD FORGED AHEAD, I WAS FOLLOWING. AND I WAS NOT ALONE.
BY LATE 1964, STILL ON THE TRAIL, I'D RELOCATED TO SAN FRANCISCO.
BECAUSE THAT'S WHERE THE BEATS WERE QUICKENING.
DEFINING A RHYTHM THAT WAS BUILDING TOWARDS A PROFOUND DISSONANCE.
AND GOD KNOWS I WANTED TO HEAR IT FOR MYSELF.

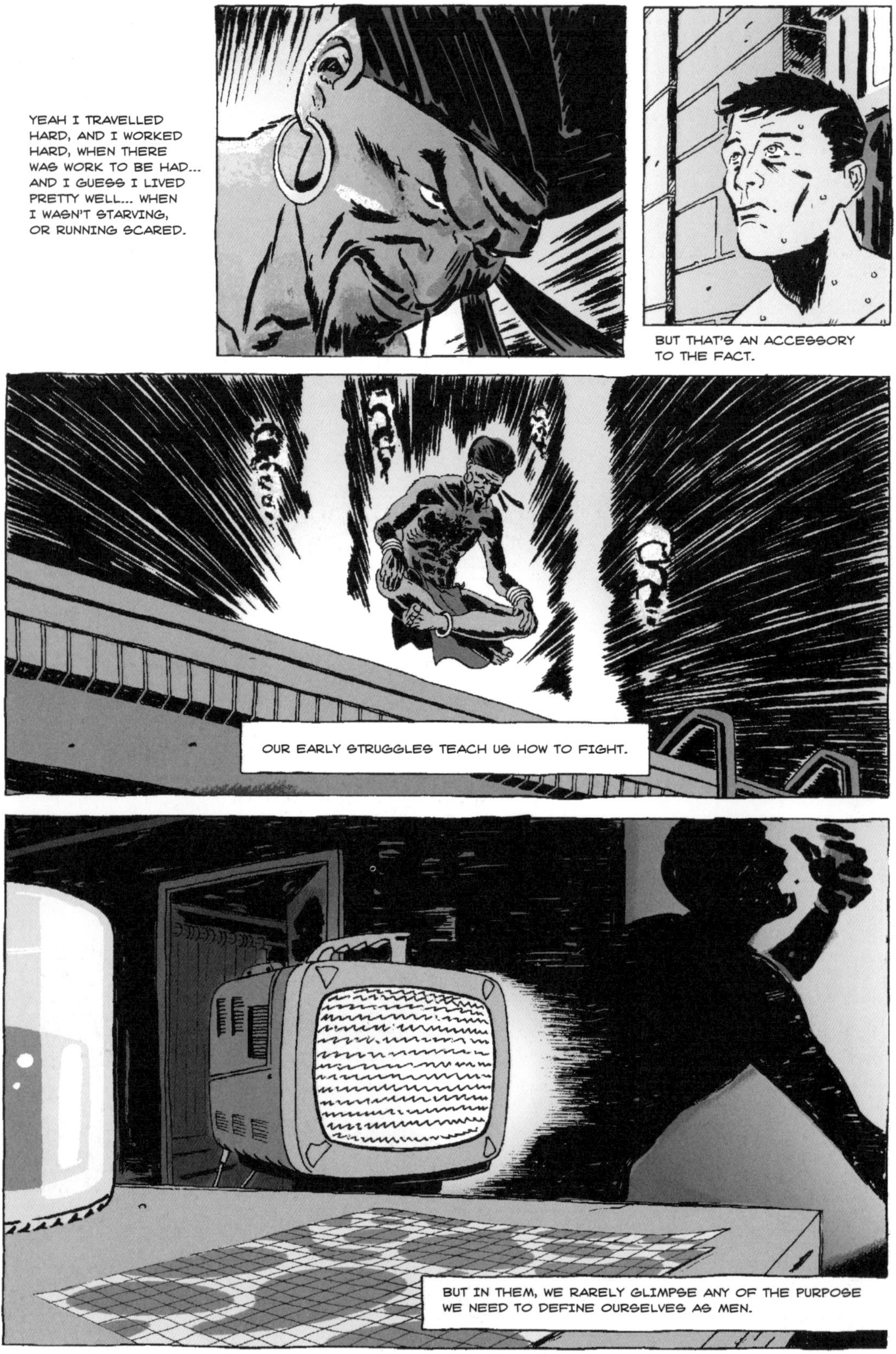
YEAH I TRAVELLED HARD, AND I WORKED HARD, WHEN THERE WAS WORK TO BE HAD... AND I GUESS I LIVED PRETTY WELL... WHEN I WASN'T STARVING, OR RUNNING SCARED.
BUT THAT'S AN ACCESSORY TO THE FACT.
OUR EARLY STRUGGLES TEACH US HOW TO FIGHT.
BUT IN THEM, WE RARELY GLIMPSE ANY OF THE PURPOSE WE NEED TO DEFINE OURSELVES AS MEN.

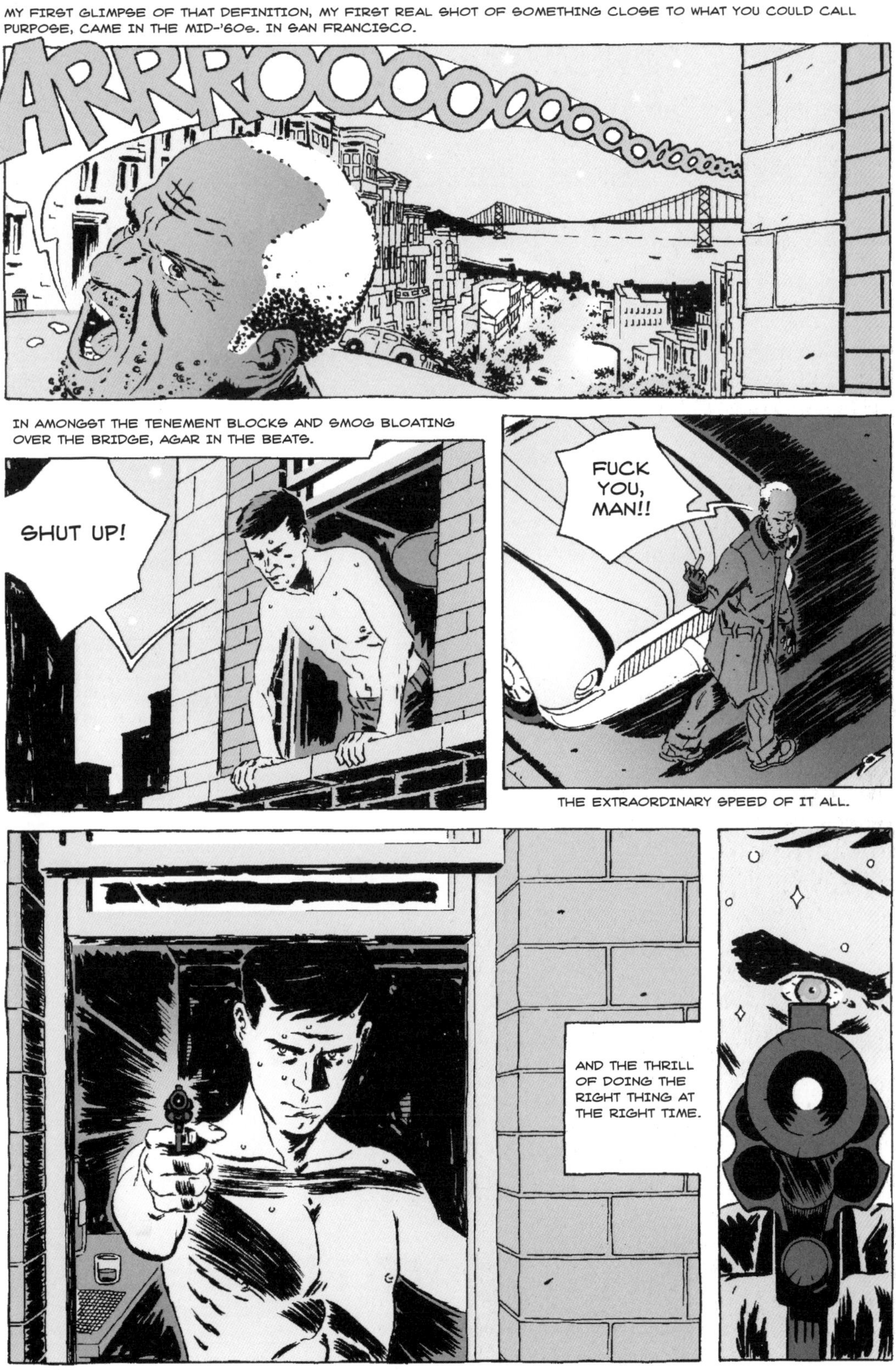
MY FIRST GLIMPSE OF THAT DEFINITION, MY FIRST REAL SHOT OF SOMETHING CLOSE TO WHAT YOU COULD CALL PURPOSE, CAME IN THE MID-'60s. IN SAN FRANCISCO.
ARRROOOOOooooooooooo
IN AMONGST THE TENEMENT BLOCKS AND SMOG BLOATING OVER THE BRIDGE, AGAR IN THE BEATS.
SHUT UP!
FUCK YOU, MAN!!
THE EXTRAORDINARY SPEED OF IT ALL.
AND THE THRILL OF DOING THE RIGHT THING AT THE RIGHT TIME.

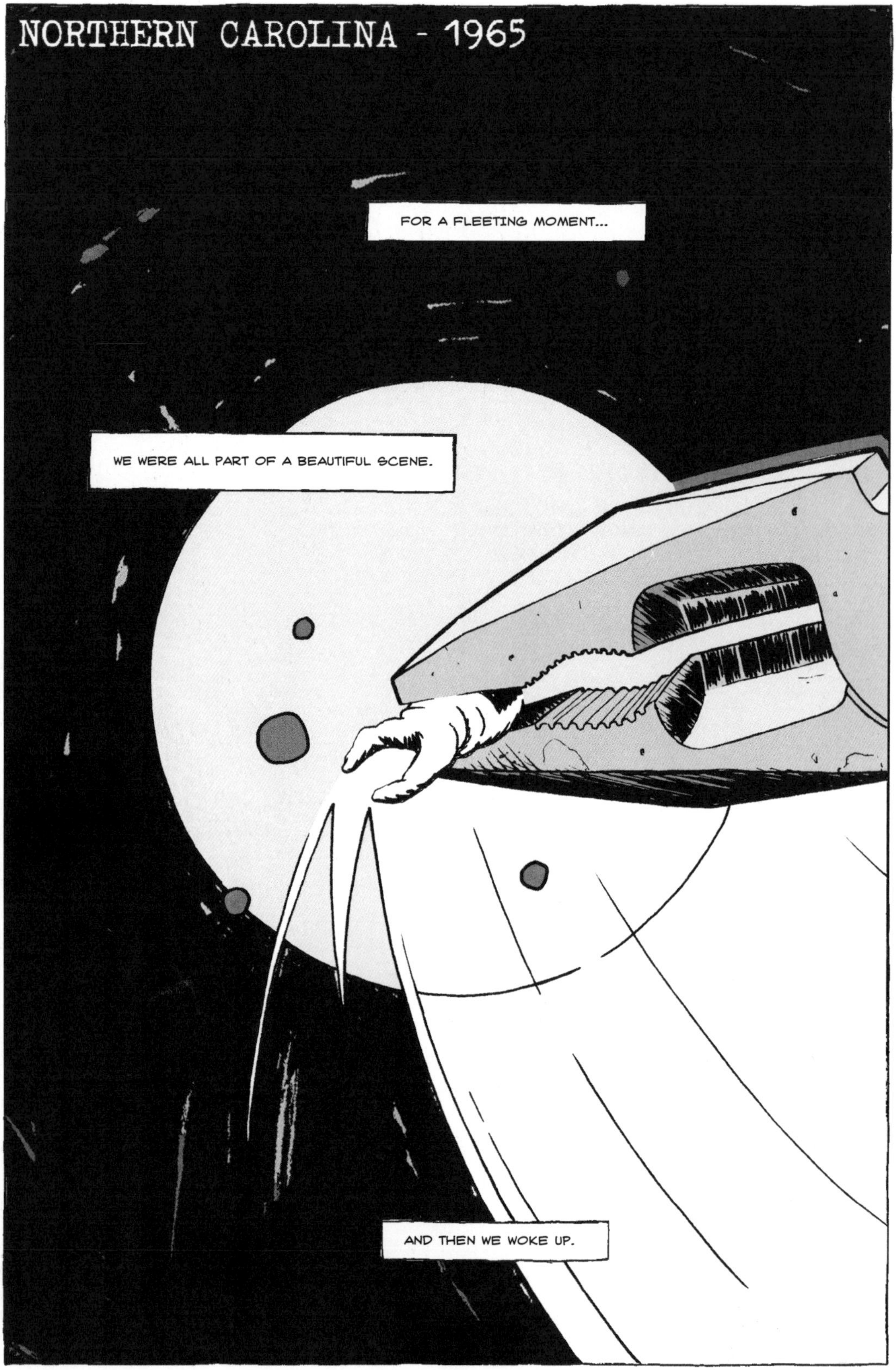
NORTHERN CAROLINA - 1965
FOR A FLEETING MOMENT...
WE WERE ALL PART OF A BEAUTIFUL SCENE.
AND THEN WE WOKE UP.

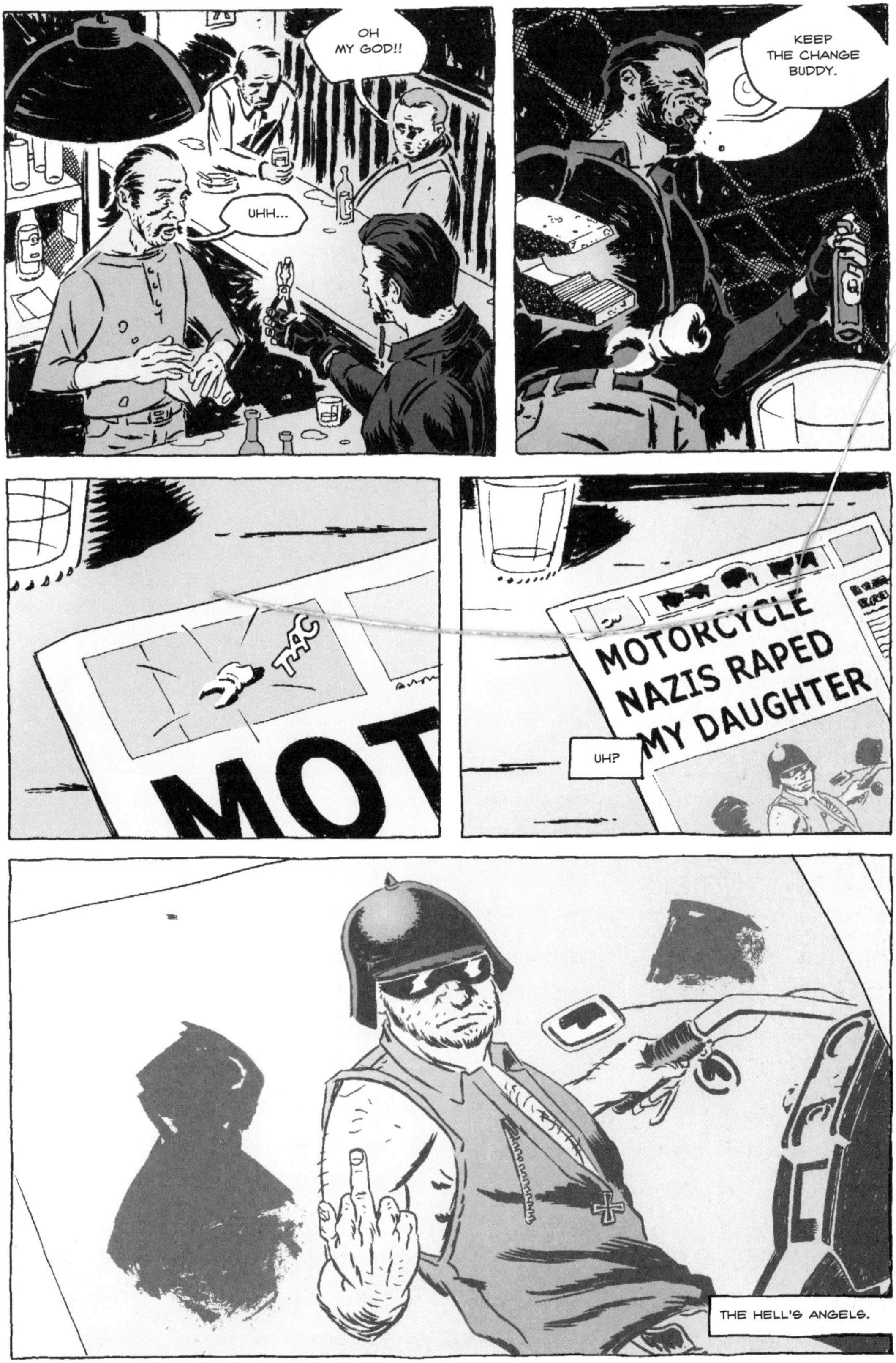
OH MY GOD!!
UHH...
KEEP THE CHANGE BUDDY.
TAC
MOT
MOTORCYCLE NAZIS RAPED MY DAUGHTER
UH?
THE HELL'S ANGELS.

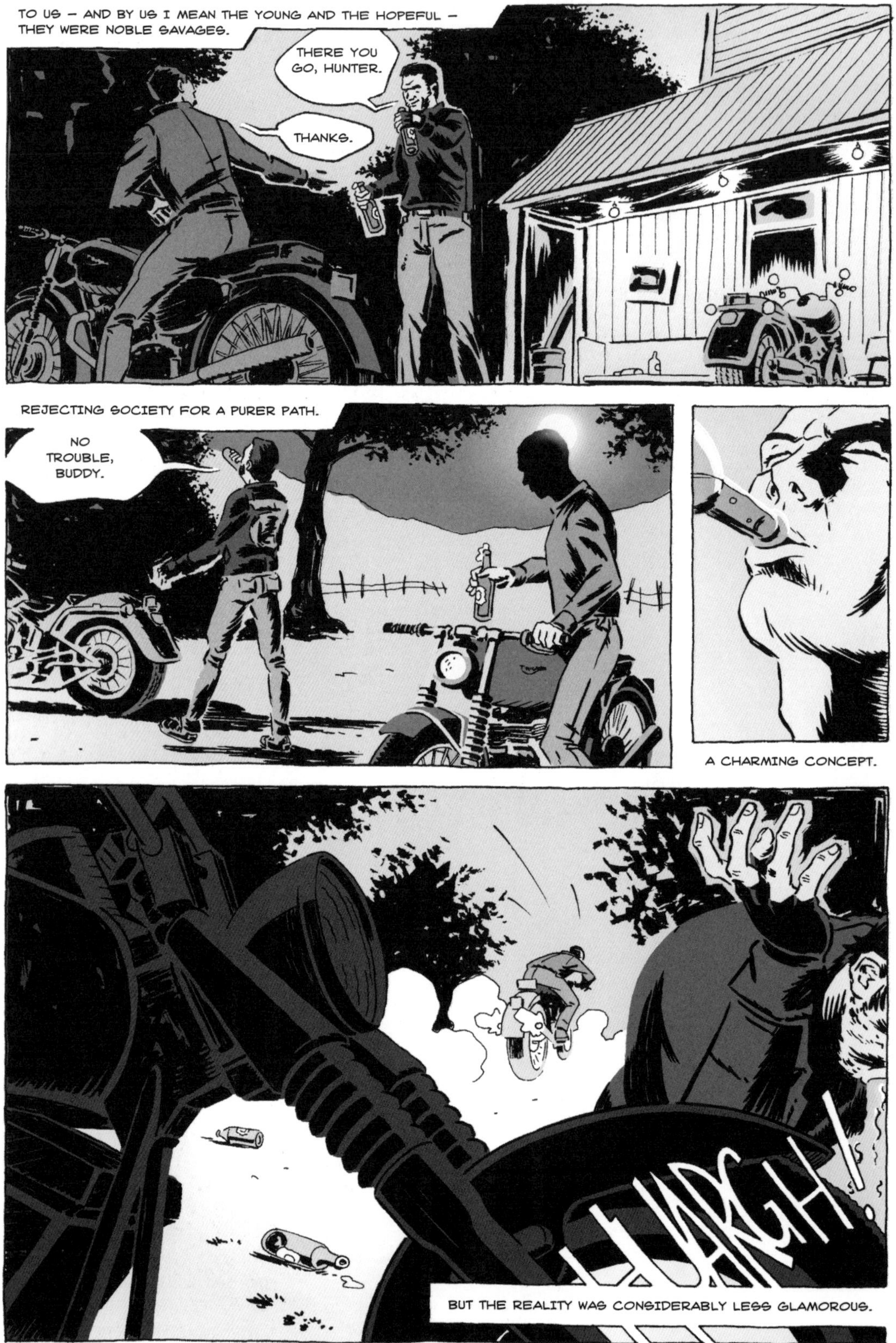
TO US – AND BY US I MEAN THE YOUNG AND THE HOPEFUL – THEY WERE NOBLE SAVAGES.
THERE YOU GO, HUNTER.
THANKS.
REJECTING SOCIETY FOR A PURER PATH.
NO TROUBLE, BUDDY.
A CHARMING CONCEPT.
HAARGH!
BUT THE REALITY WAS CONSIDERABLY LESS GLAMOROUS.

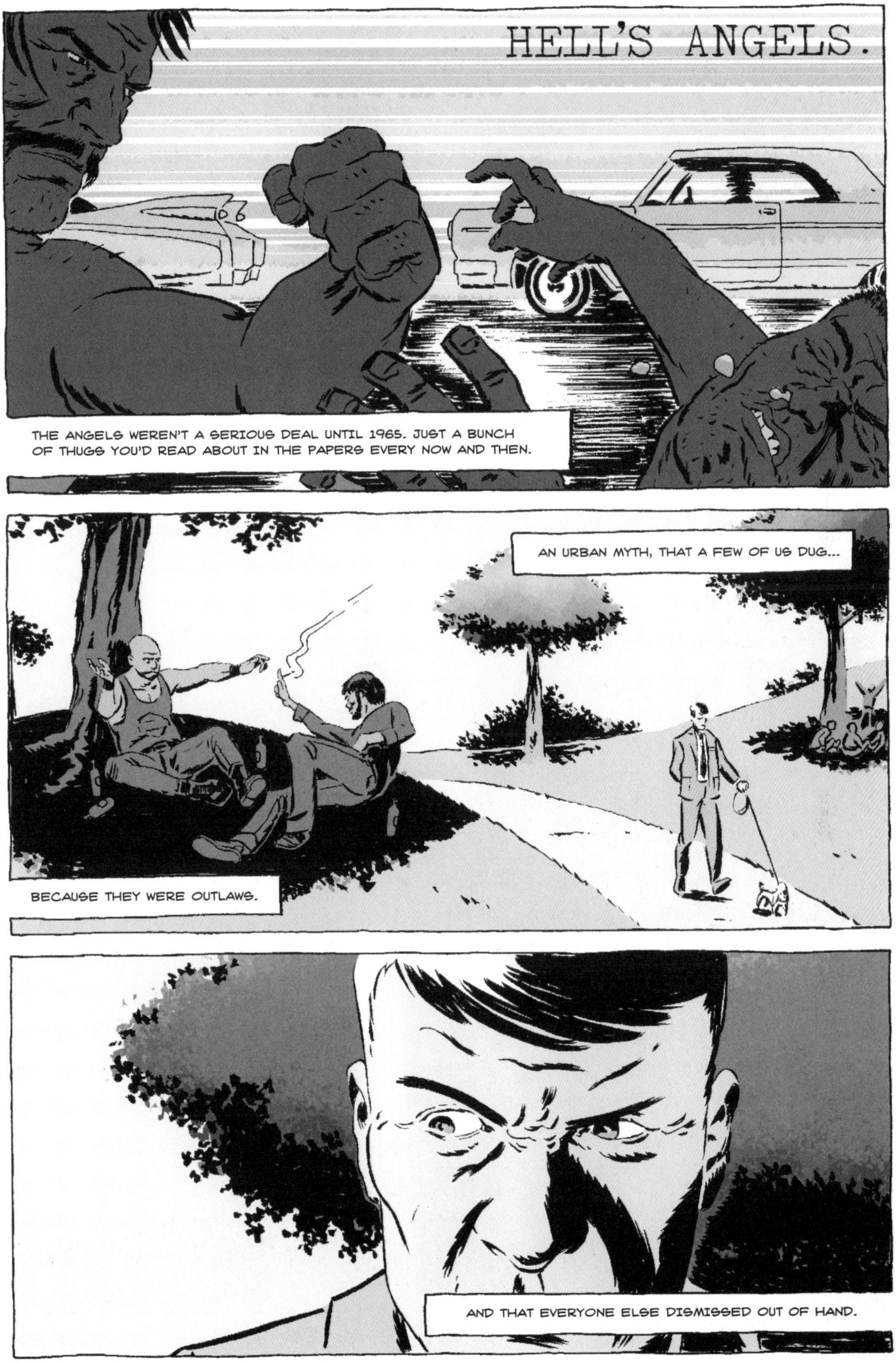
HELL'S ANGELS.
THE ANGELS WEREN'T A SERIOUS DEAL UNTIL 1965. JUST A BUNCH OF THUGS YOU'D READ ABOUT IN THE PAPERS EVERY NOW AND THEN.
AN URBAN MYTH, THAT A FEW OF US DUG...
BECAUSE THEY WERE OUTLAWS.
AND THAT EVERYONE ELSE DISMISSED OUT OF HAND.

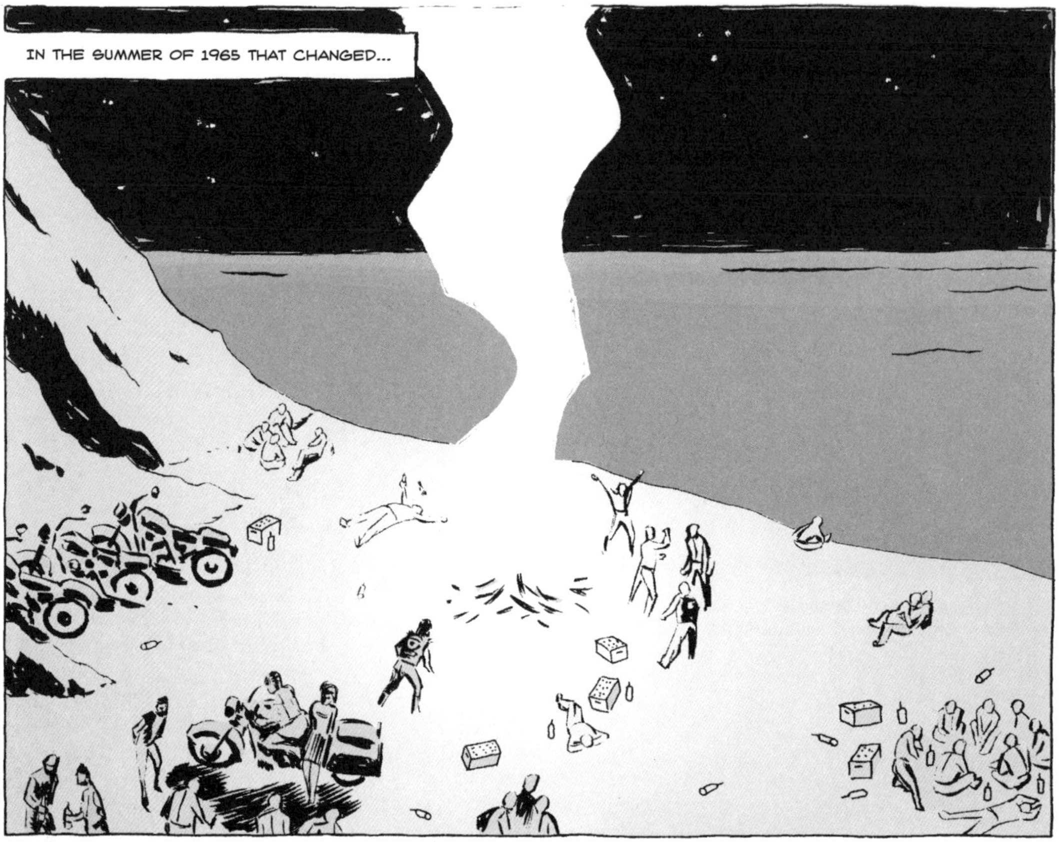
IN THE SUMMER OF 1965 THAT CHANGED...

WHEN A GROUP OF FIVE WERE ACCUSED OF RAPING TWO YOUNG GIRLS IN A TOWN IN MONTEREY.

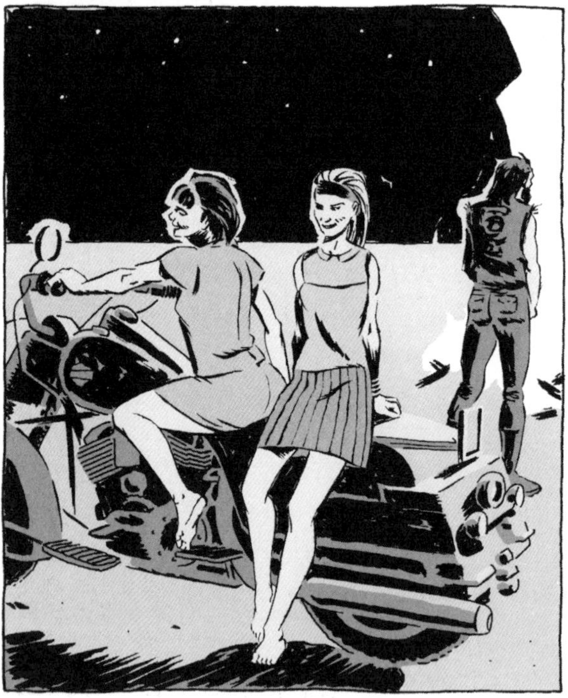

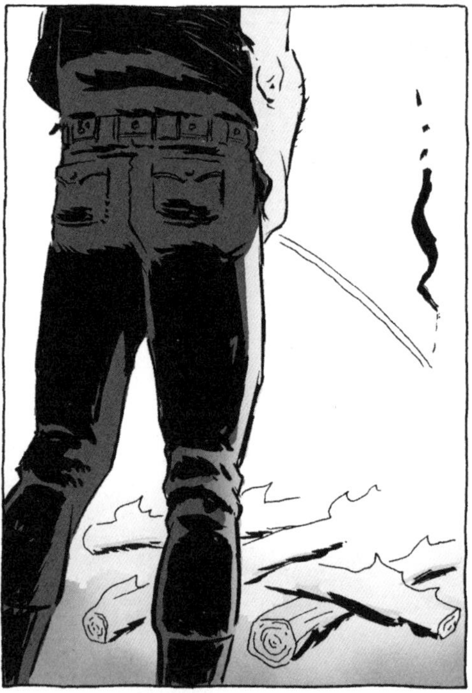

I COVERED THE STORY FOR A MAGAZINE CALLED ***THE NATION***.

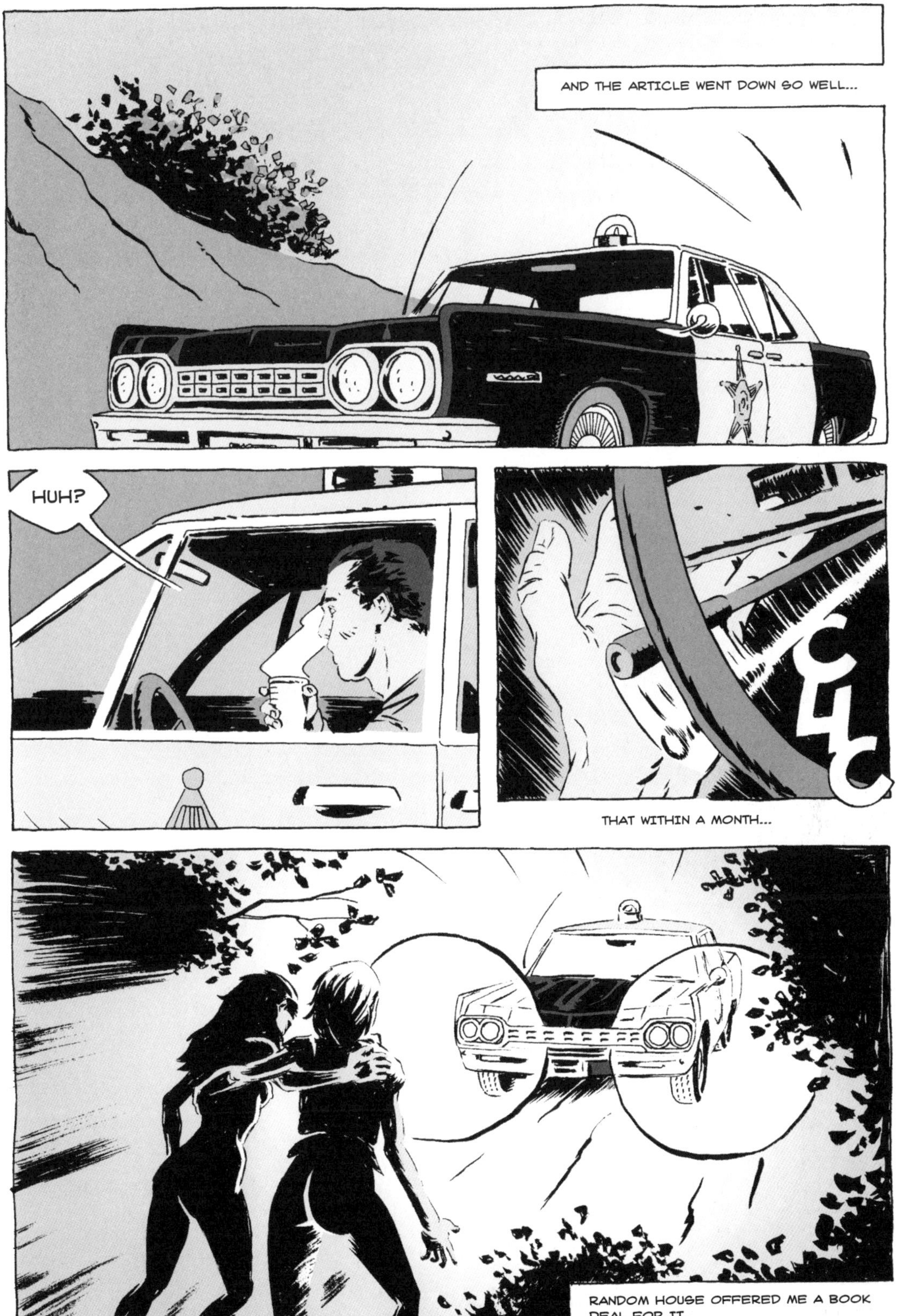
AND THE ARTICLE WENT DOWN SO WELL...
HUH?
CLIC
THAT WITHIN A MONTH...
RANDOM HOUSE OFFERED ME A BOOK DEAL FOR IT.

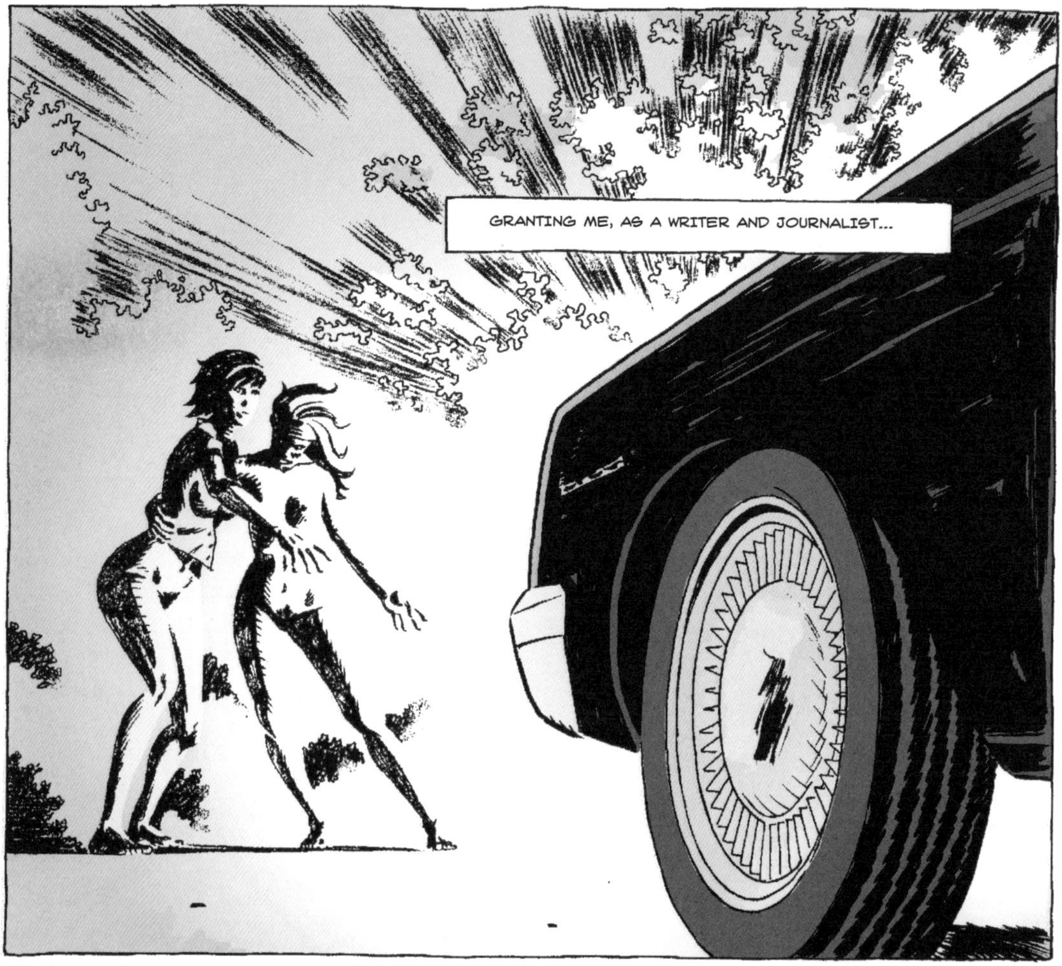
GRANTING ME, AS A WRITER AND JOURNALIST...

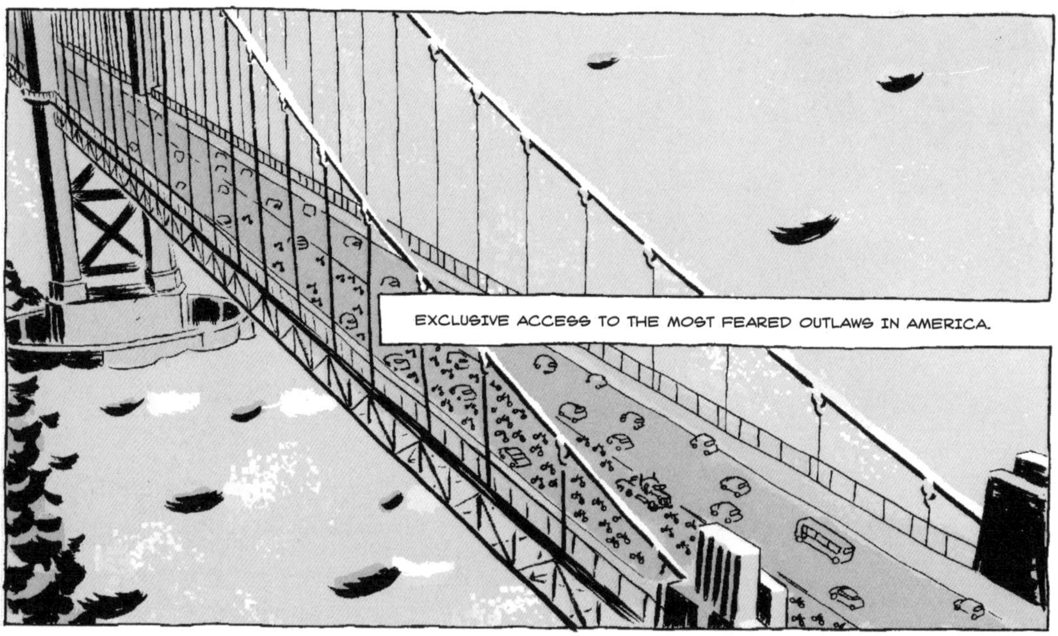
EXCLUSIVE ACCESS TO THE MOST FEARED OUTLAWS IN AMERICA.

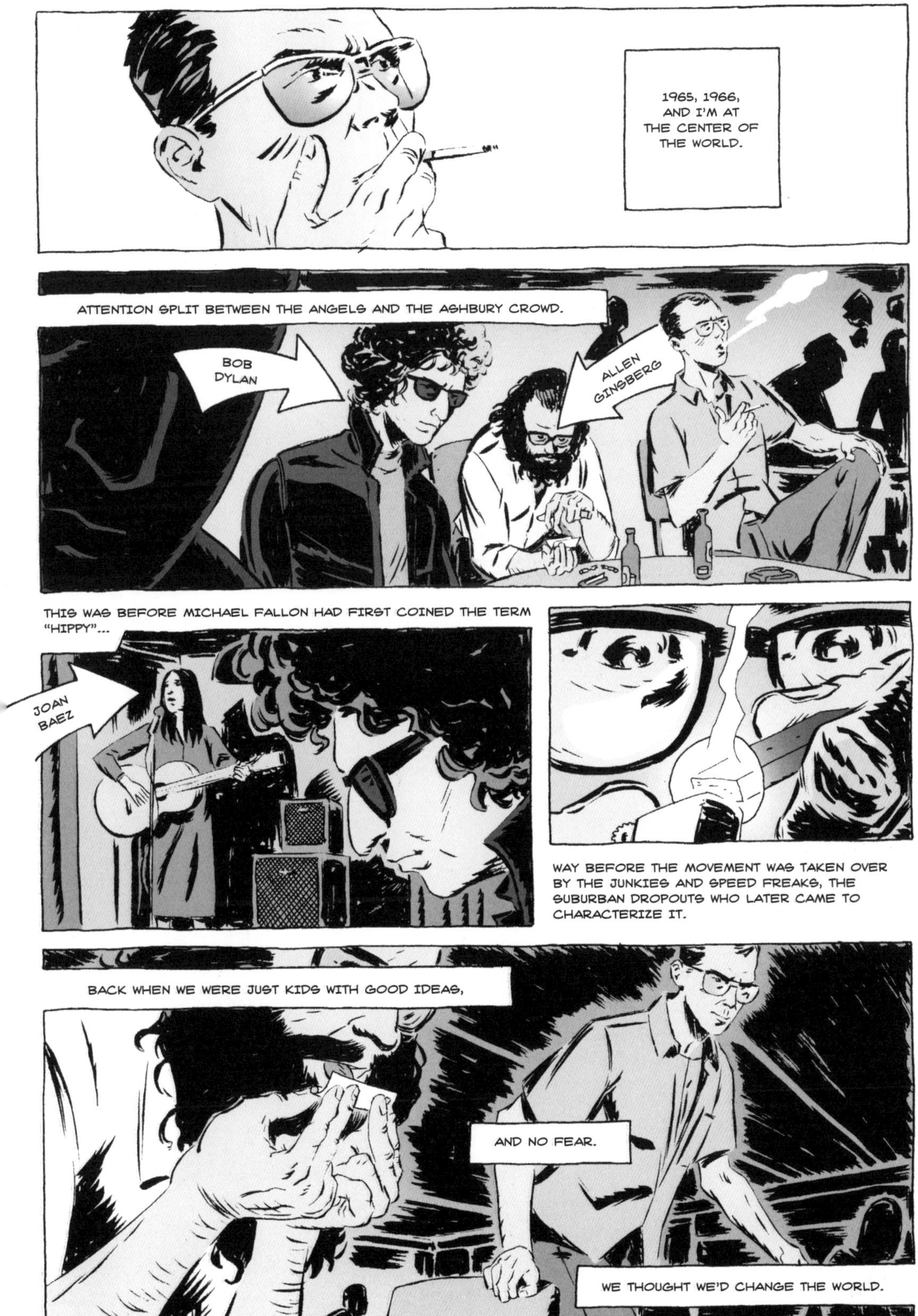
1965, 1966, AND I'M AT THE CENTER OF THE WORLD.
ATTENTION SPLIT BETWEEN THE ANGELS AND THE ASHBURY CROWD.
BOB DYLAN
ALLEN GINSBERG
THIS WAS BEFORE MICHAEL FALLON HAD FIRST COINED THE TERM "HIPPY"...
JOAN BAEZ
WAY BEFORE THE MOVEMENT WAS TAKEN OVER BY THE JUNKIES AND SPEED FREAKS, THE SUBURBAN DROPOUTS WHO LATER CAME TO CHARACTERIZE IT.
BACK WHEN WE WERE JUST KIDS WITH GOOD IDEAS,
AND NO FEAR.
WE THOUGHT WE'D CHANGE THE WORLD.

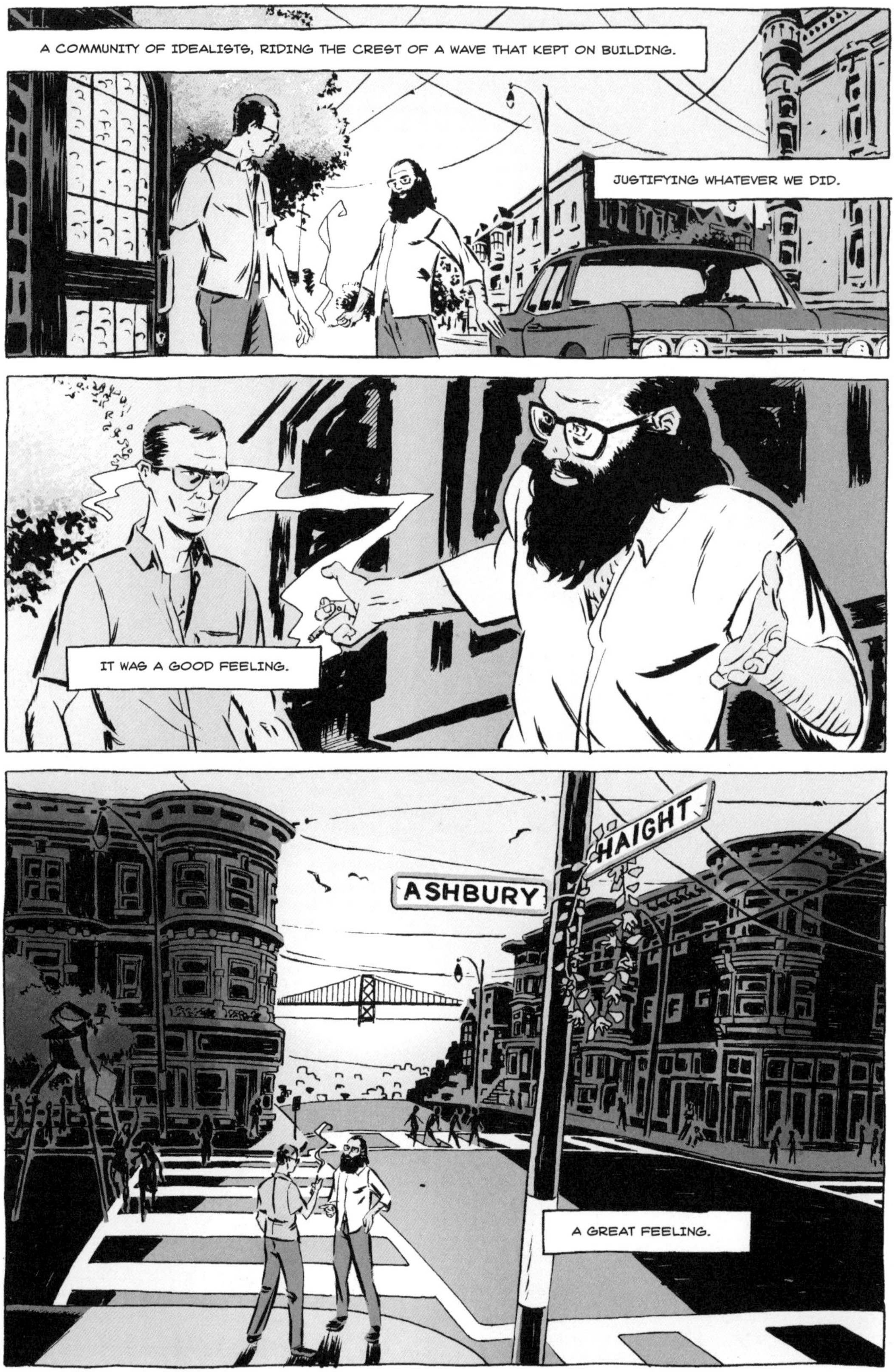
A COMMUNITY OF IDEALISTS, RIDING THE CREST OF A WAVE THAT KEPT ON BUILDING.
JUSTIFYING WHATEVER WE DID.
IT WAS A GOOD FEELING.
ASHBURY
HAIGHT
A GREAT FEELING.

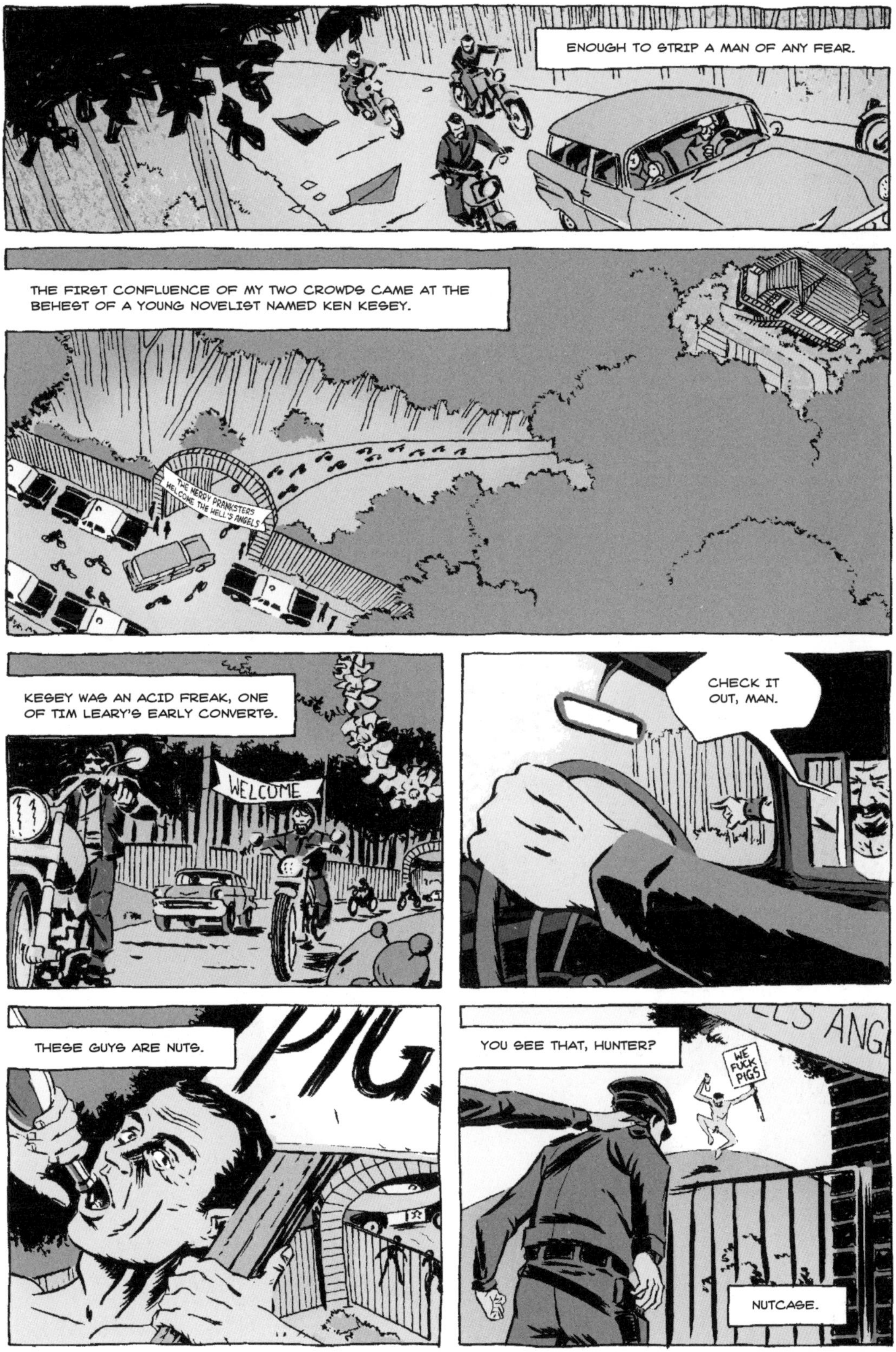
ENOUGH TO STRIP A MAN OF ANY FEAR.
THE FIRST CONFLUENCE OF MY TWO CROWDS CAME AT THE BEHEST OF A YOUNG NOVELIST NAMED KEN KESEY.
THE MERRY PRANKSTERS WELCOME THE HELL'S ANGELS
KESEY WAS AN ACID FREAK, ONE OF TIM LEARY'S EARLY CONVERTS.
WELCOME
CHECK IT OUT, MAN.
THESE GUYS ARE NUTS.
PIG.
YOU SEE THAT, HUNTER?
WE FUCK PIGS
NUTCASE.

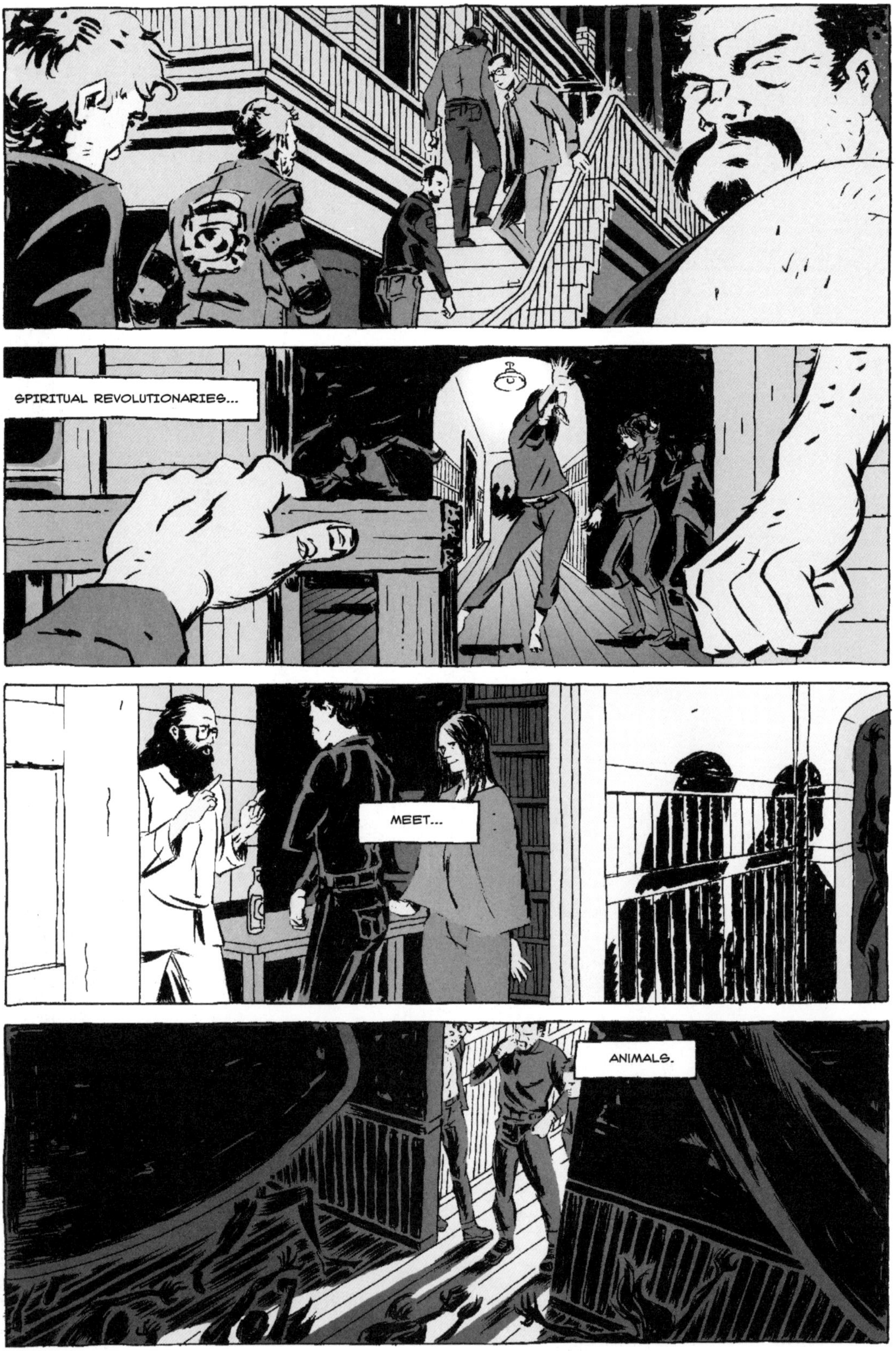
SPIRITUAL REVOLUTIONARIES...
MEET...
ANIMALS.

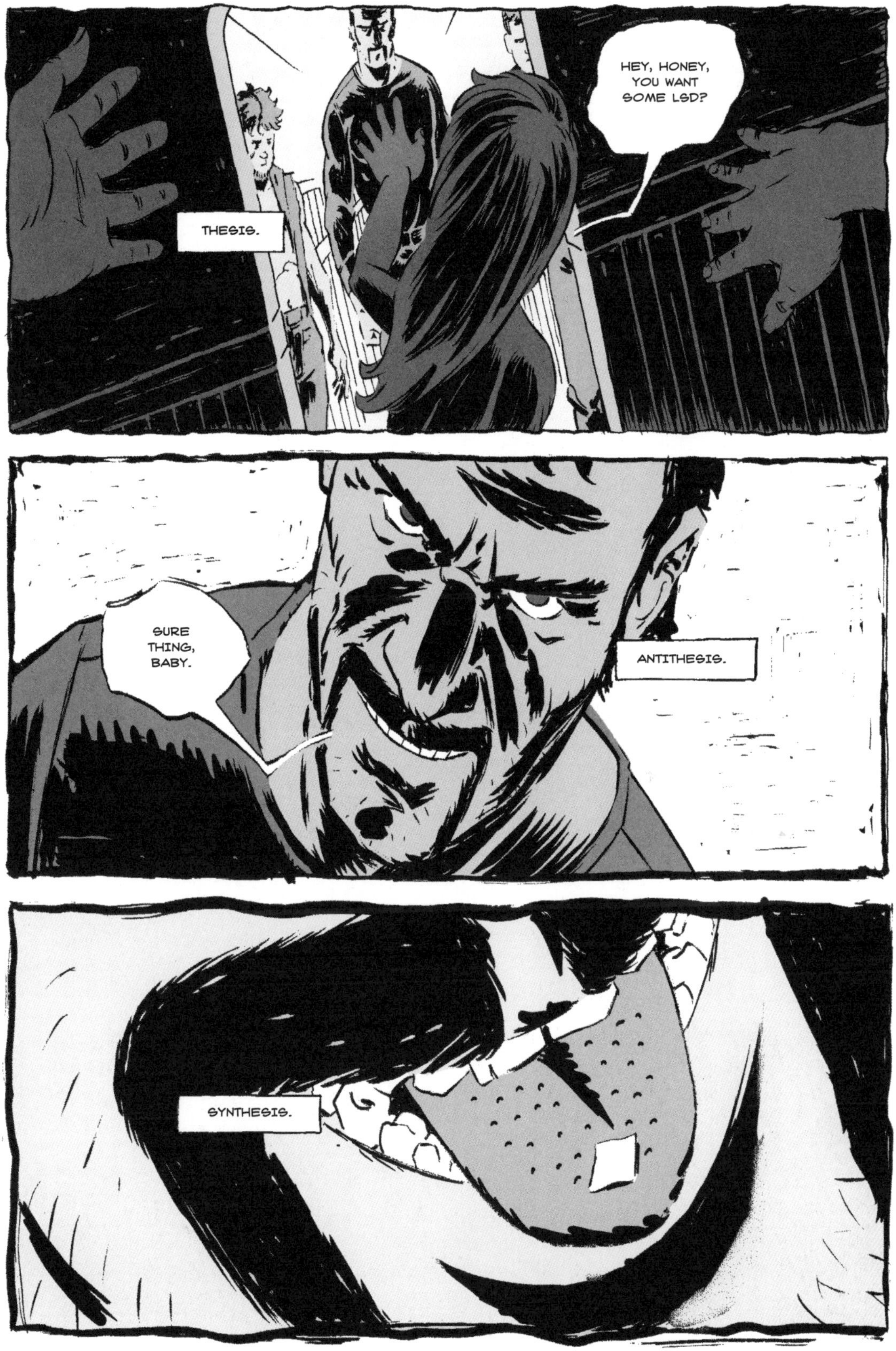
THESIS.
HEY, HONEY, YOU WANT SOME LSD?
SURE THING, BABY.
ANTITHESIS.
SYNTHESIS.

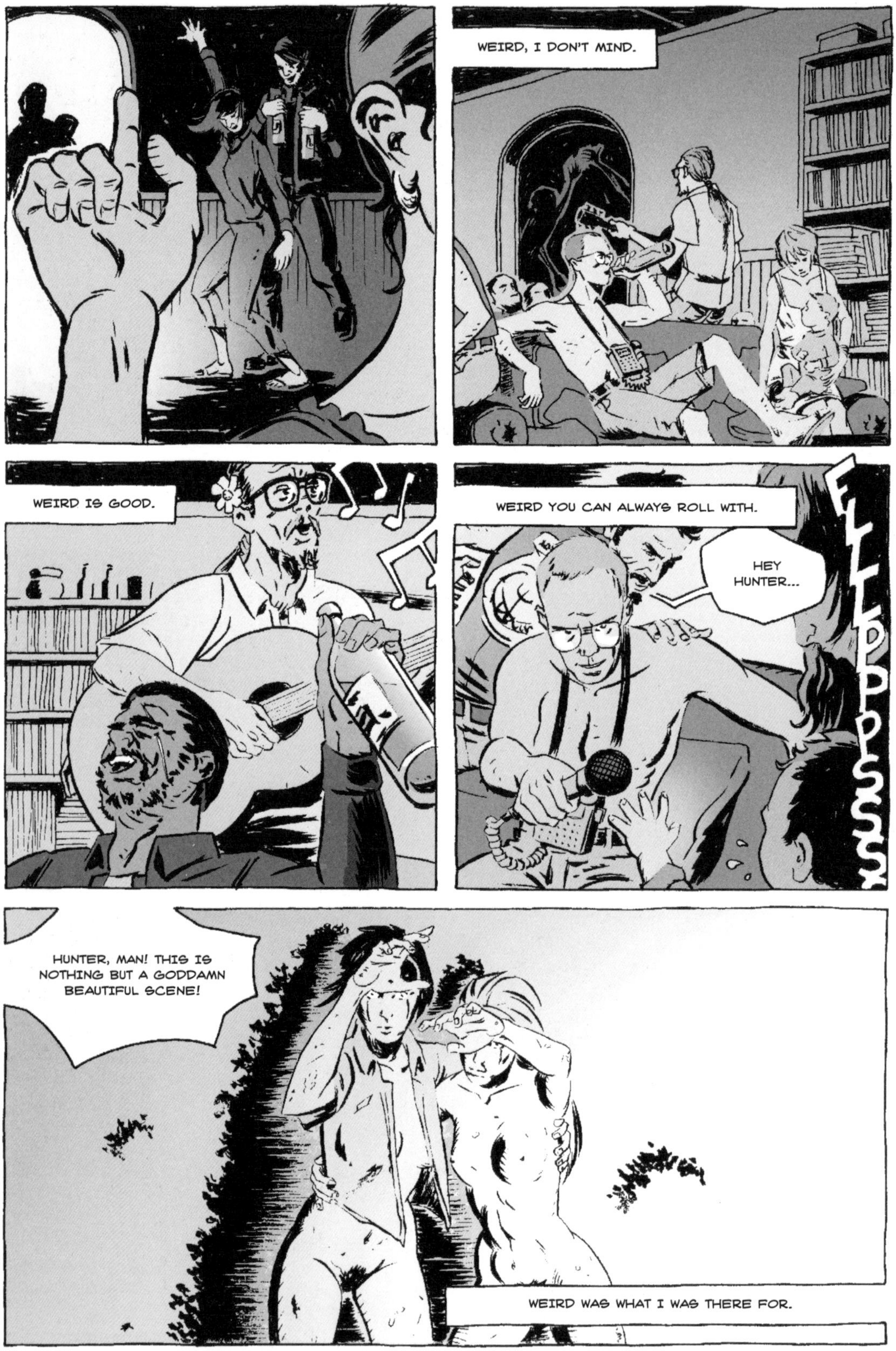
WEIRD, I DON'T MIND.
WEIRD IS GOOD.
WEIRD YOU CAN ALWAYS ROLL WITH.
HEY HUNTER...
FLLIPPPSSSX
HUNTER, MAN! THIS IS NOTHING BUT A GODDAMN BEAUTIFUL SCENE!
WEIRD WAS WHAT I WAS THERE FOR.

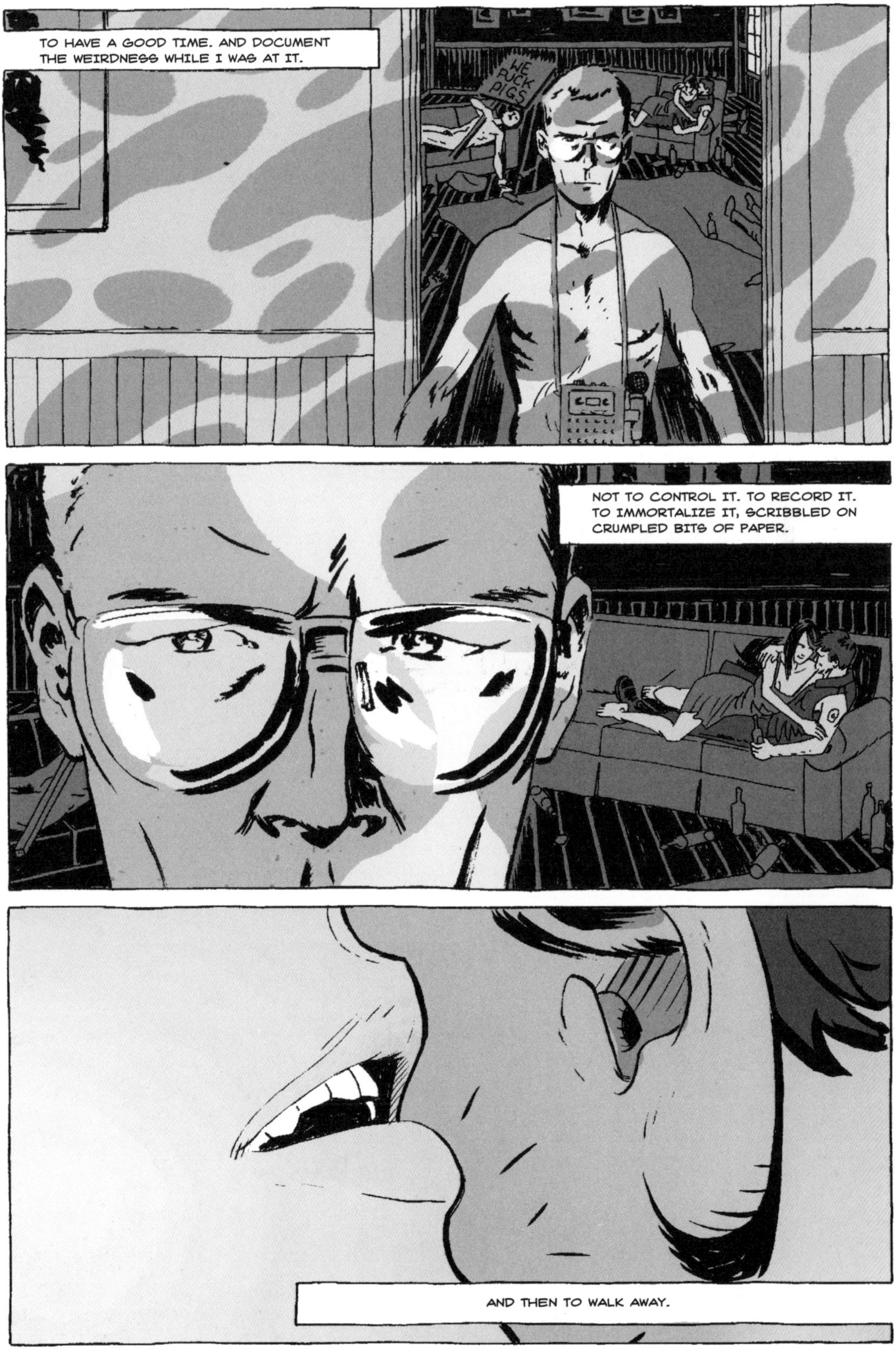
TO HAVE A GOOD TIME. AND DOCUMENT THE WEIRDNESS WHILE I WAS AT IT.
NOT TO CONTROL IT. TO RECORD IT. TO IMMORTALIZE IT, SCRIBBLED ON CRUMPLED BITS OF PAPER.
AND THEN TO WALK AWAY.

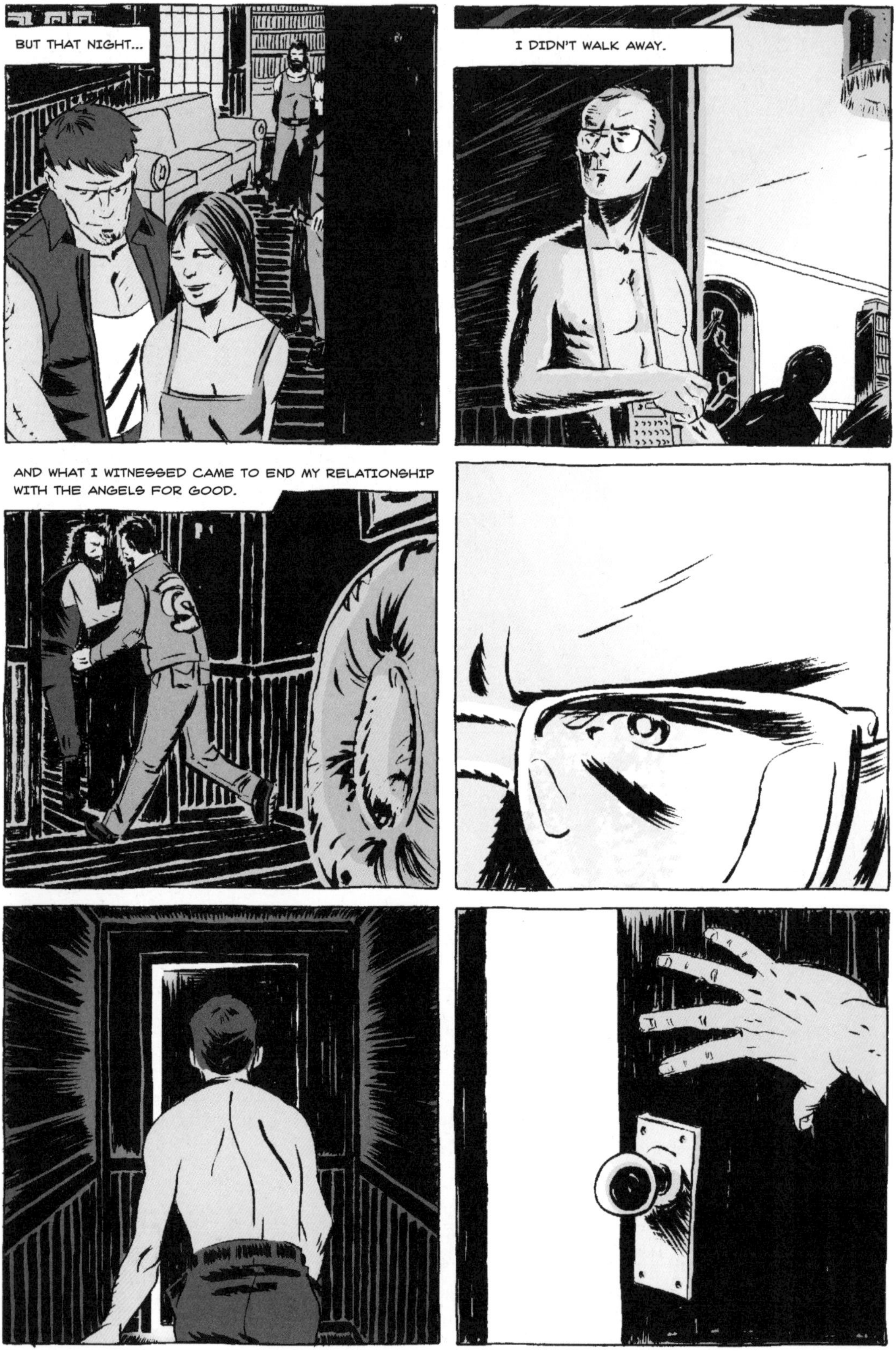
BUT THAT NIGHT...
I DIDN'T WALK AWAY.
AND WHAT I WITNESSED CAME TO END MY RELATIONSHIP WITH THE ANGELS FOR GOOD.

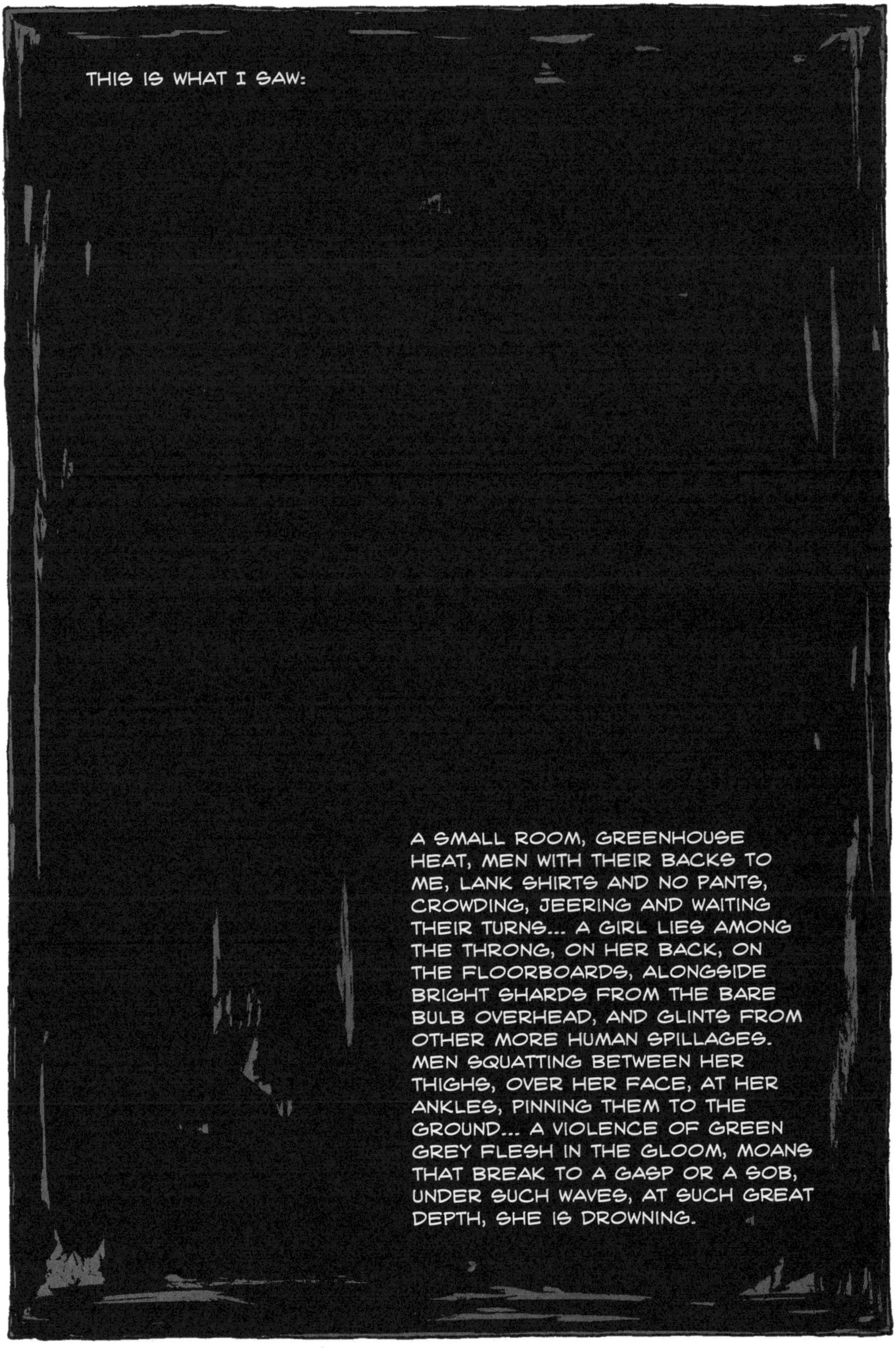
THIS IS WHAT I SAW:
A SMALL ROOM, GREENHOUSE HEAT, MEN WITH THEIR BACKS TO ME, LANK SHIRTS AND NO PANTS, CROWDING, JEERING AND WAITING THEIR TURNS... A GIRL LIES AMONG THE THRONG, ON HER BACK, ON THE FLOORBOARDS, ALONGSIDE BRIGHT SHARDS FROM THE BARE BULB OVERHEAD, AND GLINTS FROM OTHER MORE HUMAN SPILLAGES. MEN SQUATTING BETWEEN HER THIGHS, OVER HER FACE, AT HER ANKLES, PINNING THEM TO THE GROUND... A VIOLENCE OF GREEN GREY FLESH IN THE GLOOM, MOANS THAT BREAK TO A GASP OR A SOB, UNDER SUCH WAVES, AT SUCH GREAT DEPTH, SHE IS DROWNING.

I KNOW WHAT YOU'RE THINKING NOW.

BUT BACK AT KESEY'S PLACE... I DIDN'T GO SAVE THAT GIRL.

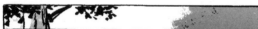

THIS IS MONTHS LATER... AFTER I SHOT MY MOUTH OFF.

AFTER SOME VICIOUS FUCKER STOMPED ME...

AND STOMPED ME GOOD.

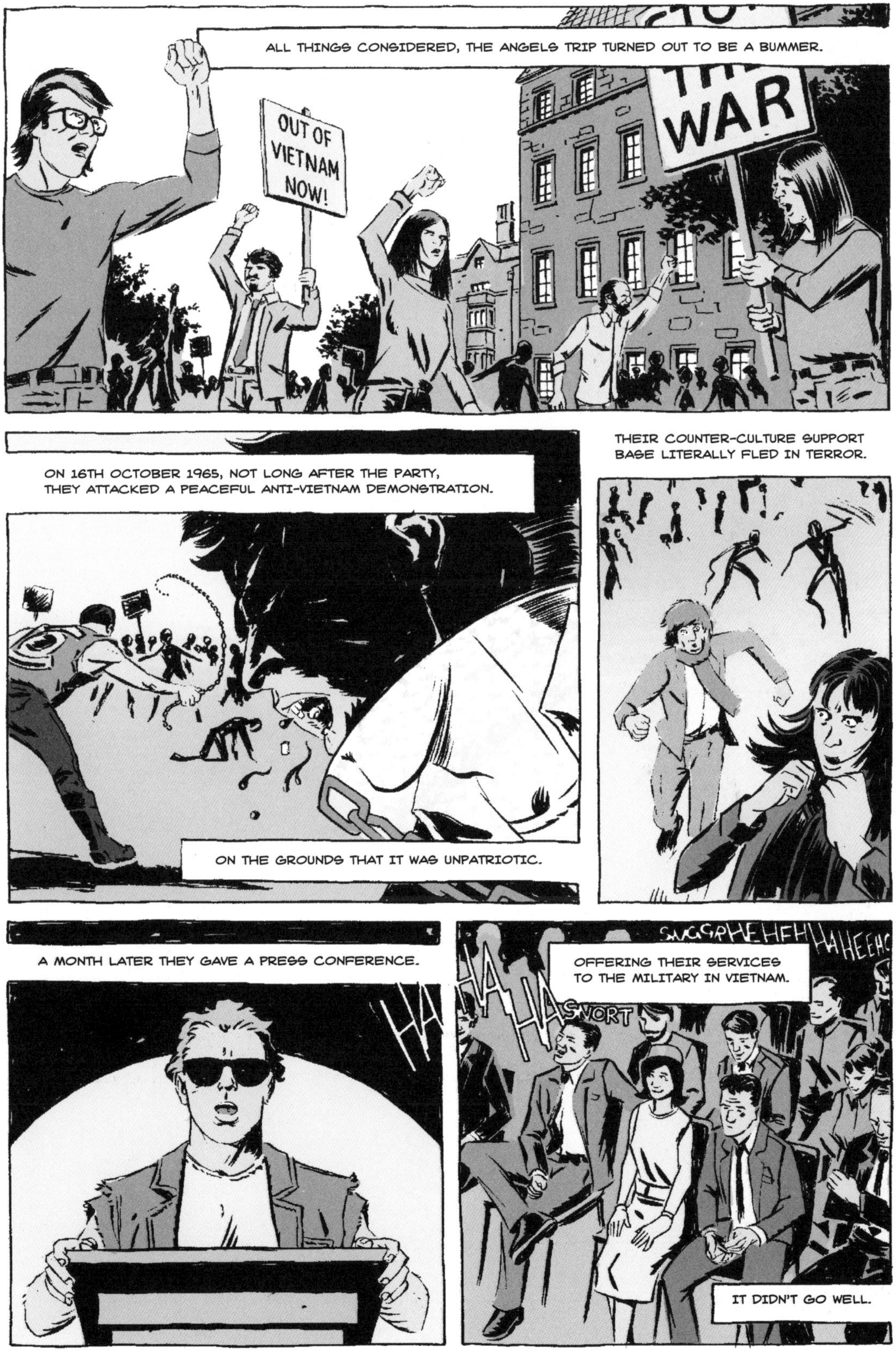
ALL THINGS CONSIDERED, THE ANGELS TRIP TURNED OUT TO BE A BUMMER.
OUT OF VIETNAM NOW!
WAR
ON 16TH OCTOBER 1965, NOT LONG AFTER THE PARTY, THEY ATTACKED A PEACEFUL ANTI-VIETNAM DEMONSTRATION.
ON THE GROUNDS THAT IT WAS UNPATRIOTIC.
THEIR COUNTER-CULTURE SUPPORT BASE LITERALLY FLED IN TERROR.
A MONTH LATER THEY GAVE A PRESS CONFERENCE.
HA
OFFERING THEIR SERVICES TO THE MILITARY IN VIETNAM.
HAHAHA
SNORT
SNGGRHEHEH
HAHEEHC
IT DIDN'T GO WELL.

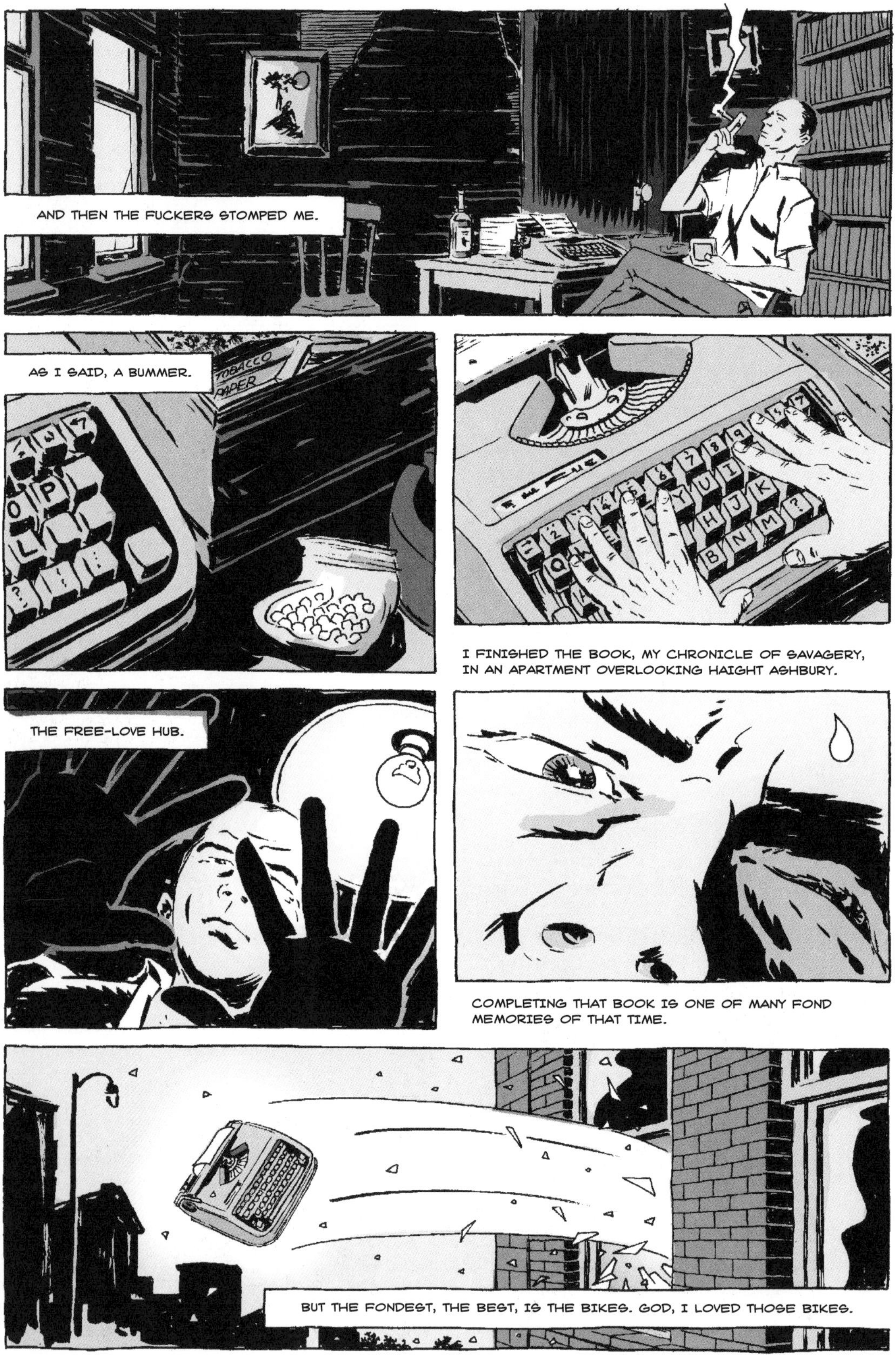
AND THEN THE FUCKERS STOMPED ME.
AS I SAID, A BUMMER.
TOBACCO PAPER
I FINISHED THE BOOK, MY CHRONICLE OF SAVAGERY, IN AN APARTMENT OVERLOOKING HAIGHT ASHBURY.
THE FREE-LOVE HUB.
COMPLETING THAT BOOK IS ONE OF MANY FOND MEMORIES OF THAT TIME.
BUT THE FONDEST, THE BEST, IS THE BIKES. GOD, I LOVED THOSE BIKES.

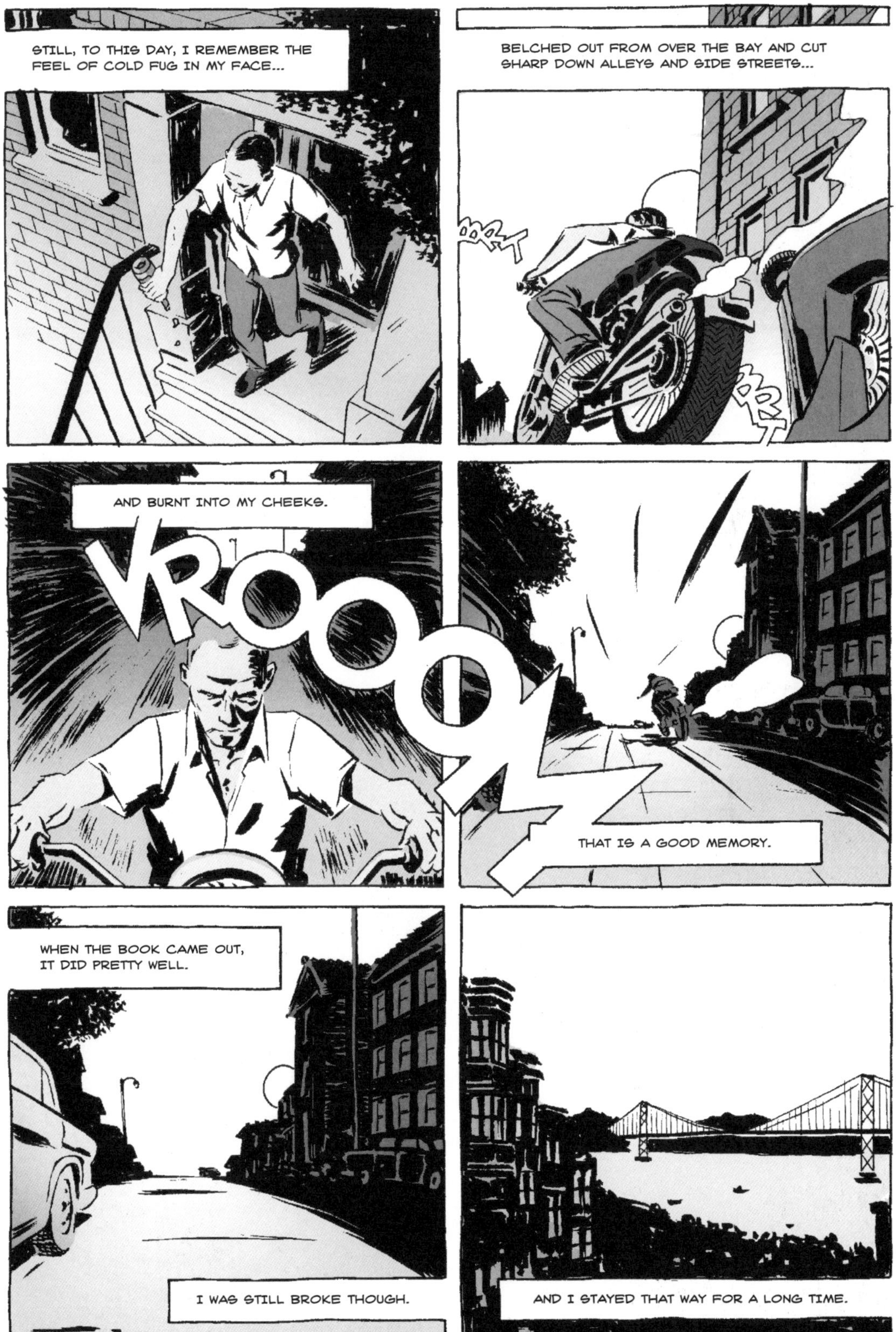
STILL, TO THIS DAY, I REMEMBER THE FEEL OF COLD FUG IN MY FACE...
BELCHED OUT FROM OVER THE BAY AND CUT SHARP DOWN ALLEYS AND SIDE STREETS...
AND BURNT INTO MY CHEEKS.
VROOOM
THAT IS A GOOD MEMORY.
WHEN THE BOOK CAME OUT, IT DID PRETTY WELL.
I WAS STILL BROKE THOUGH.
AND I STAYED THAT WAY FOR A LONG TIME.

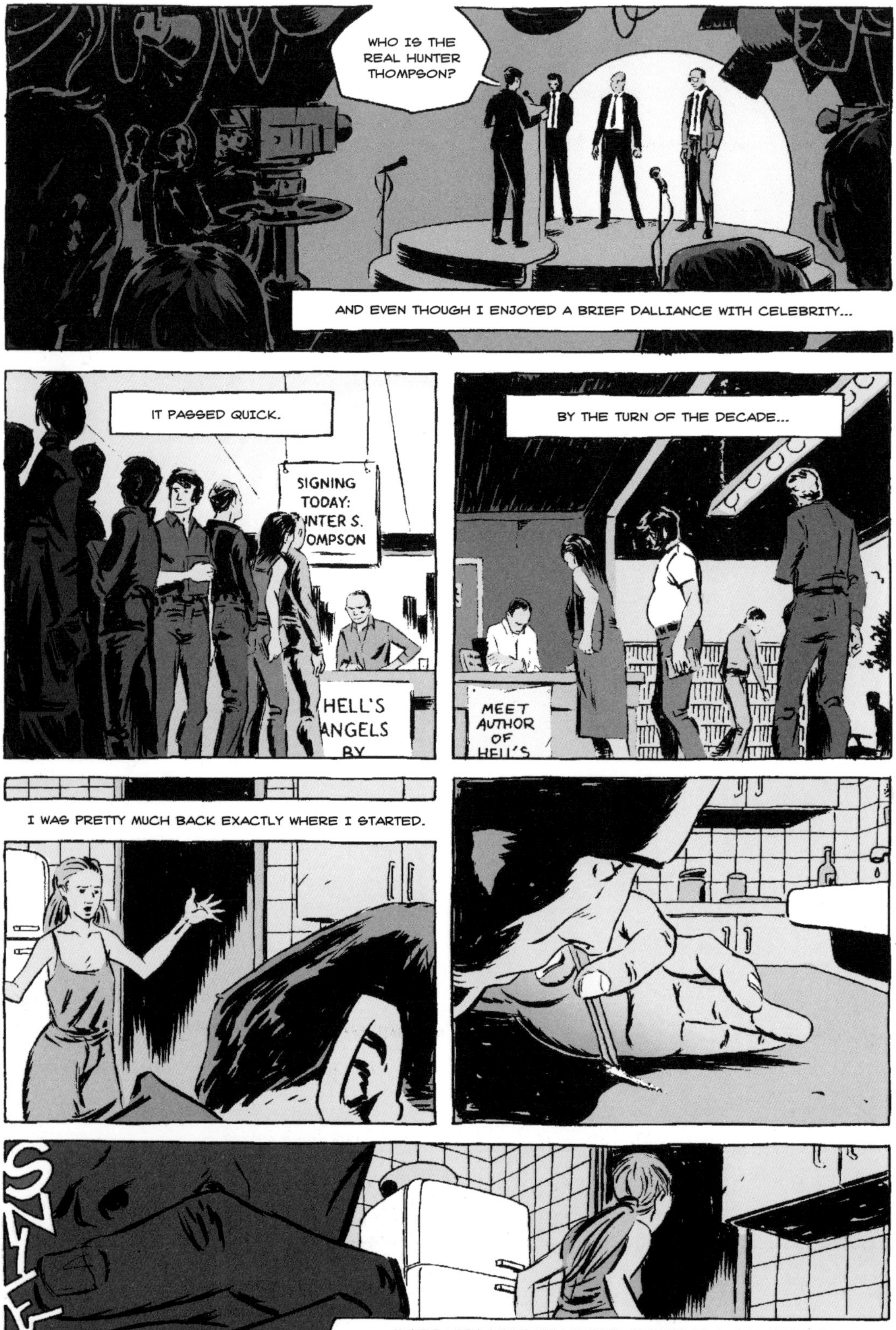
WHO IS THE REAL HUNTER THOMPSON?
AND EVEN THOUGH I ENJOYED A BRIEF DALLIANCE WITH CELEBRITY...
IT PASSED QUICK.
SIGNING TODAY: NTER S. OMPSON
HELL'S ANGELS BY
BY THE TURN OF THE DECADE...
MEET AUTHOR OF
I WAS PRETTY MUCH BACK EXACTLY WHERE I STARTED.
SNIFF
MAYBE WITH SOME NEW HABITS PICKED UP ALONG THE WAY.

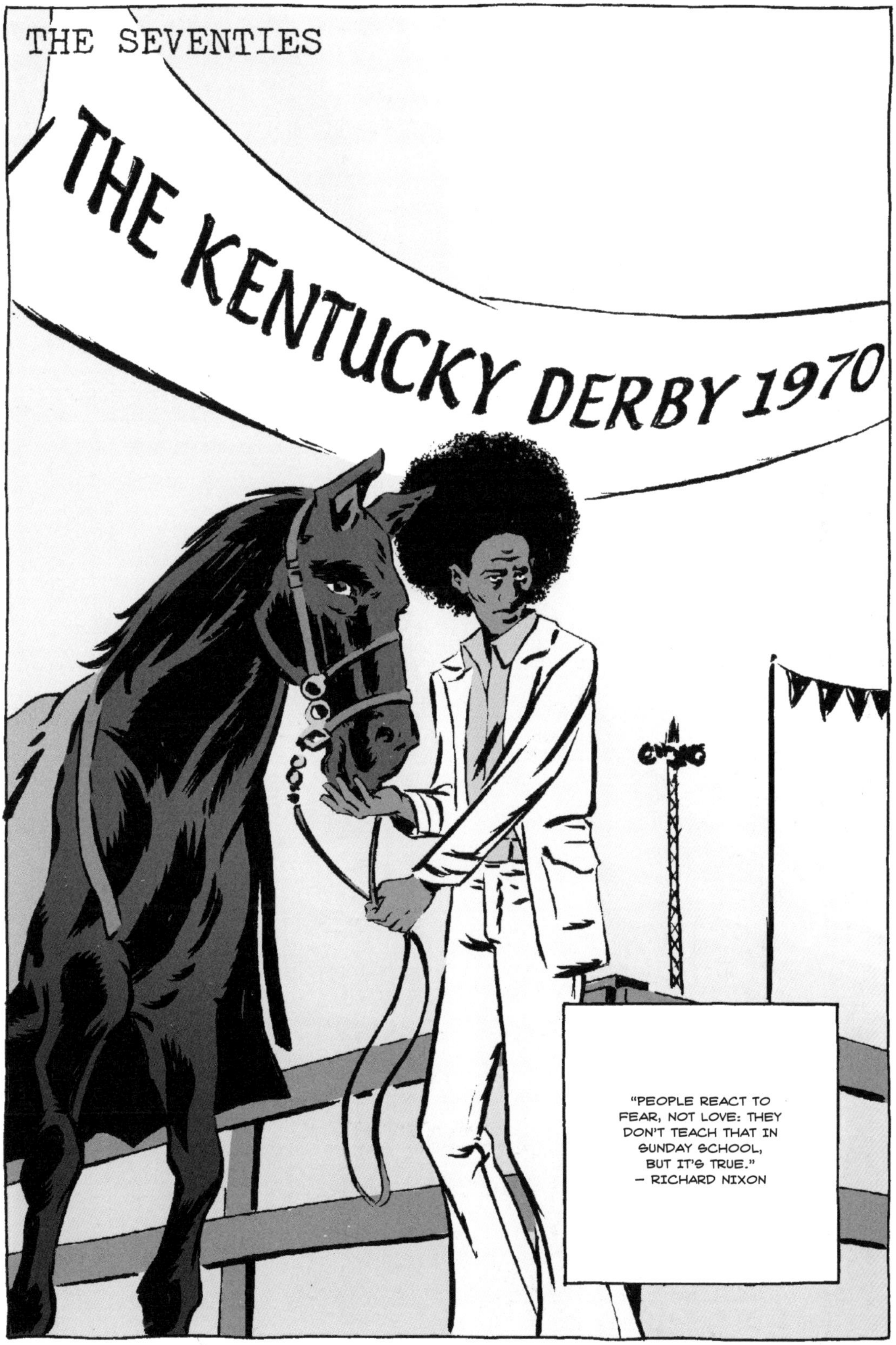
THE SEVENTIES
THE KENTUCKY DERBY 1970
"PEOPLE REACT TO FEAR, NOT LOVE: THEY DON'T TEACH THAT IN SUNDAY SCHOOL, BUT IT'S TRUE."
— RICHARD NIXON

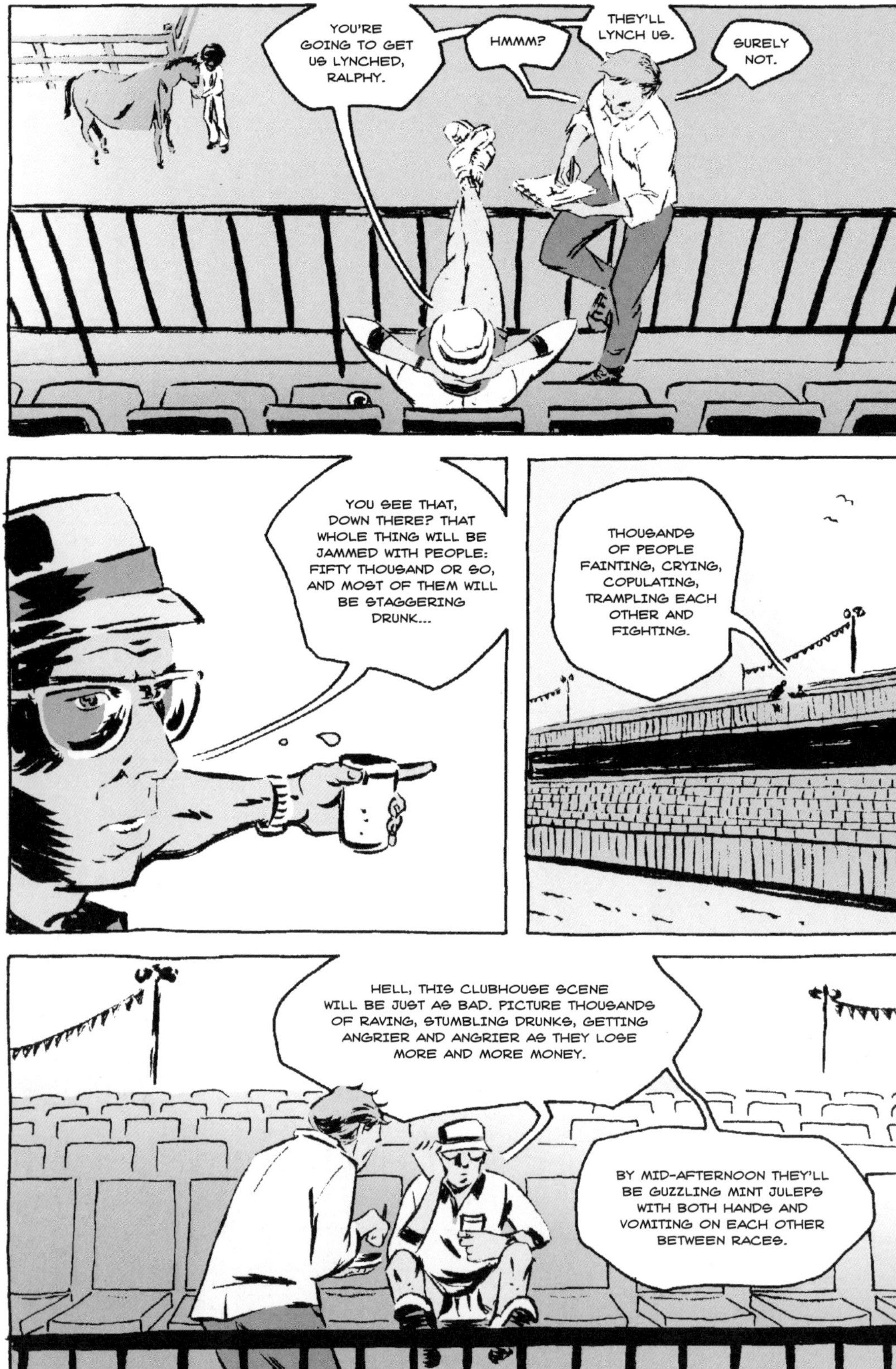
YOU'RE GOING TO GET US LYNCHED, RALPHY.
HMMM?
THEY'LL LYNCH US.
SURELY NOT.
YOU SEE THAT, DOWN THERE? THAT WHOLE THING WILL BE JAMMED WITH PEOPLE: FIFTY THOUSAND OR SO, AND MOST OF THEM WILL BE STAGGERING DRUNK...
THOUSANDS OF PEOPLE FAINTING, CRYING, COPULATING, TRAMPLING EACH OTHER AND FIGHTING.
HELL, THIS CLUBHOUSE SCENE WILL BE JUST AS BAD. PICTURE THOUSANDS OF RAVING, STUMBLING DRUNKS, GETTING ANGRIER AND ANGRIER AS THEY LOSE MORE AND MORE MONEY.
BY MID-AFTERNOON THEY'LL BE GUZZLING MINT JULEPS WITH BOTH HANDS AND VOMITING ON EACH OTHER BETWEEN RACES.

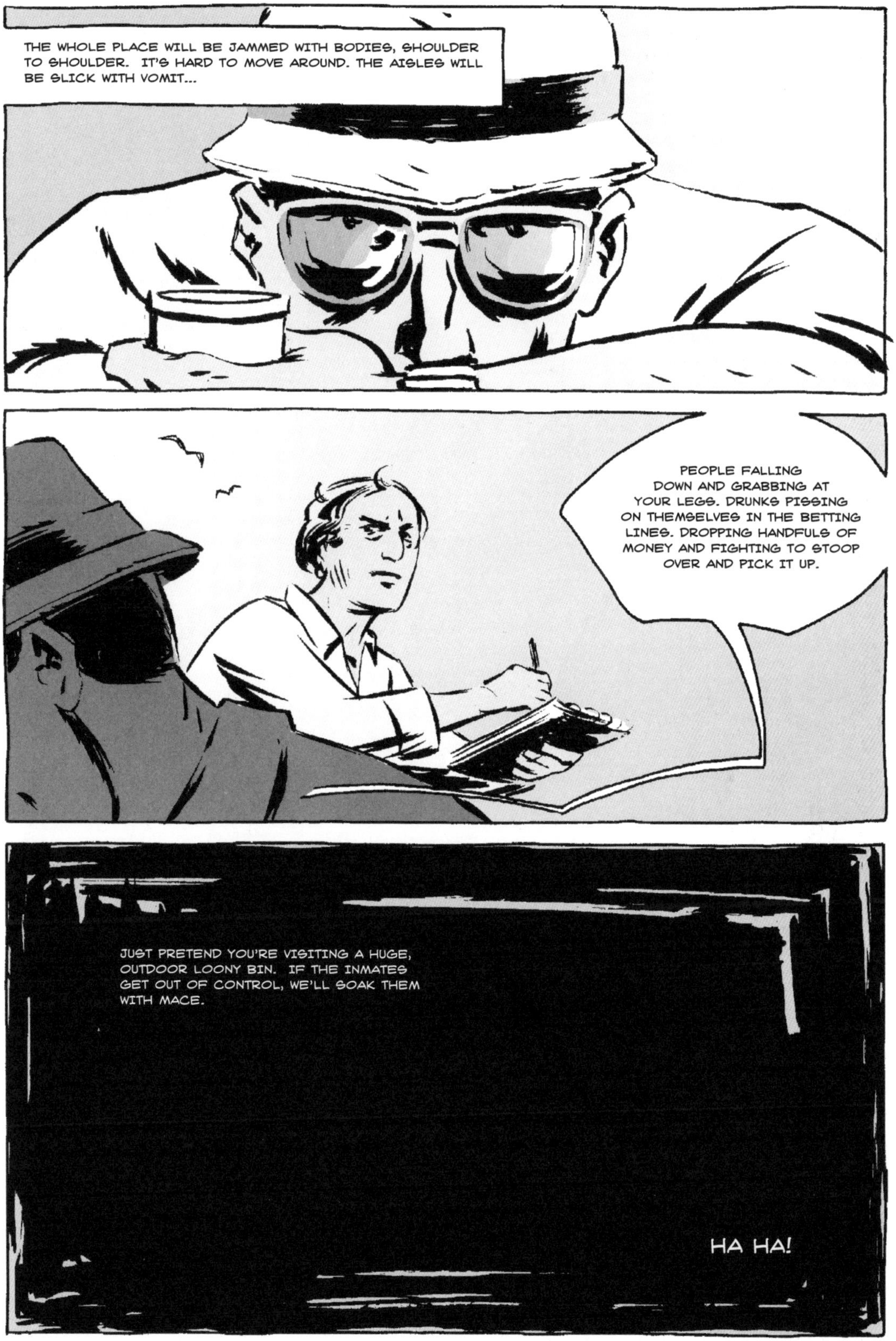
THE WHOLE PLACE WILL BE JAMMED WITH BODIES, SHOULDER TO SHOULDER. IT'S HARD TO MOVE AROUND. THE AISLES WILL BE SLICK WITH VOMIT...
PEOPLE FALLING DOWN AND GRABBING AT YOUR LEGS. DRUNKS PISSING ON THEMSELVES IN THE BETTING LINES. DROPPING HANDFULS OF MONEY AND FIGHTING TO STOOP OVER AND PICK IT UP.
JUST PRETEND YOU'RE VISITING A HUGE, OUTDOOR LOONY BIN. IF THE INMATES GET OUT OF CONTROL, WE'LL SOAK THEM WITH MACE.
HA HA!

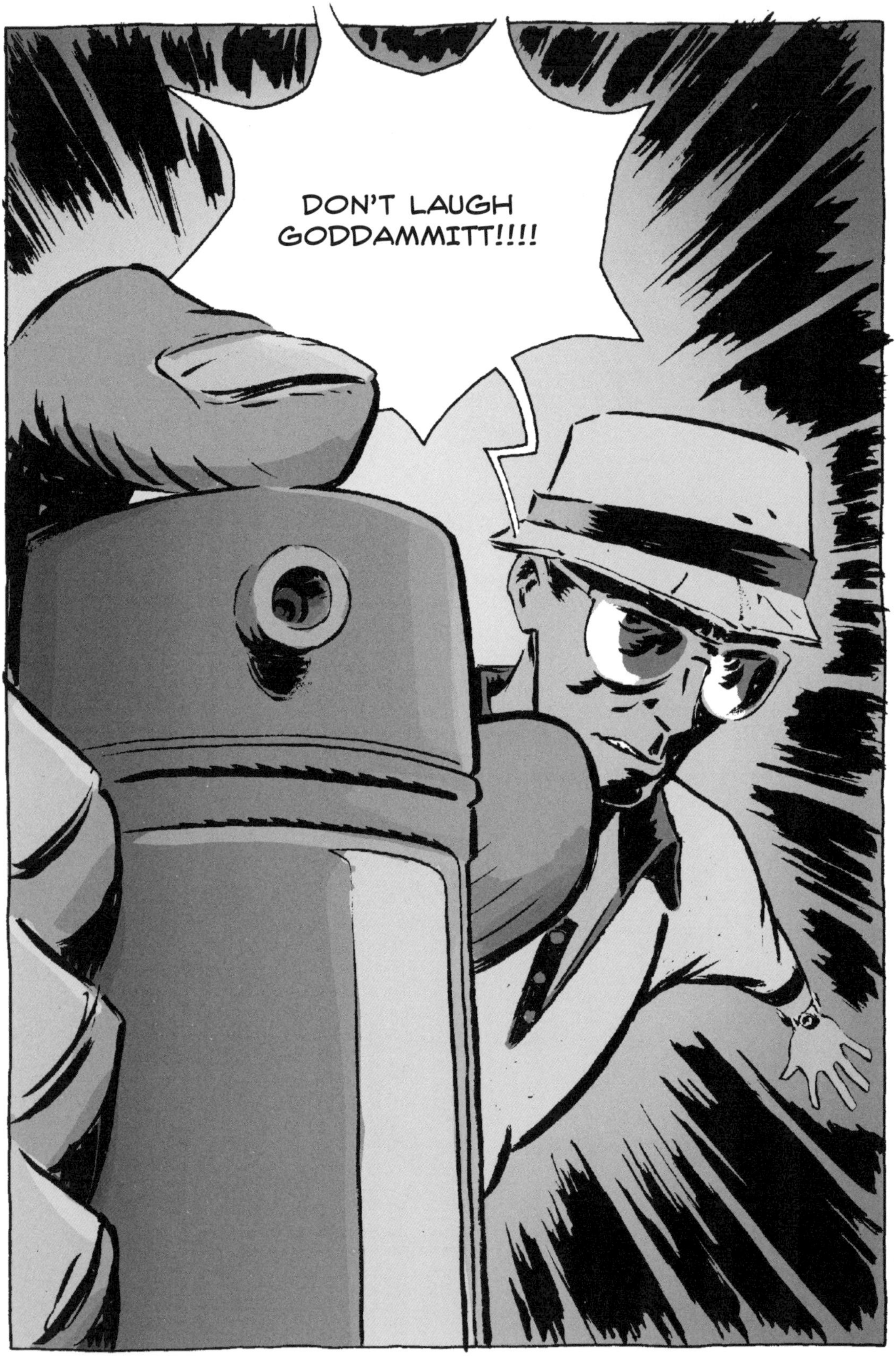
DON'T LAUGH
GODDAMMITT!!!!

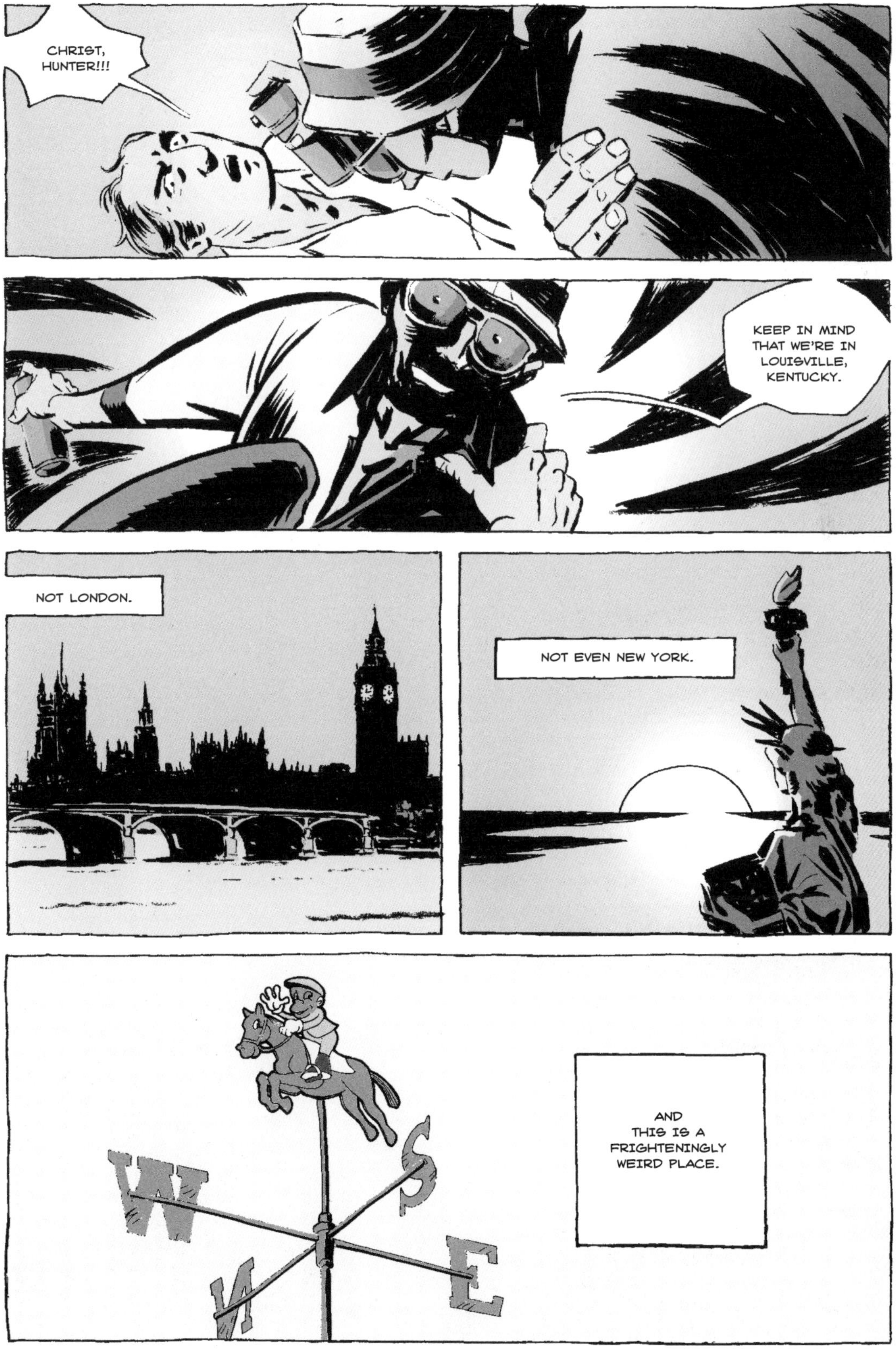
CHRIST, HUNTER!!!
KEEP IN MIND THAT WE'RE IN LOUISVILLE, KENTUCKY.
NOT LONDON.
NOT EVEN NEW YORK.
AND THIS IS A FRIGHTENINGLY WEIRD PLACE.
W
S
E
N

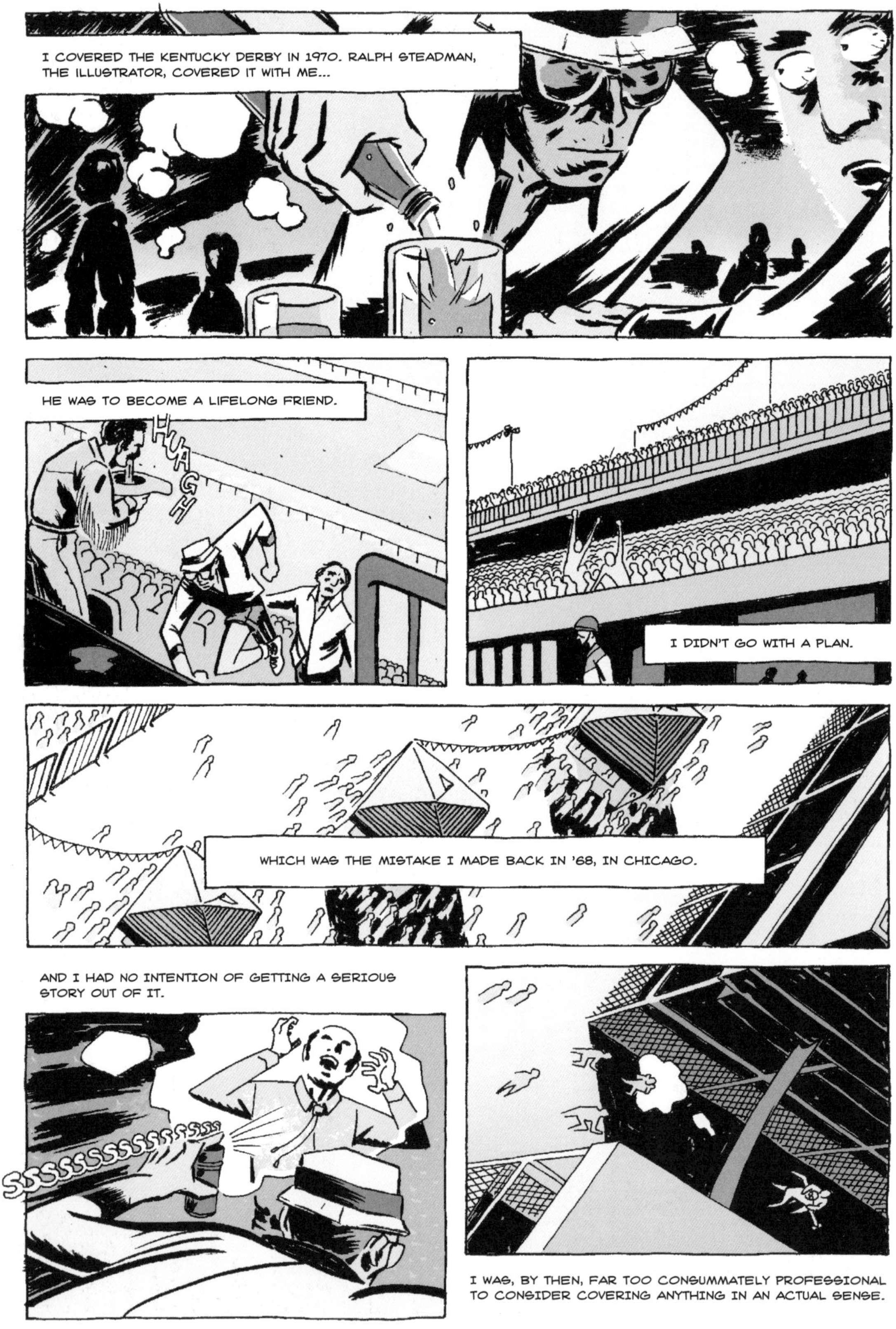

I COVERED THE KENTUCKY DERBY IN 1970. RALPH STEADMAN, THE ILLUSTRATOR, COVERED IT WITH ME...
HE WAS TO BECOME A LIFELONG FRIEND.
HUAGH
I DIDN'T GO WITH A PLAN.
WHICH WAS THE MISTAKE I MADE BACK IN '68, IN CHICAGO.
AND I HAD NO INTENTION OF GETTING A SERIOUS STORY OUT OF IT.
SSSSSSSSSSSSSSSSS
I WAS, BY THEN, FAR TOO CONSUMMATELY PROFESSIONAL TO CONSIDER COVERING ANYTHING IN AN ACTUAL SENSE.

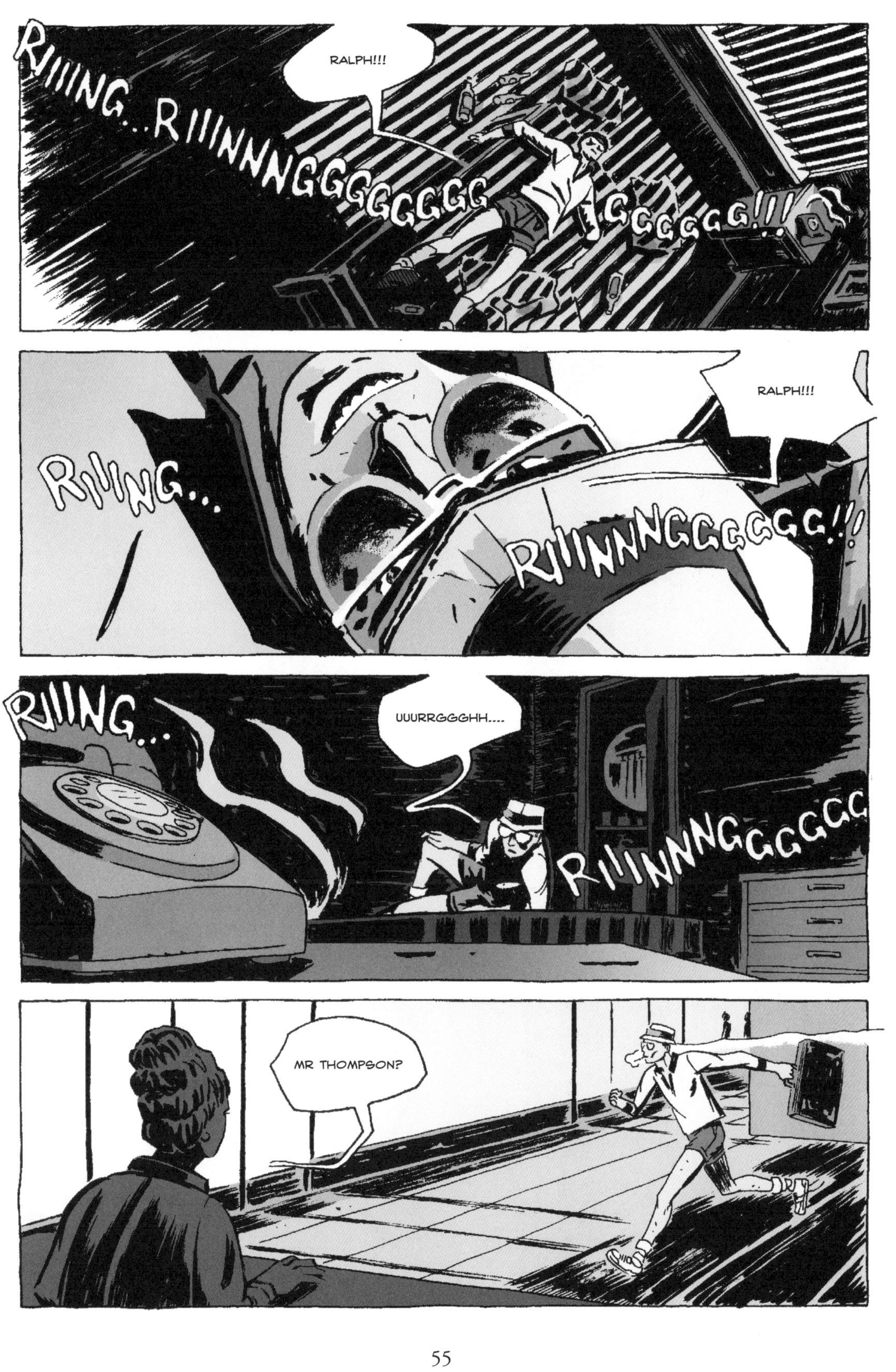
RIIING...RIIINNNGGGGGGGG
RALPH!!!
GGGGGG!!!
RIIING...
RALPH!!!
RIIINNNGGGGGG!!!
RIIING...
UUURRGGGHH....
RIIINNNGGGGG
MR THOMPSON?

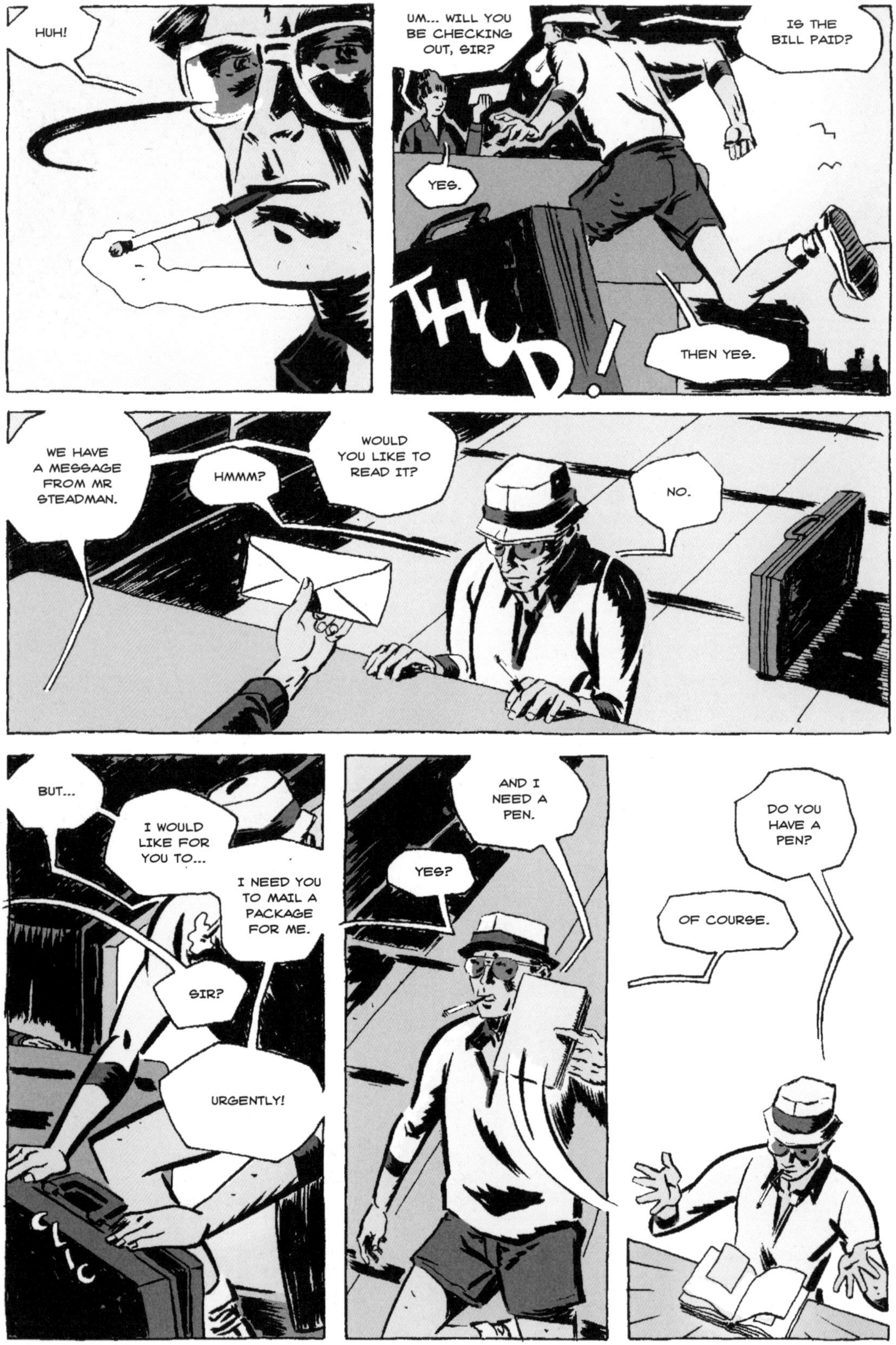
HUH!
UM... WILL YOU BE CHECKING OUT, SIR?
IS THE BILL PAID?
YES.
THUD!
THEN YES.
WE HAVE A MESSAGE FROM MR STEADMAN.
HMMM?
WOULD YOU LIKE TO READ IT?
NO.
BUT...
I WOULD LIKE FOR YOU TO...
I NEED YOU TO MAIL A PACKAGE FOR ME.
SIR?
URGENTLY!
CLIC
AND I NEED A PEN.
YES?
DO YOU HAVE A PEN?
OF COURSE.

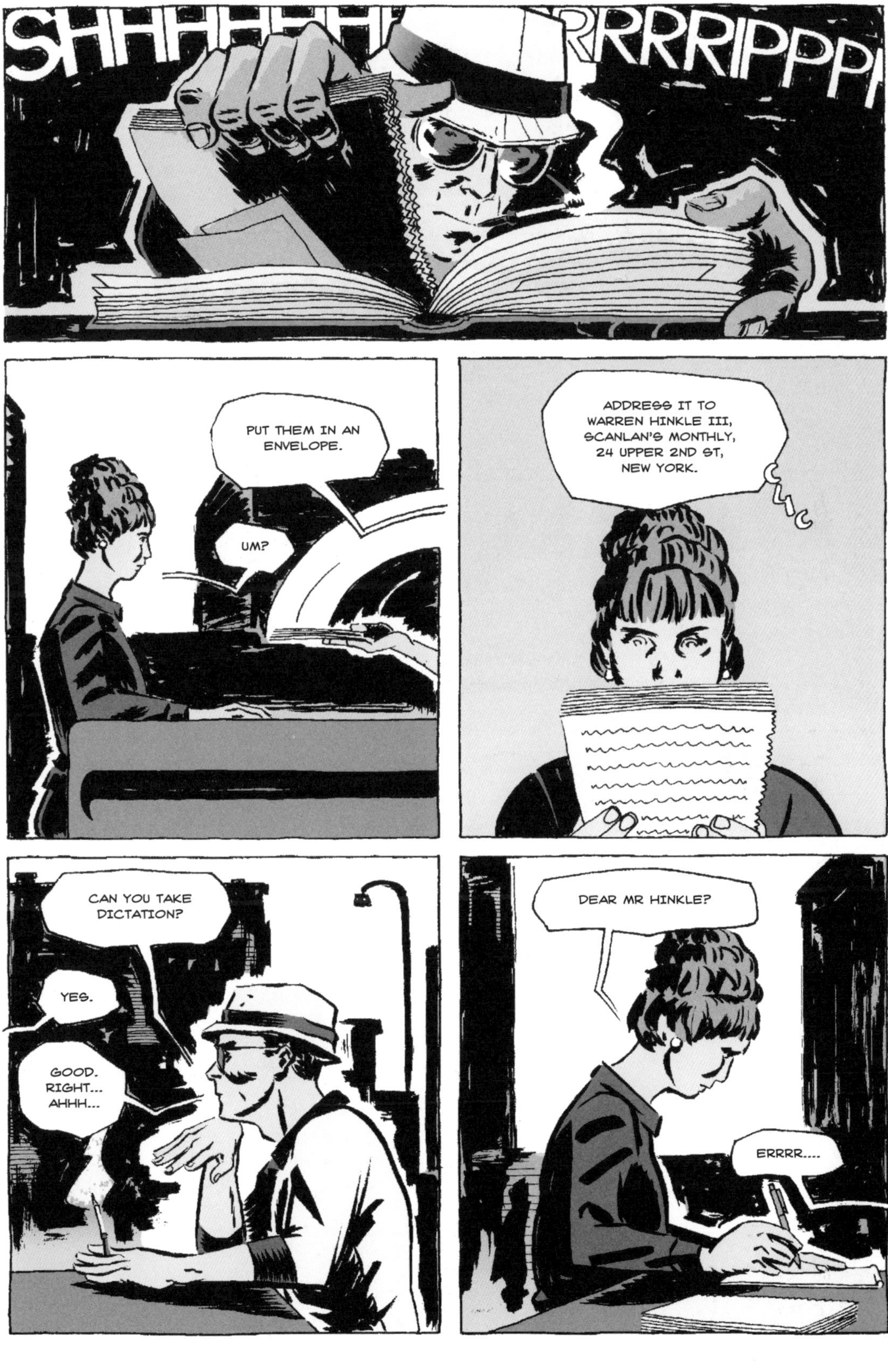
SHHHHHH RRRRRIPPPP
PUT THEM IN AN ENVELOPE.
UM?
ADDRESS IT TO WARREN HINKLE III, SCANLAN'S MONTHLY, 24 UPPER 2ND ST, NEW YORK.
CLIC
CAN YOU TAKE DICTATION?
YES.
GOOD. RIGHT... AHHH...
DEAR MR HINKLE?
ERRRR....

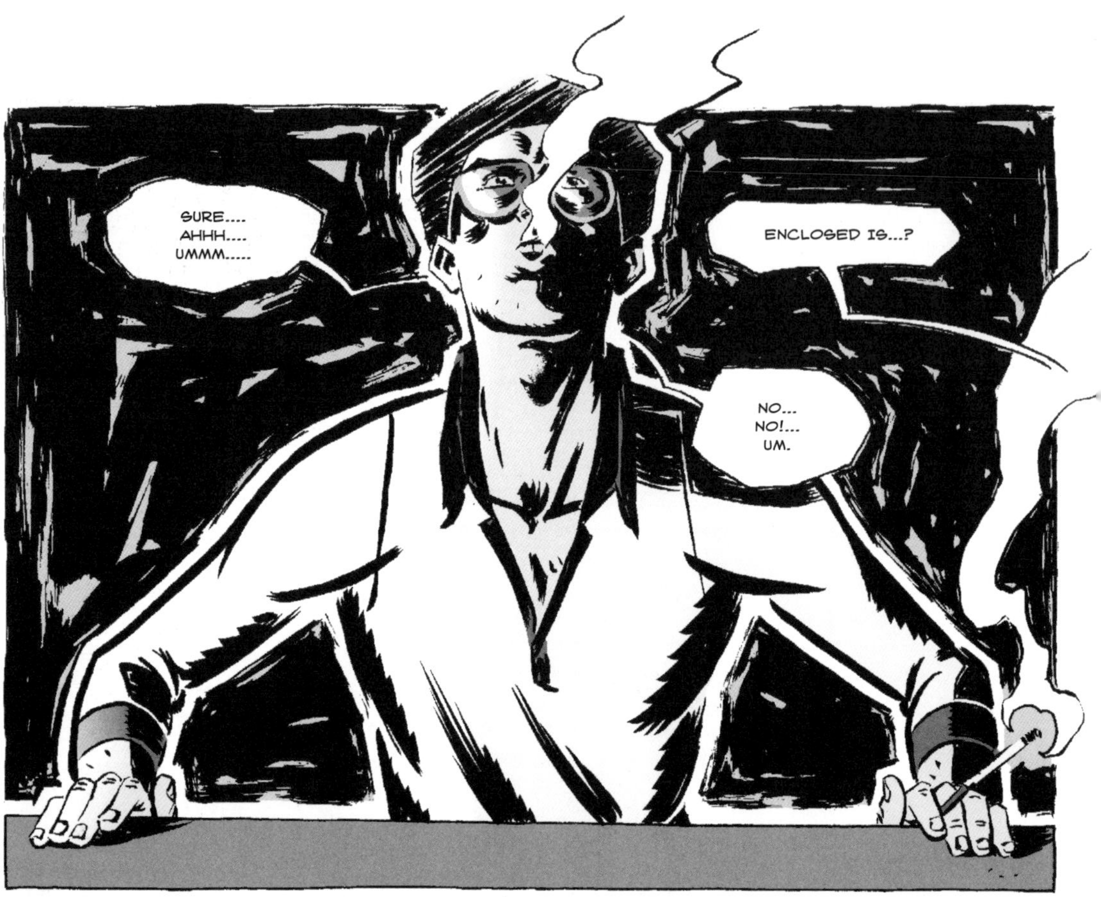
SURE....
AHHH....
UMMM.....
ENCLOSED IS...?
NO...
NO!...
UM.

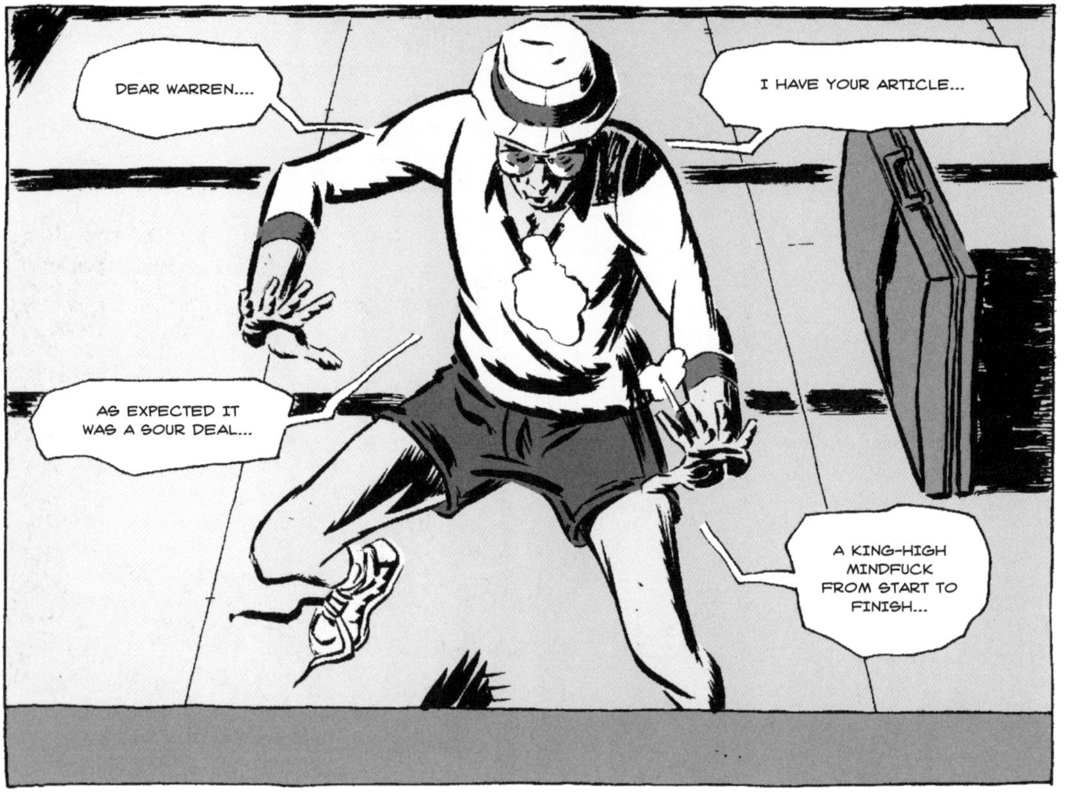
DEAR WARREN....
I HAVE YOUR ARTICLE...
AS EXPECTED IT WAS A SOUR DEAL...
A KING-HIGH MINDFUCK FROM START TO FINISH...

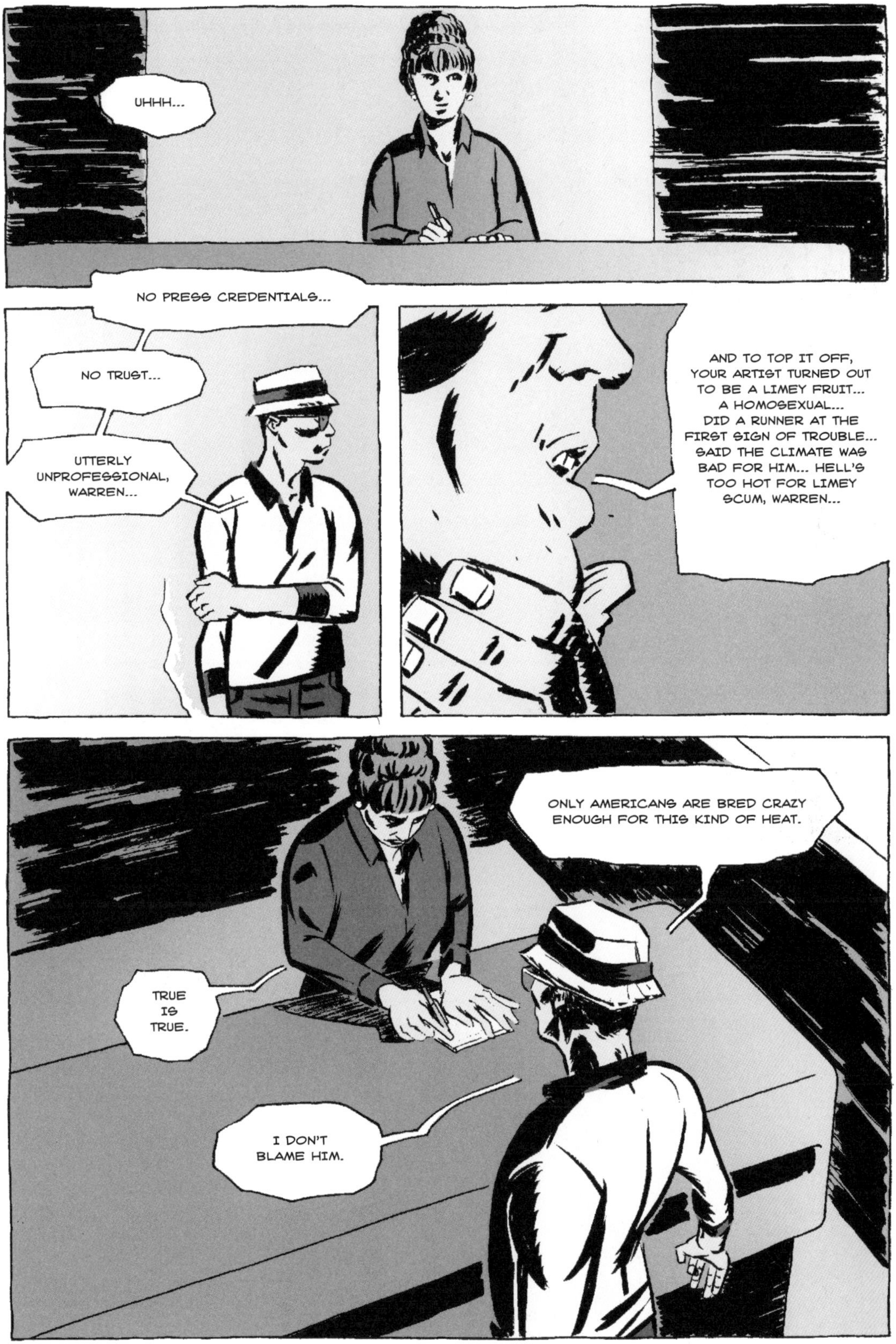
UHHH...
NO PRESS CREDENTIALS...
NO TRUST...
UTTERLY UNPROFESSIONAL, WARREN...
AND TO TOP IT OFF, YOUR ARTIST TURNED OUT TO BE A LIMEY FRUIT... A HOMOSEXUAL... DID A RUNNER AT THE FIRST SIGN OF TROUBLE... SAID THE CLIMATE WAS BAD FOR HIM... HELL'S TOO HOT FOR LIMEY SCUM, WARREN...
ONLY AMERICANS ARE BRED CRAZY ENOUGH FOR THIS KIND OF HEAT.
TRUE IS TRUE.
I DON'T BLAME HIM.

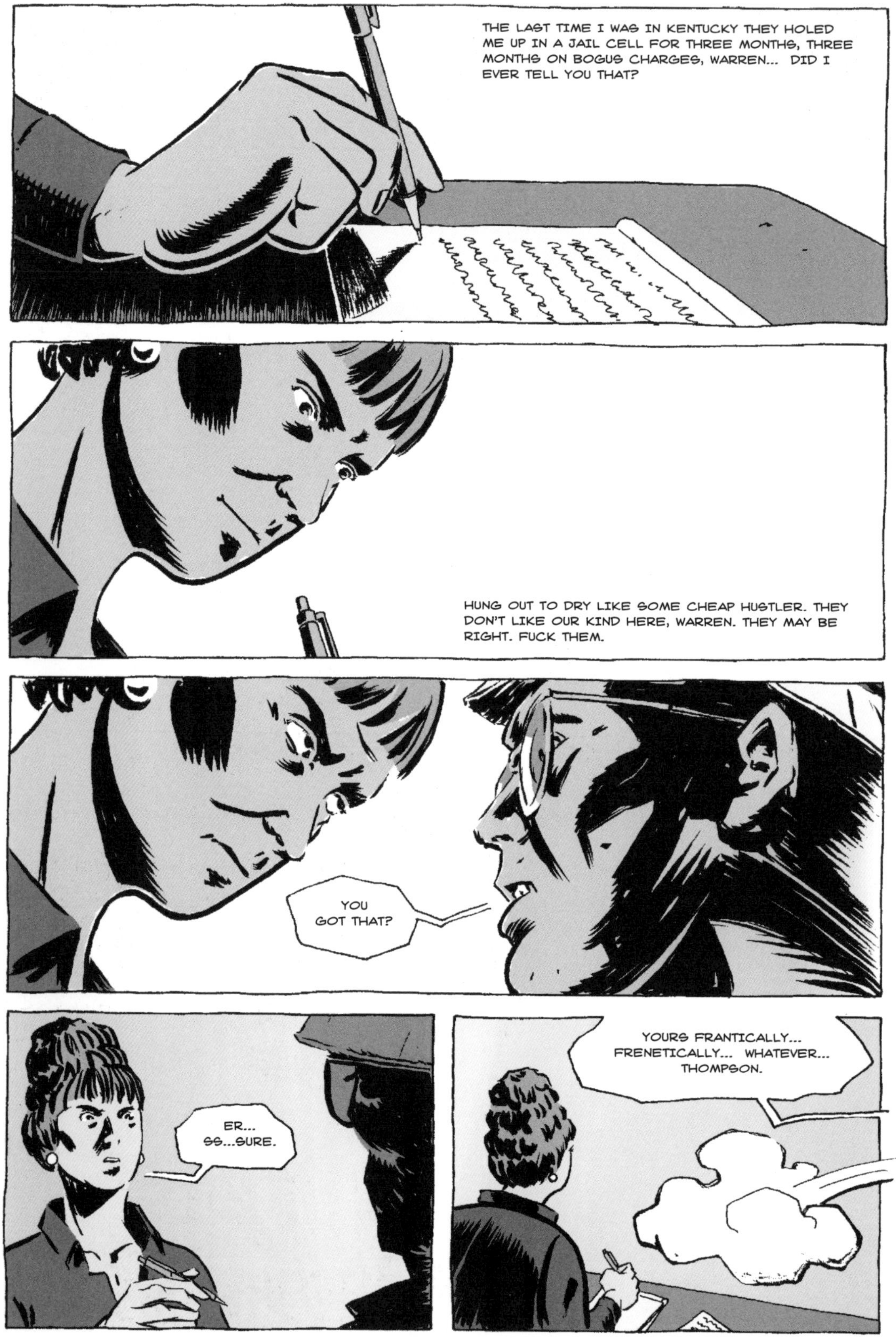
THE LAST TIME I WAS IN KENTUCKY THEY HOLED ME UP IN A JAIL CELL FOR THREE MONTHS, THREE MONTHS ON BOGUS CHARGES, WARREN... DID I EVER TELL YOU THAT?
HUNG OUT TO DRY LIKE SOME CHEAP HUSTLER. THEY DON'T LIKE OUR KIND HERE, WARREN. THEY MAY BE RIGHT. FUCK THEM.
YOU GOT THAT?
ER... SS...SURE.
YOURS FRANTICALLY... FRENETICALLY... WHATEVER... THOMPSON.

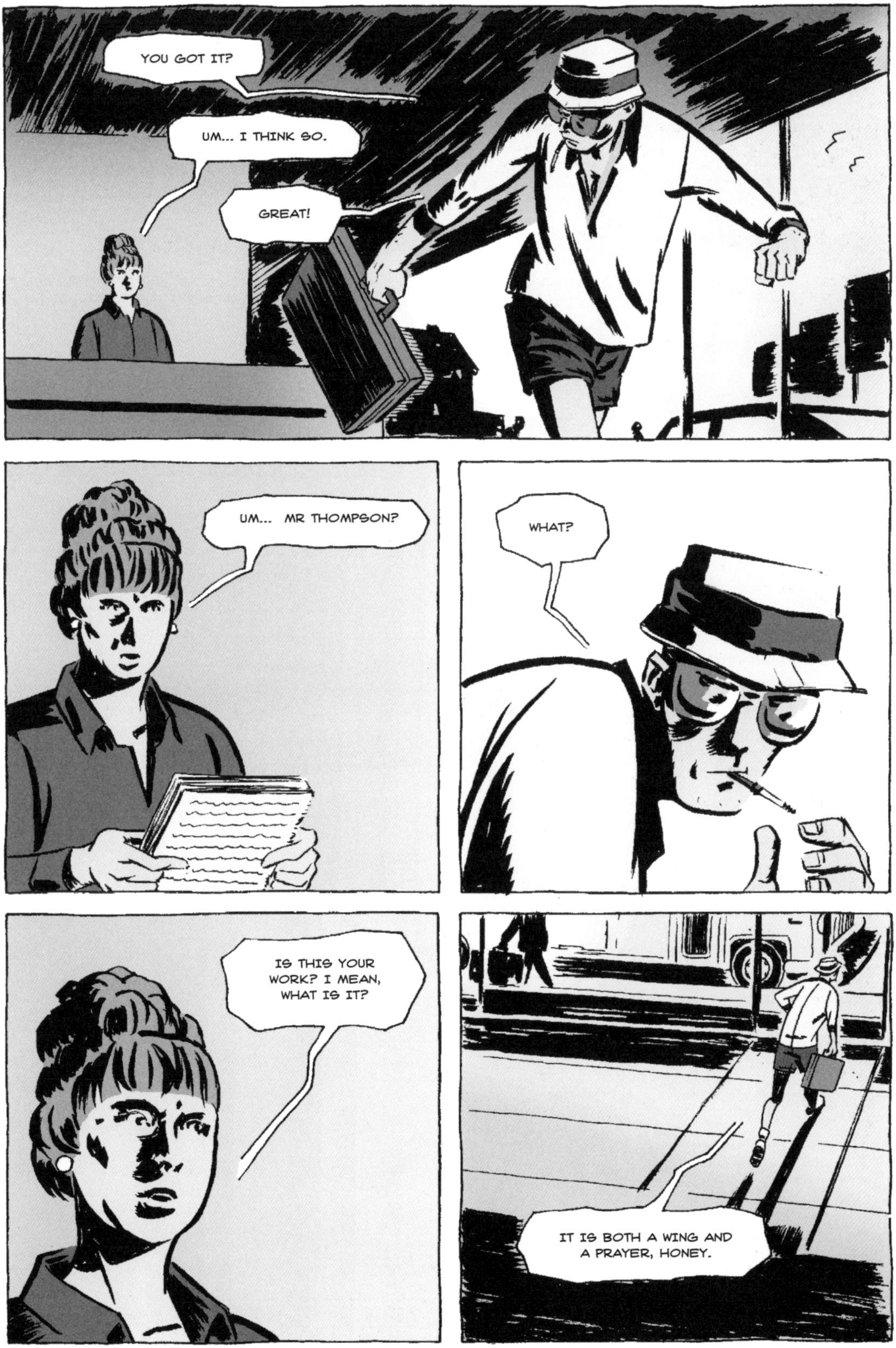
YOU GOT IT?
UM... I THINK SO.
GREAT!
UM... MR THOMPSON?
WHAT?
IS THIS YOUR WORK? I MEAN, WHAT IS IT?
IT IS BOTH A WING AND A PRAYER, HONEY.

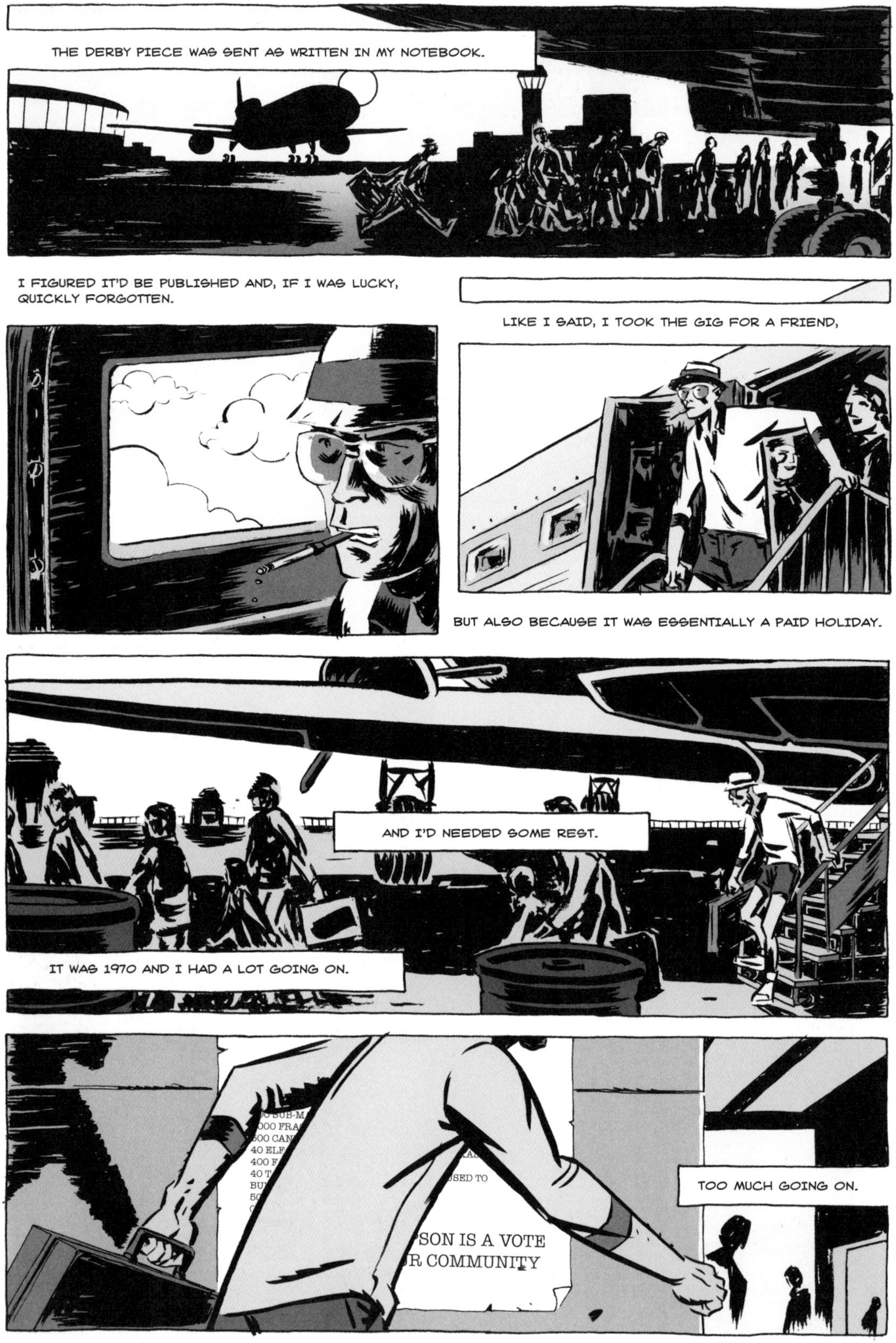
THE DERBY PIECE WAS SENT AS WRITTEN IN MY NOTEBOOK.
I FIGURED IT'D BE PUBLISHED AND, IF I WAS LUCKY, QUICKLY FORGOTTEN.
LIKE I SAID, I TOOK THE GIG FOR A FRIEND,
BUT ALSO BECAUSE IT WAS ESSENTIALLY A PAID HOLIDAY.
AND I'D NEEDED SOME REST.
IT WAS 1970 AND I HAD A LOT GOING ON.
SON IS A VOTE
R COMMUNITY
TOO MUCH GOING ON.

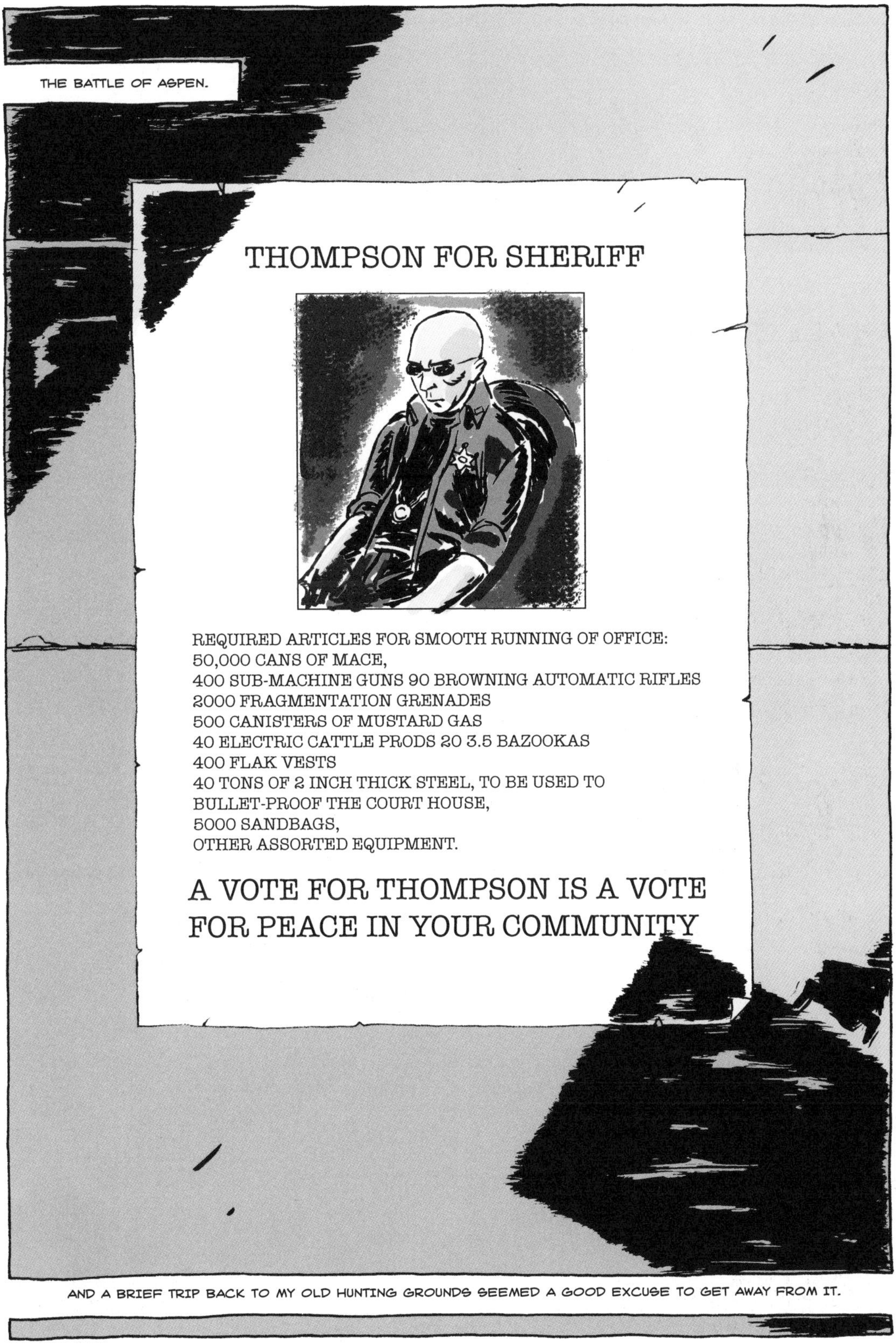
THE BATTLE OF ASPEN.
THOMPSON FOR SHERIFF
REQUIRED ARTICLES FOR SMOOTH RUNNING OF OFFICE:
50,000 CANS OF MACE,
400 SUB-MACHINE GUNS 90 BROWNING AUTOMATIC RIFLES
2000 FRAGMENTATION GRENADES
500 CANISTERS OF MUSTARD GAS
40 ELECTRIC CATTLE PRODS 20 3.5 BAZOOKAS
400 FLAK VESTS
40 TONS OF 2 INCH THICK STEEL, TO BE USED TO
BULLET-PROOF THE COURT HOUSE,
5000 SANDBAGS,
OTHER ASSORTED EQUIPMENT.
A VOTE FOR THOMPSON IS A VOTE
FOR PEACE IN YOUR COMMUNITY
AND A BRIEF TRIP BACK TO MY OLD HUNTING GROUNDS SEEMED A GOOD EXCUSE TO GET AWAY FROM IT.

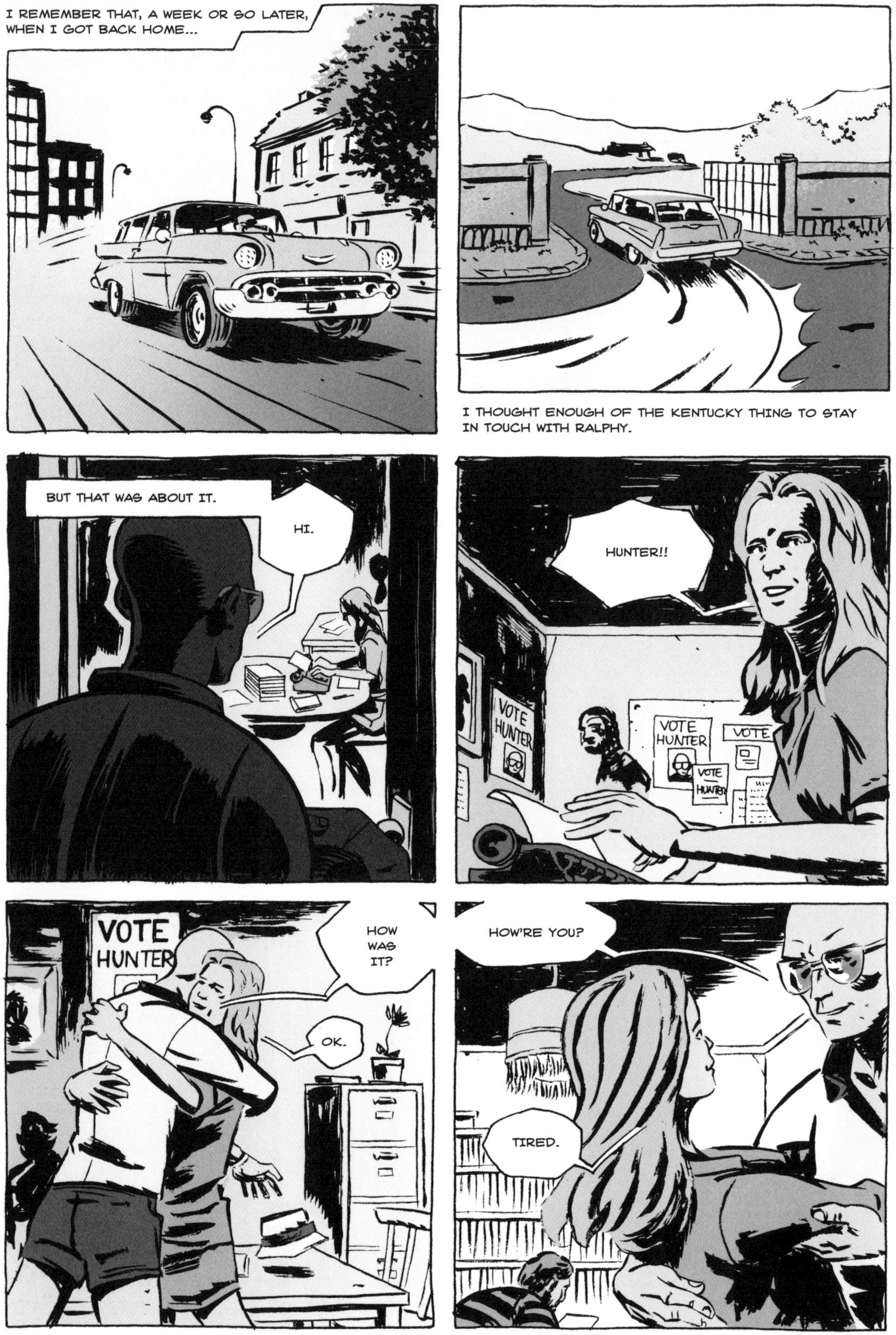
I REMEMBER THAT, A WEEK OR SO LATER, WHEN I GOT BACK HOME...
I THOUGHT ENOUGH OF THE KENTUCKY THING TO STAY IN TOUCH WITH RALPHY.
BUT THAT WAS ABOUT IT.
HI.
HUNTER!!
VOTE HUNTER
VOTE HUNTER
VOTE
HOW WAS IT?
OK.
VOTE HUNTER
HOW'RE YOU?
TIRED.

VERY NICE.

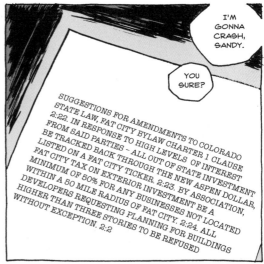

I'M GONNA CRASH, SANDY.

YOU SURE?

SUGGESTIONS FOR AMENDMENTS TO COLORADO STATE LAW, FAT CITY BYLAW CHARTER 1 CLAUSE 2:22. IN RESPONSE TO HIGH LEVELS OF INTEREST FROM SAID PARTIES – ALL OUT OF STATE INVESTMENT BE TRACKED BACK THROUGH THE NEW ASPEN DOLLAR, LISTED ON A FAT CITY TICKER. 2:23. BY ASSOCIATION, FAT CITY TAX ON EXTERIOR INVESTMENT BE A MINIMUM OF 50% FOR ANY BUSINESSES NOT LOCATED WITHIN A 50 MILE RADIUS OF FAT CITY. 2:24. ALL DEVELOPERS REQUESTING PLANNING FOR BUILDINGS HIGHER THAN THREE STORIES TO BE REFUSED WITHOUT EXCEPTION. 2:2

IF I'M NOT UP AT SIX, COME WAKE ME.

HEY, HUNTER!

YEAH?

I MISSED YOU, HUNTER

WELL THEN, UH...

YOU SHOULD COME AND TELL ME ABOUT IT.

GUYS.

LET'S CALL IT A DAY, OK?

I NEED SOME REST.

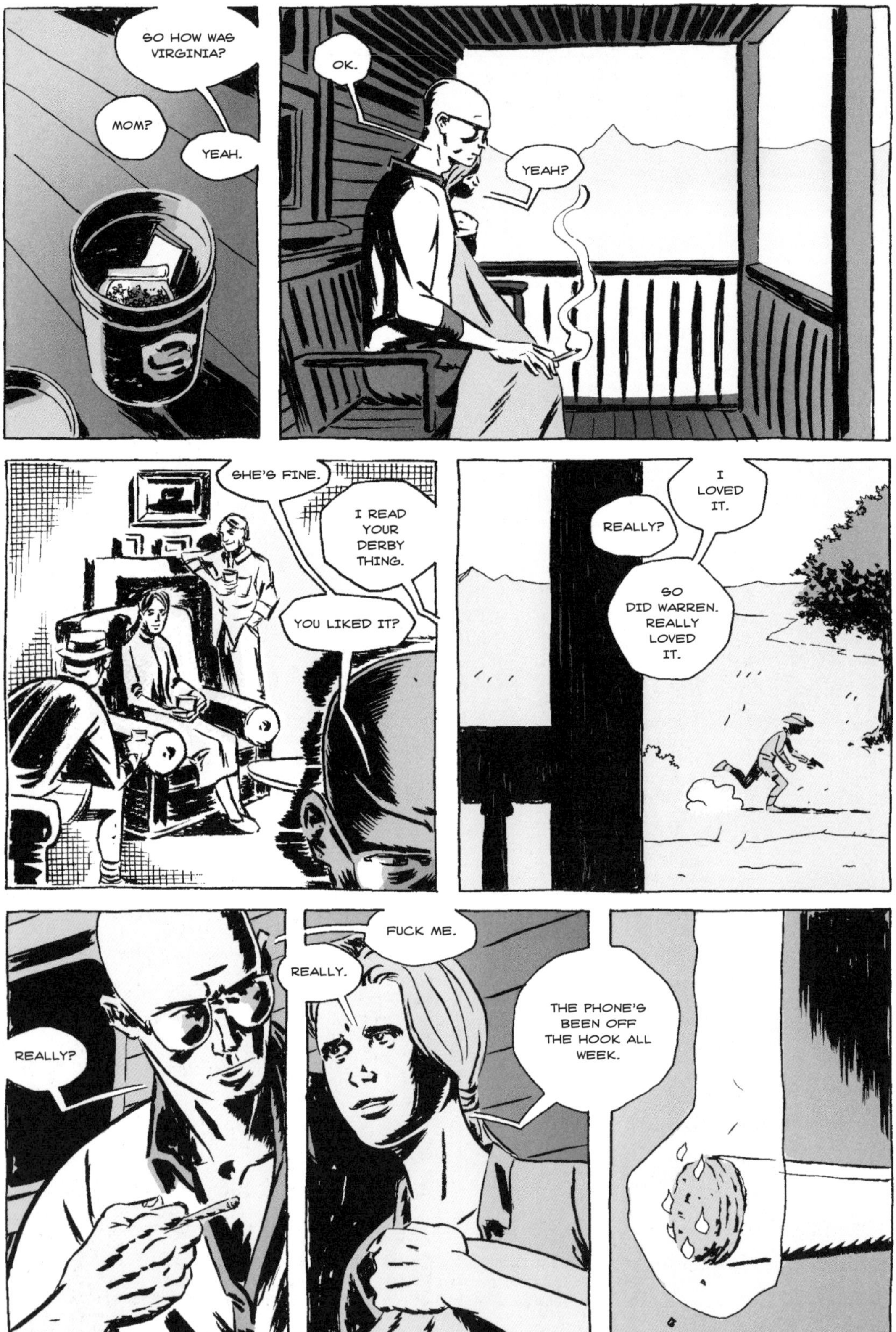
SO HOW WAS VIRGINIA?
MOM?
YEAH.
OK.
YEAH?
SHE'S FINE.
I READ YOUR DERBY THING.
YOU LIKED IT?
REALLY?
I LOVED IT.
SO DID WARREN. REALLY LOVED IT.
REALLY?
FUCK ME.
REALLY.
THE PHONE'S BEEN OFF THE HOOK ALL WEEK.

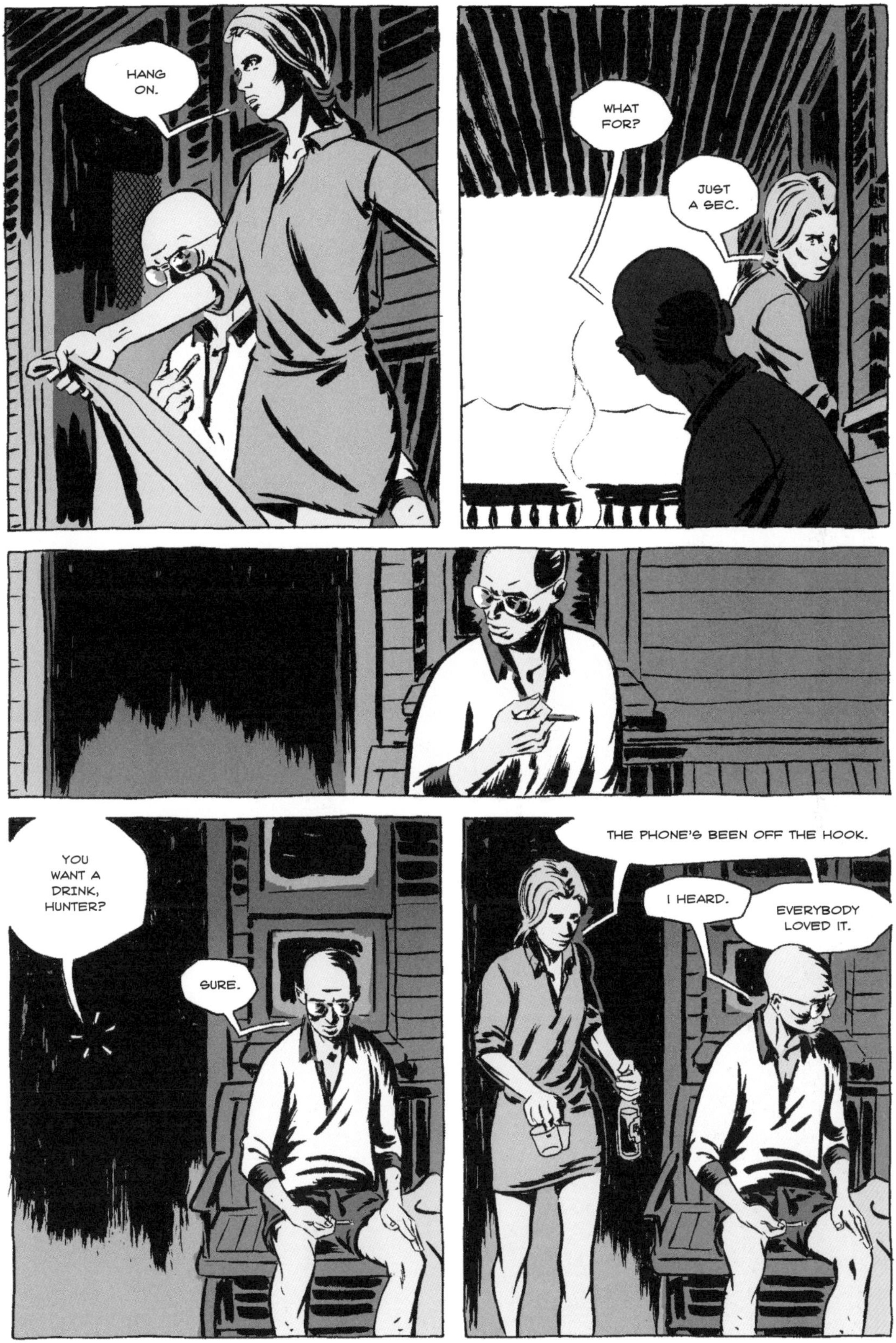
HANG ON.
WHAT FOR?
JUST A SEC.
YOU WANT A DRINK, HUNTER?
SURE.
THE PHONE'S BEEN OFF THE HOOK.
I HEARD.
EVERYBODY LOVED IT.

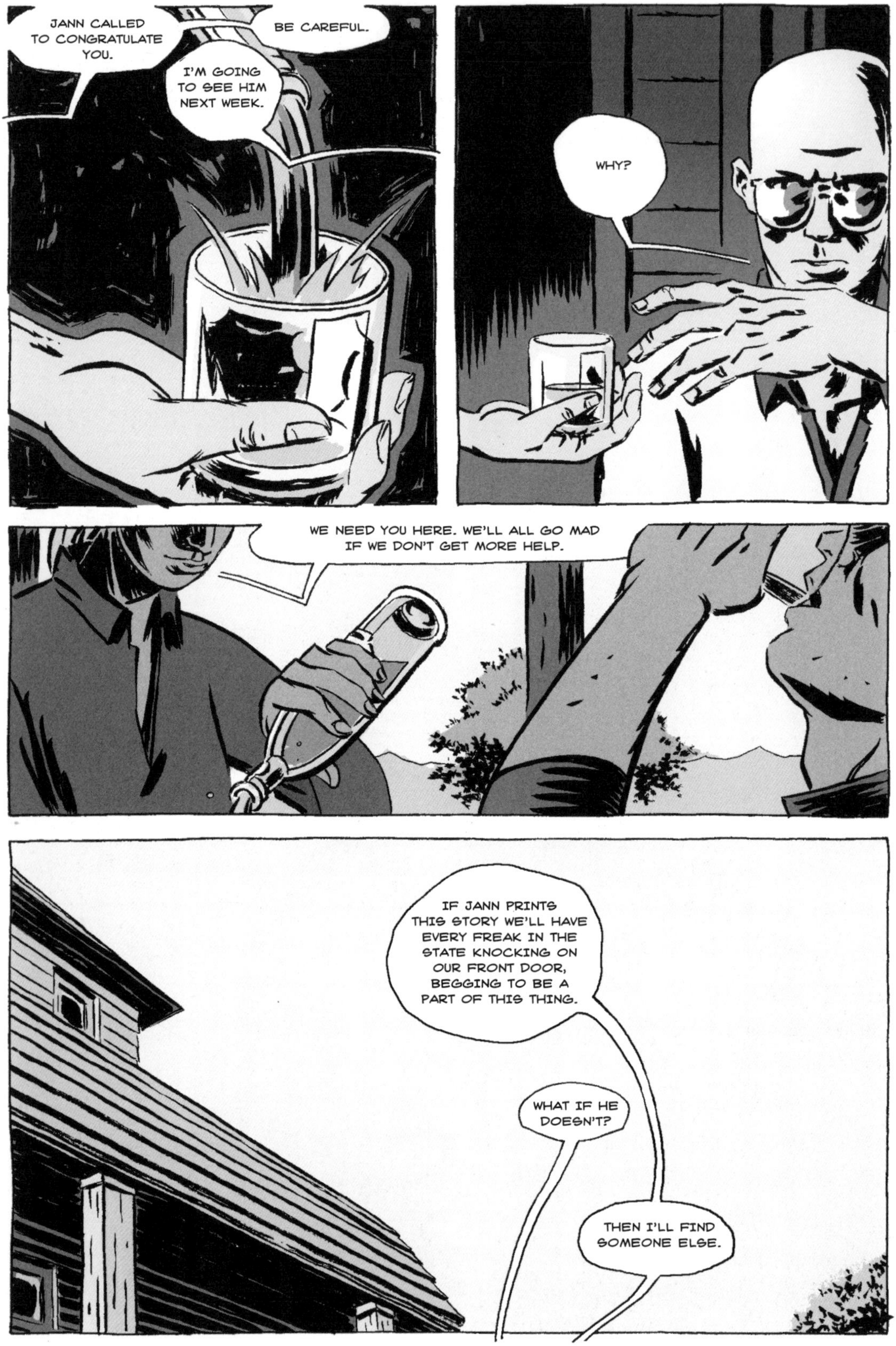
JANN CALLED TO CONGRATULATE YOU.
BE CAREFUL.
I'M GOING TO SEE HIM NEXT WEEK.
WHY?
WE NEED YOU HERE. WE'LL ALL GO MAD IF WE DON'T GET MORE HELP.
IF JANN PRINTS THIS STORY WE'LL HAVE EVERY FREAK IN THE STATE KNOCKING ON OUR FRONT DOOR, BEGGING TO BE A PART OF THIS THING.
WHAT IF HE DOESN'T?
THEN I'LL FIND SOMEONE ELSE.

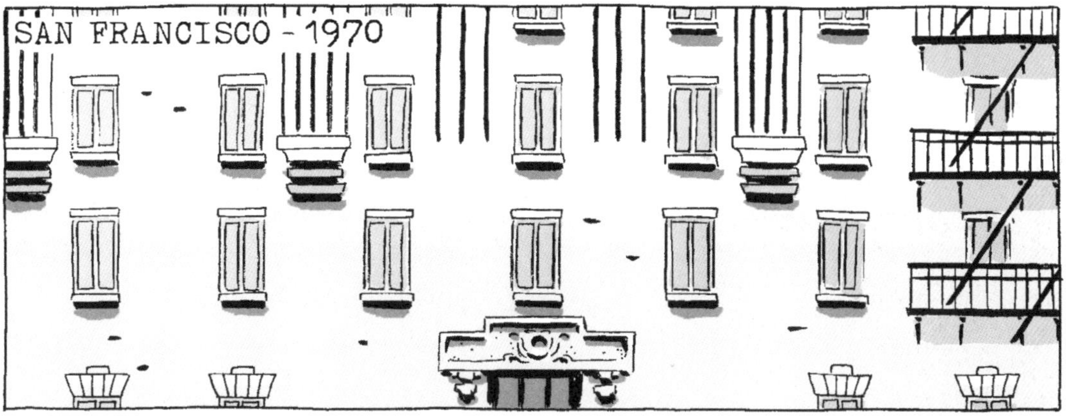
SAN FRANCISCO - 1970

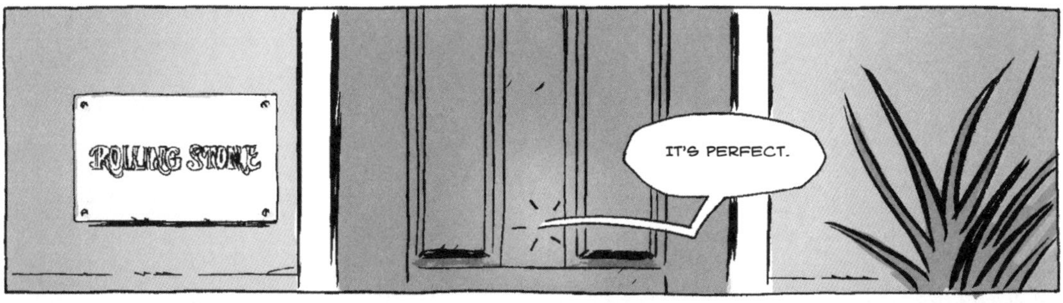
ROLLING STONE
IT'S PERFECT.

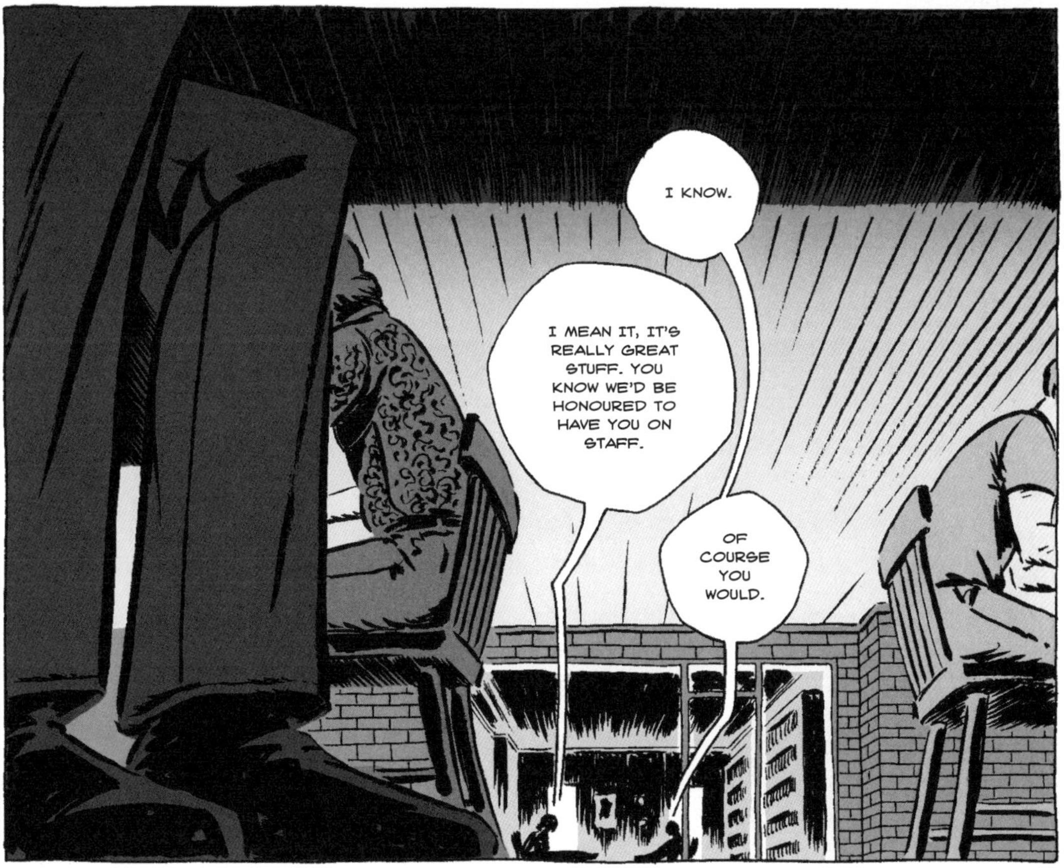
I KNOW.
I MEAN IT, IT'S REALLY GREAT STUFF. YOU KNOW WE'D BE HONOURED TO HAVE YOU ON STAFF.
OF COURSE YOU WOULD.

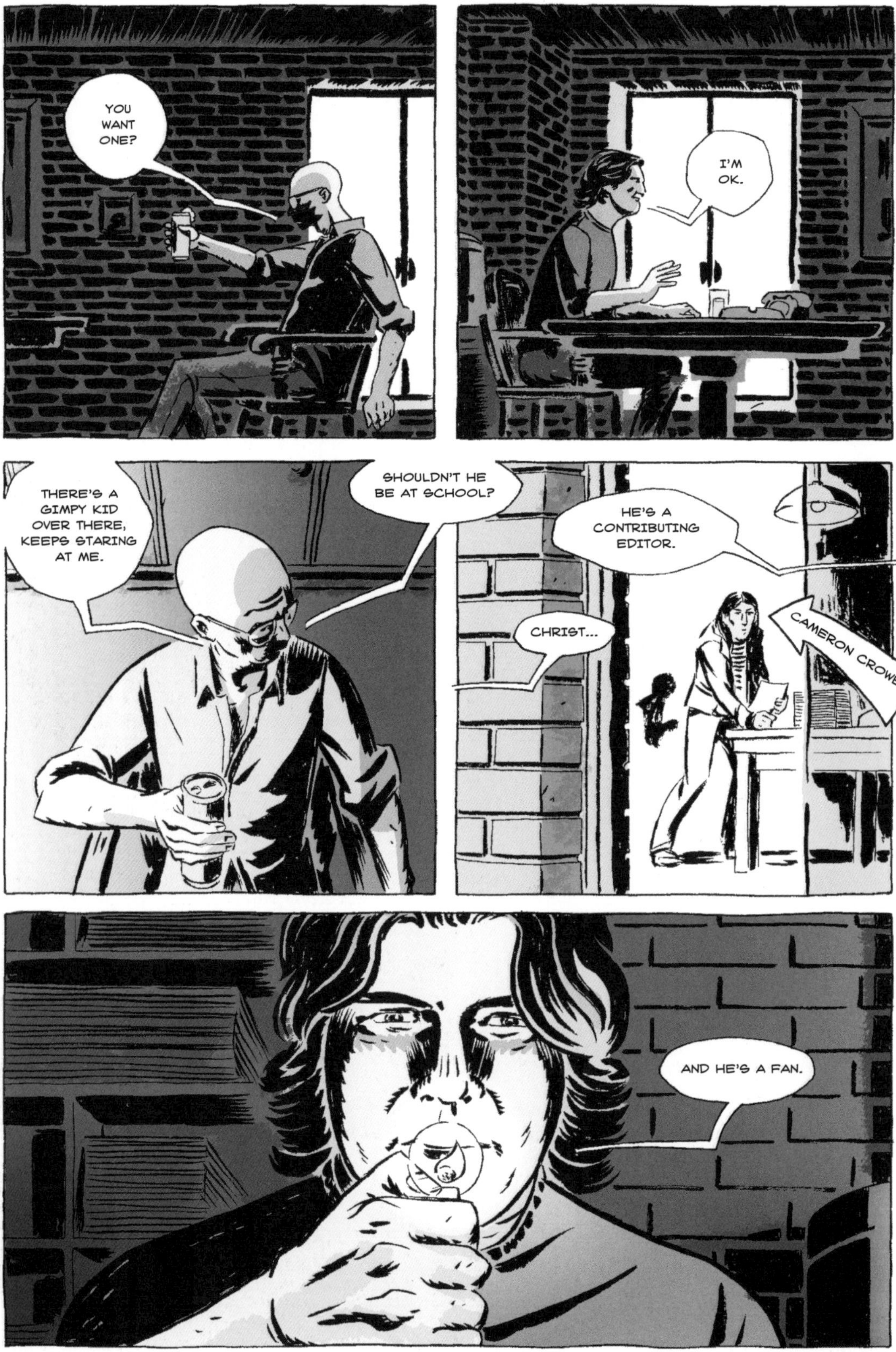
YOU WANT ONE?
I'M OK.
THERE'S A GIMPY KID OVER THERE, KEEPS STARING AT ME.
SHOULDN'T HE BE AT SCHOOL?
HE'S A CONTRIBUTING EDITOR.
CHRIST...
CAMERON CROWE
AND HE'S A FAN.

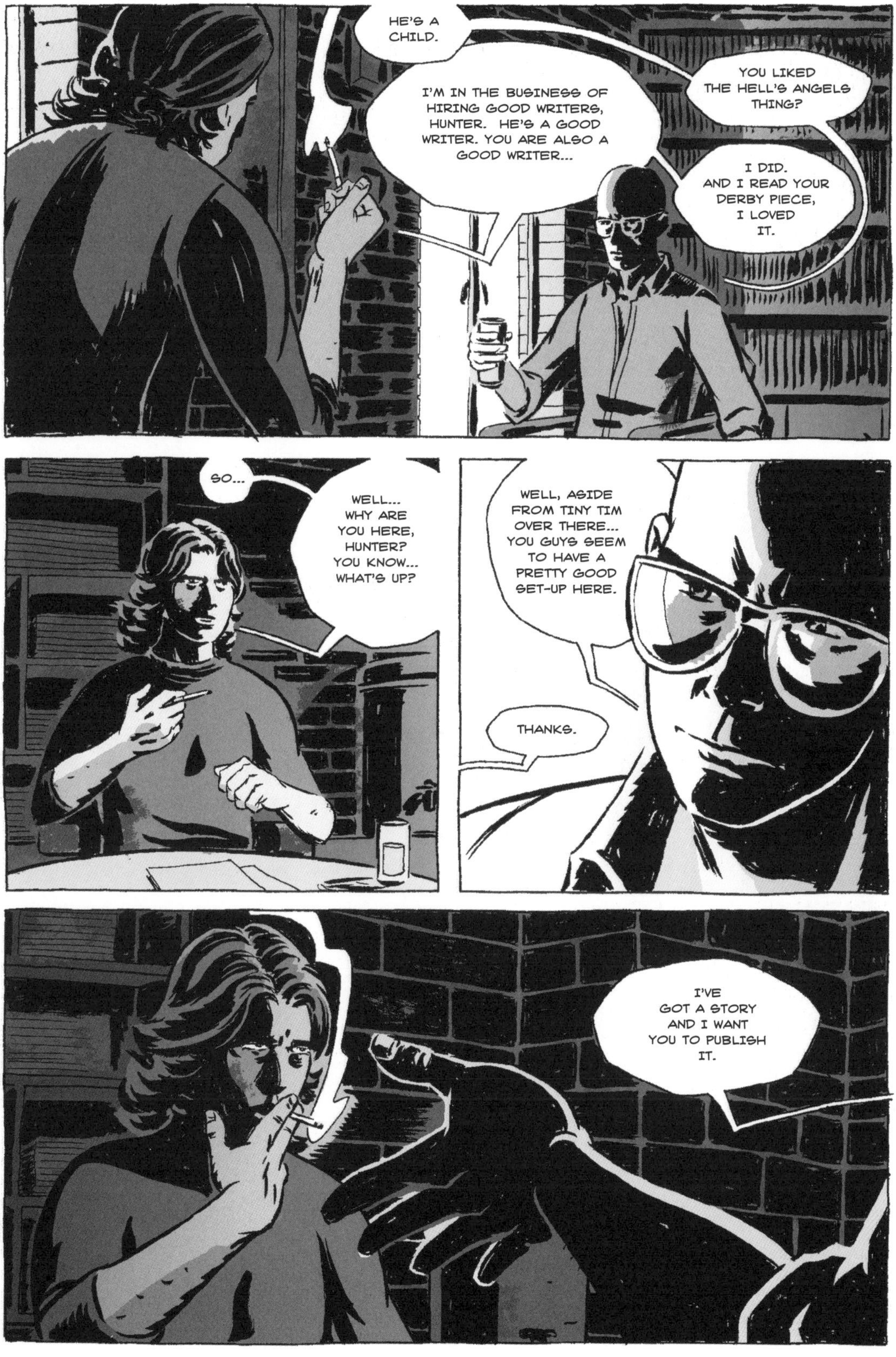
HE'S A CHILD.
I'M IN THE BUSINESS OF HIRING GOOD WRITERS, HUNTER. HE'S A GOOD WRITER. YOU ARE ALSO A GOOD WRITER...
YOU LIKED THE HELL'S ANGELS THING?
I DID. AND I READ YOUR DERBY PIECE, I LOVED IT.
SO...
WELL... WHY ARE YOU HERE, HUNTER? YOU KNOW... WHAT'S UP?
WELL, ASIDE FROM TINY TIM OVER THERE... YOU GUYS SEEM TO HAVE A PRETTY GOOD SET-UP HERE.
THANKS.
I'VE GOT A STORY AND I WANT YOU TO PUBLISH IT.

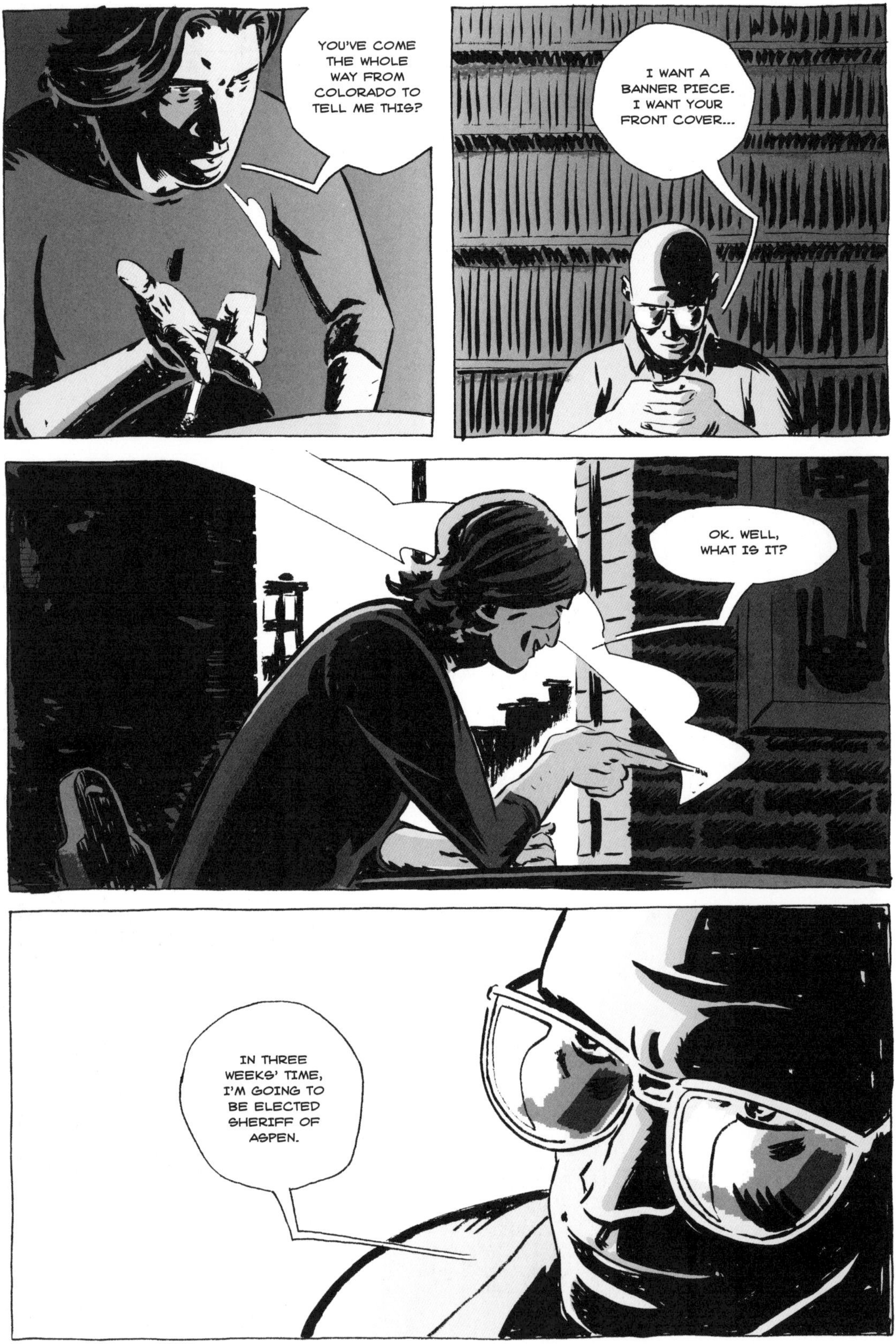
YOU'VE COME THE WHOLE WAY FROM COLORADO TO TELL ME THIS?
I WANT A BANNER PIECE. I WANT YOUR FRONT COVER...
OK. WELL, WHAT IS IT?
IN THREE WEEKS' TIME, I'M GOING TO BE ELECTED SHERIFF OF ASPEN.

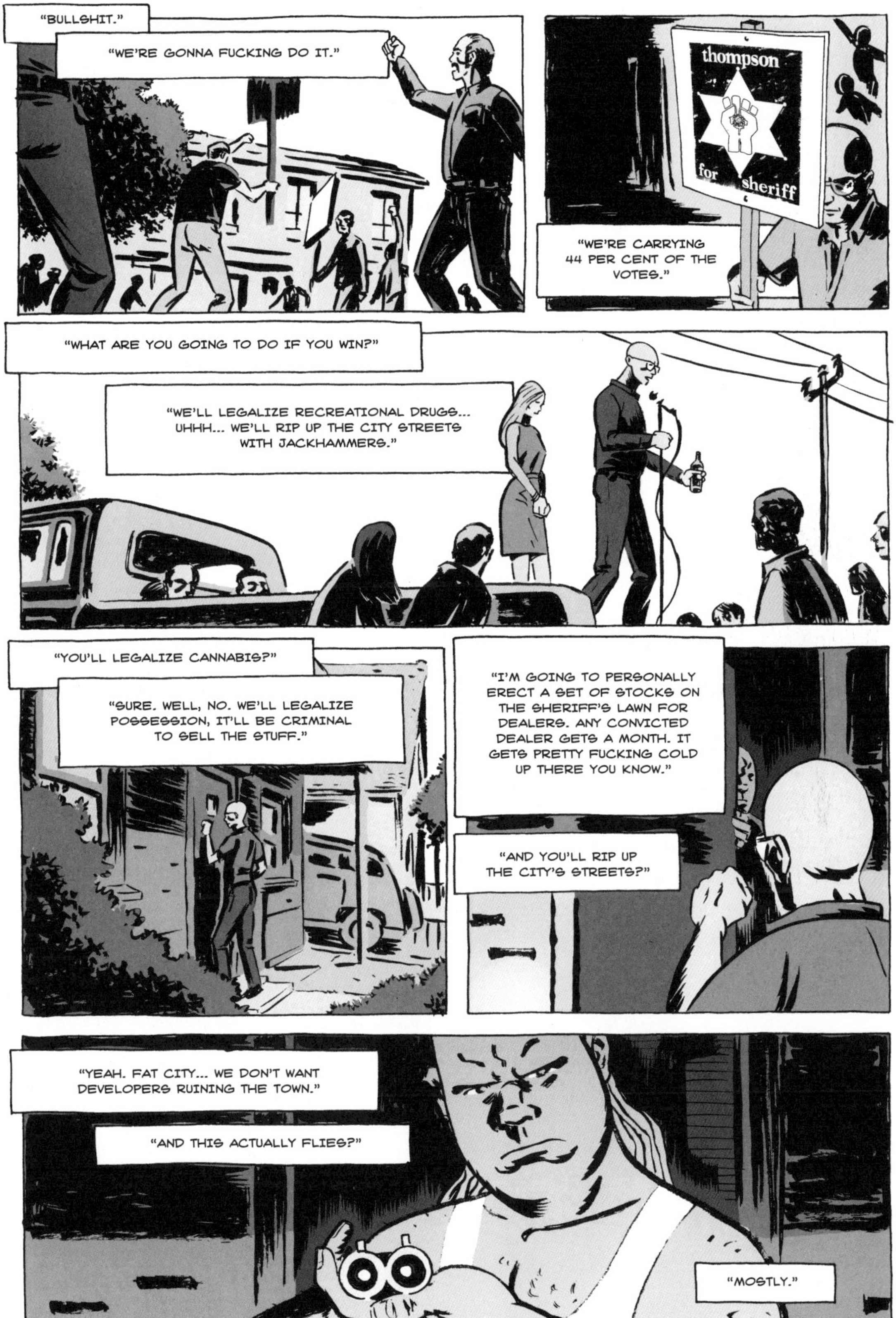
"BULLSHIT."
"WE'RE GONNA FUCKING DO IT."
thompson
for sheriff
"WE'RE CARRYING 44 PER CENT OF THE VOTES."
"WHAT ARE YOU GOING TO DO IF YOU WIN?"
"WE'LL LEGALIZE RECREATIONAL DRUGS... UHHH... WE'LL RIP UP THE CITY STREETS WITH JACKHAMMERS."
"YOU'LL LEGALIZE CANNABIS?"
"SURE. WELL, NO. WE'LL LEGALIZE POSSESSION, IT'LL BE CRIMINAL TO SELL THE STUFF."
"I'M GOING TO PERSONALLY ERECT A SET OF STOCKS ON THE SHERIFF'S LAWN FOR DEALERS. ANY CONVICTED DEALER GETS A MONTH. IT GETS PRETTY FUCKING COLD UP THERE YOU KNOW."
"AND YOU'LL RIP UP THE CITY'S STREETS?"
"YEAH. FAT CITY... WE DON'T WANT DEVELOPERS RUINING THE TOWN."
"AND THIS ACTUALLY FLIES?"
"MOSTLY."

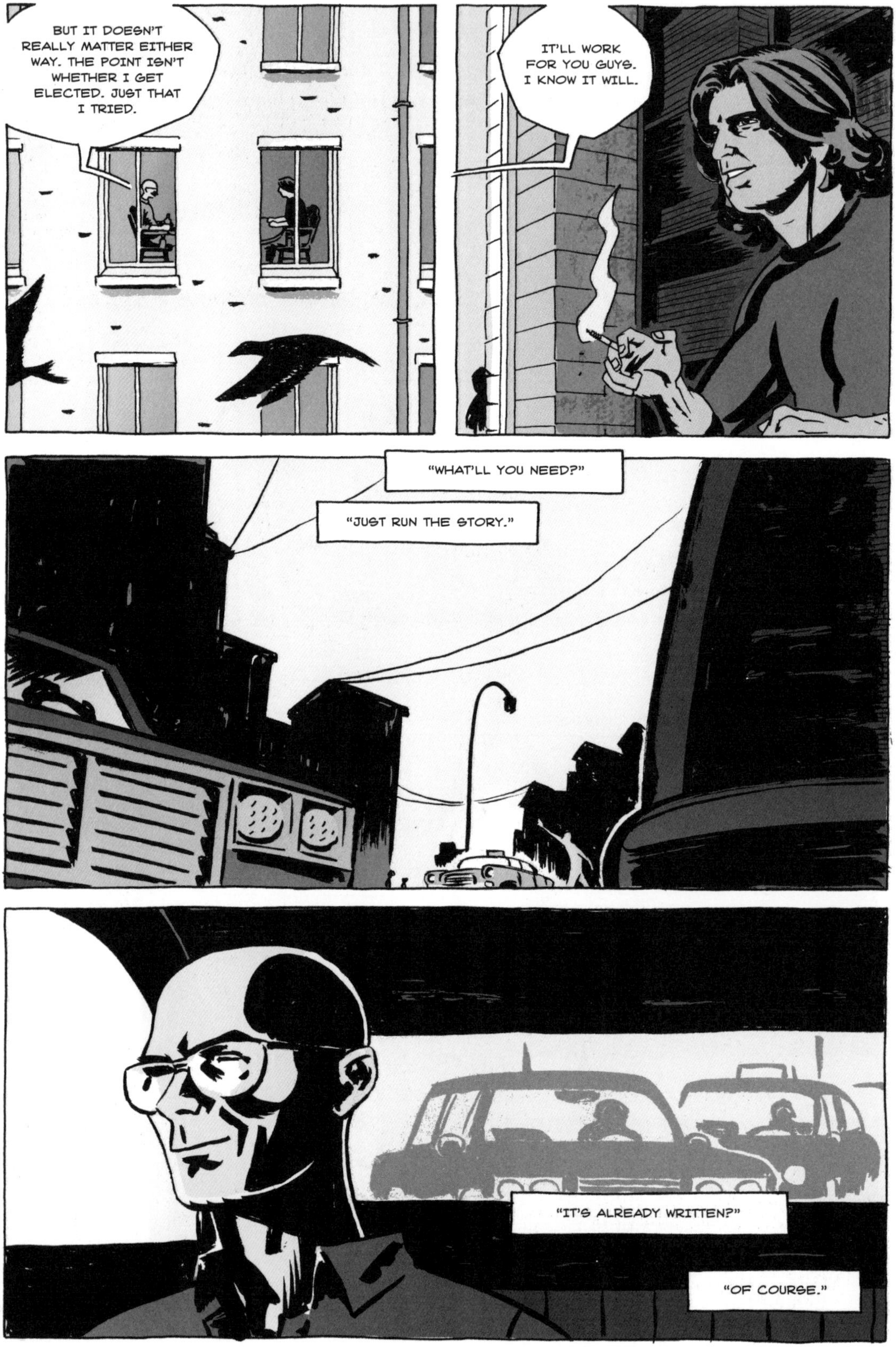
BUT IT DOESN'T REALLY MATTER EITHER WAY. THE POINT ISN'T WHETHER I GET ELECTED. JUST THAT I TRIED.
IT'LL WORK FOR YOU GUYS. I KNOW IT WILL.
"WHAT'LL YOU NEED?"
"JUST RUN THE STORY."
"IT'S ALREADY WRITTEN?"
"OF COURSE."

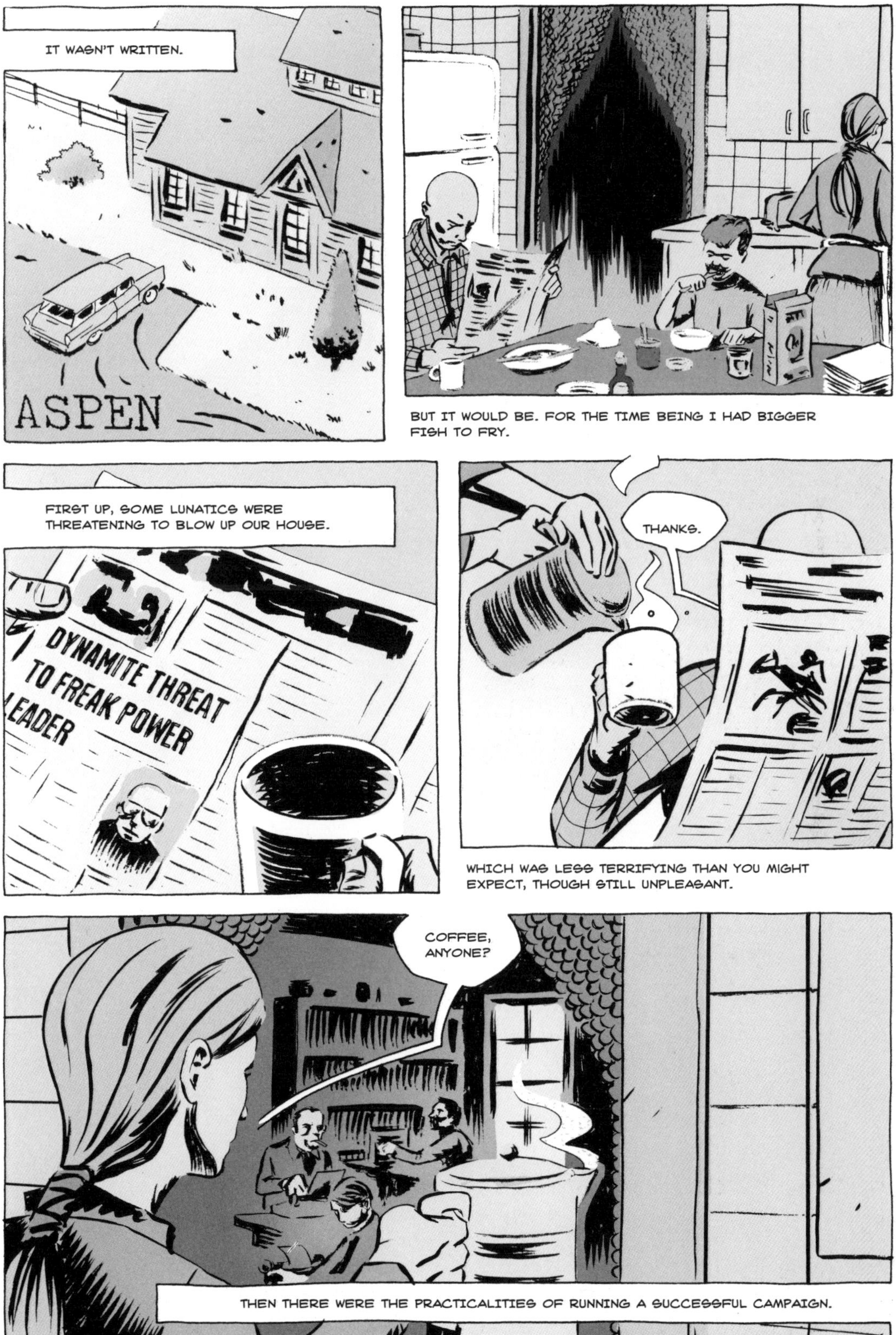
IT WASN'T WRITTEN.
ASPEN
BUT IT WOULD BE. FOR THE TIME BEING I HAD BIGGER FISH TO FRY.
FIRST UP, SOME LUNATICS WERE THREATENING TO BLOW UP OUR HOUSE.
DYNAMITE THREAT TO FREAK POWER LEADER
THANKS.
WHICH WAS LESS TERRIFYING THAN YOU MIGHT EXPECT, THOUGH STILL UNPLEASANT.
COFFEE, ANYONE?
THEN THERE WERE THE PRACTICALITIES OF RUNNING A SUCCESSFUL CAMPAIGN.

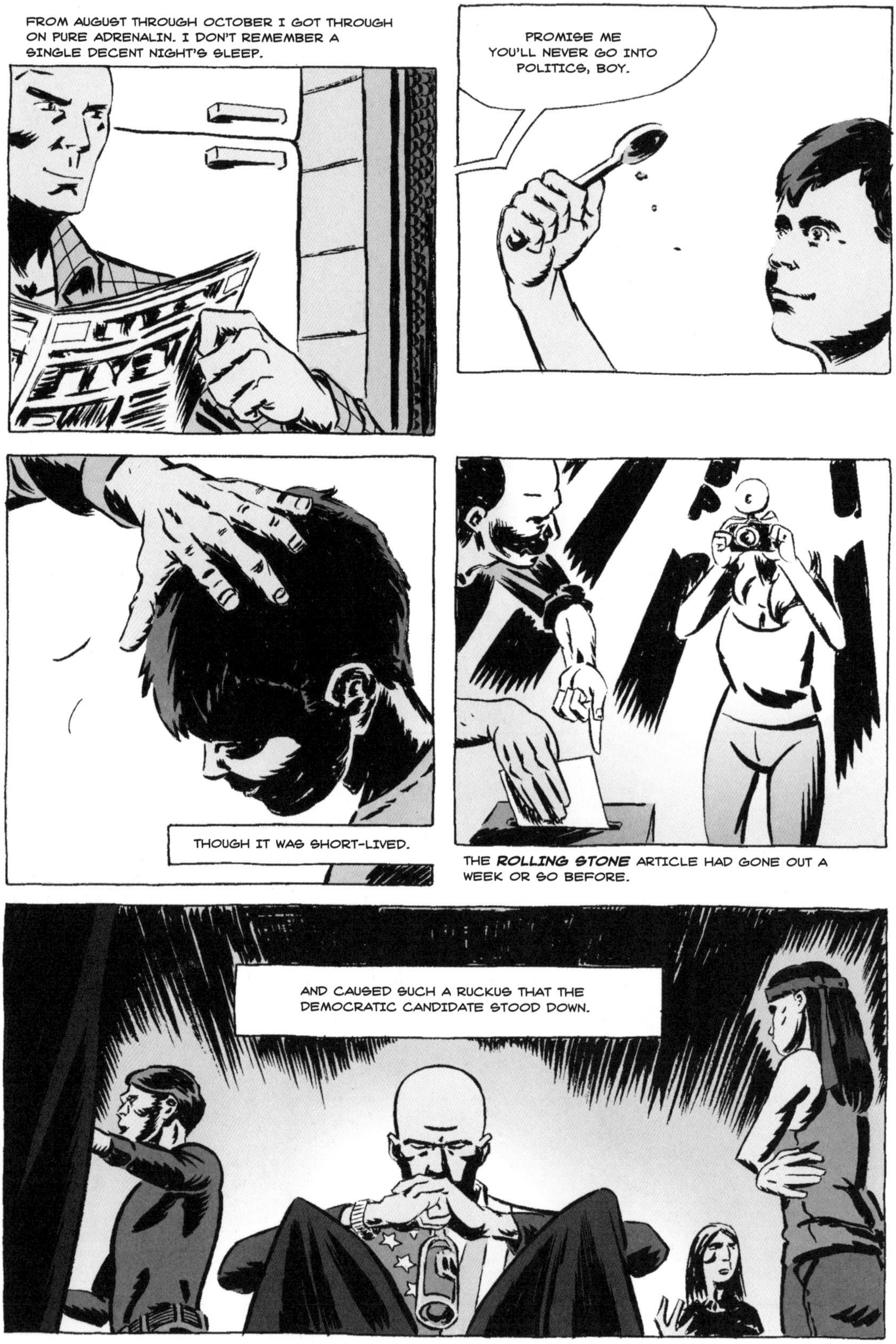
FROM AUGUST THROUGH OCTOBER I GOT THROUGH ON PURE ADRENALIN. I DON'T REMEMBER A SINGLE DECENT NIGHT'S SLEEP.
PROMISE ME YOU'LL NEVER GO INTO POLITICS, BOY.
THOUGH IT WAS SHORT-LIVED.
THE ROLLING STONE ARTICLE HAD GONE OUT A WEEK OR SO BEFORE.
AND CAUSED SUCH A RUCKUS THAT THE DEMOCRATIC CANDIDATE STOOD DOWN.

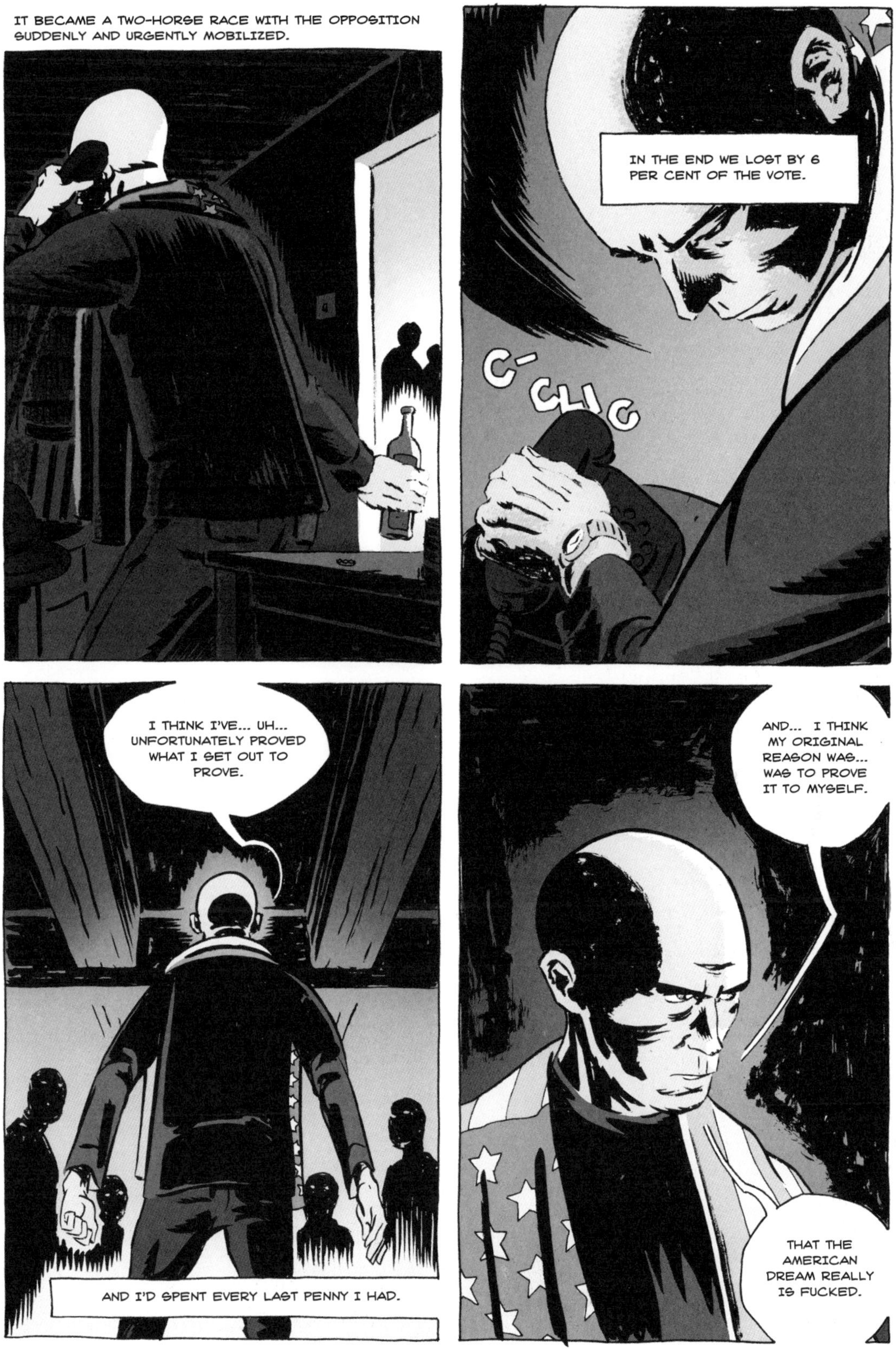
IT BECAME A TWO-HORSE RACE WITH THE OPPOSITION SUDDENLY AND URGENTLY MOBILIZED.
IN THE END WE LOST BY 6 PER CENT OF THE VOTE.
C-CLIC
I THINK I'VE... UH... UNFORTUNATELY PROVED WHAT I SET OUT TO PROVE.
AND I'D SPENT EVERY LAST PENNY I HAD.
AND... I THINK MY ORIGINAL REASON WAS... WAS TO PROVE IT TO MYSELF.
THAT THE AMERICAN DREAM REALLY IS FUCKED.

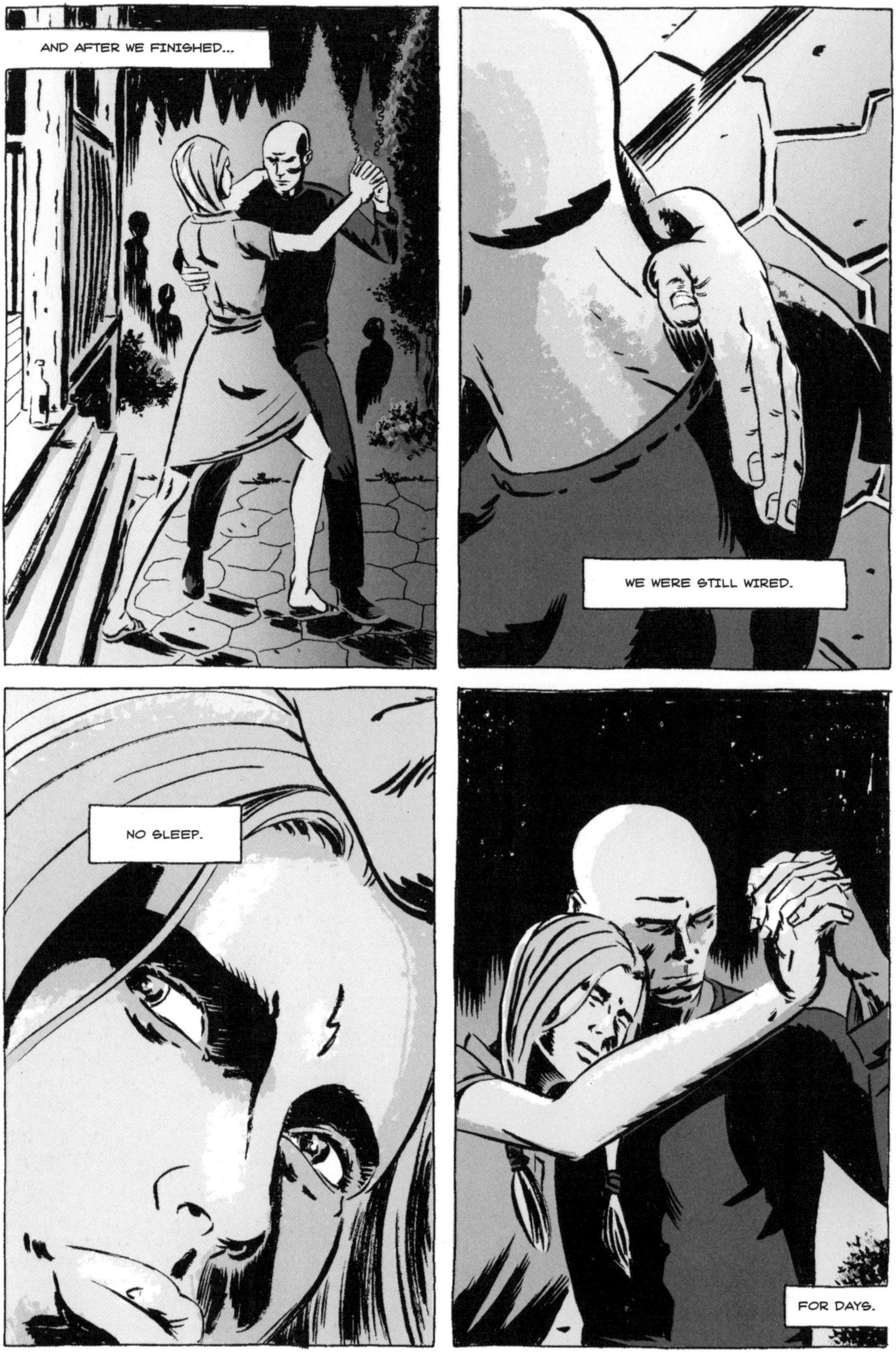
AND AFTER WE FINISHED...
WE WERE STILL WIRED.
NO SLEEP.
FOR DAYS.

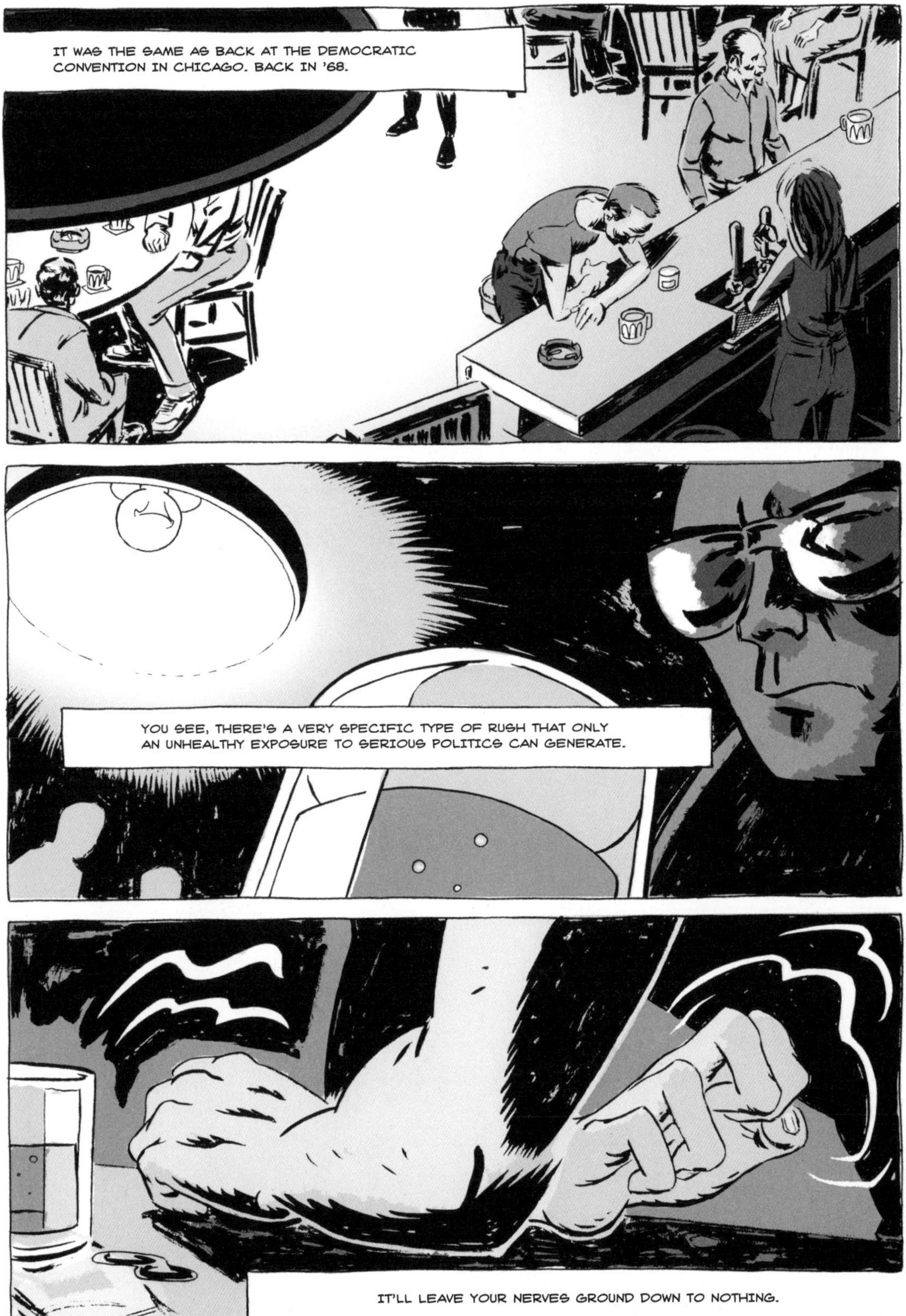

IT WAS THE SAME AS BACK AT THE DEMOCRATIC CONVENTION IN CHICAGO. BACK IN '68.
YOU SEE, THERE'S A VERY SPECIFIC TYPE OF RUSH THAT ONLY AN UNHEALTHY EXPOSURE TO SERIOUS POLITICS CAN GENERATE.
IT'LL LEAVE YOUR NERVES GROUND DOWN TO NOTHING.

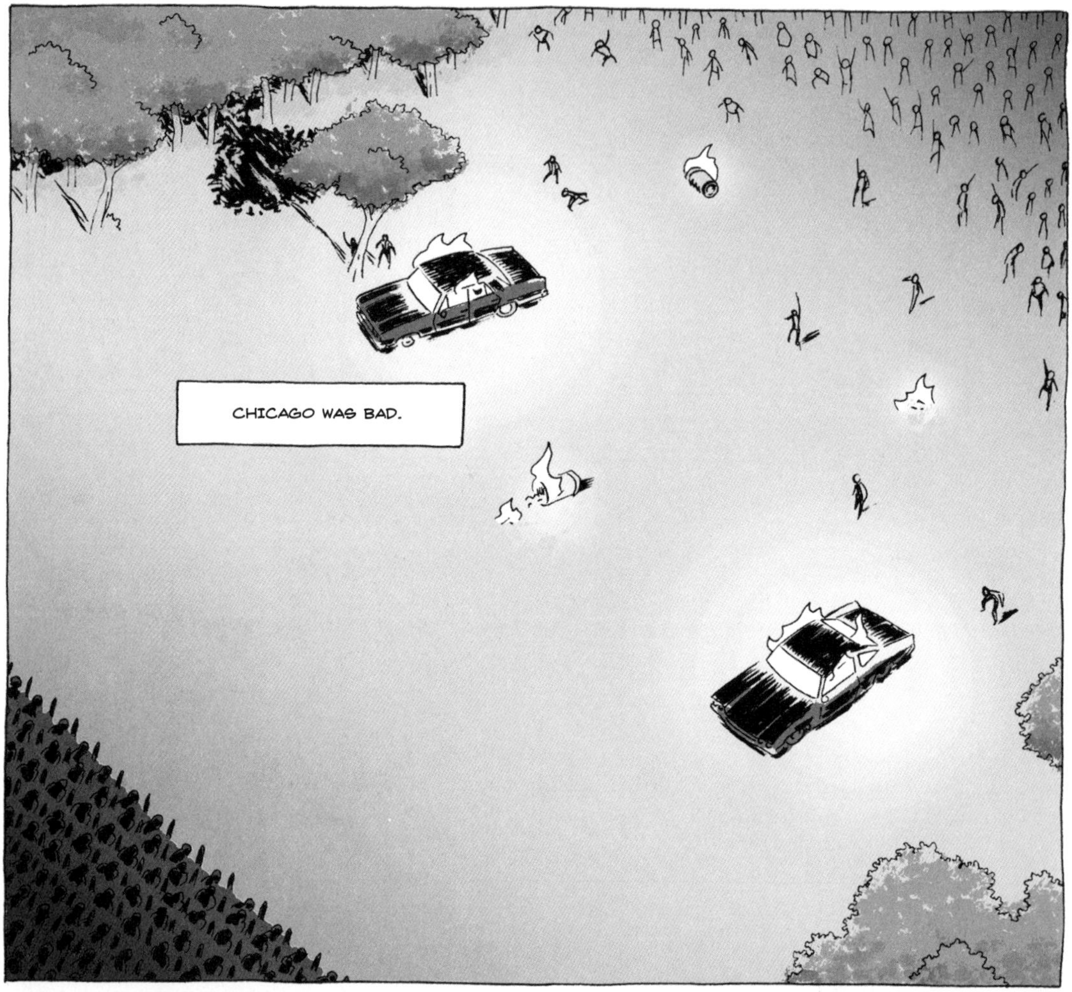
CHICAGO WAS BAD.

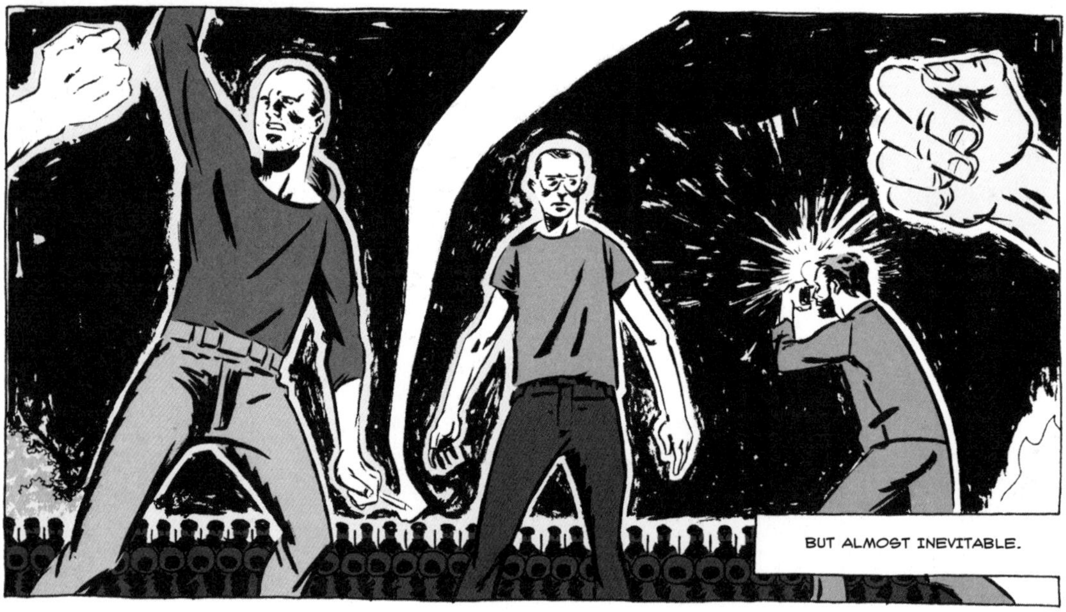
BUT ALMOST INEVITABLE.

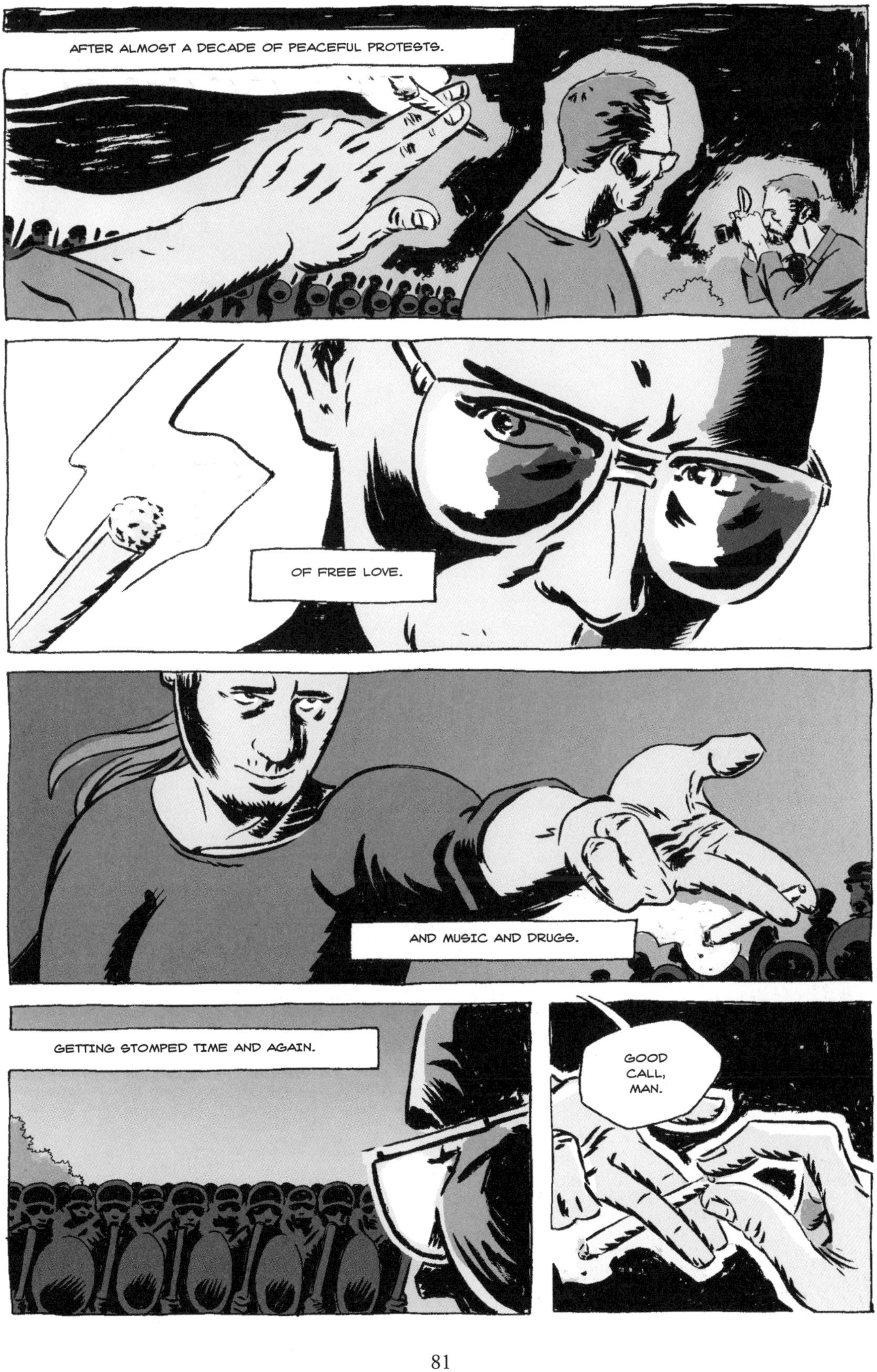
AFTER ALMOST A DECADE OF PEACEFUL PROTESTS.
OF FREE LOVE.
AND MUSIC AND DRUGS.
GETTING STOMPED TIME AND AGAIN.
GOOD CALL, MAN.

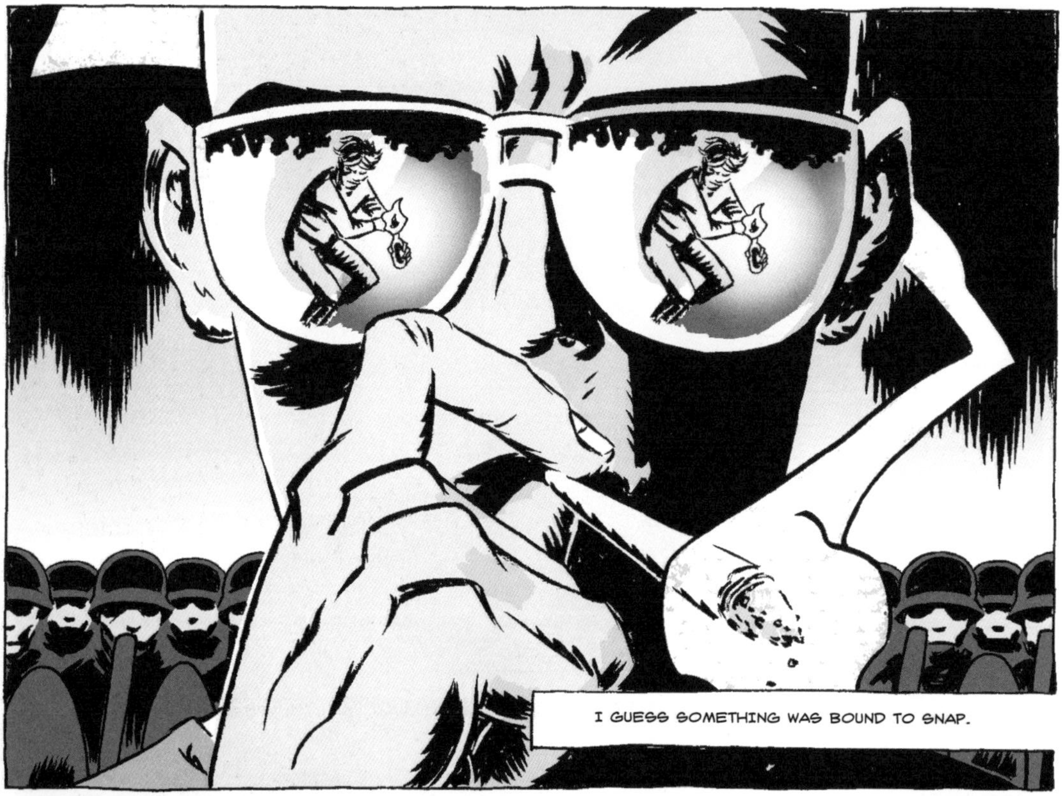
I GUESS SOMETHING WAS BOUND TO SNAP.

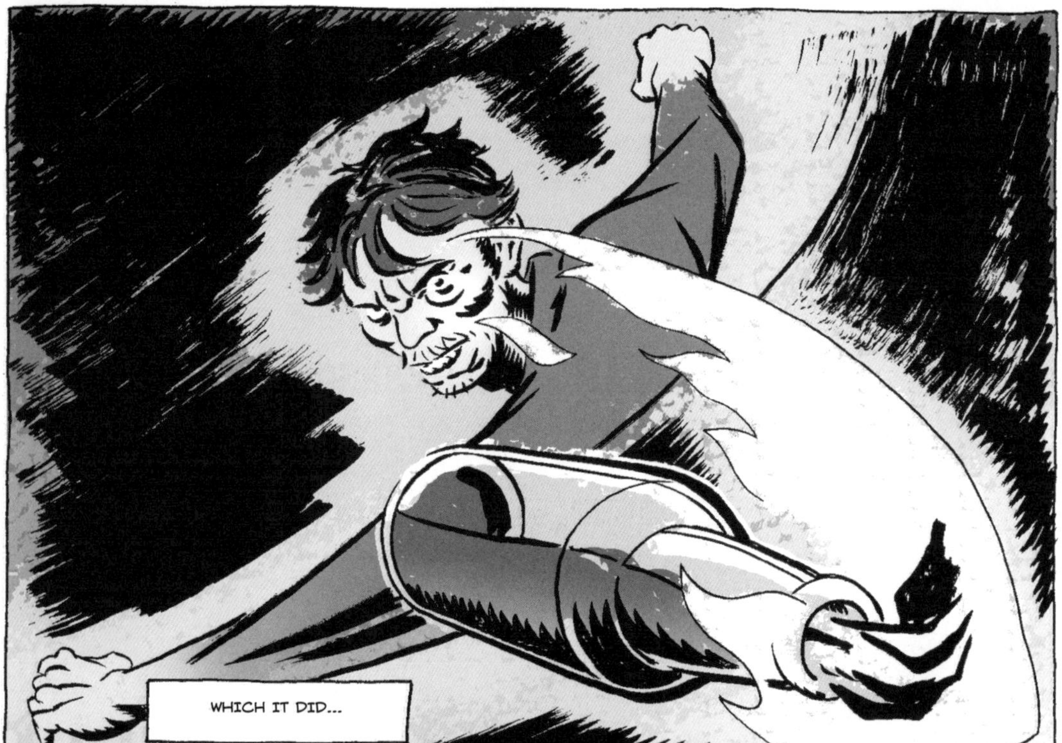
WHICH IT DID...

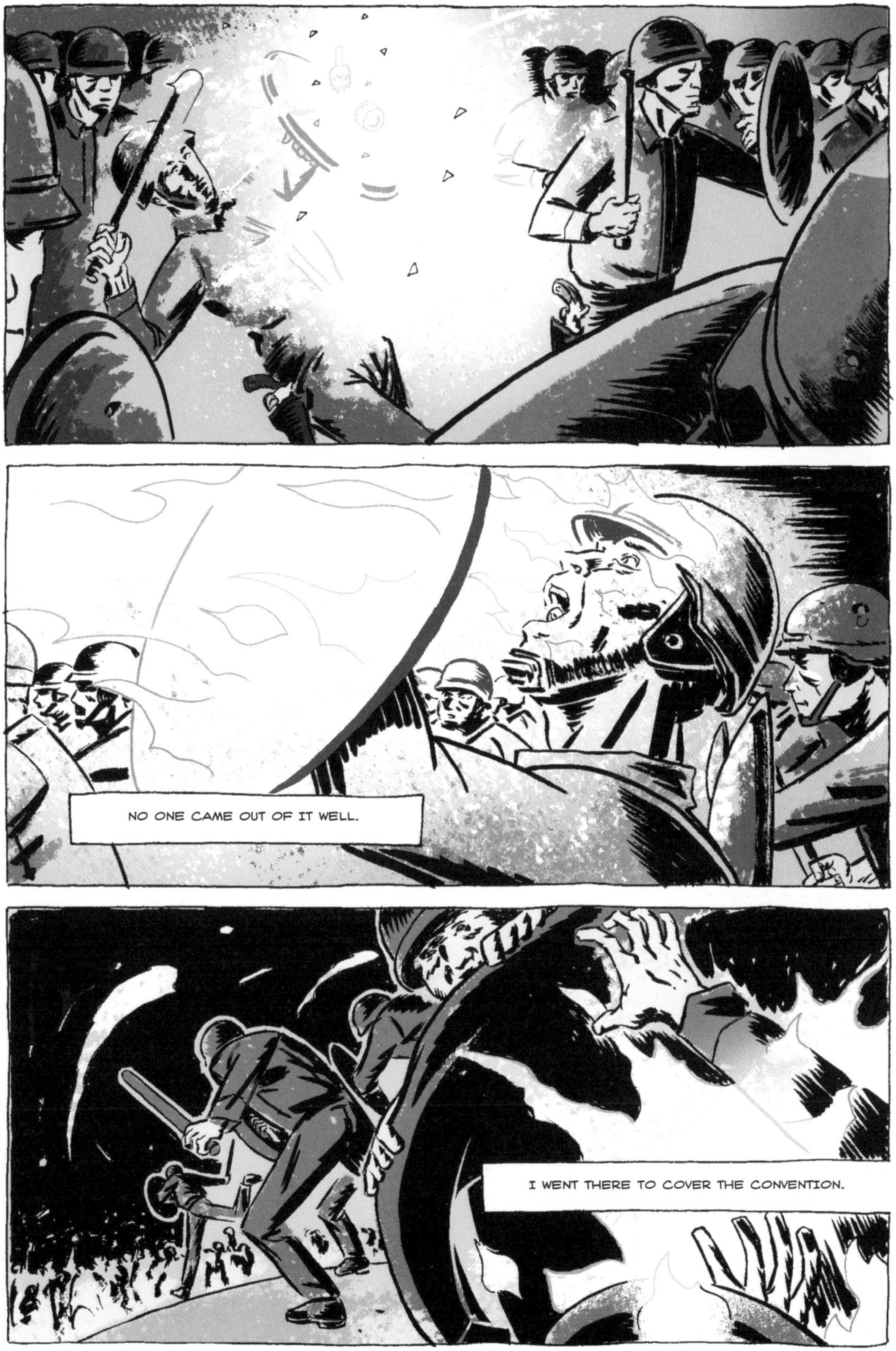
NO ONE CAME OUT OF IT WELL.
I WENT THERE TO COVER THE CONVENTION.

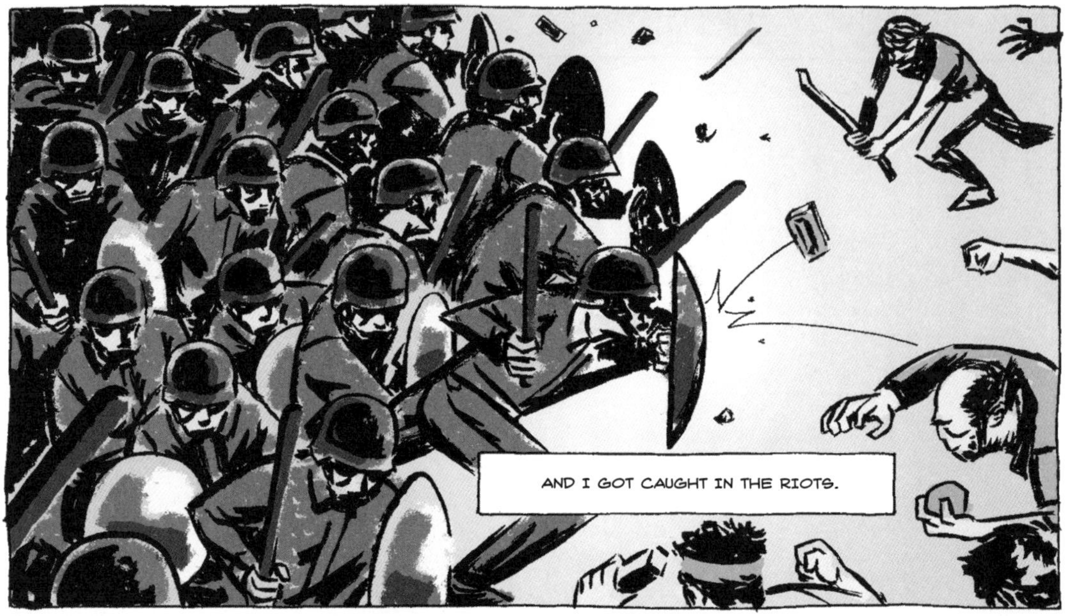
AND I GOT CAUGHT IN THE RIOTS.

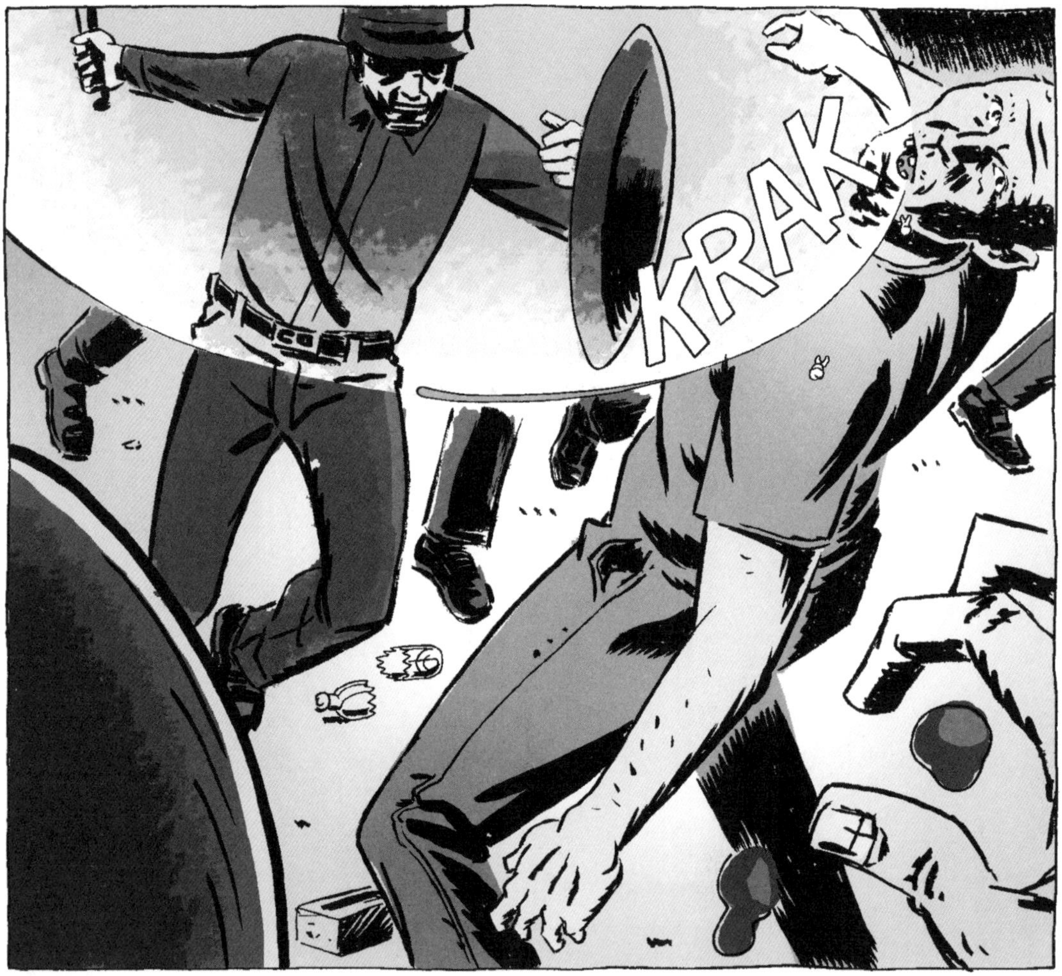
KRAK

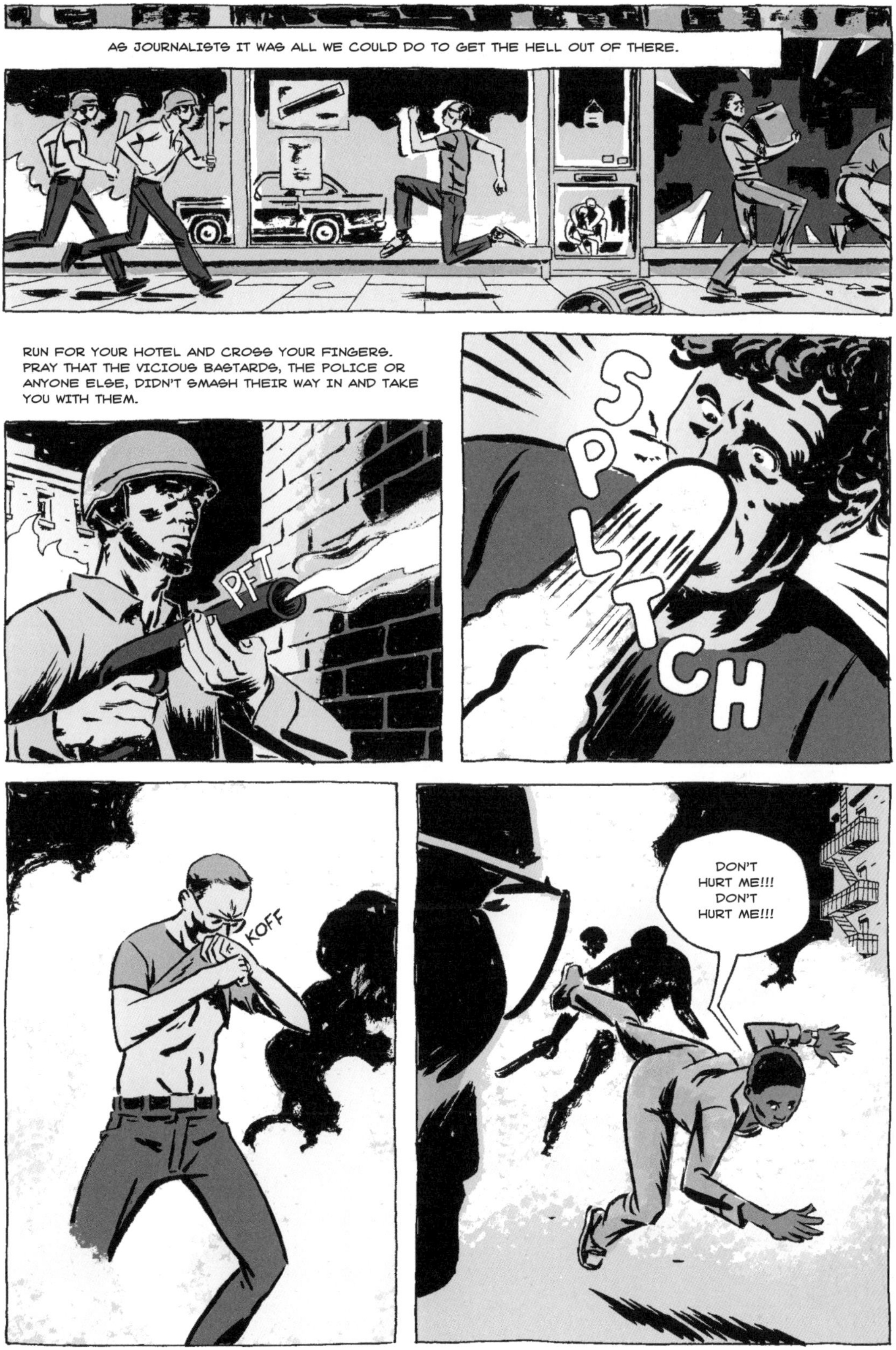
AS JOURNALISTS IT WAS ALL WE COULD DO TO GET THE HELL OUT OF THERE.
RUN FOR YOUR HOTEL AND CROSS YOUR FINGERS. PRAY THAT THE VICIOUS BASTARDS, THE POLICE OR ANYONE ELSE, DIDN'T SMASH THEIR WAY IN AND TAKE YOU WITH THEM.
PFT
SPLTCH
KOFF
DON'T HURT ME!!! DON'T HURT ME!!!

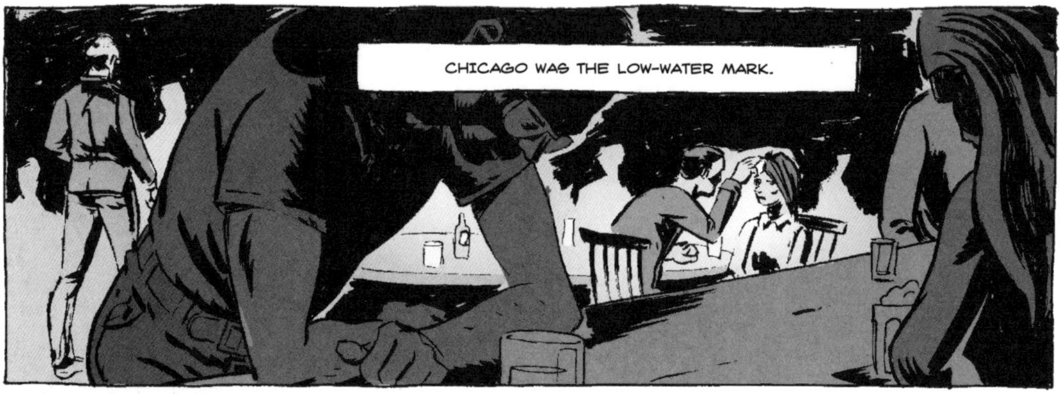
CHICAGO WAS THE LOW-WATER MARK.

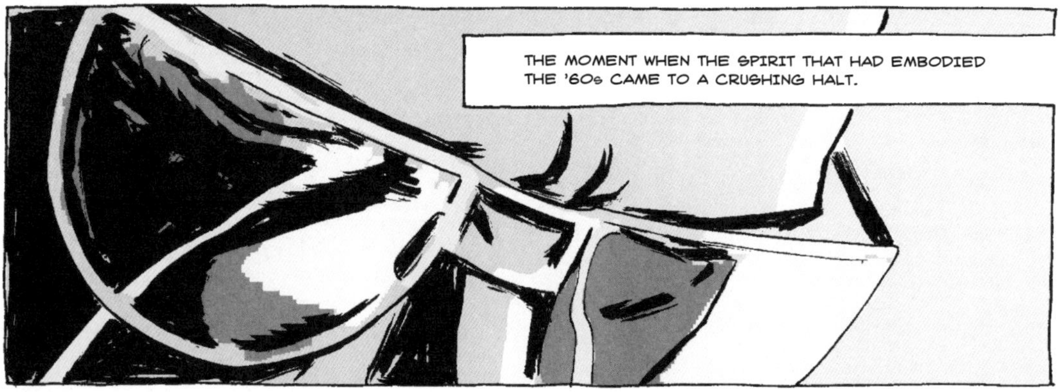
THE MOMENT WHEN THE SPIRIT THAT HAD EMBODIED THE '60s CAME TO A CRUSHING HALT.

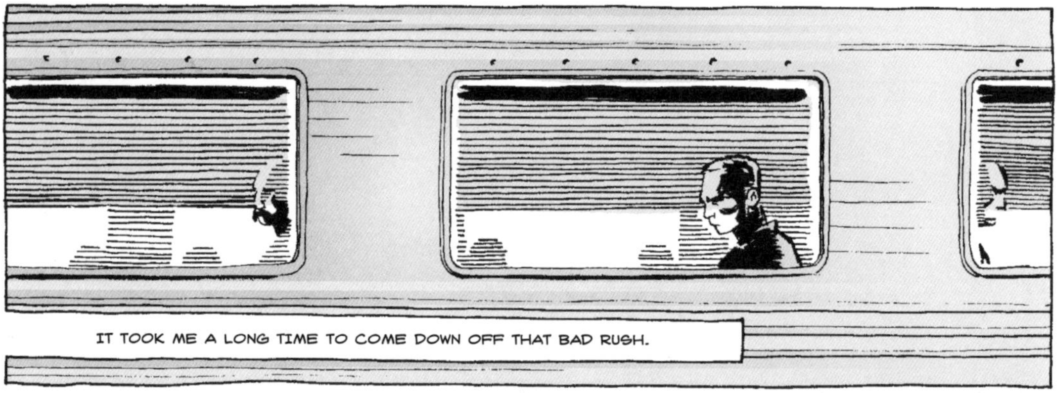
IT TOOK ME A LONG TIME TO COME DOWN OFF THAT BAD RUSH.

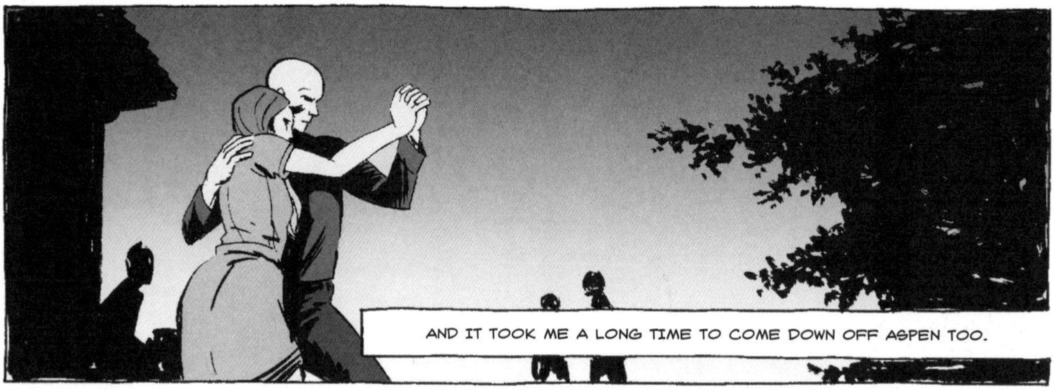
AND IT TOOK ME A LONG TIME TO COME DOWN OFF ASPEN TOO.

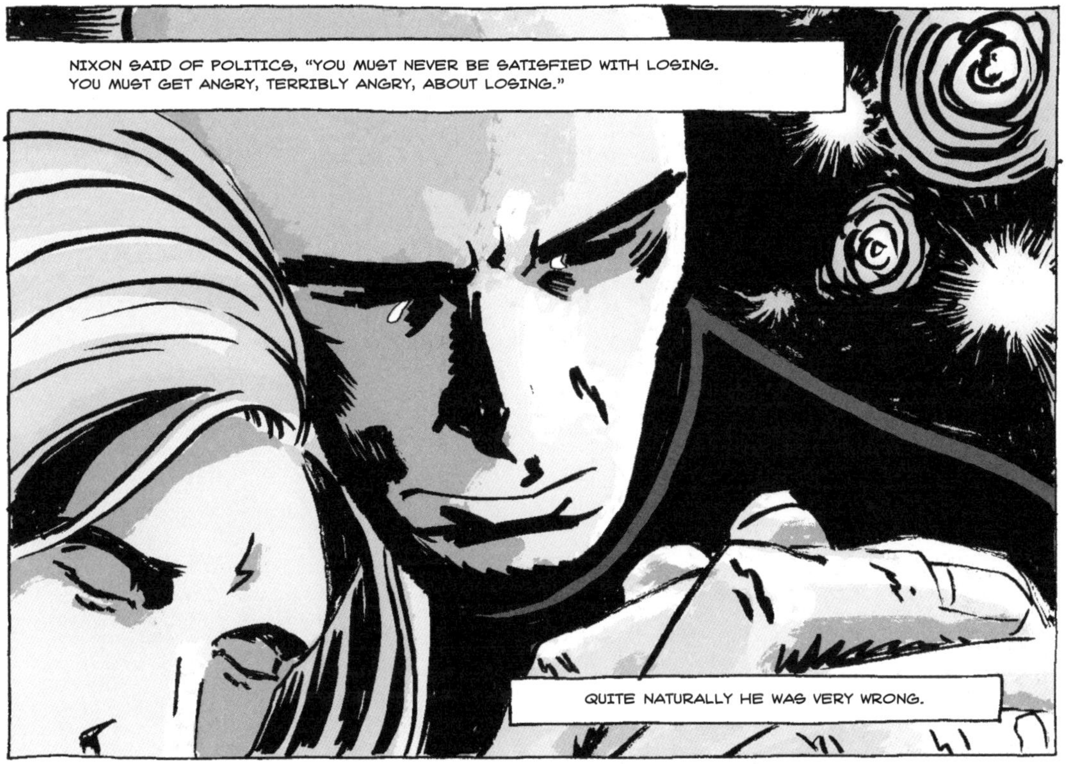
NIXON SAID OF POLITICS, "YOU MUST NEVER BE SATISFIED WITH LOSING. YOU MUST GET ANGRY, TERRIBLY ANGRY, ABOUT LOSING."
QUITE NATURALLY HE WAS VERY WRONG.

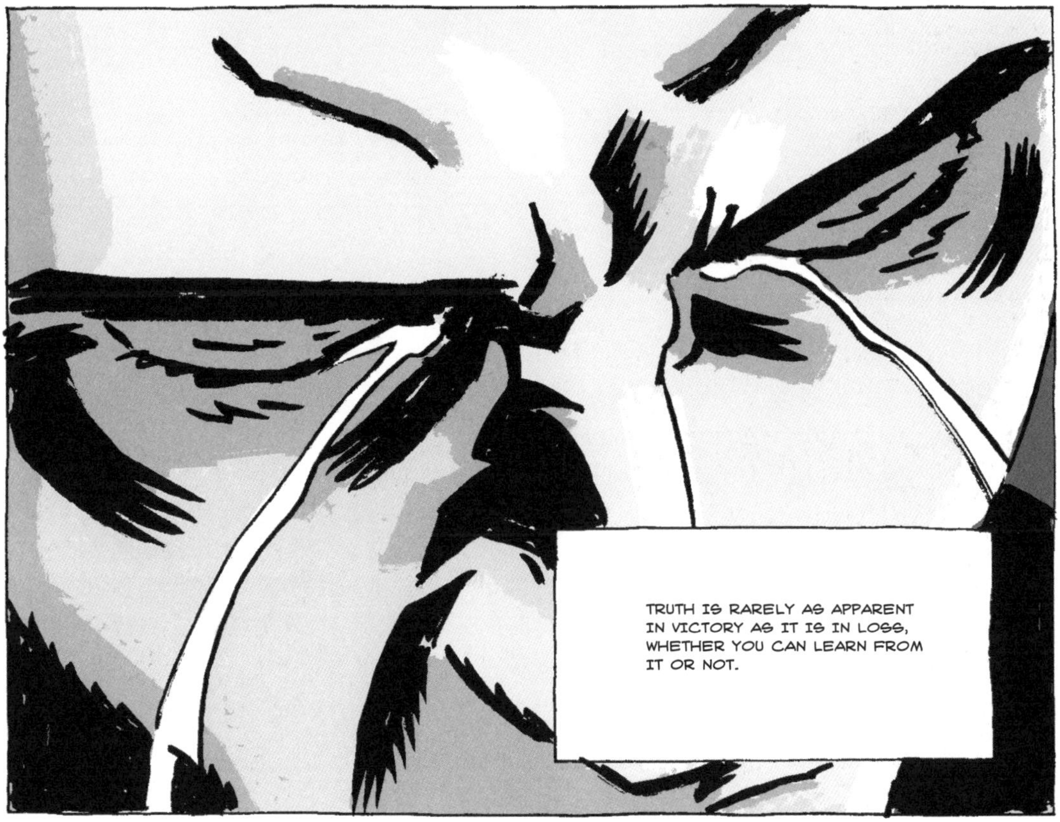
TRUTH IS RARELY AS APPARENT IN VICTORY AS IT IS IN LOSS, WHETHER YOU CAN LEARN FROM IT OR NOT.

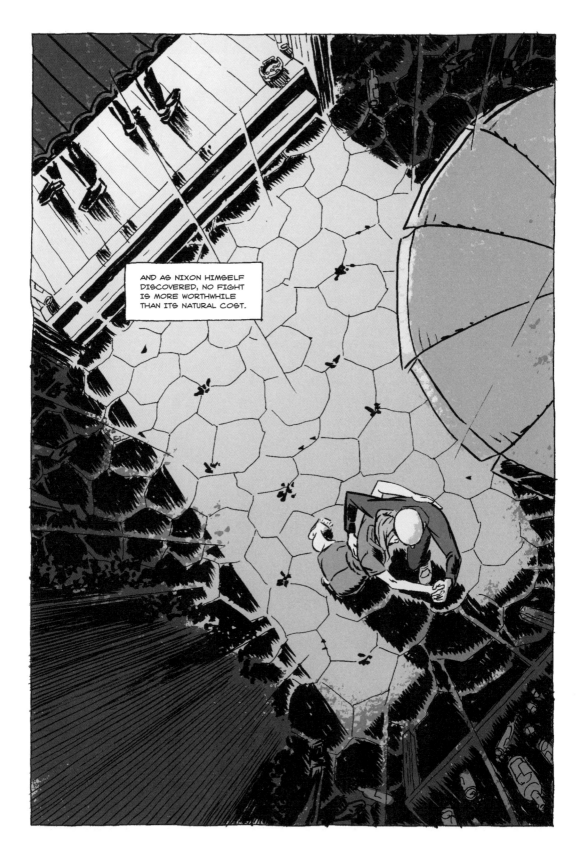

AND AS NIXON HIMSELF DISCOVERED, NO FIGHT IS MORE WORTHWHILE THAN ITS NATURAL COST.

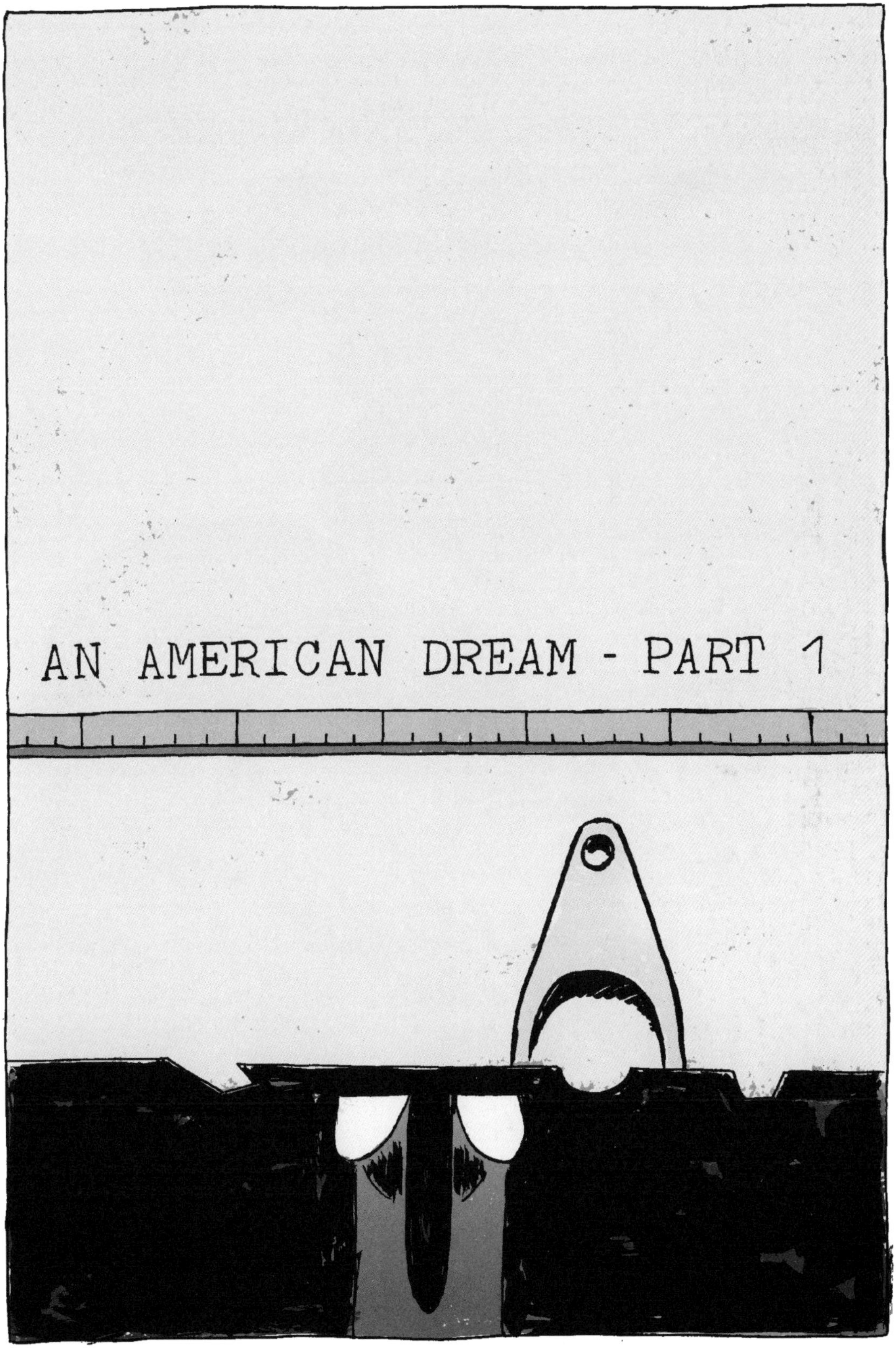
AN AMERICAN DREAM - PART 1

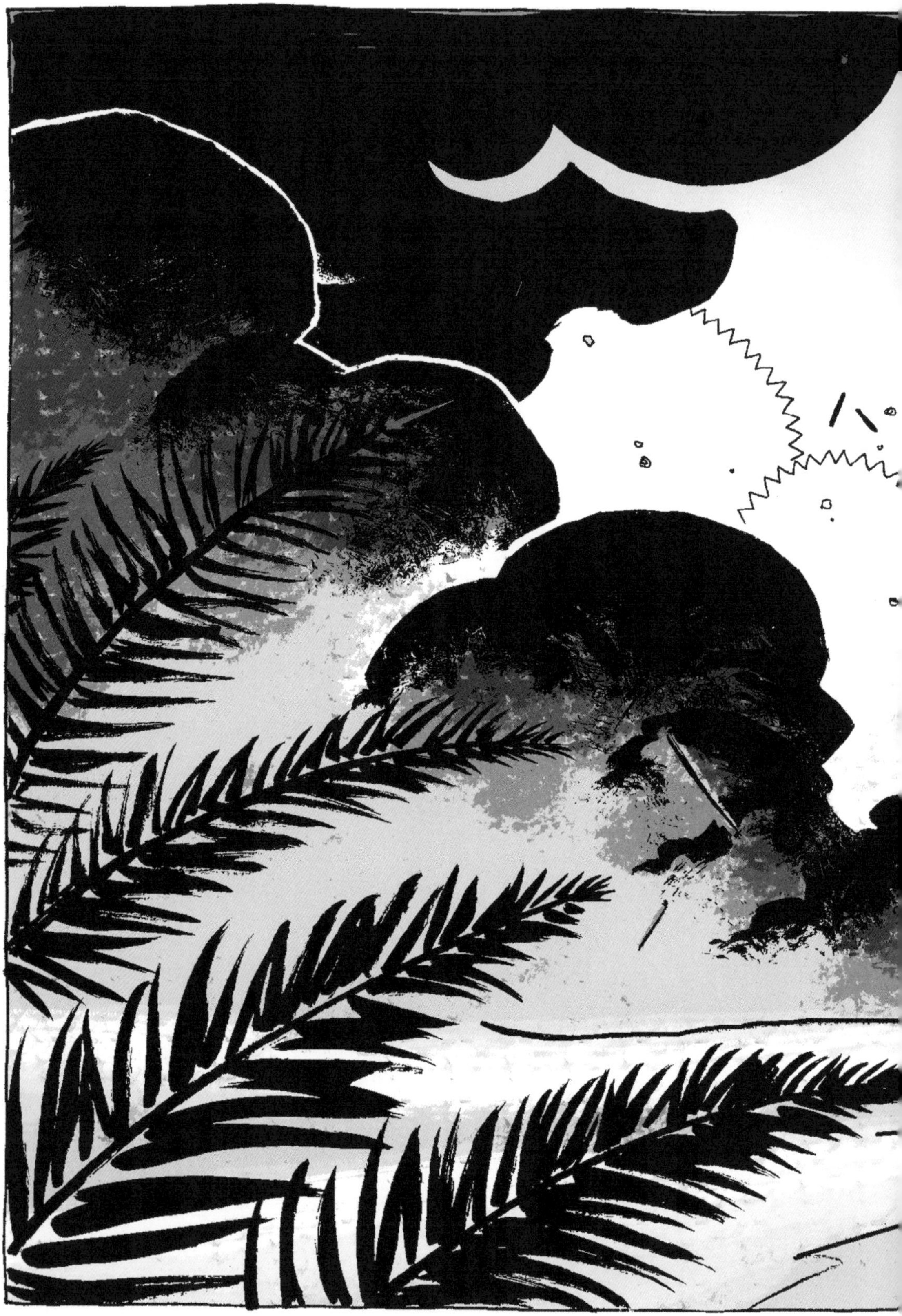

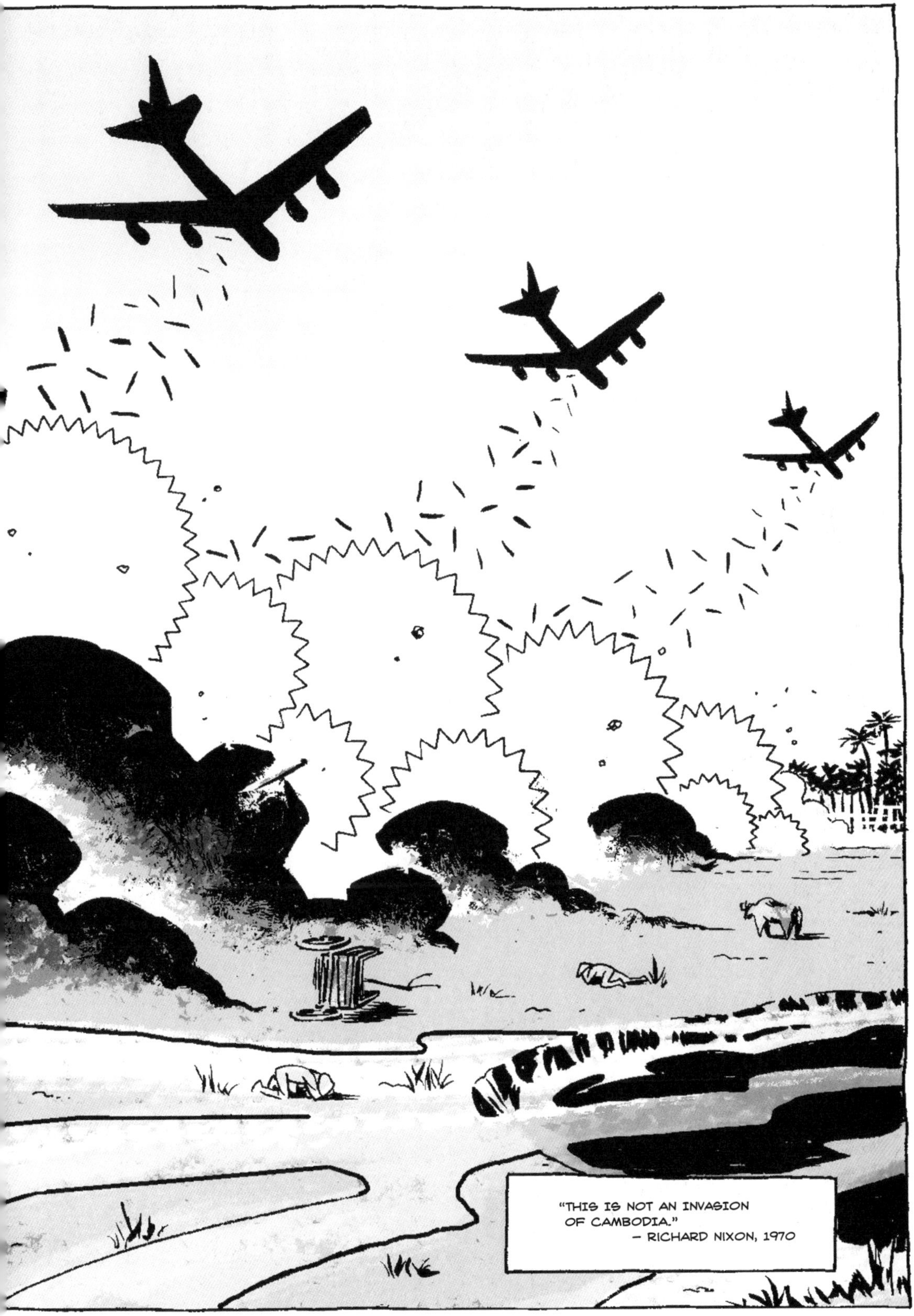
"THIS IS NOT AN INVASION
OF CAMBODIA."
– RICHARD NIXON, 1970

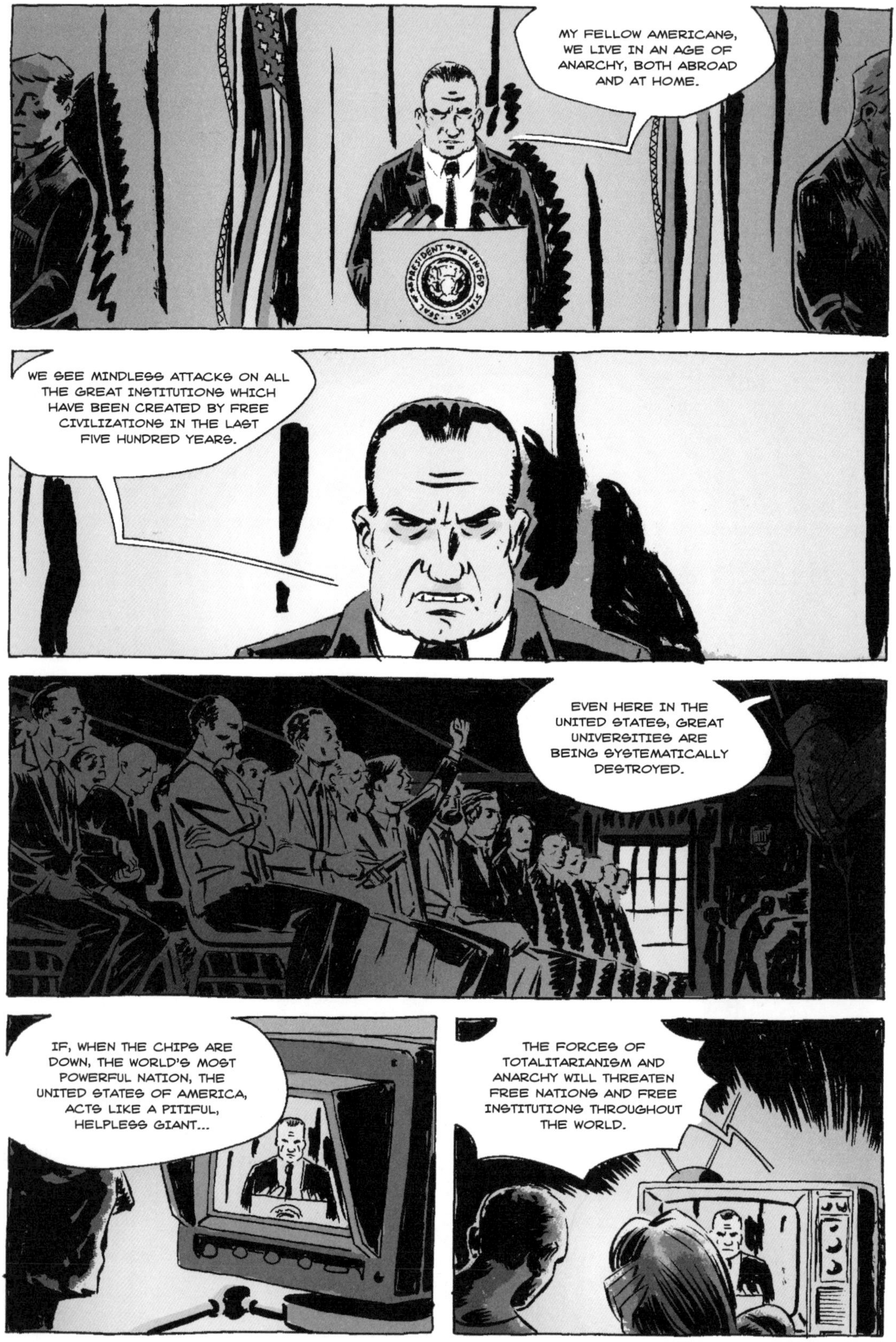

MY FELLOW AMERICANS, WE LIVE IN AN AGE OF ANARCHY, BOTH ABROAD AND AT HOME.
SEAL OF THE PRESIDENT OF THE UNITED STATES
WE SEE MINDLESS ATTACKS ON ALL THE GREAT INSTITUTIONS WHICH HAVE BEEN CREATED BY FREE CIVILIZATIONS IN THE LAST FIVE HUNDRED YEARS.
EVEN HERE IN THE UNITED STATES, GREAT UNIVERSITIES ARE BEING SYSTEMATICALLY DESTROYED.
IF, WHEN THE CHIPS ARE DOWN, THE WORLD'S MOST POWERFUL NATION, THE UNITED STATES OF AMERICA, ACTS LIKE A PITIFUL, HELPLESS GIANT...
THE FORCES OF TOTALITARIANISM AND ANARCHY WILL THREATEN FREE NATIONS AND FREE INSTITUTIONS THROUGHOUT THE WORLD.

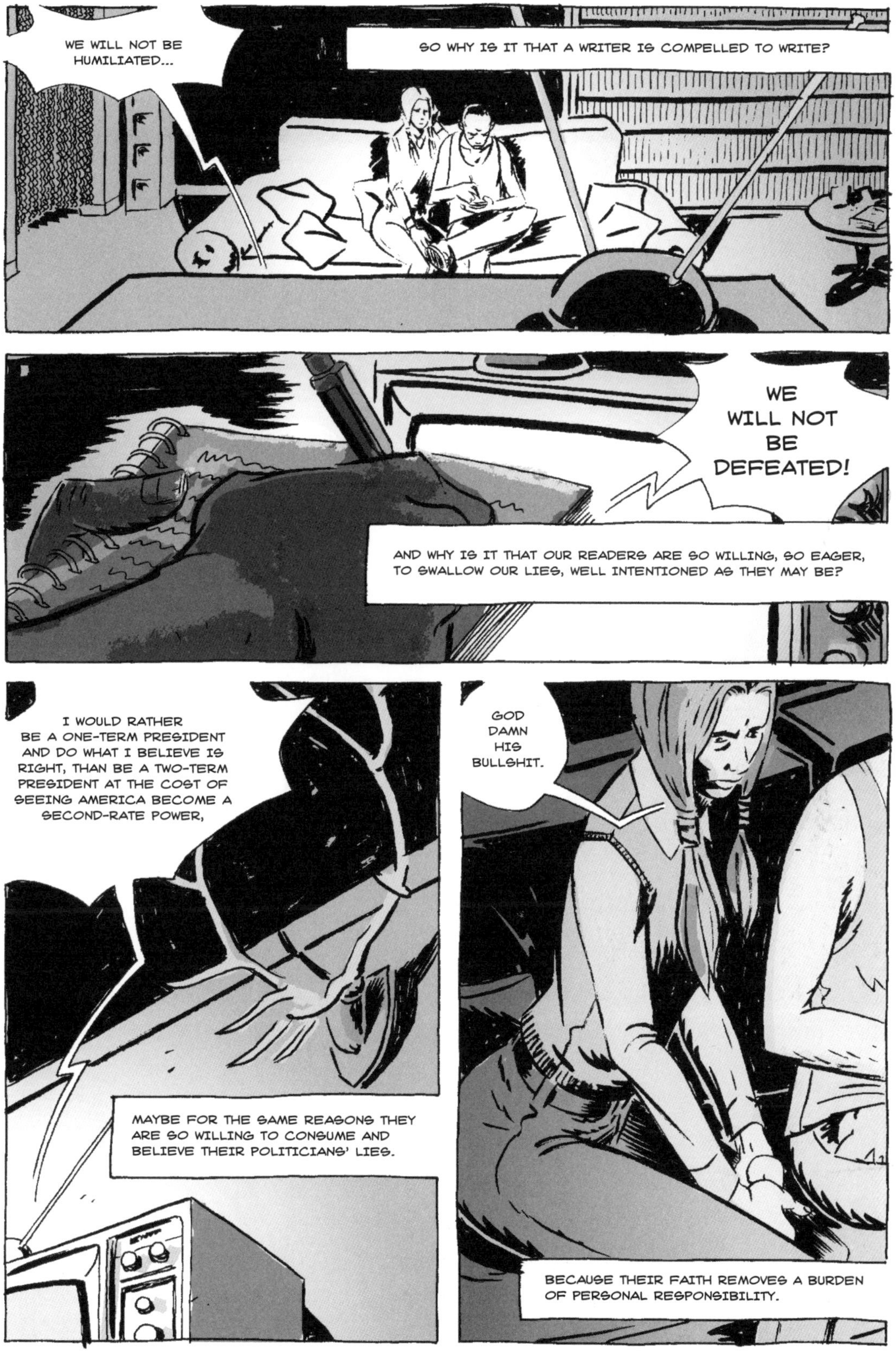
WE WILL NOT BE HUMILIATED...
SO WHY IS IT THAT A WRITER IS COMPELLED TO WRITE?
WE WILL NOT BE DEFEATED!
AND WHY IS IT THAT OUR READERS ARE SO WILLING, SO EAGER, TO SWALLOW OUR LIES, WELL INTENTIONED AS THEY MAY BE?
I WOULD RATHER BE A ONE-TERM PRESIDENT AND DO WHAT I BELIEVE IS RIGHT, THAN BE A TWO-TERM PRESIDENT AT THE COST OF SEEING AMERICA BECOME A SECOND-RATE POWER,
MAYBE FOR THE SAME REASONS THEY ARE SO WILLING TO CONSUME AND BELIEVE THEIR POLITICIANS' LIES.
GOD DAMN HIS BULLSHIT.
BECAUSE THEIR FAITH REMOVES A BURDEN OF PERSONAL RESPONSIBILITY.

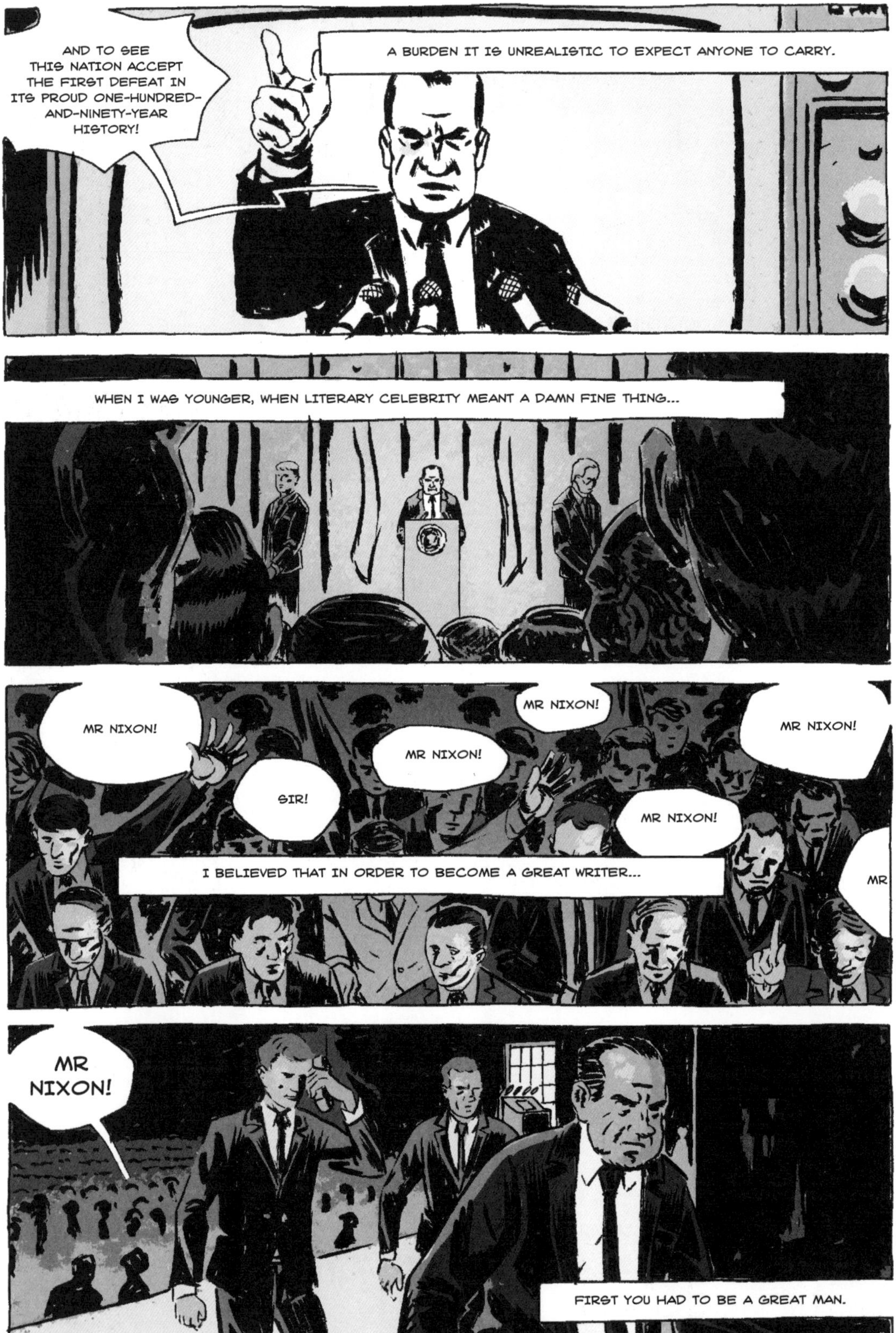
AND TO SEE THIS NATION ACCEPT THE FIRST DEFEAT IN ITS PROUD ONE-HUNDRED-AND-NINETY-YEAR HISTORY!
A BURDEN IT IS UNREALISTIC TO EXPECT ANYONE TO CARRY.
WHEN I WAS YOUNGER, WHEN LITERARY CELEBRITY MEANT A DAMN FINE THING...
MR NIXON!
MR NIXON!
MR NIXON!
MR NIXON!
SIR!
MR NIXON!
I BELIEVED THAT IN ORDER TO BECOME A GREAT WRITER...
MR
MR NIXON!
FIRST YOU HAD TO BE A GREAT MAN.

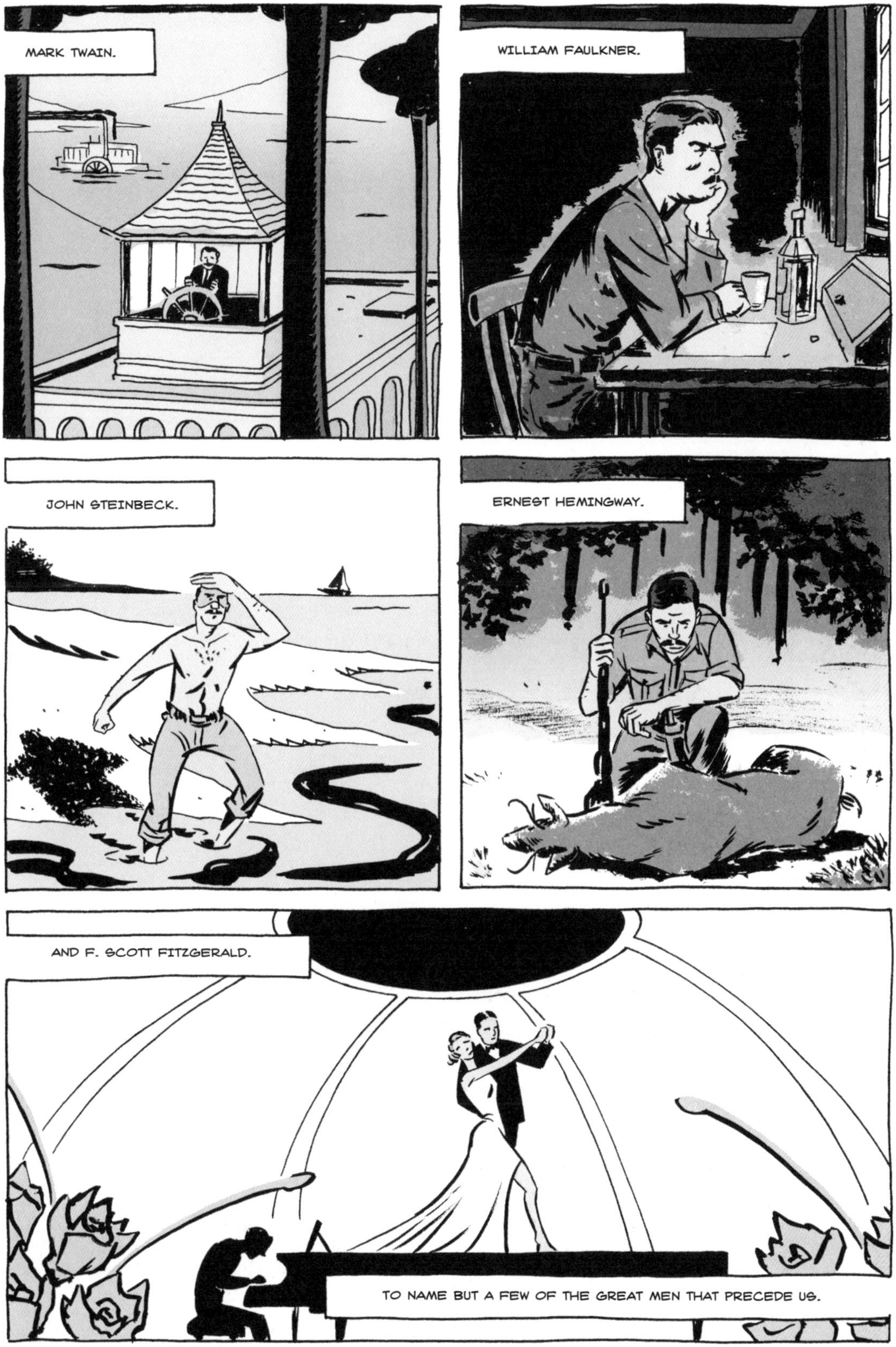
MARK TWAIN.
WILLIAM FAULKNER.
JOHN STEINBECK.
ERNEST HEMINGWAY.
AND F. SCOTT FITZGERALD.
TO NAME BUT A FEW OF THE GREAT MEN THAT PRECEDE US.

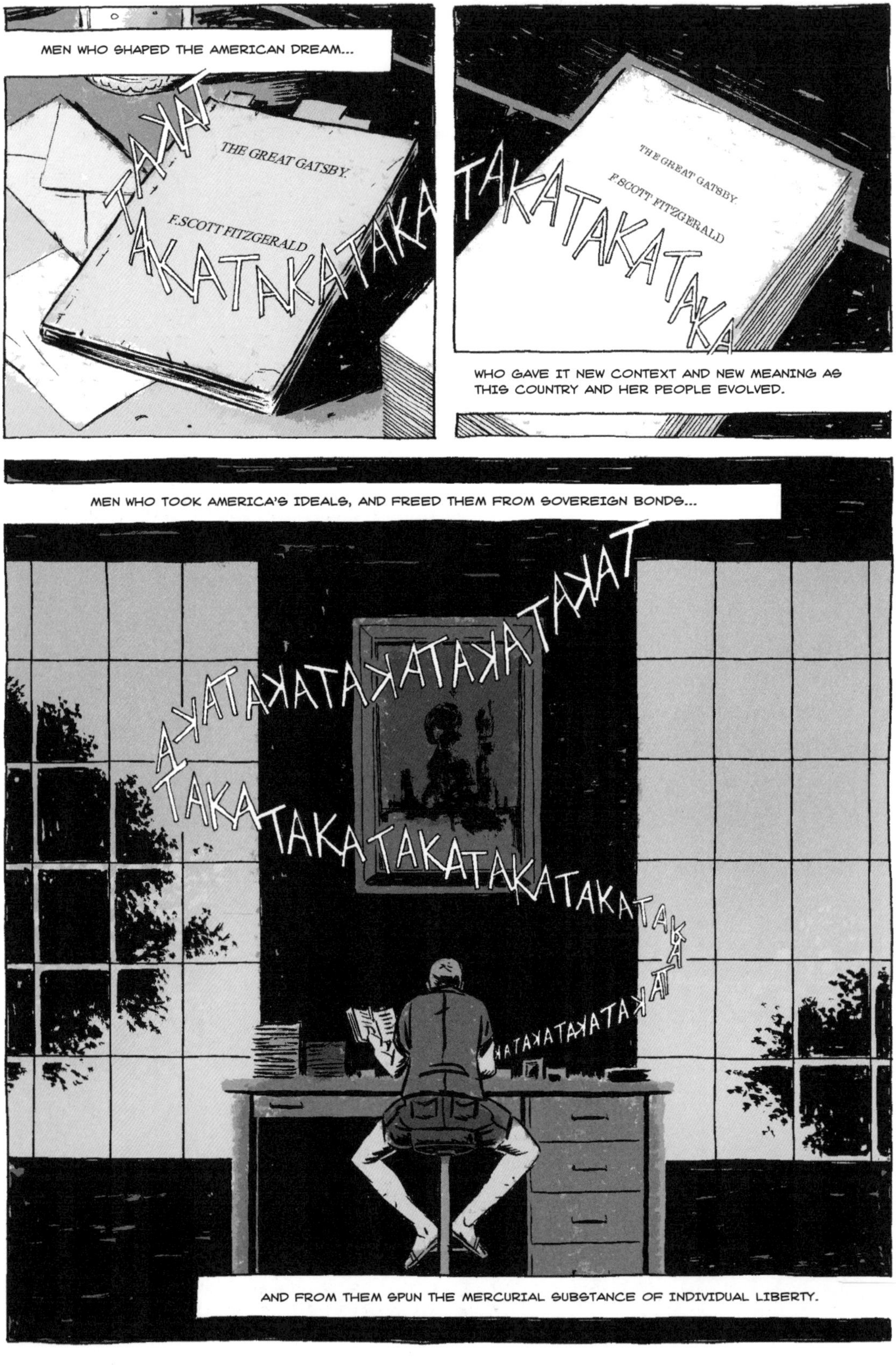
MEN WHO SHAPED THE AMERICAN DREAM...
THE GREAT GATSBY.
F.SCOTT FITZGERALD
THE GREAT GATSBY.
F.SCOTT FITZGERALD
WHO GAVE IT NEW CONTEXT AND NEW MEANING AS THIS COUNTRY AND HER PEOPLE EVOLVED.
MEN WHO TOOK AMERICA'S IDEALS, AND FREED THEM FROM SOVEREIGN BONDS...
AND FROM THEM SPUN THE MERCURIAL SUBSTANCE OF INDIVIDUAL LIBERTY.

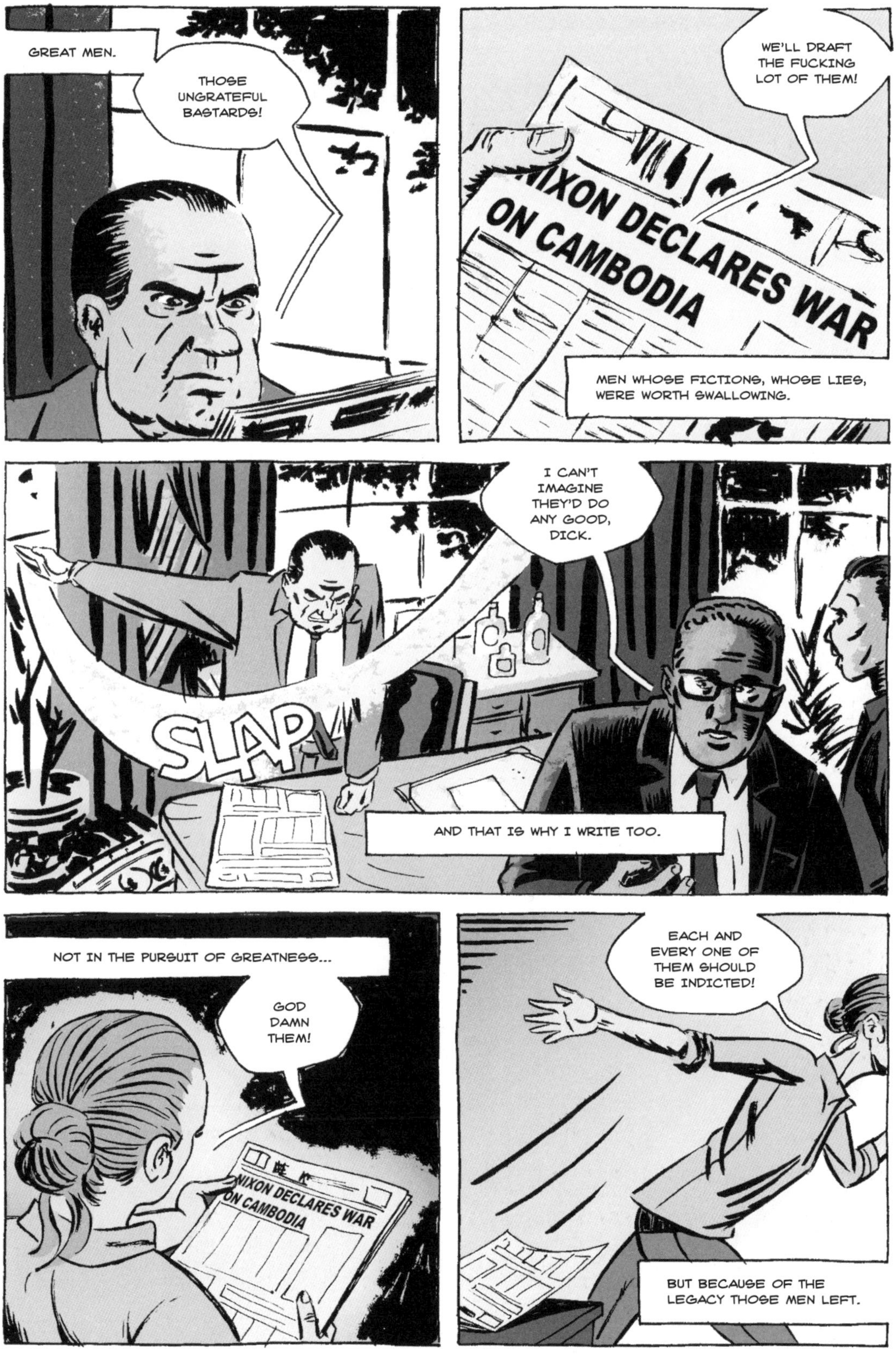
GREAT MEN.
THOSE UNGRATEFUL BASTARDS!
WE'LL DRAFT THE FUCKING LOT OF THEM!
NIXON DECLARES WAR ON CAMBODIA
MEN WHOSE FICTIONS, WHOSE LIES, WERE WORTH SWALLOWING.
I CAN'T IMAGINE THEY'D DO ANY GOOD, DICK.
SLAP
AND THAT IS WHY I WRITE TOO.
NOT IN THE PURSUIT OF GREATNESS...
GOD DAMN THEM!
NIXON DECLARES WAR ON CAMBODIA
EACH AND EVERY ONE OF THEM SHOULD BE INDICTED!
BUT BECAUSE OF THE LEGACY THOSE MEN LEFT.

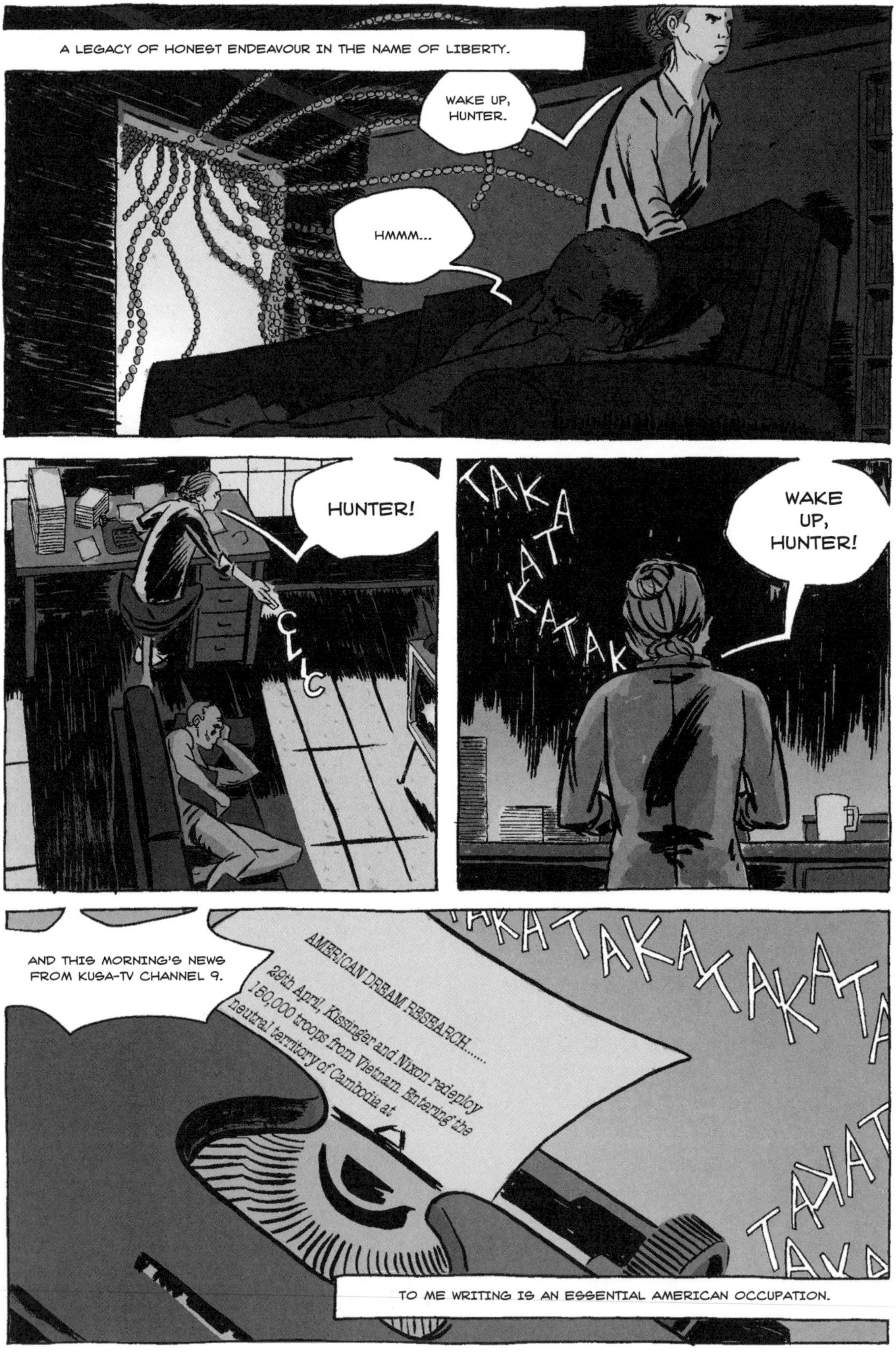
A LEGACY OF HONEST ENDEAVOUR IN THE NAME OF LIBERTY.
WAKE UP, HUNTER.
HMMM...
HUNTER!
CLIC
TAKA TAKA TAKA TAK
WAKE UP, HUNTER!
AND THIS MORNING'S NEWS FROM KUSA-TV CHANNEL 9.
AMERICAN DREAM RESEARCH......
29th April, Kissinger and Nixon redeploy 150,000 troops from Vietnam. Entering the neutral territory of Cambodia at
TAKA TAKA TAKA
TO ME WRITING IS AN ESSENTIAL AMERICAN OCCUPATION.

AN ACT OF PAINSTAKING CONSERVATION.

TAKATAKATHKATAKATAKATAKA

IT WAS ANNOUNCED AT TEN O'CLOCK THIS MORNING THAT AMERICAN TANKS HAVE CROSSED THE CAMBODIAN BORDER. WE'RE HEARING REPORTS OF LOCAL...

CRS NEWS

TAKAT TAYATAYA

THIS IS NOT AN INVASION OF CAMBODIA.

AN AMERICAN WRITER'S PURPOSE?

TO LOCATE AND DOCUMENT THOSE SAME STRANDS OF LIBERTY.

TAKA TA TAKA TAKATAKA

WHEREVER THEY MAY BE.

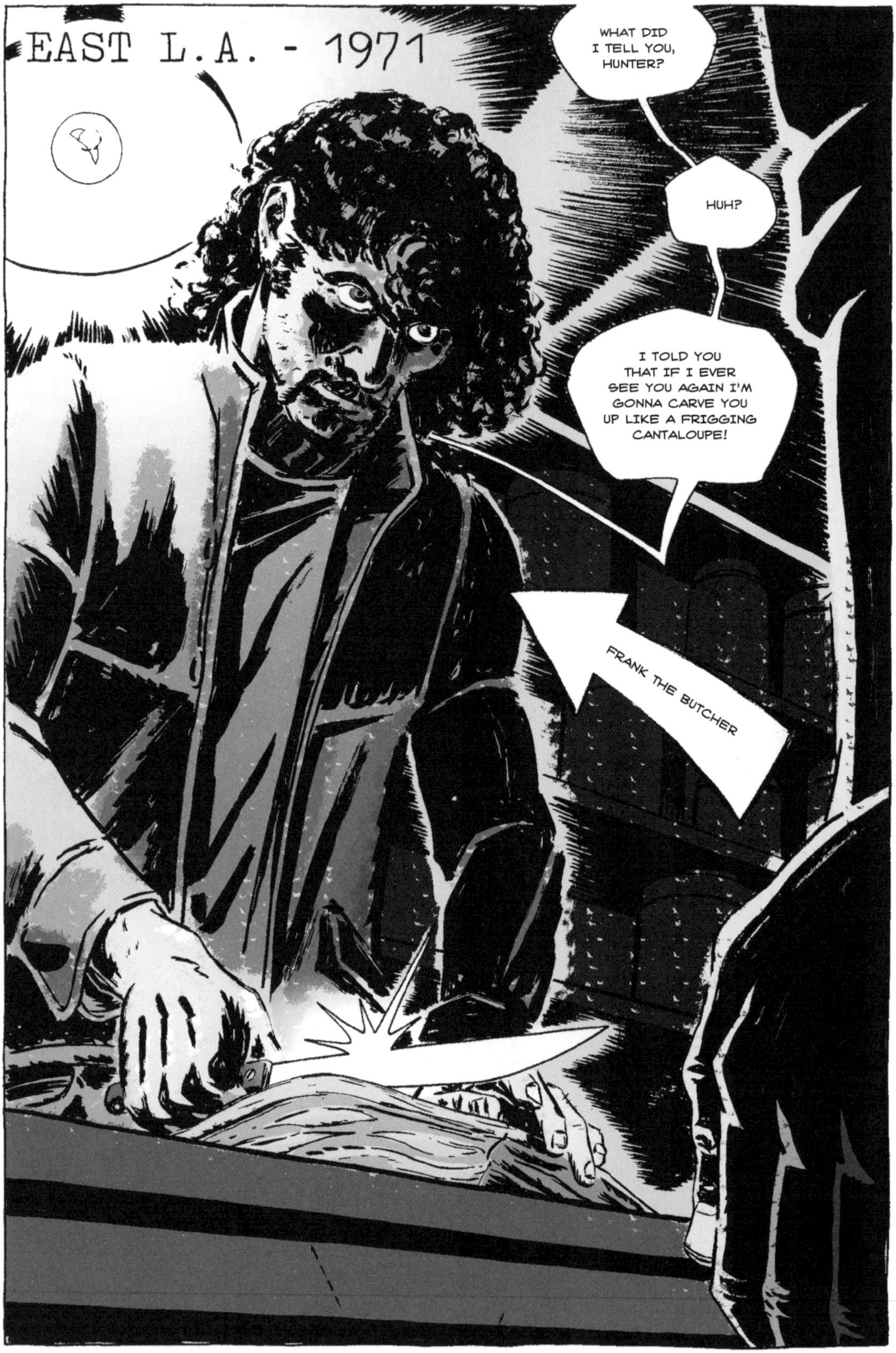
EAST L.A. - 1971
WHAT DID I TELL YOU, HUNTER?
HUH?
I TOLD YOU THAT IF I EVER SEE YOU AGAIN I'M GONNA CARVE YOU UP LIKE A FRIGGING CANTALOUPE!
FRANK THE BUTCHER

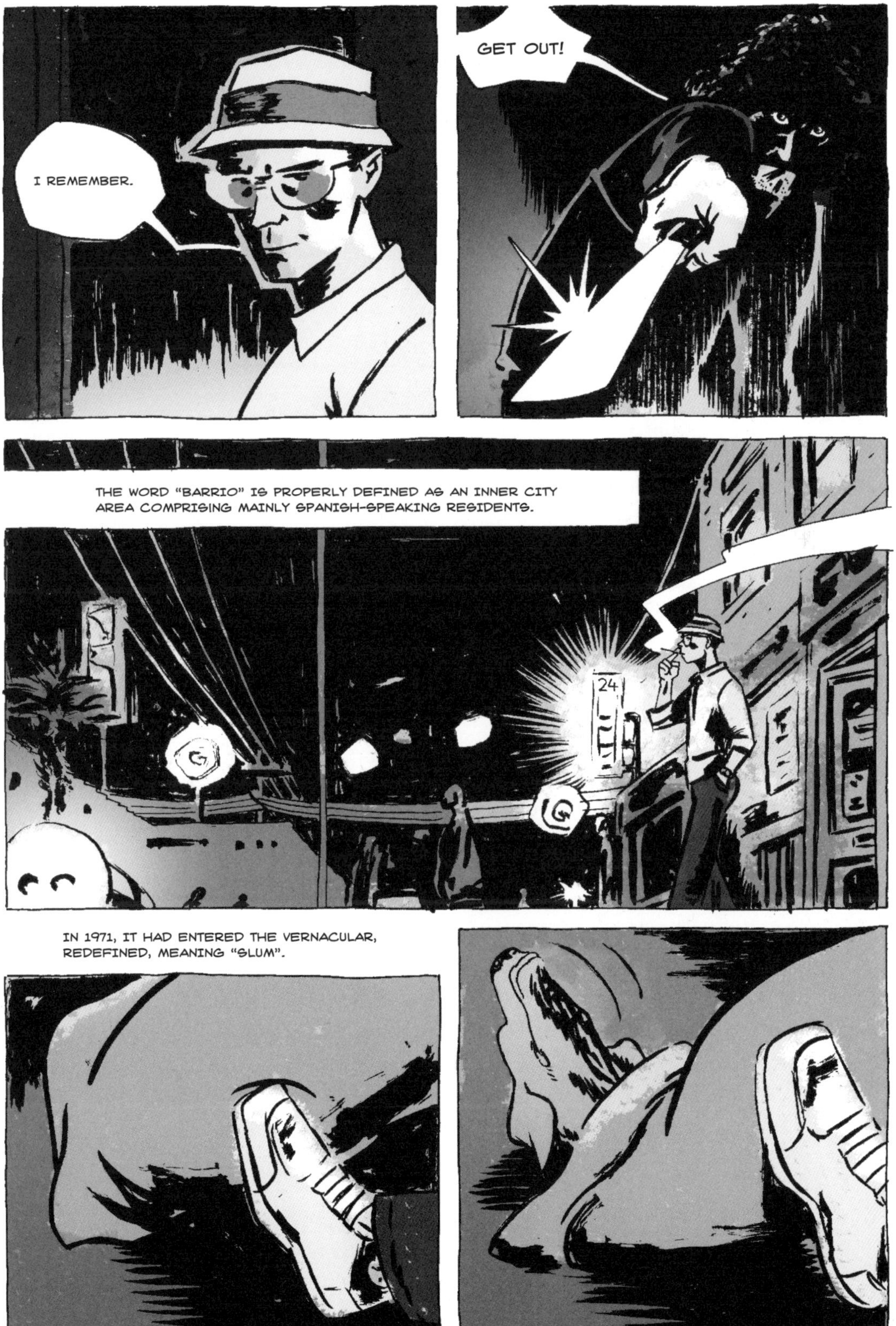
I REMEMBER.
GET OUT!
THE WORD "BARRIO" IS PROPERLY DEFINED AS AN INNER CITY AREA COMPRISING MAINLY SPANISH-SPEAKING RESIDENTS.
24
IN 1971, IT HAD ENTERED THE VERNACULAR, REDEFINED, MEANING "SLUM".

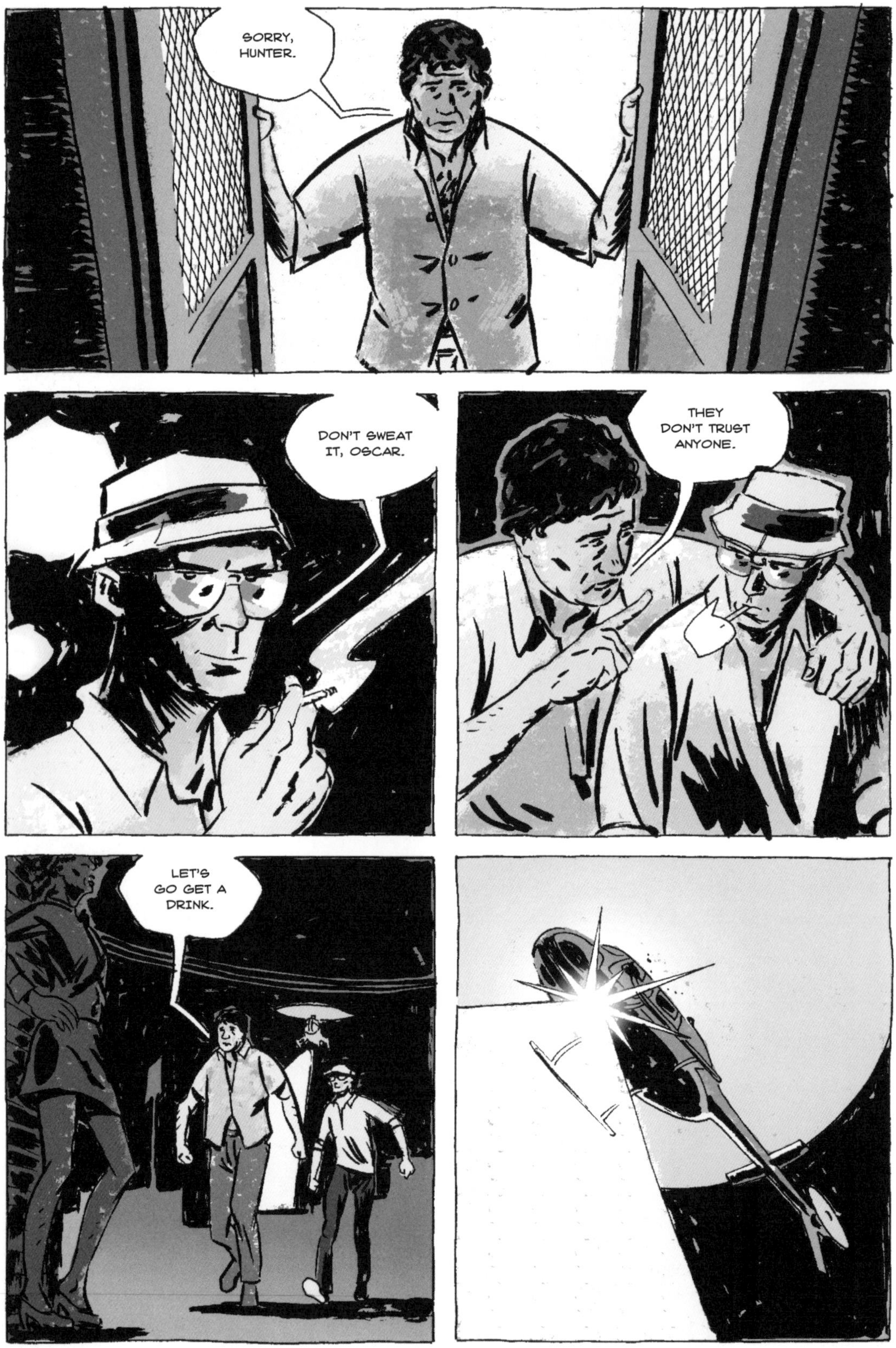
SORRY, HUNTER.
DON'T SWEAT IT, OSCAR.
THEY DON'T TRUST ANYONE.
LET'S GO GET A DRINK.

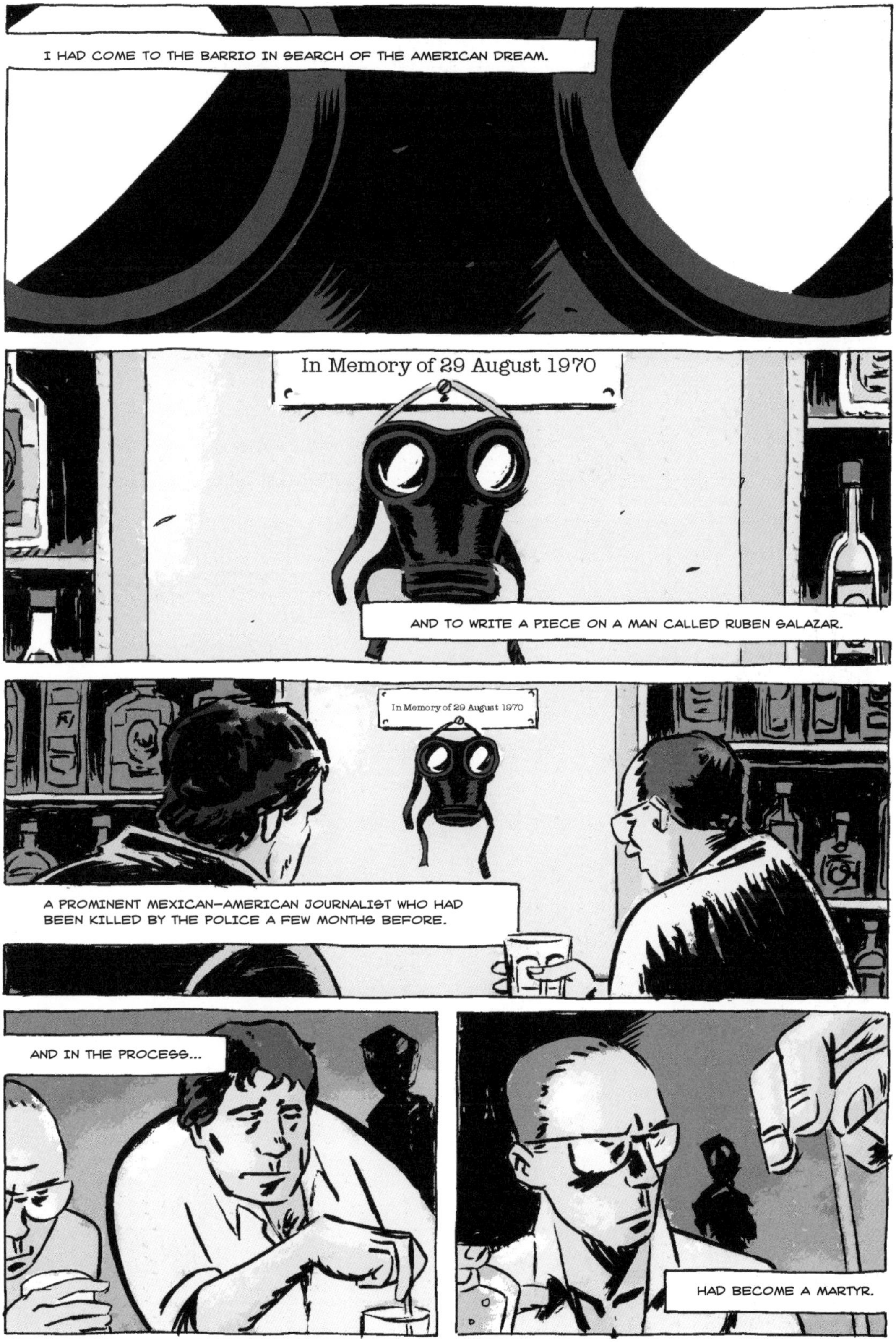
I HAD COME TO THE BARRIO IN SEARCH OF THE AMERICAN DREAM.
In Memory of 29 August 1970
AND TO WRITE A PIECE ON A MAN CALLED RUBEN SALAZAR.
In Memory of 29 August 1970
A PROMINENT MEXICAN-AMERICAN JOURNALIST WHO HAD BEEN KILLED BY THE POLICE A FEW MONTHS BEFORE.
AND IN THE PROCESS...
HAD BECOME A MARTYR.

"ON THE 29 AUGUST, THROUGH ALL OUR BARRIOS
WERE DEMONSTRATIONS FOR PEACE AND JUSTICE
AND THE POLICE RIOTED AND ATTACKED...
ARRESTING AND ABUSING HUNDREDS OF COMMUNITY
PEOPLE. THEY KILLED GILBERTO DIAZ, LYNN WARD
AND RUBEN SALAZAR, THE MAN WHO COULD TELL OUR
STORY TO THE NATION AND THE WORLD.

"WE MUST NOT FORGET THE LESSON OF 29 AUGUST,
THAT THE MAJOR SOCIAL AND POLITICAL ISSUE
WE FACE IS POLICE BRUTALITY. SINCE THE 29TH,
POLICE ATTACKS HAVE BEEN WORSE, EITHER THE
PEOPLE CONTROL THE POLICE, OR WE ARE LIVING
IN A POLICE STATE."

NATIONAL CHICANO
MORATORIUM COMMITTEE, 31 JANUARY 1971

"FOR THIRTEEN DEVASTATED BLOCKS,
DARKENED STORES STOOD GAPING, SHOW
WINDOWS SMASHED. TRAFFIC SIGNS, SPENT
SHOTGUN SHELLS, CHUNKS OF BRICK AND
CONCRETE LITTERED THE PAVEMENT. A PAIR
OF SOFAS, GUTTED BY FIRE, SMOULDERED AT A
KERBSIDE SPLASHED WITH BLOOD. IN THE HOT
BLAZE OF POLICE FLARES, THREE CHICANO
YOUTHS SWAGGERED DOWN THE RUINED STREET.
'HEY BROTHER,' ONE YELLED TO A BLACK
REPORTER, 'WAS THIS BETTER THAN WATTS?' "

NEWSWEEK,
15 FEBRUARY 1971

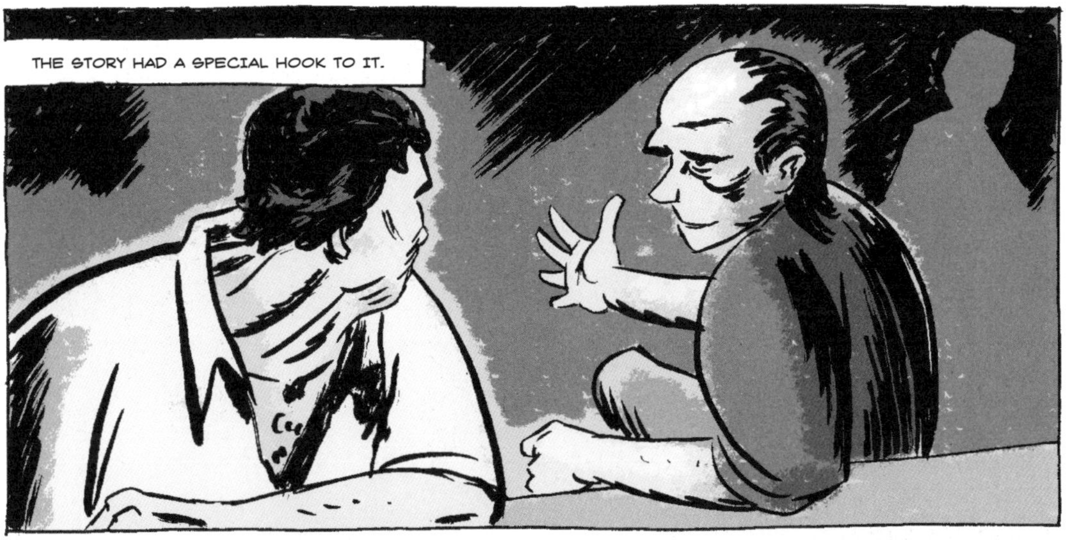
THE STORY HAD A SPECIAL HOOK TO IT.

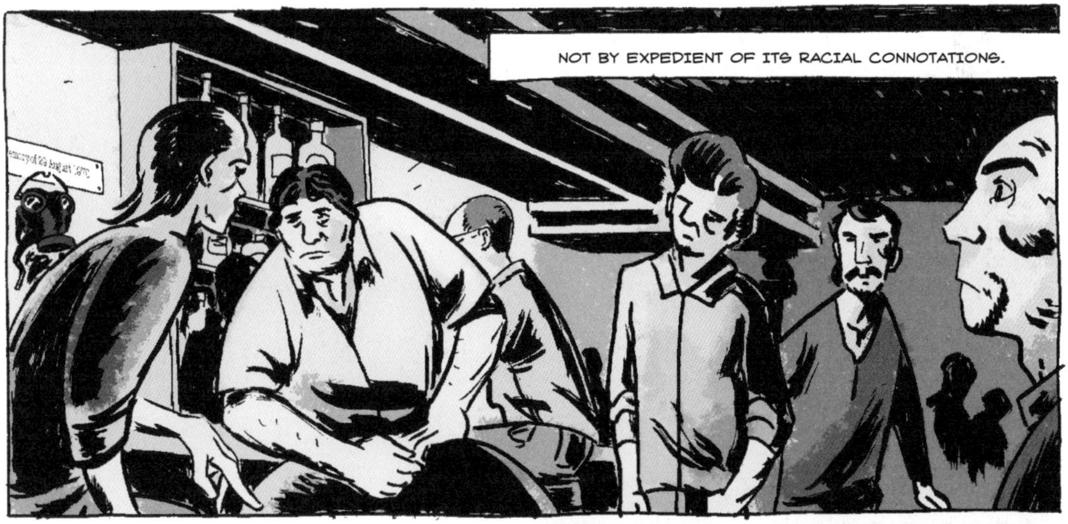
NOT BY EXPEDIENT OF ITS RACIAL CONNOTATIONS.

BUT BECAUSE THE POLICE HAD DELIBERATELY GONE OUT ONTO THE STREETS TO KILL A PUBLIC FIGURE WHO HAD BEEN MAKING THEIR LIVES MORE DIFFICULT.

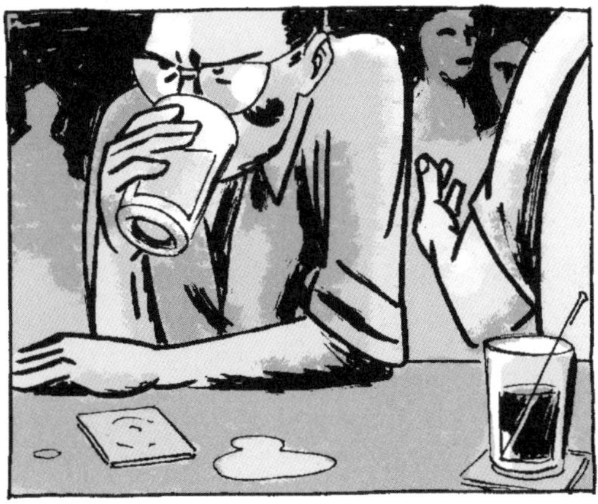

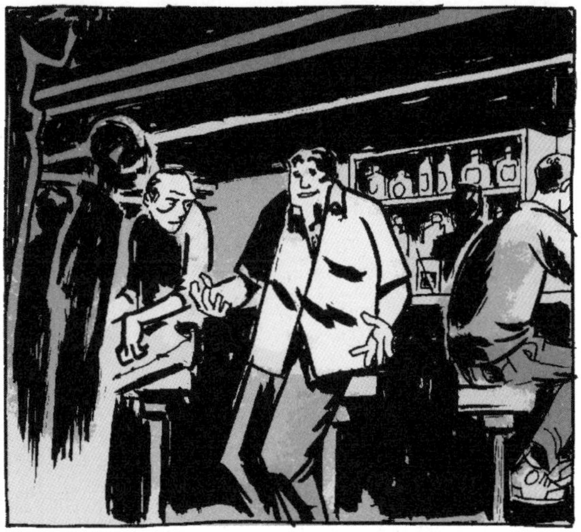

WHICH, I SUPPOSE, BRINGS ME TO OSCAR.

OSCAR WAS A LAWYER BY TRADE.

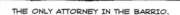

THE ONLY ATTORNEY IN THE BARRIO.

A GOOD MAN, AND AN HONEST ADVOCATE OF AMERICAN IDEALS.

YA ES TIEMPO!!!

THE TIME IS NOW!!!

WE ARE GOING TO BE CLUBBED OVER OUR HEADS FOR AS LONG AS WE LIVE!! NOT BECAUSE WE ARE CRIMINALS, BUT BECAUSE WE ARE CHICANOS!!

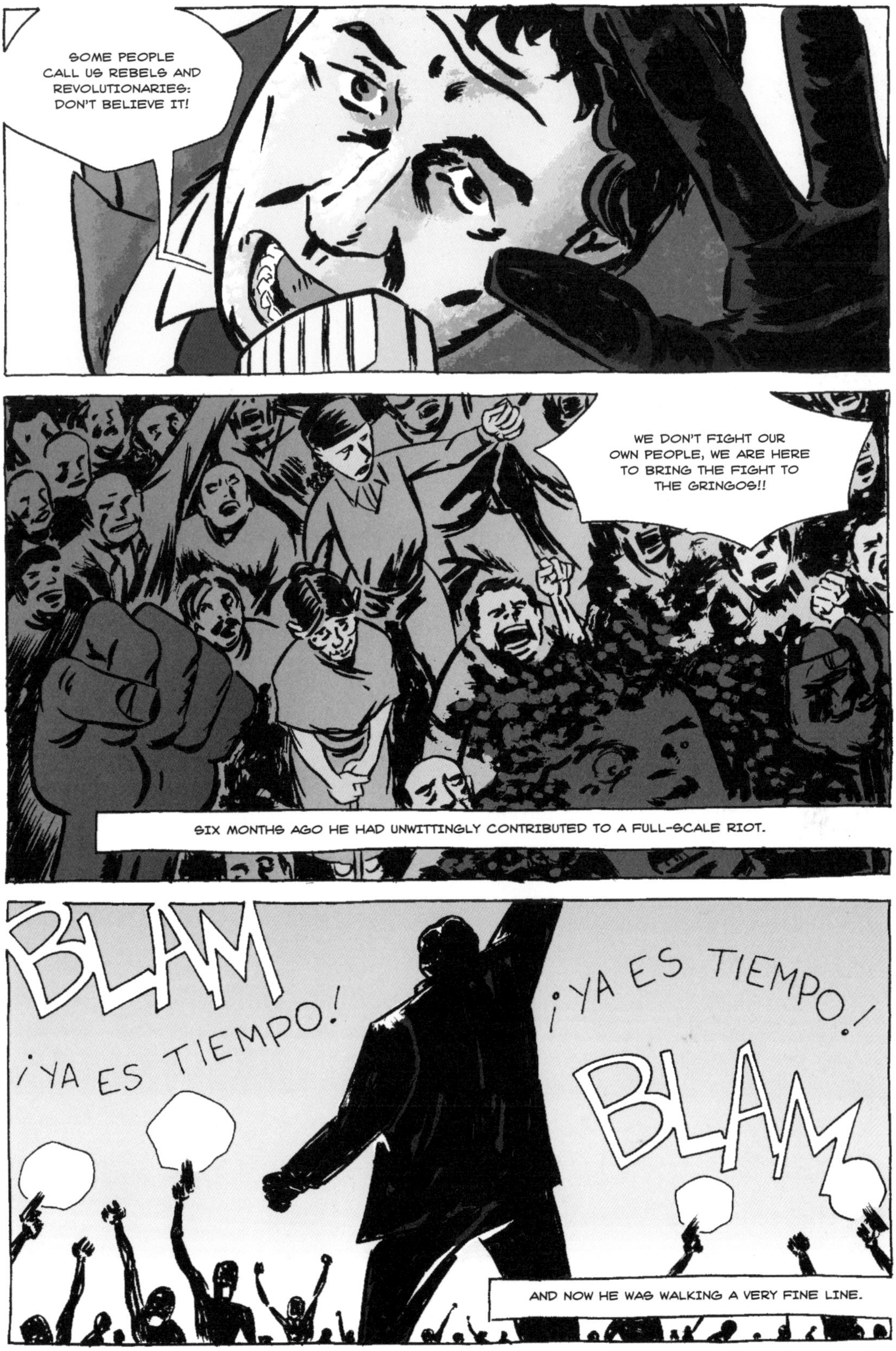
SOME PEOPLE CALL US REBELS AND REVOLUTIONARIES: DON'T BELIEVE IT!
WE DON'T FIGHT OUR OWN PEOPLE, WE ARE HERE TO BRING THE FIGHT TO THE GRINGOS!!
SIX MONTHS AGO HE HAD UNWITTINGLY CONTRIBUTED TO A FULL-SCALE RIOT.
BLAM
¡YA ES TIEMPO!
¡YA ES TIEMPO!
BLAM
AND NOW HE WAS WALKING A VERY FINE LINE.

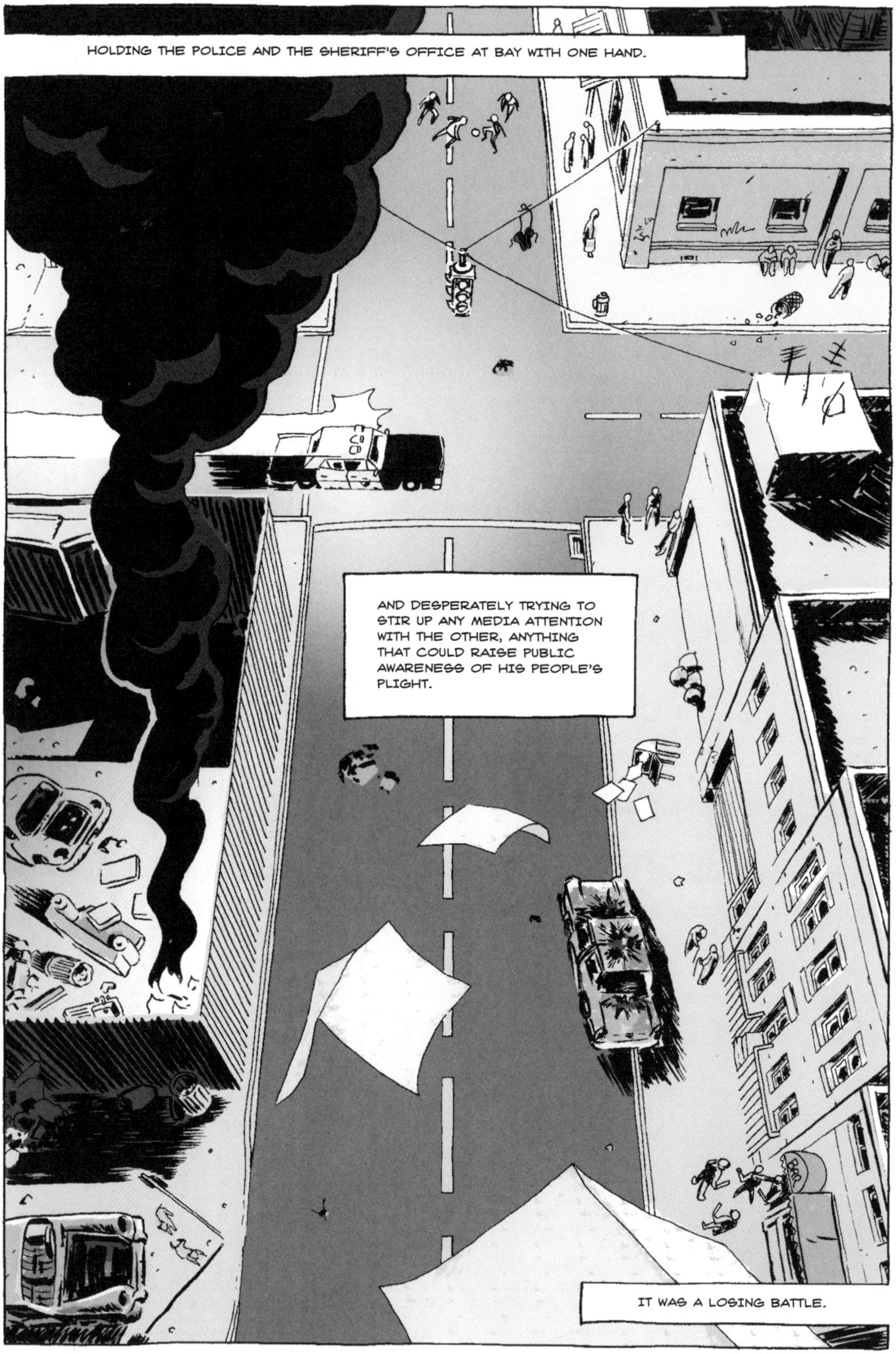
HOLDING THE POLICE AND THE SHERIFF'S OFFICE AT BAY WITH ONE HAND.
AND DESPERATELY TRYING TO STIR UP ANY MEDIA ATTENTION WITH THE OTHER, ANYTHING THAT COULD RAISE PUBLIC AWARENESS OF HIS PEOPLE'S PLIGHT.
IT WAS A LOSING BATTLE.

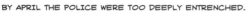

BY APRIL THE POLICE WERE TOO DEEPLY ENTRENCHED.

AND EVEN WITH OSCAR ON MY SIDE, THE CHICANOS WERE TOO SCARED TO ALLOW ME THE ACCESS I NEEDED TO TELL THEIR STORY.

IT WAS GRUELLING.

AND IT WAS GETTING ME DOWN.

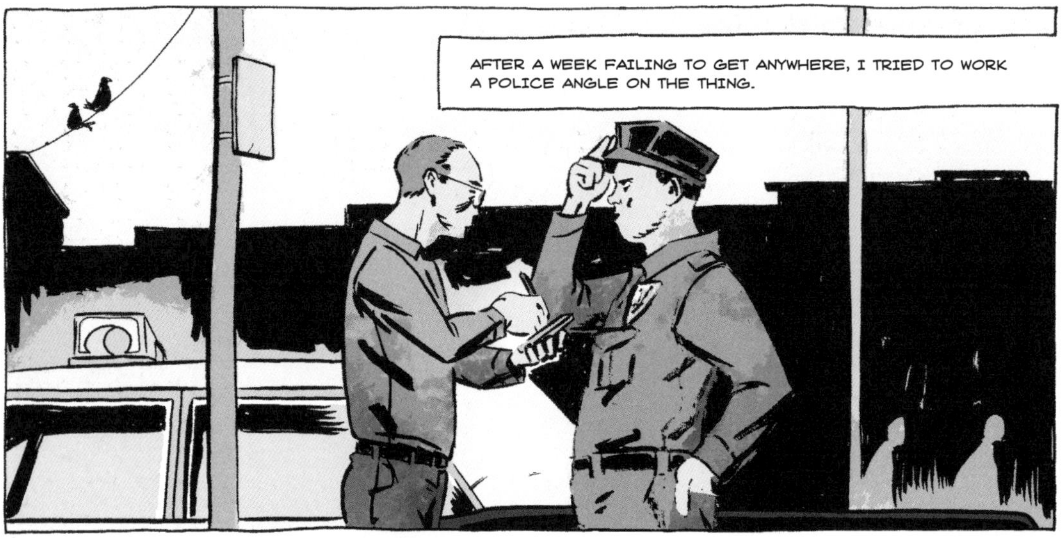
AFTER A WEEK FAILING TO GET ANYWHERE, I TRIED TO WORK A POLICE ANGLE ON THE THING.

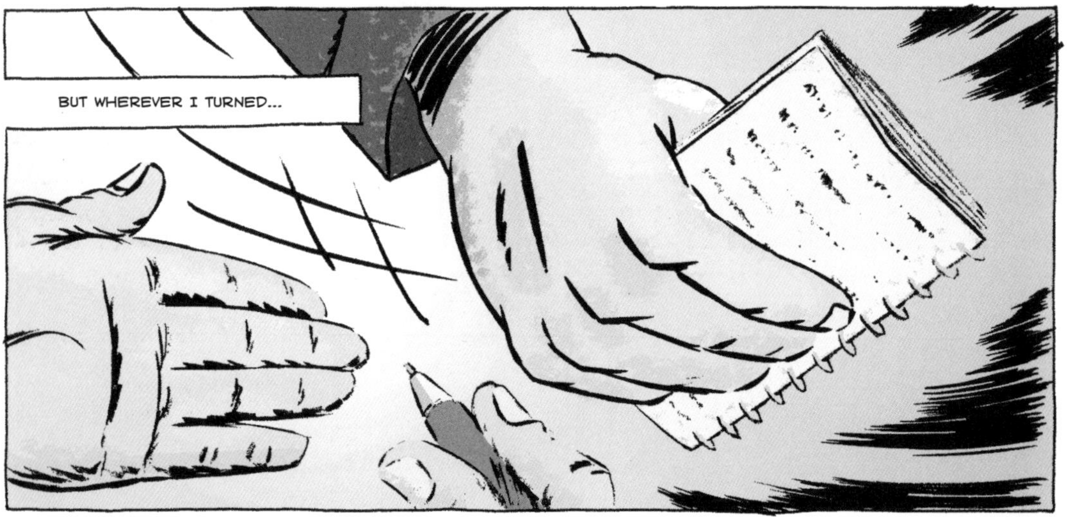
BUT WHEREVER I TURNED...

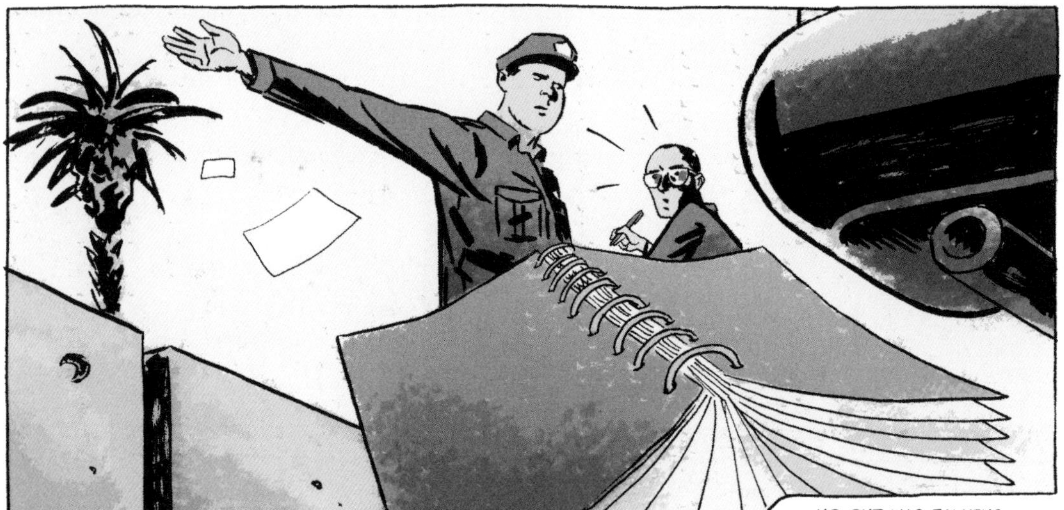
NO ONE WAS TALKING.

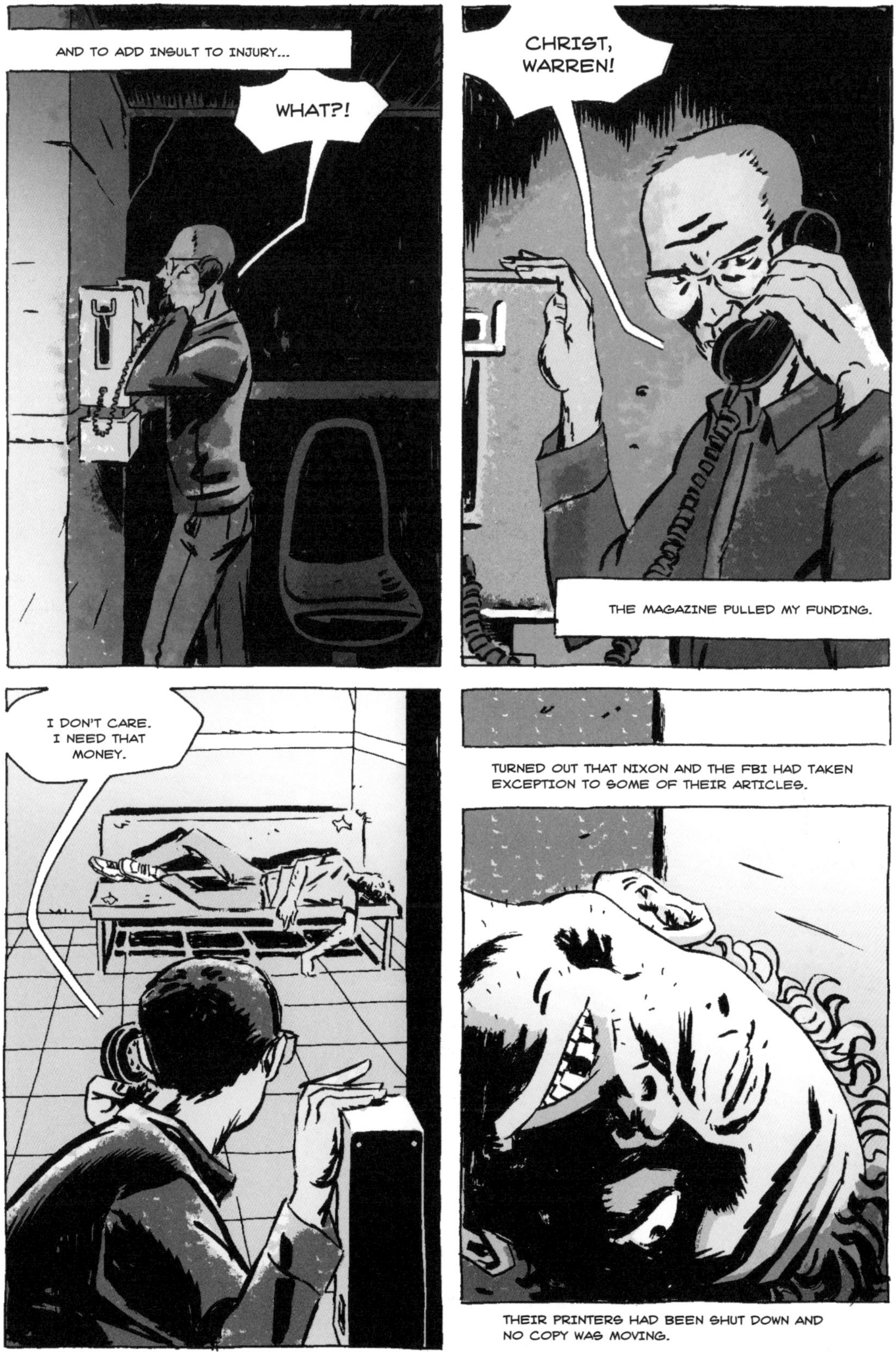
AND TO ADD INSULT TO INJURY...
WHAT?!
CHRIST, WARREN!
THE MAGAZINE PULLED MY FUNDING.
I DON'T CARE. I NEED THAT MONEY.
TURNED OUT THAT NIXON AND THE FBI HAD TAKEN EXCEPTION TO SOME OF THEIR ARTICLES.
THEIR PRINTERS HAD BEEN SHUT DOWN AND NO COPY WAS MOVING.

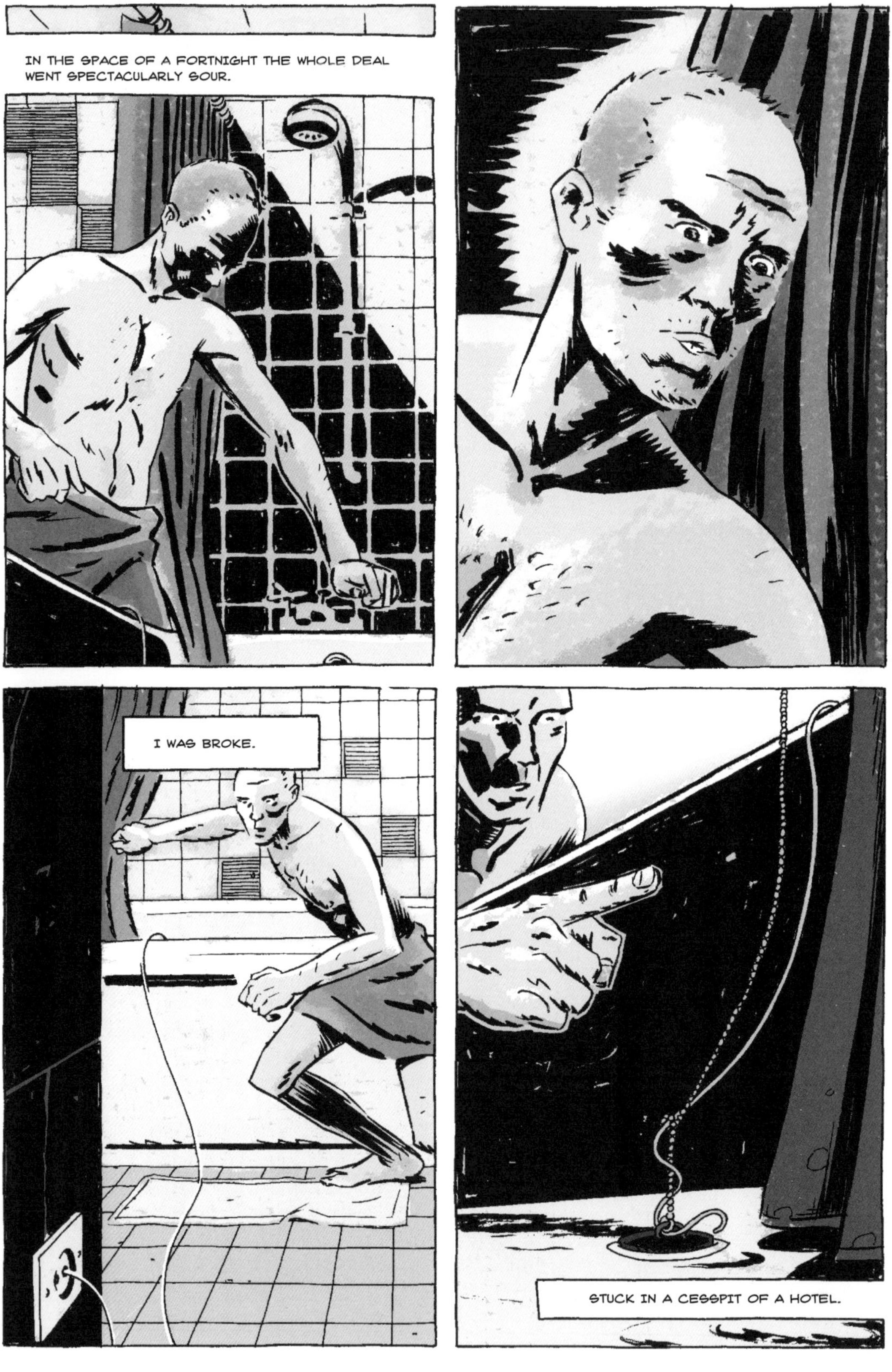
IN THE SPACE OF A FORTNIGHT THE WHOLE DEAL WENT SPECTACULARLY SOUR.
I WAS BROKE.
STUCK IN A CESSPIT OF A HOTEL.

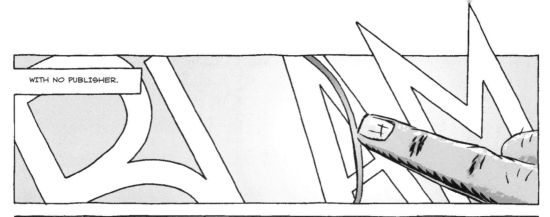

WITH NO PUBLISHER.

AND IT SEEMED THE SAME PEOPLE I WAS WORKING SO HARD TO HELP...

WERE ACTIVELY TRYING TO KILL ME.

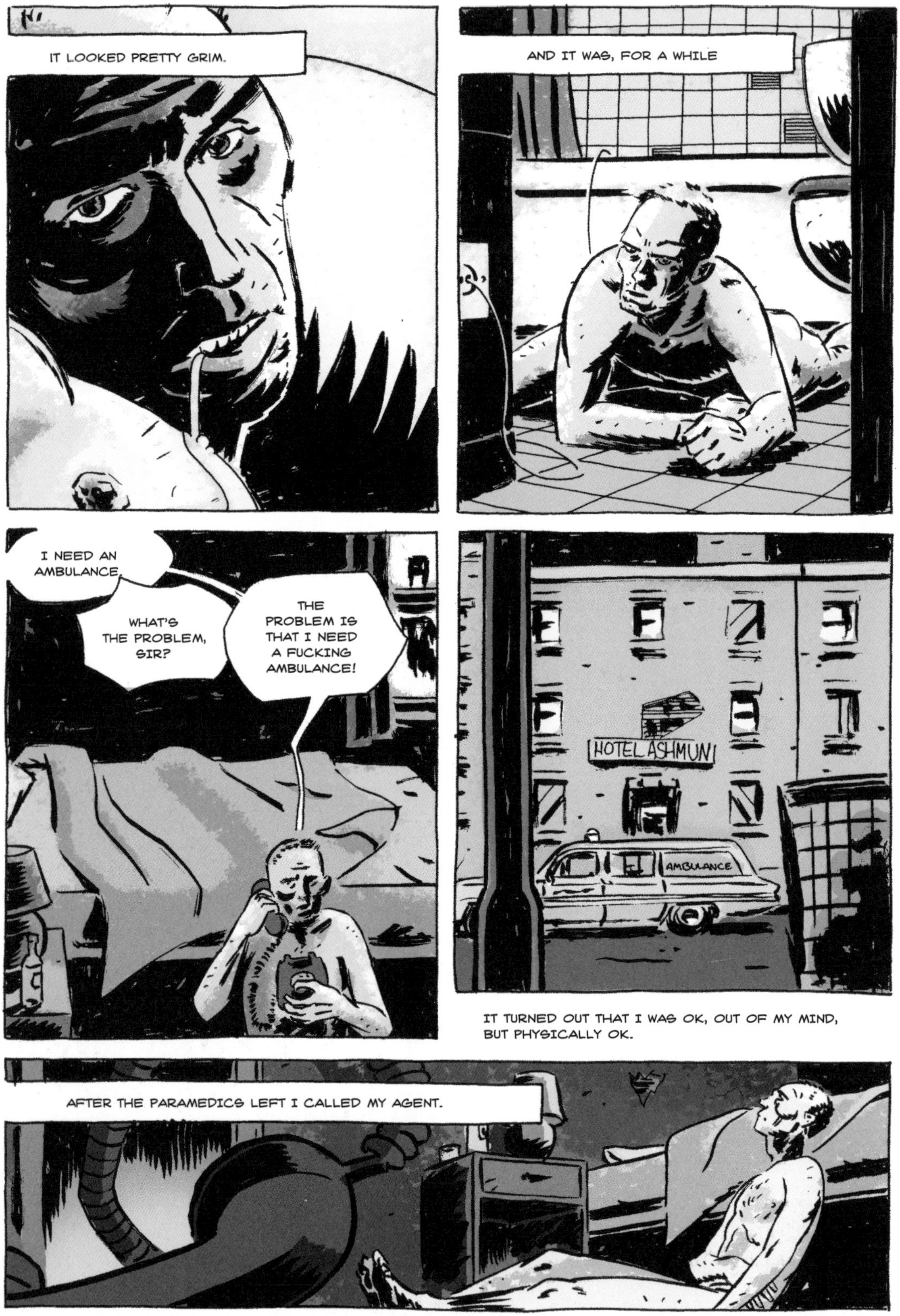
IT LOOKED PRETTY GRIM.
AND IT WAS, FOR A WHILE
I NEED AN AMBULANCE.
WHAT'S THE PROBLEM, SIR?
THE PROBLEM IS THAT I NEED A FUCKING AMBULANCE!
HOTEL ASHMUN
AMBULANCE
IT TURNED OUT THAT I WAS OK, OUT OF MY MIND, BUT PHYSICALLY OK.
AFTER THE PARAMEDICS LEFT I CALLED MY AGENT.
ASKED HER TO FIND ME ANYTHING, ANY PAYING GIG THAT'D GET ME OUT OF THERE.

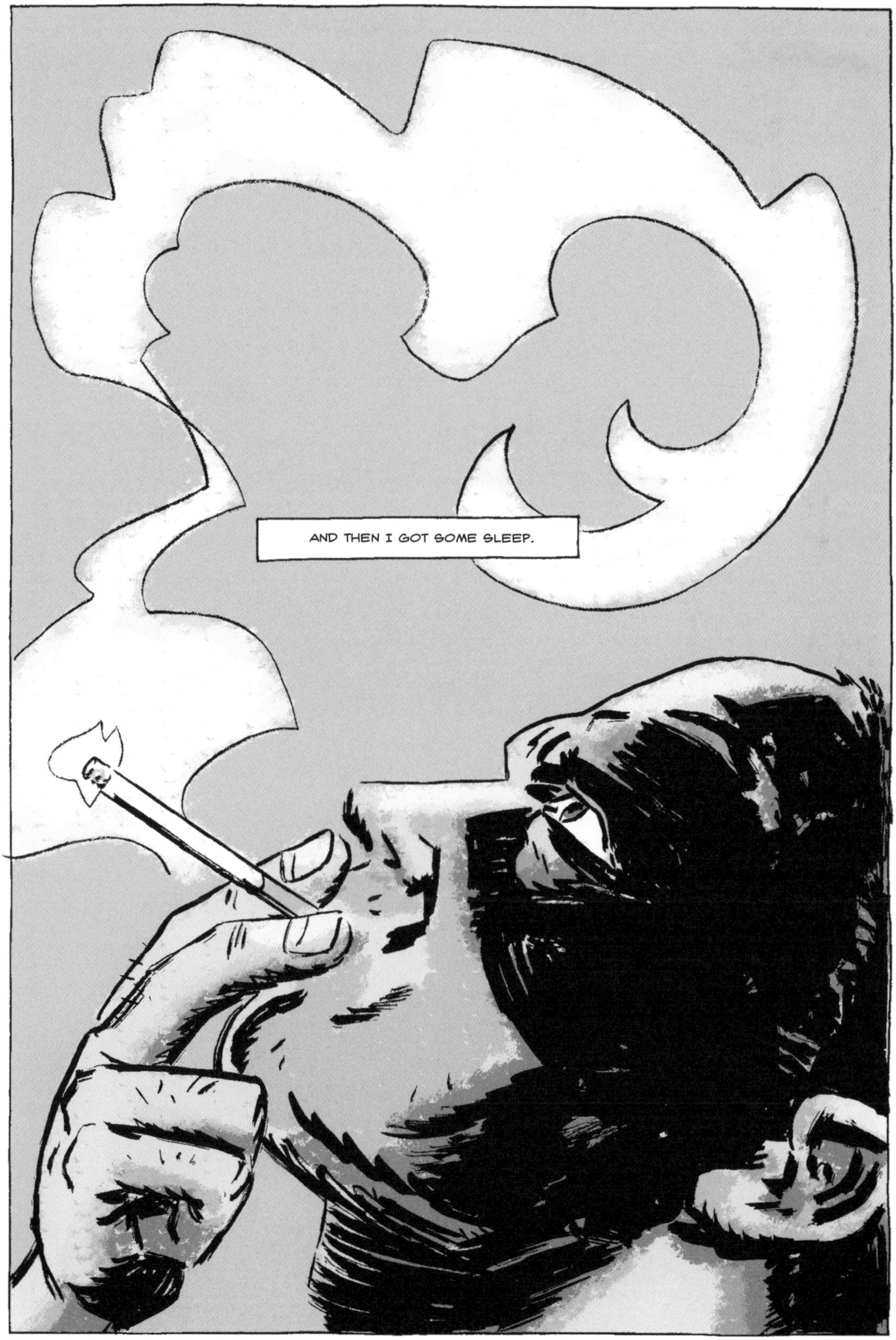
AND THEN I GOT SOME SLEEP.

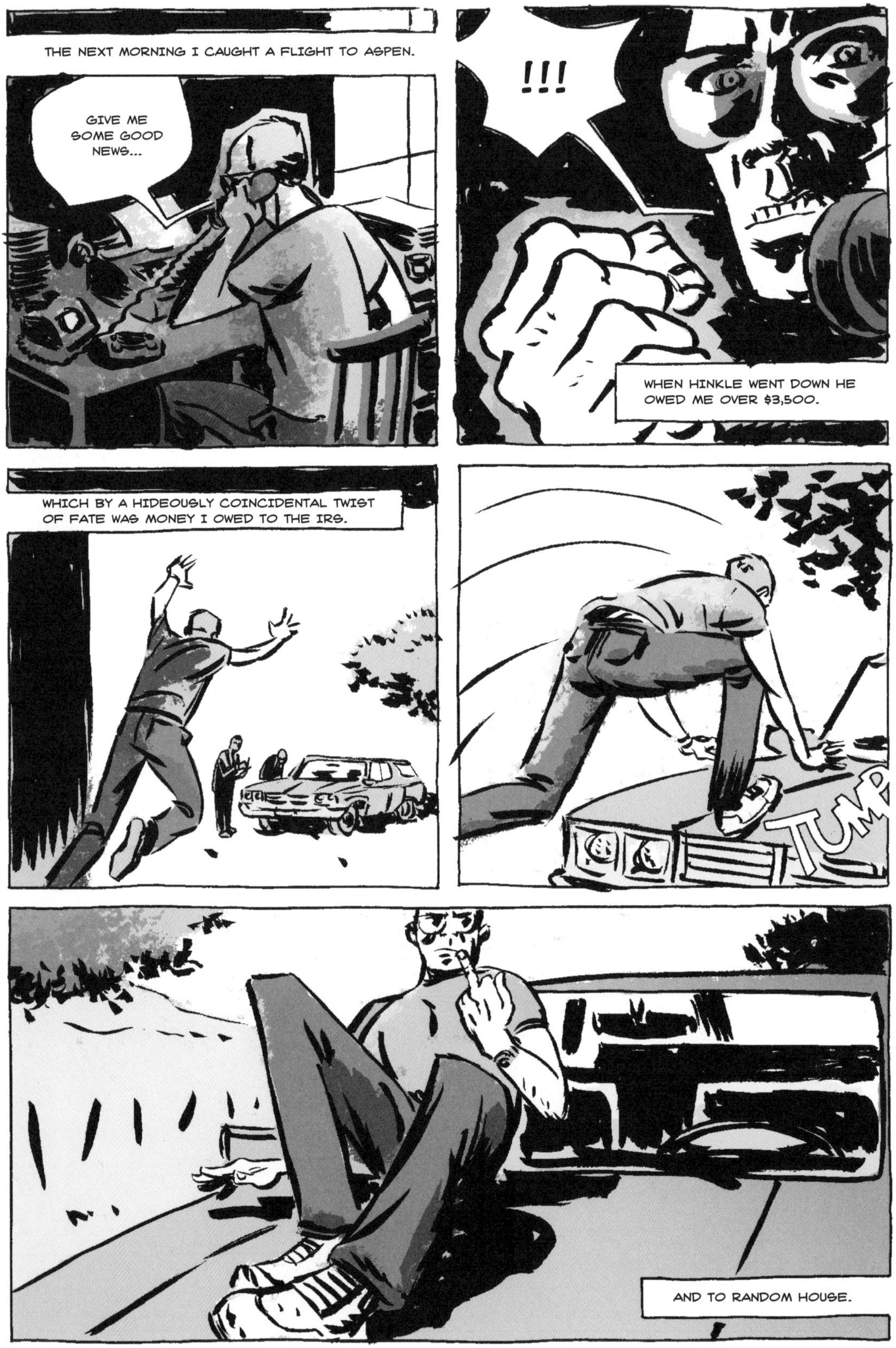
THE NEXT MORNING I CAUGHT A FLIGHT TO ASPEN.
GIVE ME SOME GOOD NEWS...
!!!
WHEN HINKLE WENT DOWN HE OWED ME OVER $3,500.
WHICH BY A HIDEOUSLY COINCIDENTAL TWIST OF FATE WAS MONEY I OWED TO THE IRS.
TUMP
AND TO RANDOM HOUSE.

AND THE BANK.

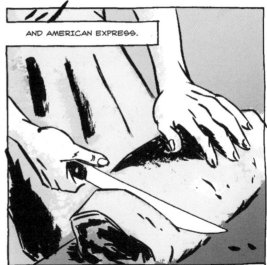

AND AMERICAN EXPRESS.

COME ON, CHEER UP, HUNTER!

IT COULD BE WORSE.

HOW?

JUST SELL IT ON, MOVE ON AND KEEP GOING, HONEY.

SO I DID.

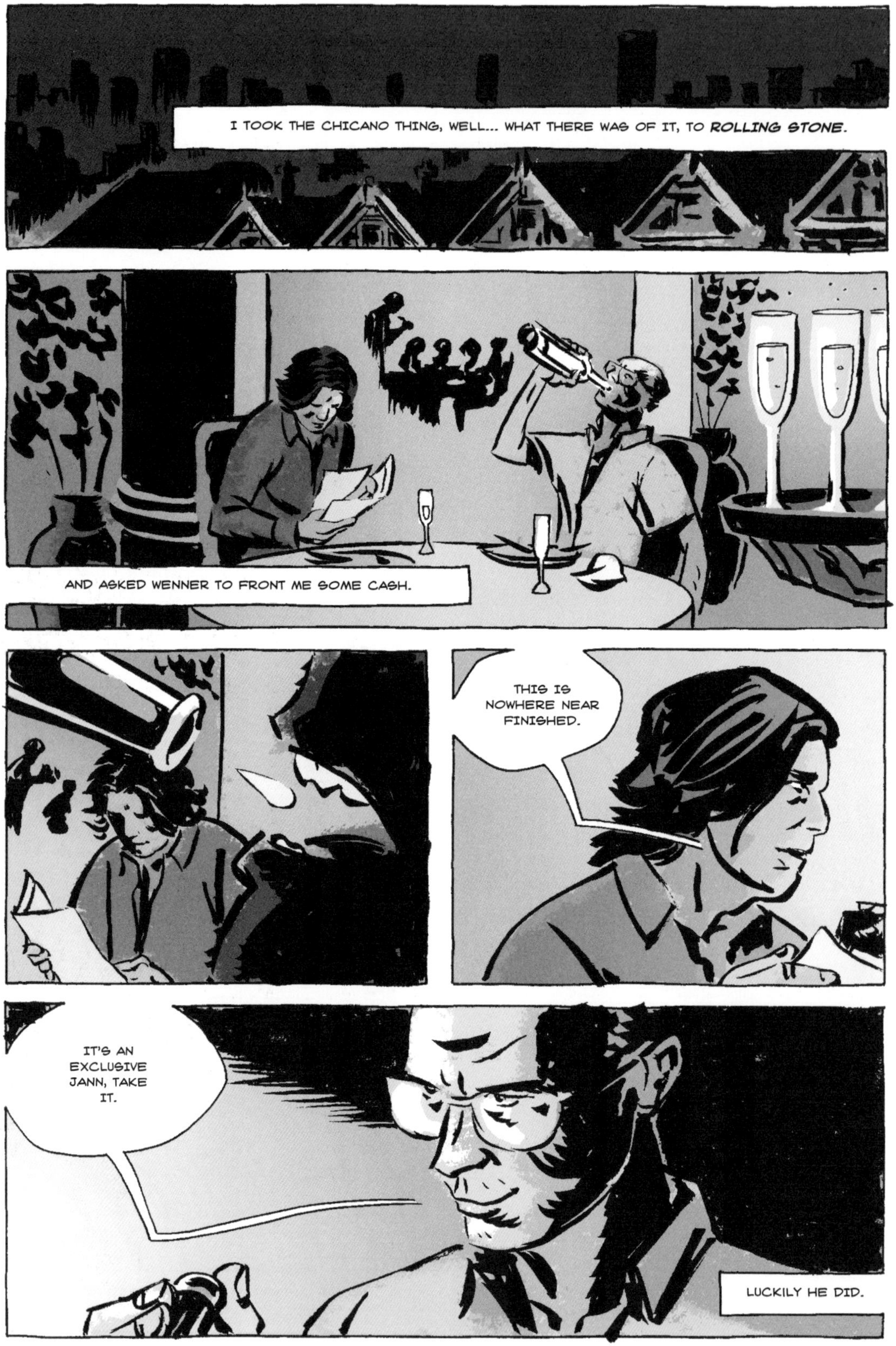
I TOOK THE CHICANO THING, WELL... WHAT THERE WAS OF IT, TO *ROLLING STONE*.
AND ASKED WENNER TO FRONT ME SOME CASH.
THIS IS NOWHERE NEAR FINISHED.
IT'S AN EXCLUSIVE JANN, TAKE IT.
LUCKILY HE DID.

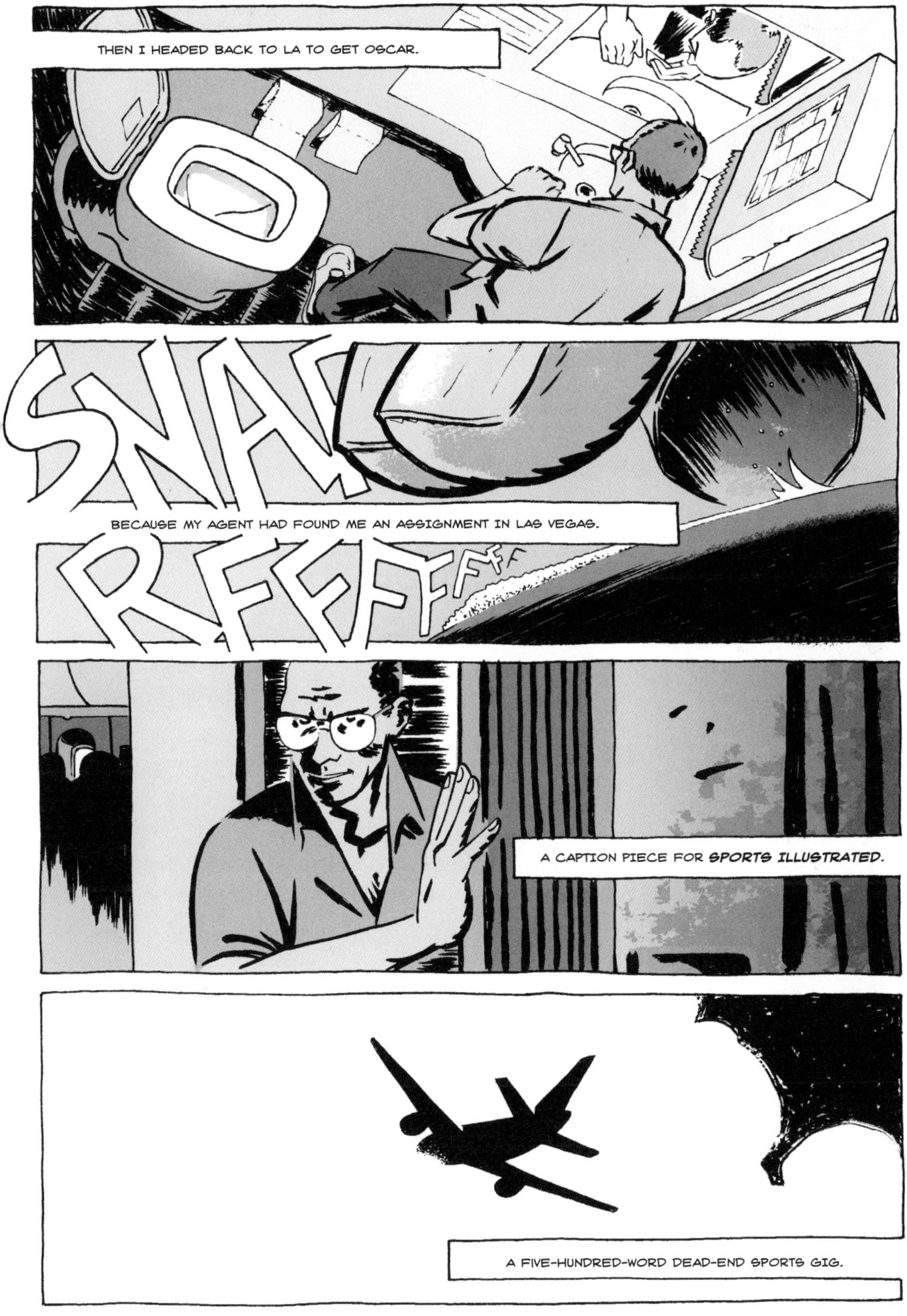
THEN I HEADED BACK TO LA TO GET OSCAR.
SNAP
BECAUSE MY AGENT HAD FOUND ME AN ASSIGNMENT IN LAS VEGAS.
RFFFFFF
A CAPTION PIECE FOR SPORTS ILLUSTRATED.
A FIVE-HUNDRED-WORD DEAD-END SPORTS GIG.

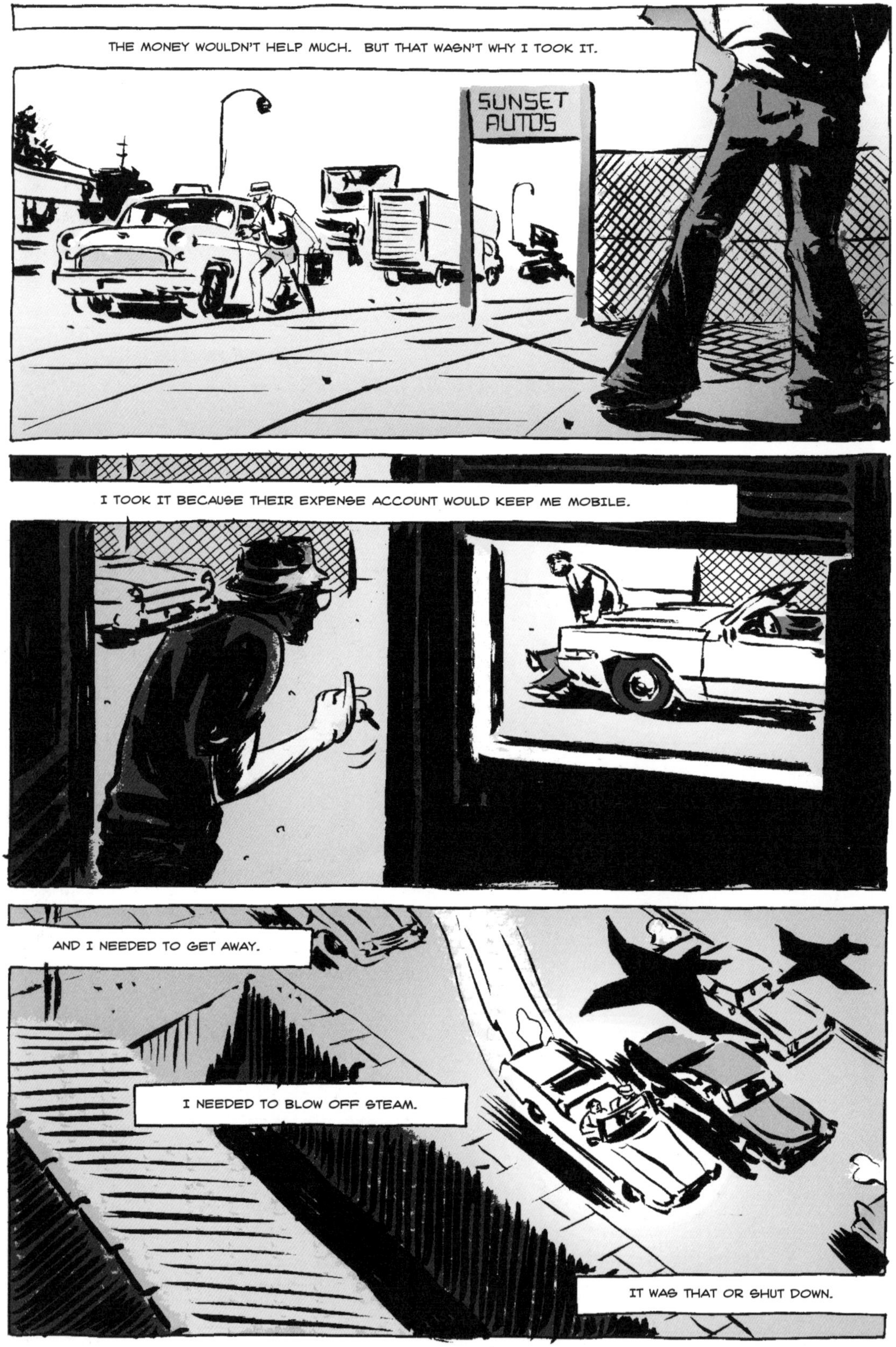
THE MONEY WOULDN'T HELP MUCH. BUT THAT WASN'T WHY I TOOK IT.
SUNSET AUTOS
I TOOK IT BECAUSE THEIR EXPENSE ACCOUNT WOULD KEEP ME MOBILE.
AND I NEEDED TO GET AWAY.
I NEEDED TO BLOW OFF STEAM.
IT WAS THAT OR SHUT DOWN.

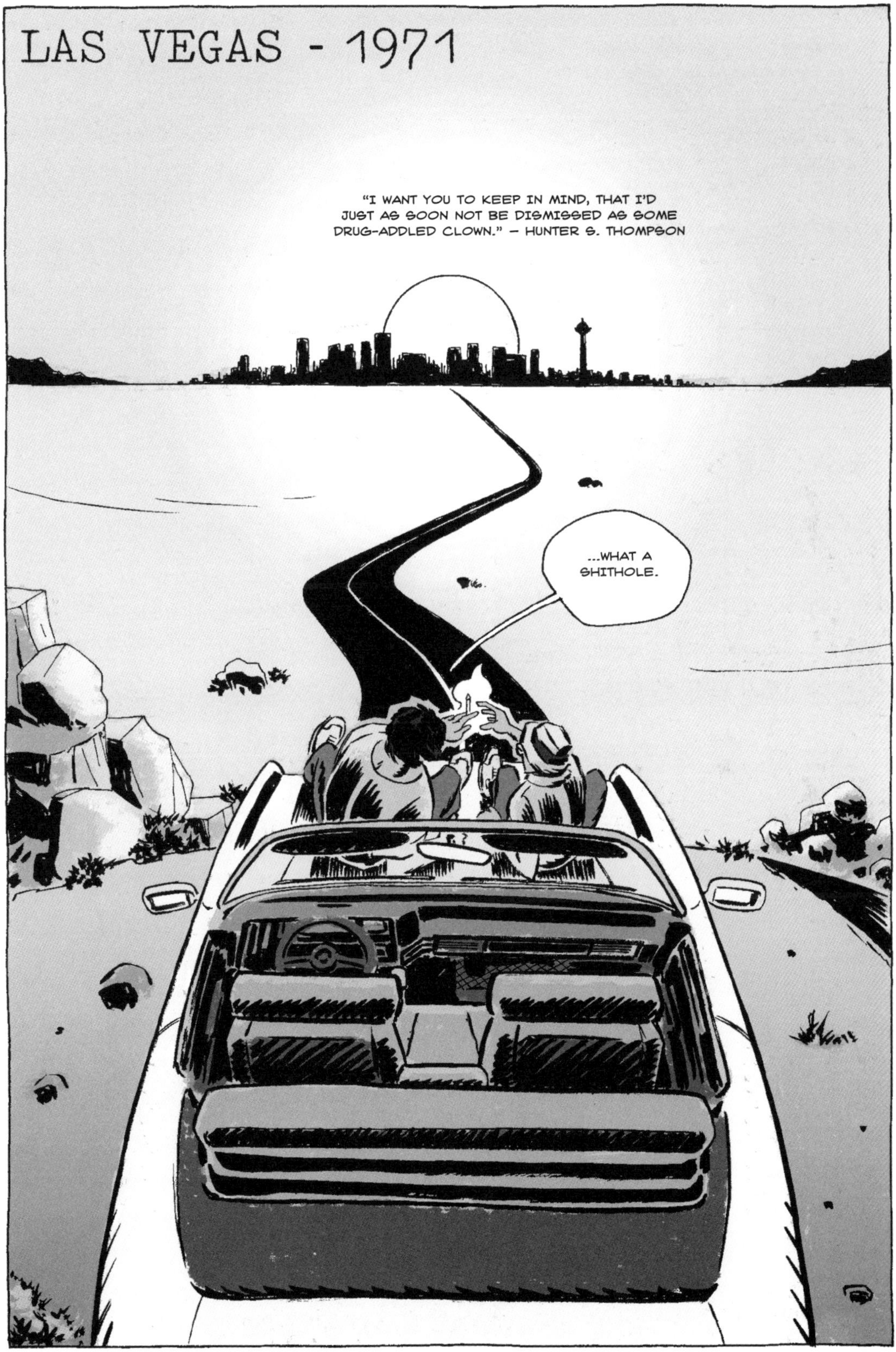
LAS VEGAS - 1971
"I WANT YOU TO KEEP IN MIND, THAT I'D JUST AS SOON NOT BE DISMISSED AS SOME DRUG-ADDLED CLOWN." – HUNTER S. THOMPSON
...WHAT A SHITHOLE.

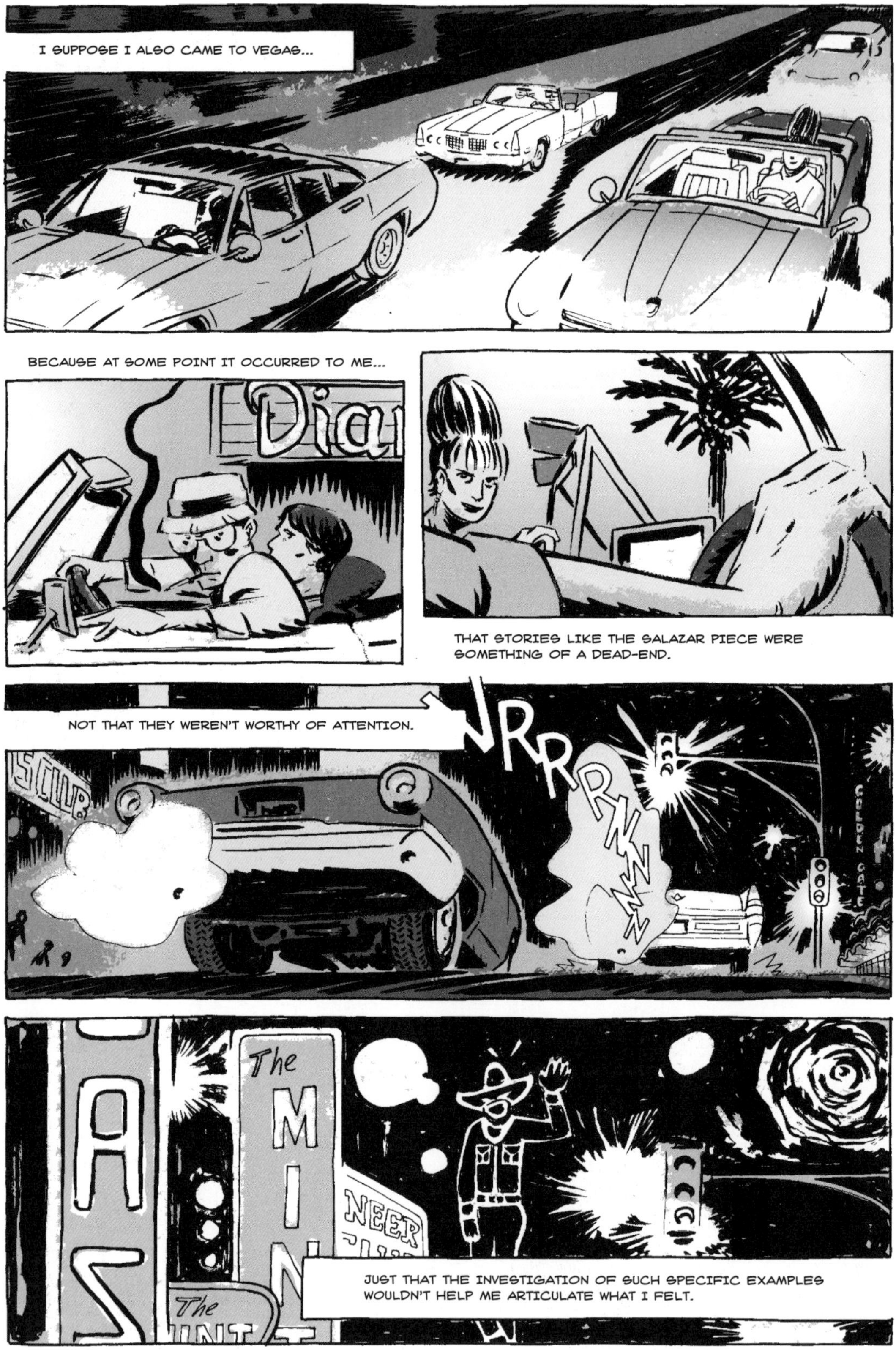
I SUPPOSE I ALSO CAME TO VEGAS...
BECAUSE AT SOME POINT IT OCCURRED TO ME...
Dia
THAT STORIES LIKE THE SALAZAR PIECE WERE SOMETHING OF A DEAD-END.
NOT THAT THEY WEREN'T WORTHY OF ATTENTION.
The
JUST THAT THE INVESTIGATION OF SUCH SPECIFIC EXAMPLES WOULDN'T HELP ME ARTICULATE WHAT I FELT.

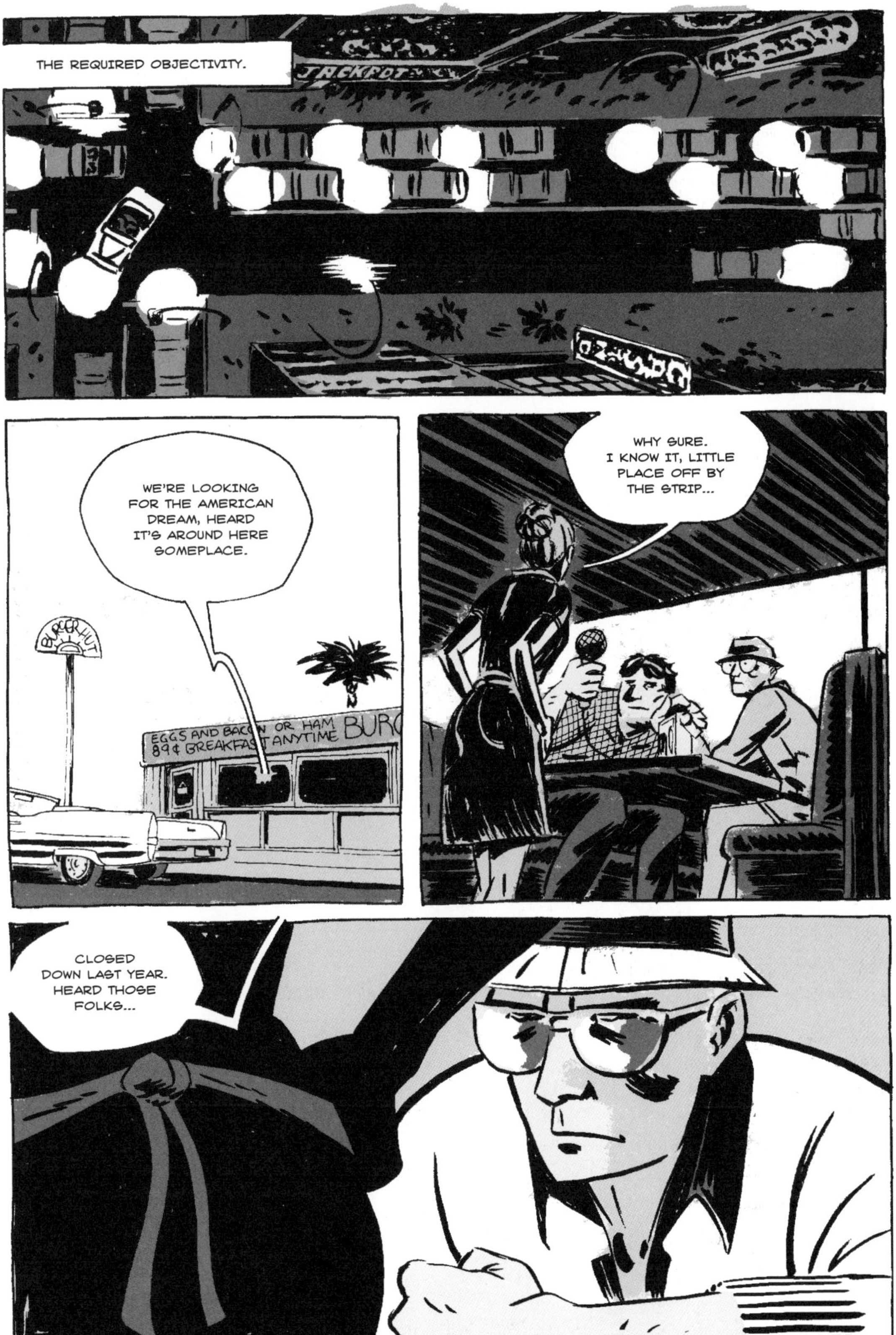
THE REQUIRED OBJECTIVITY.
JACKPOT
WE'RE LOOKING FOR THE AMERICAN DREAM, HEARD IT'S AROUND HERE SOMEPLACE.
BURGER HUT
EGGS AND BACON OR HAM 89¢ BREAKFAST ANYTIME
WHY SURE. I KNOW IT, LITTLE PLACE OFF BY THE STRIP...
CLOSED DOWN LAST YEAR. HEARD THOSE FOLKS...

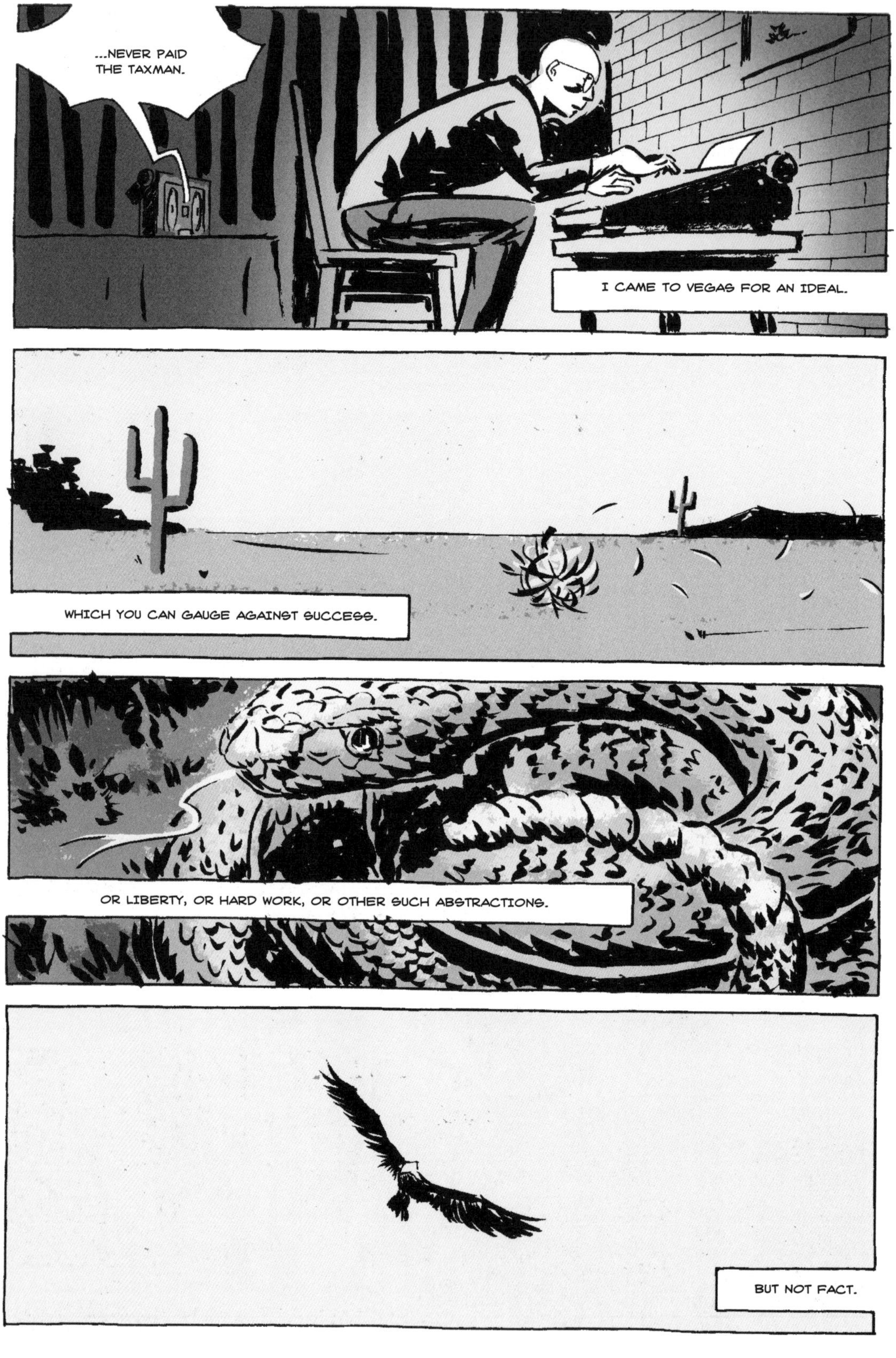
...NEVER PAID
THE TAXMAN.
I CAME TO VEGAS FOR AN IDEAL.
WHICH YOU CAN GAUGE AGAINST SUCCESS.
OR LIBERTY, OR HARD WORK, OR OTHER SUCH ABSTRACTIONS.
BUT NOT FACT.

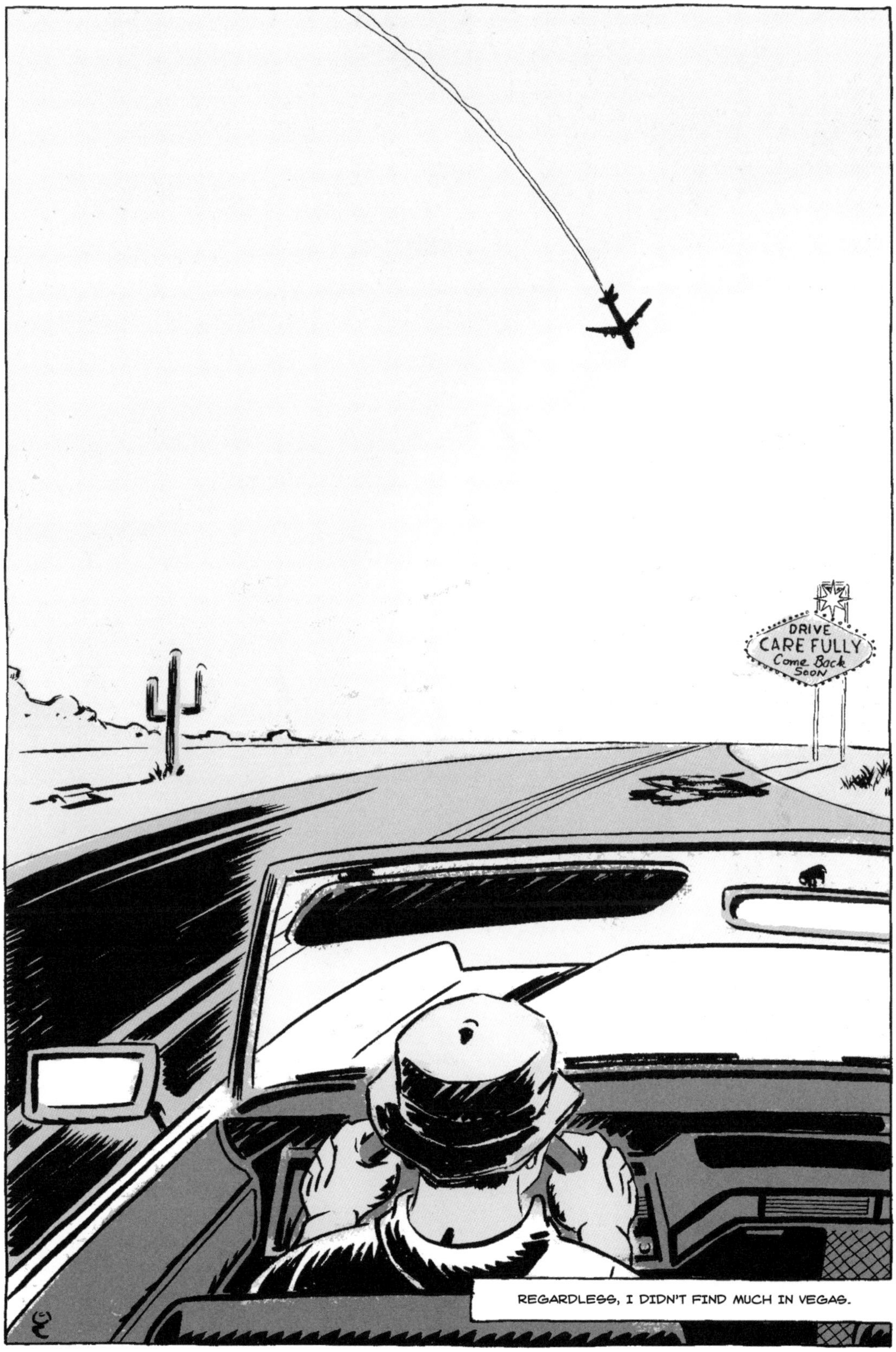
DRIVE
CARE FULLY
Come Back
SooN
REGARDLESS, I DIDN'T FIND MUCH IN VEGAS.

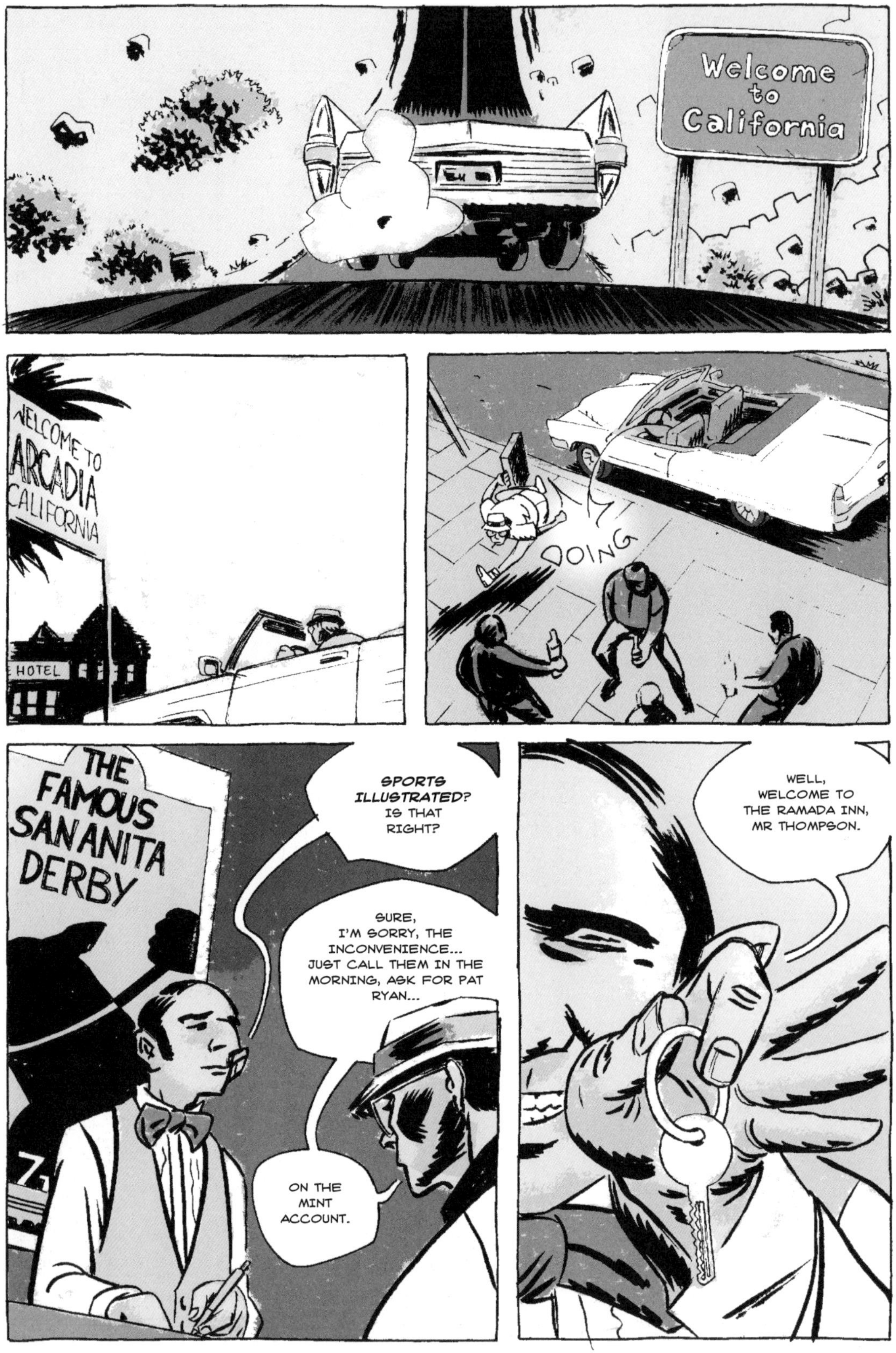
Welcome to California
WELCOME TO ARCADIA CALIFORNIA
HOTEL
DOING
THE FAMOUS SAN ANITA DERBY
SPORTS ILLUSTRATED? IS THAT RIGHT?
SURE, I'M SORRY, THE INCONVENIENCE... JUST CALL THEM IN THE MORNING, ASK FOR PAT RYAN...
ON THE MINT ACCOUNT.
WELL, WELCOME TO THE RAMADA INN, MR THOMPSON.

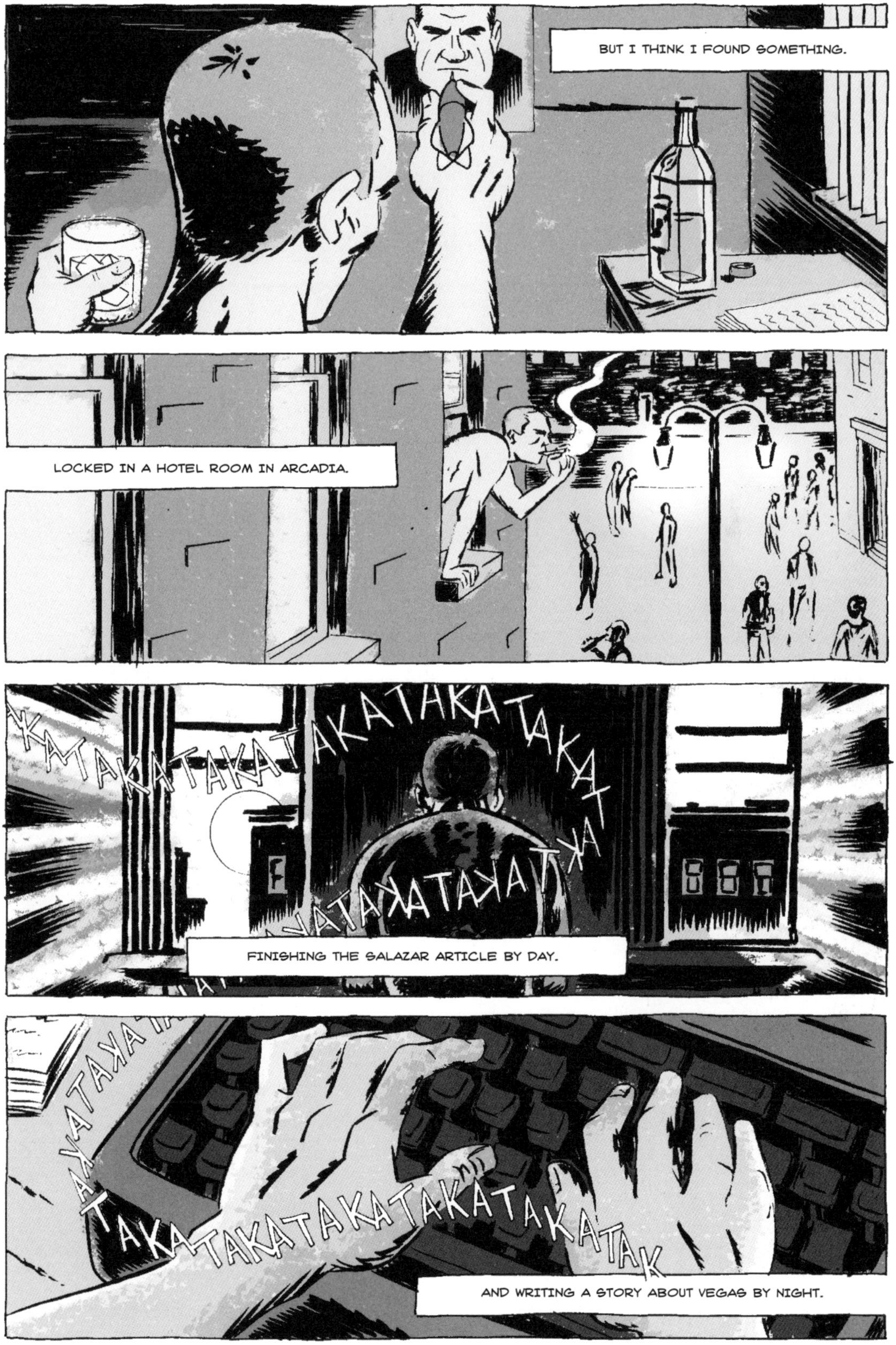
BUT I THINK I FOUND SOMETHING.
LOCKED IN A HOTEL ROOM IN ARCADIA.
TAKATAKATAKATAKATAKATAKATAKAT
FINISHING THE SALAZAR ARTICLE BY DAY.
TAKATAKATAKATAKATAKATAKATAK
AND WRITING A STORY ABOUT VEGAS BY NIGHT.

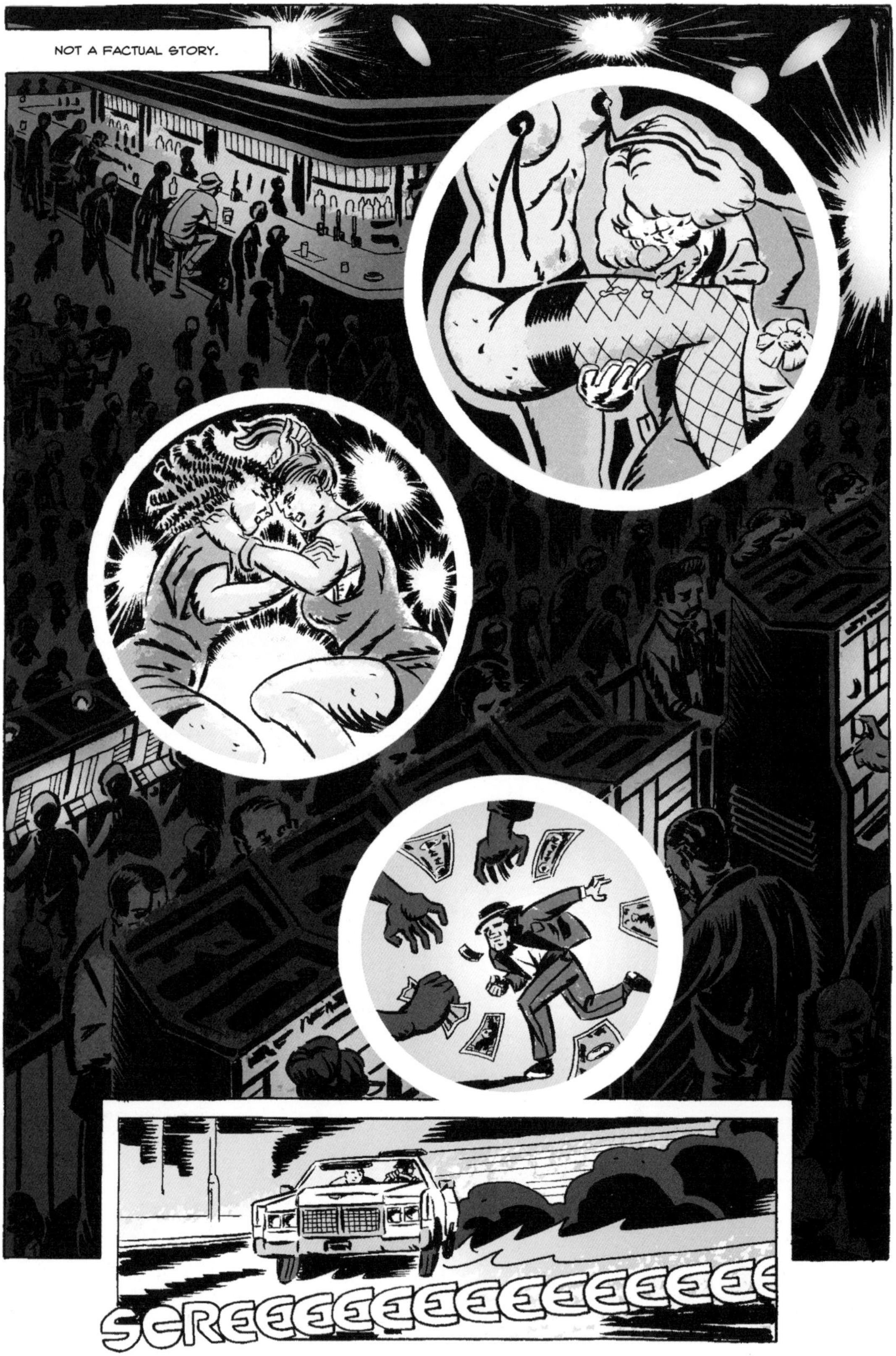
NOT A FACTUAL STORY.
SCREEEEEEEEEEEEEEEEE

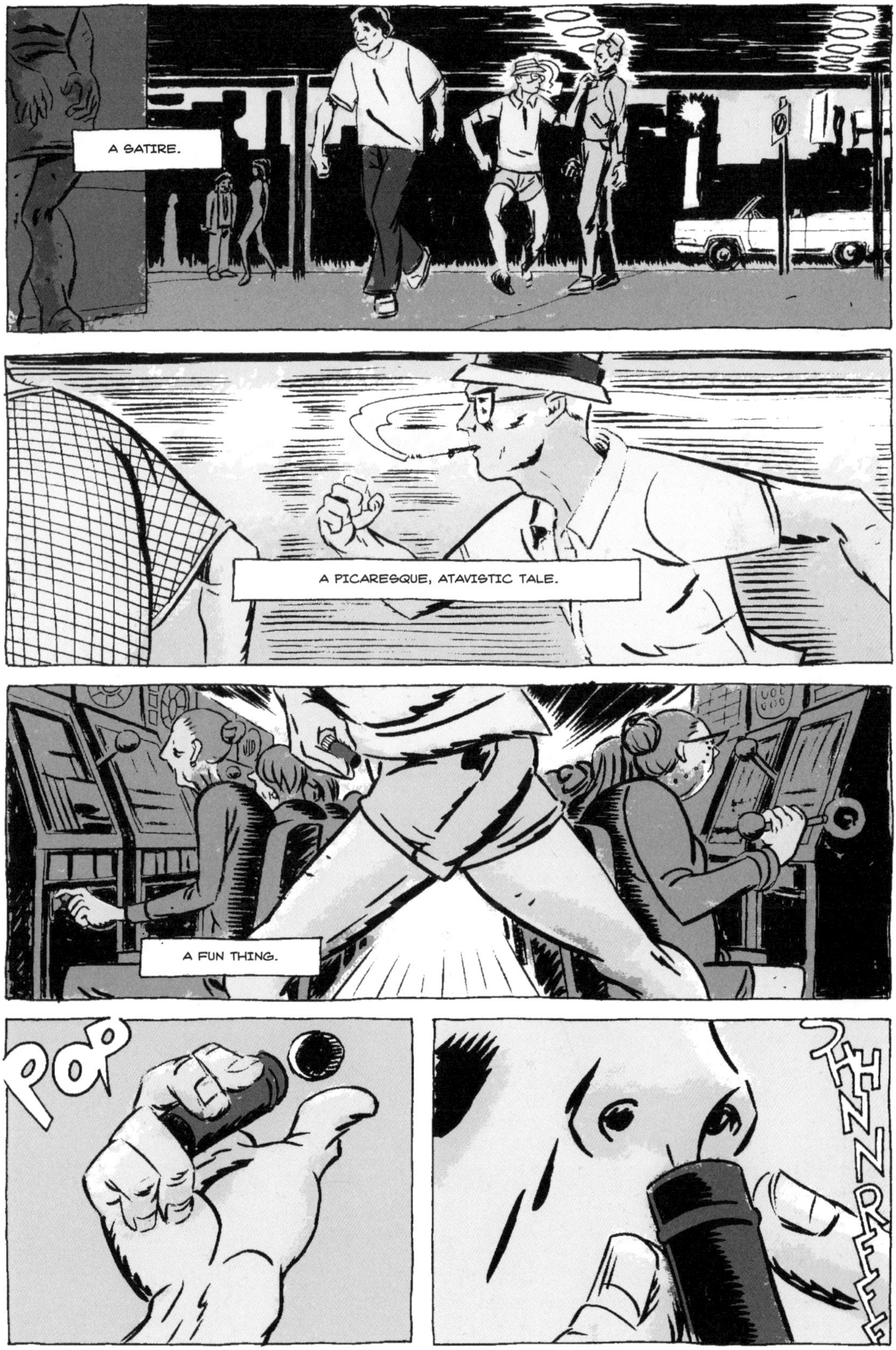

A SATIRE.
A PICARESQUE, ATAVISTIC TALE.
A FUN THING.
POP
SHHNNRFFF

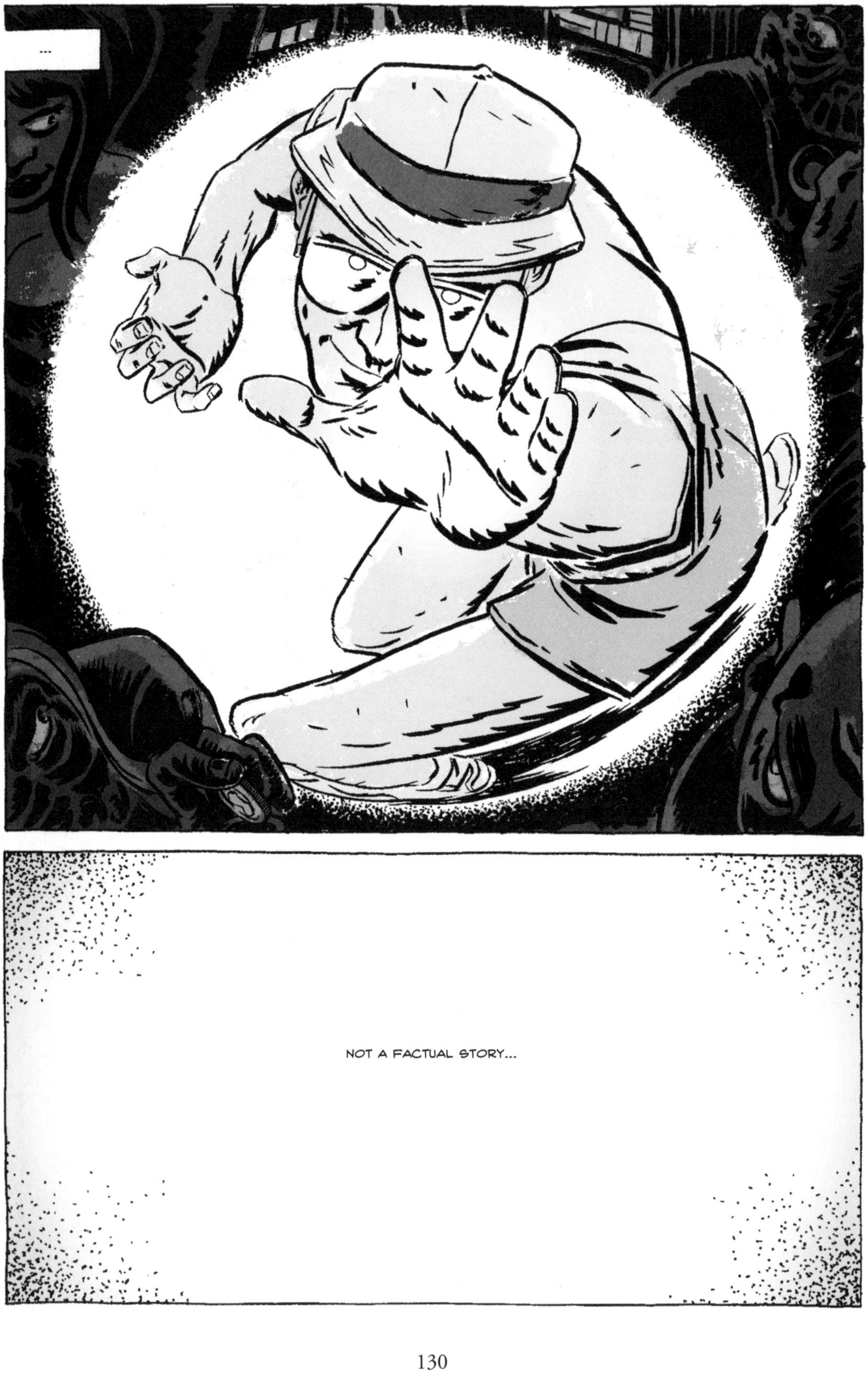
...
NOT A FACTUAL STORY...

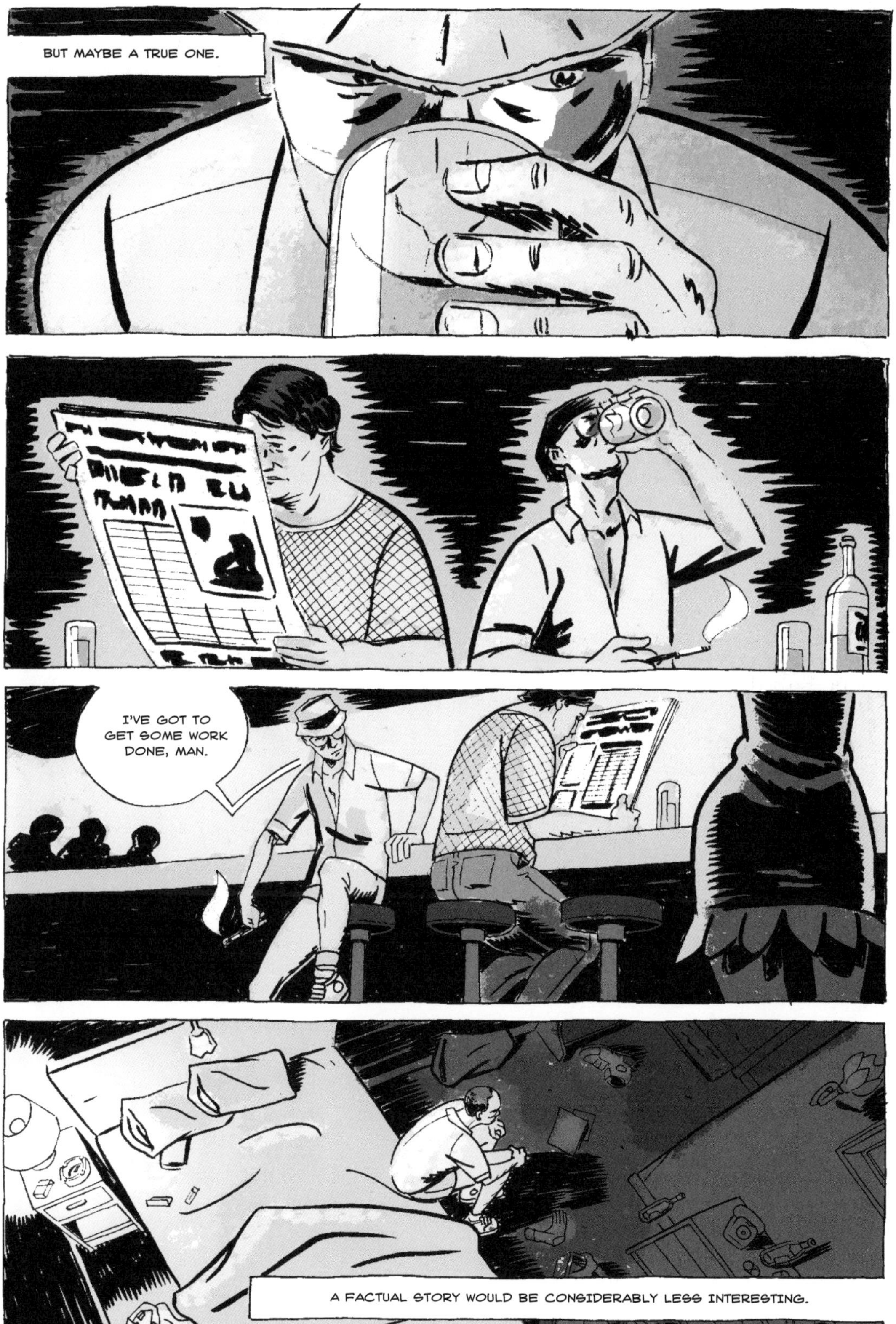

BUT MAYBE A TRUE ONE.
I'VE GOT TO GET SOME WORK DONE, MAN.
A FACTUAL STORY WOULD BE CONSIDERABLY LESS INTERESTING.

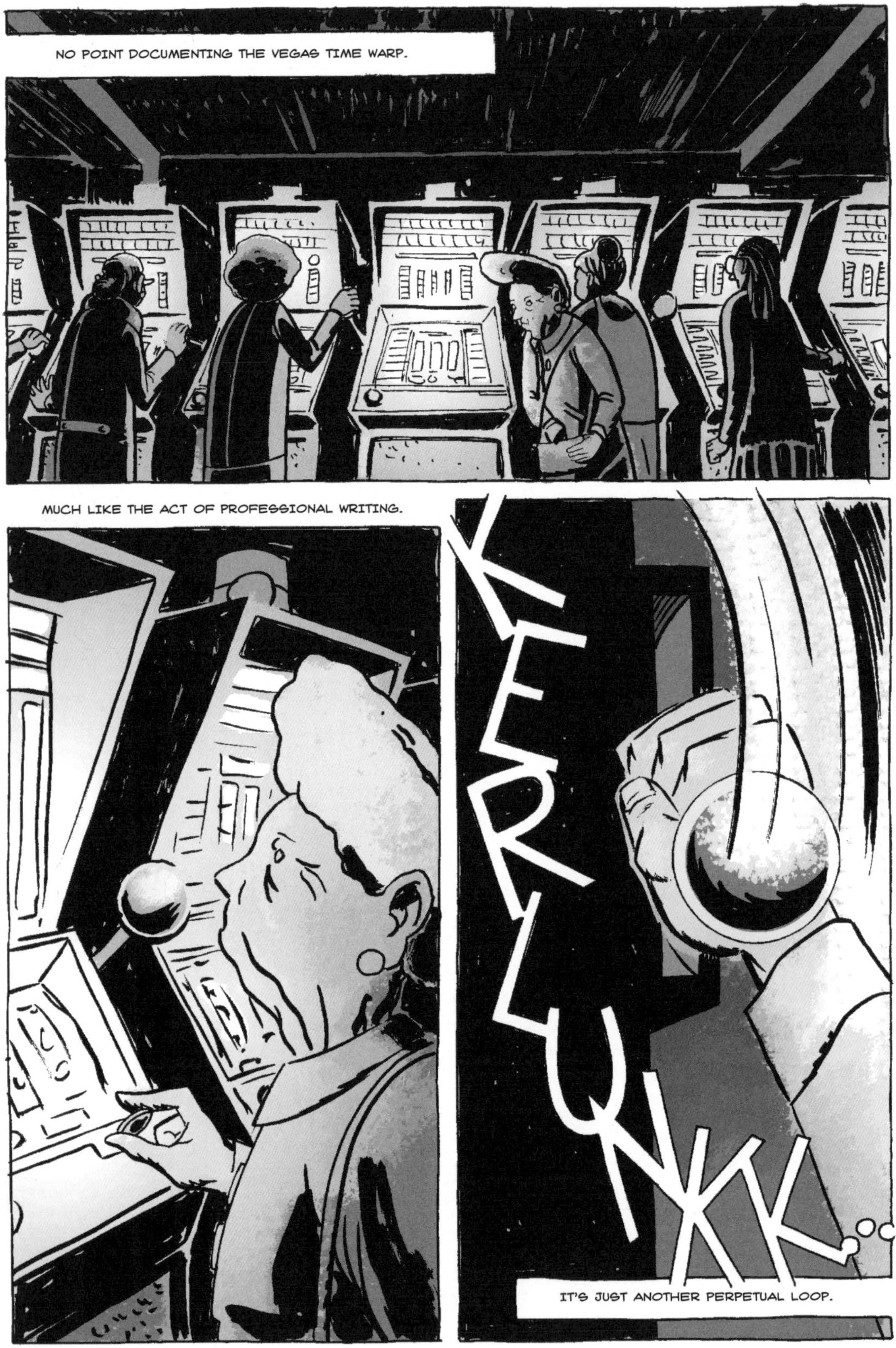
NO POINT DOCUMENTING THE VEGAS TIME WARP.
MUCH LIKE THE ACT OF PROFESSIONAL WRITING.
KERLUNKK..
IT'S JUST ANOTHER PERPETUAL LOOP.

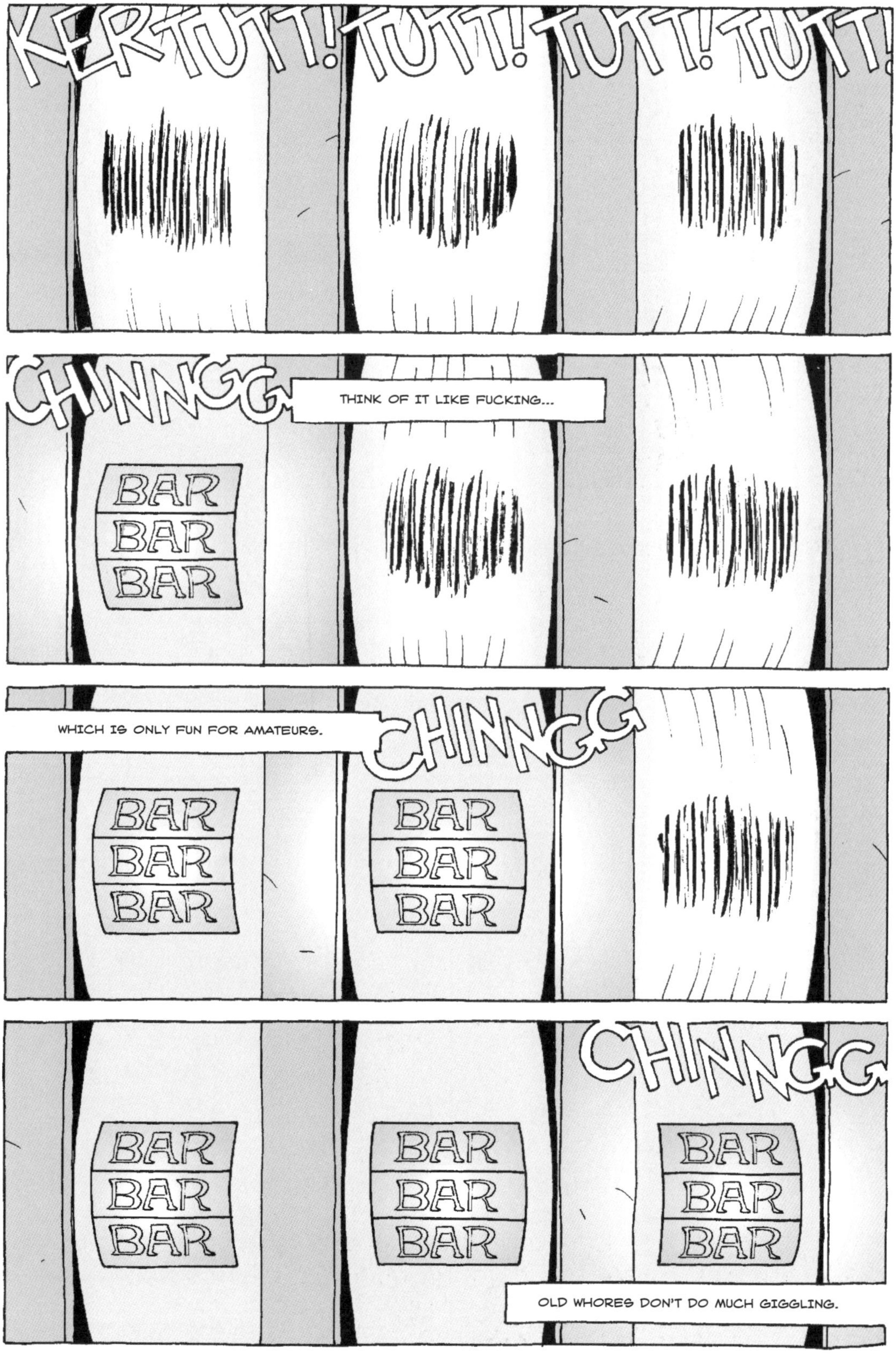
KERTUTT! TUTT! TUTT! TUTT!
CHINNGG
THINK OF IT LIKE FUCKING...
BAR
BAR
BAR
WHICH IS ONLY FUN FOR AMATEURS.
CHINNGG
BAR
BAR
BAR
BAR
BAR
BAR
CHINNGG
BAR
BAR
BAR
BAR
BAR
BAR
BAR
BAR
BAR
OLD WHORES DON'T DO MUCH GIGGLING.

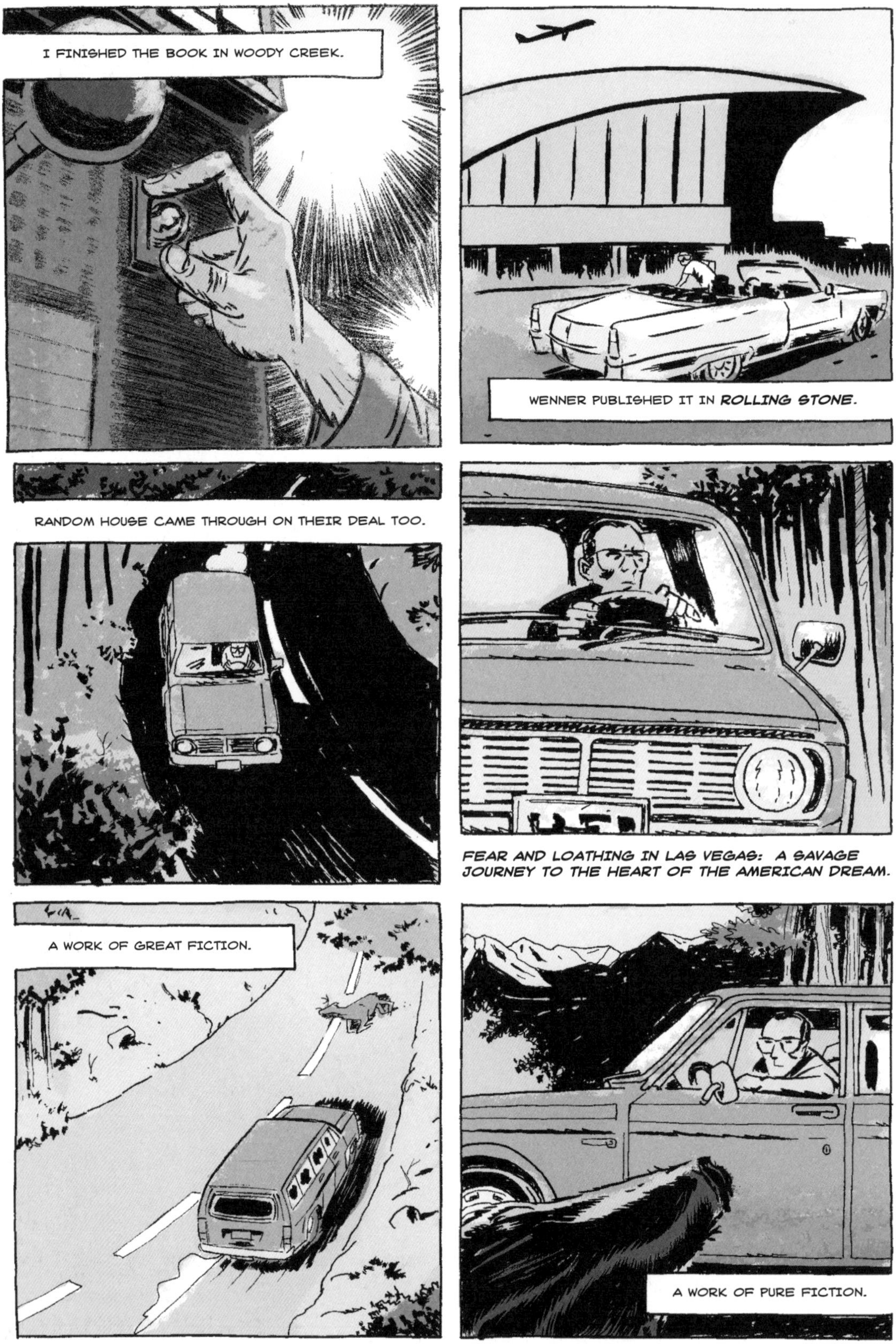
I FINISHED THE BOOK IN WOODY CREEK.
WENNER PUBLISHED IT IN ROLLING STONE.
RANDOM HOUSE CAME THROUGH ON THEIR DEAL TOO.
FEAR AND LOATHING IN LAS VEGAS: A SAVAGE JOURNEY TO THE HEART OF THE AMERICAN DREAM.
A WORK OF GREAT FICTION.
A WORK OF PURE FICTION.

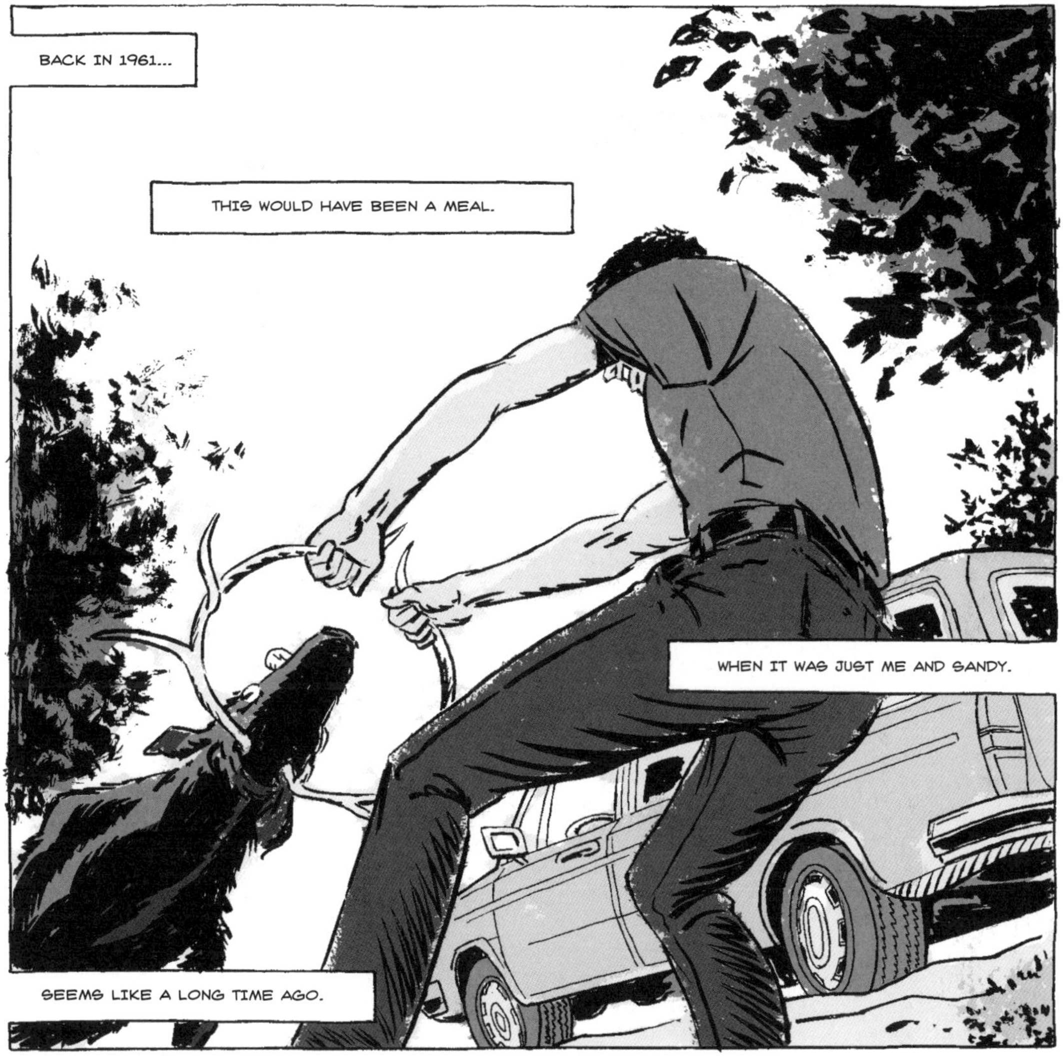
BACK IN 1961...
THIS WOULD HAVE BEEN A MEAL.
WHEN IT WAS JUST ME AND SANDY.
SEEMS LIKE A LONG TIME AGO.

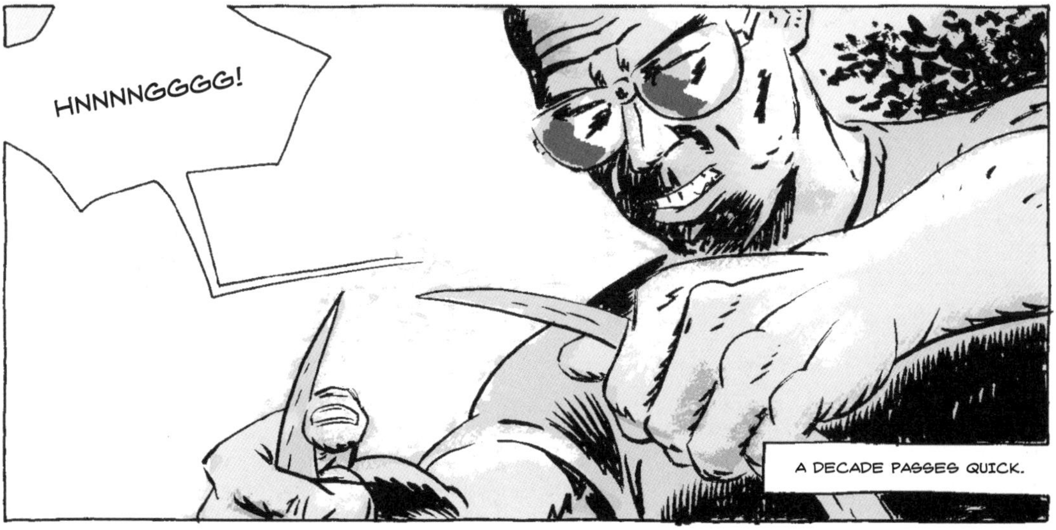
HNNNNGGGG!
A DECADE PASSES QUICK.

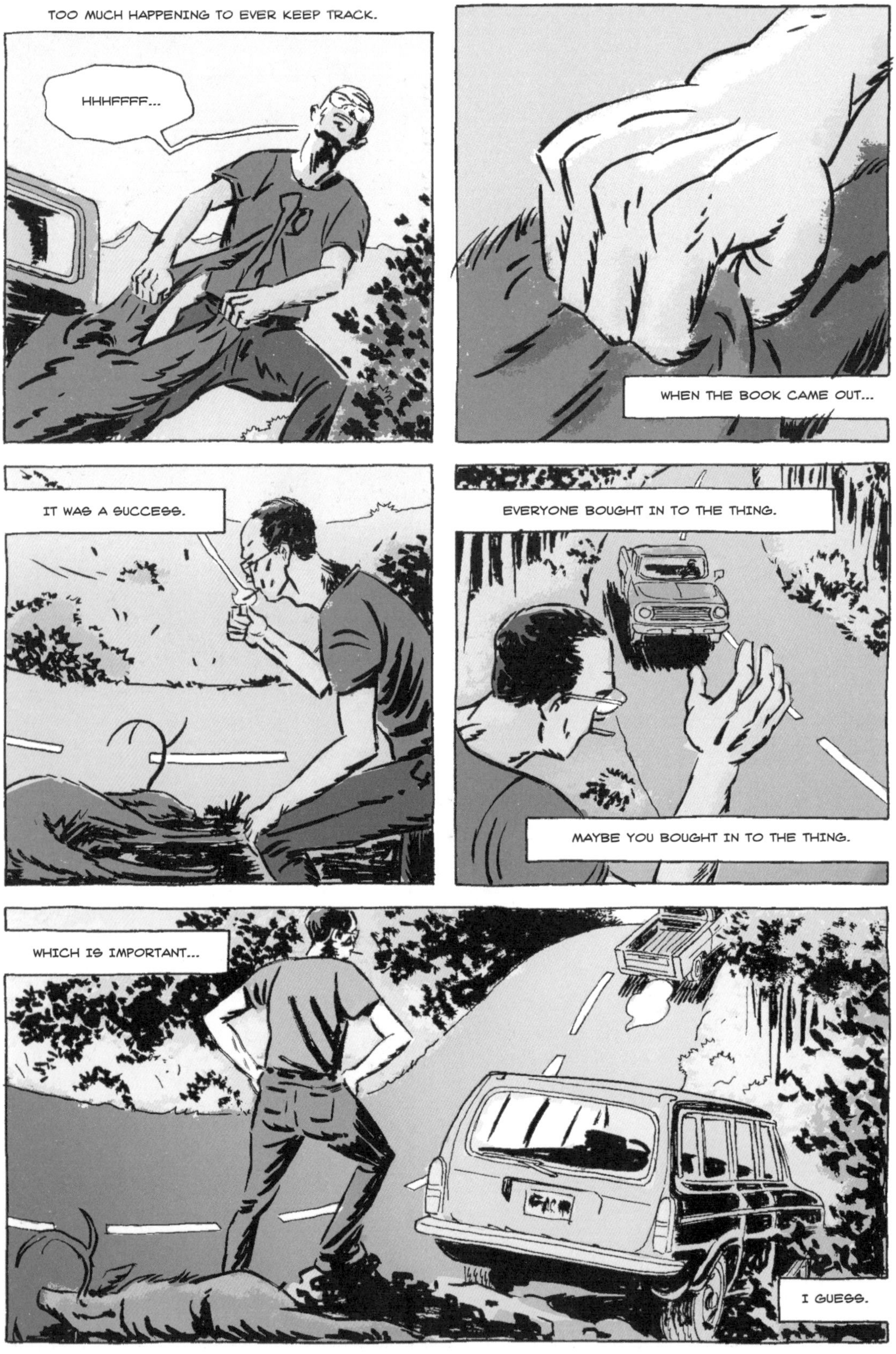
TOO MUCH HAPPENING TO EVER KEEP TRACK.
HHHFFFF...
WHEN THE BOOK CAME OUT...
IT WAS A SUCCESS.
EVERYONE BOUGHT IN TO THE THING.
MAYBE YOU BOUGHT IN TO THE THING.
WHICH IS IMPORTANT...
I GUESS.

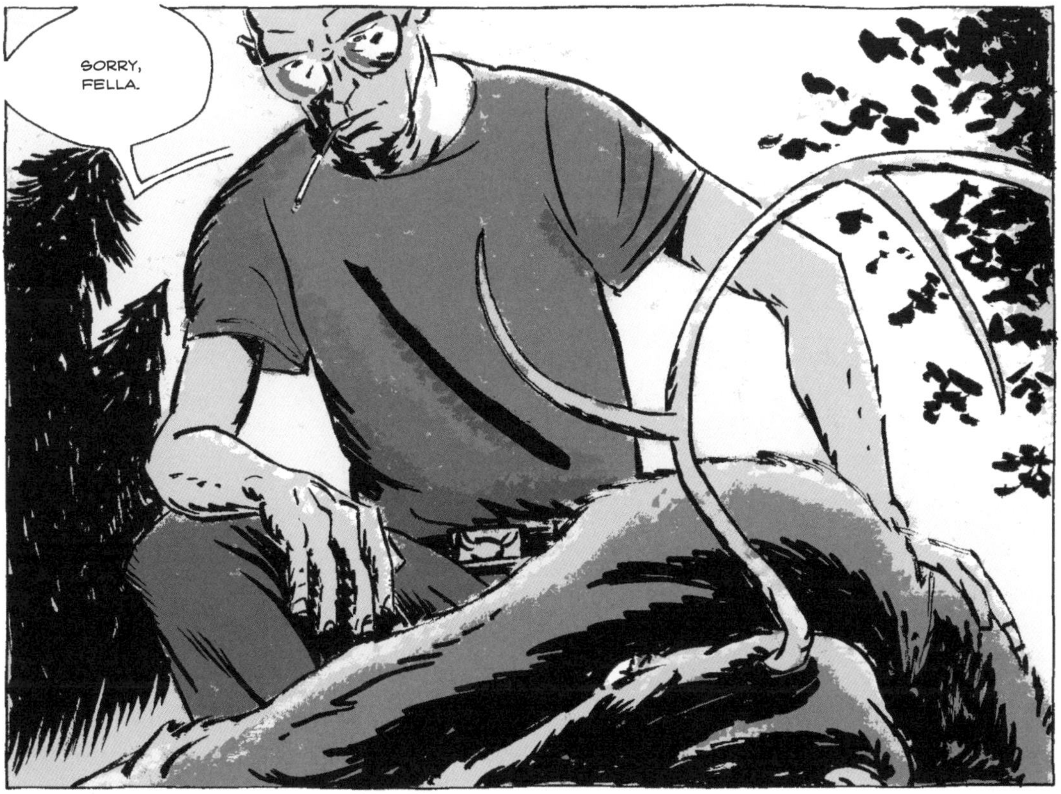
SORRY, FELLA.

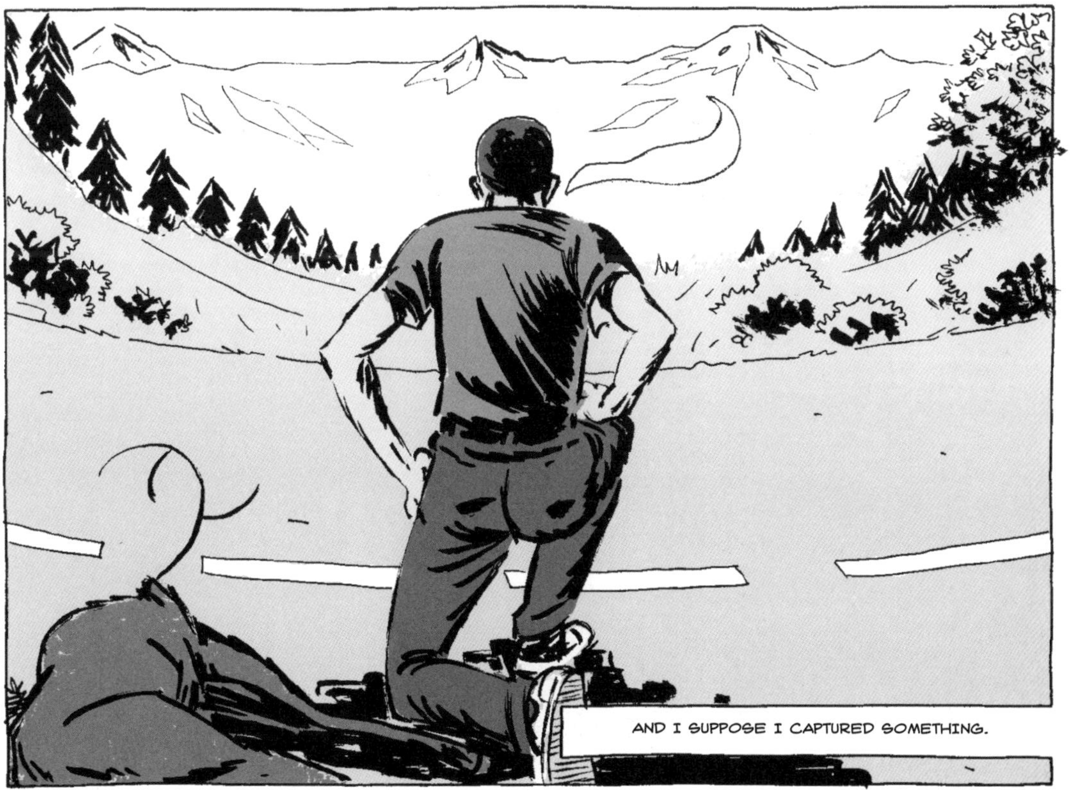
AND I SUPPOSE I CAPTURED SOMETHING.

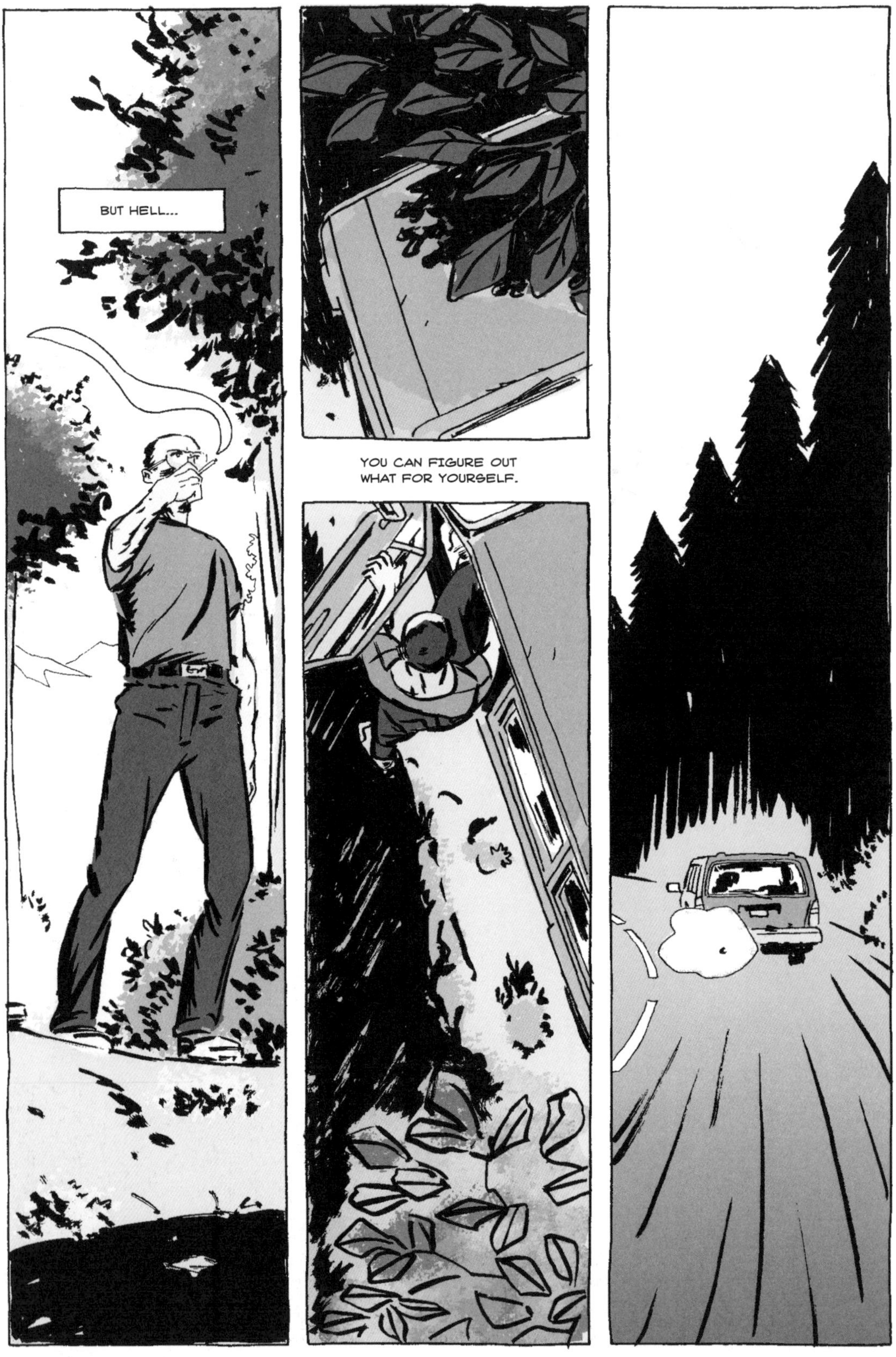
BUT HELL...
YOU CAN FIGURE OUT WHAT FOR YOURSELF.

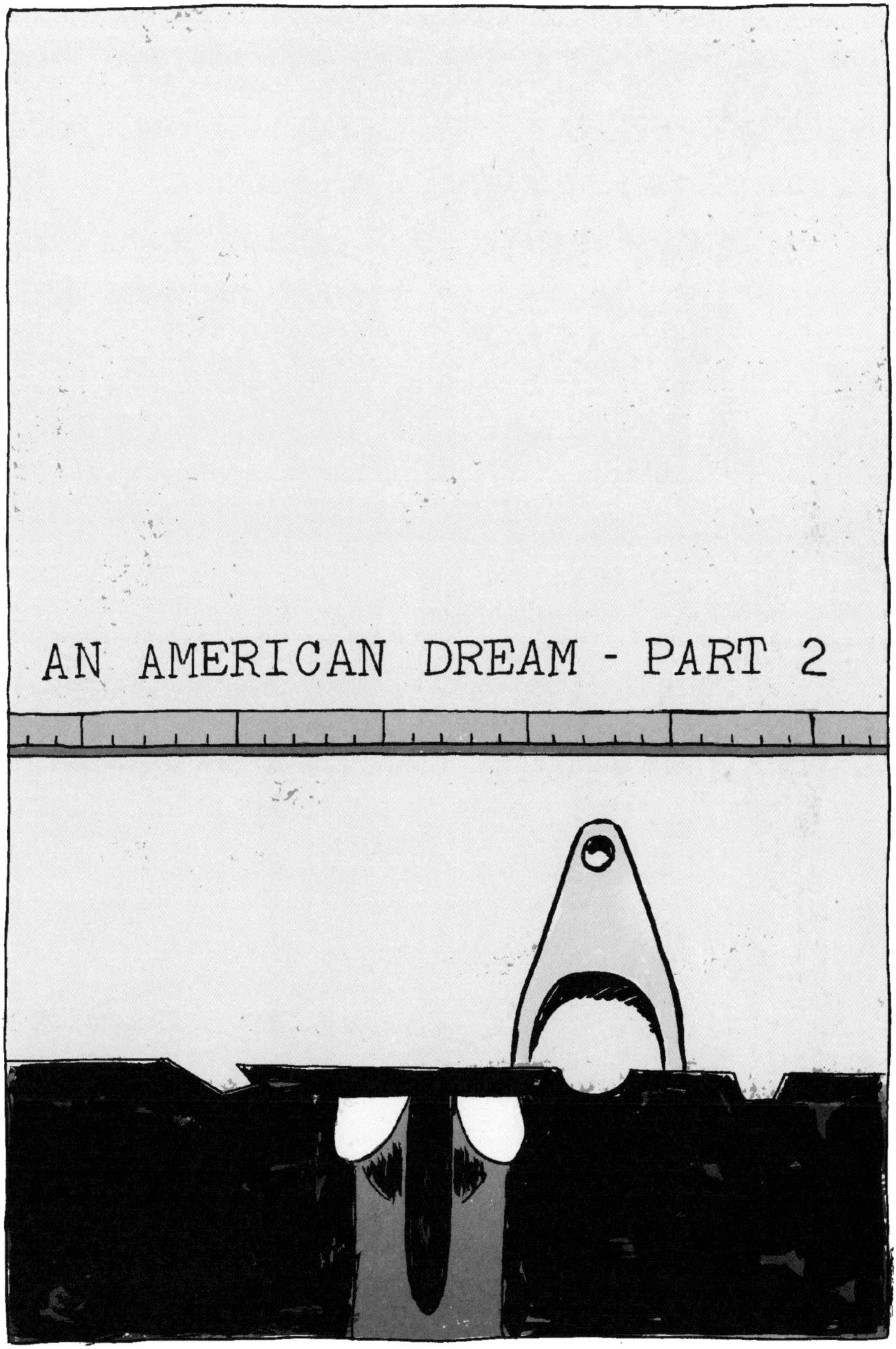
AN AMERICAN DREAM - PART 2

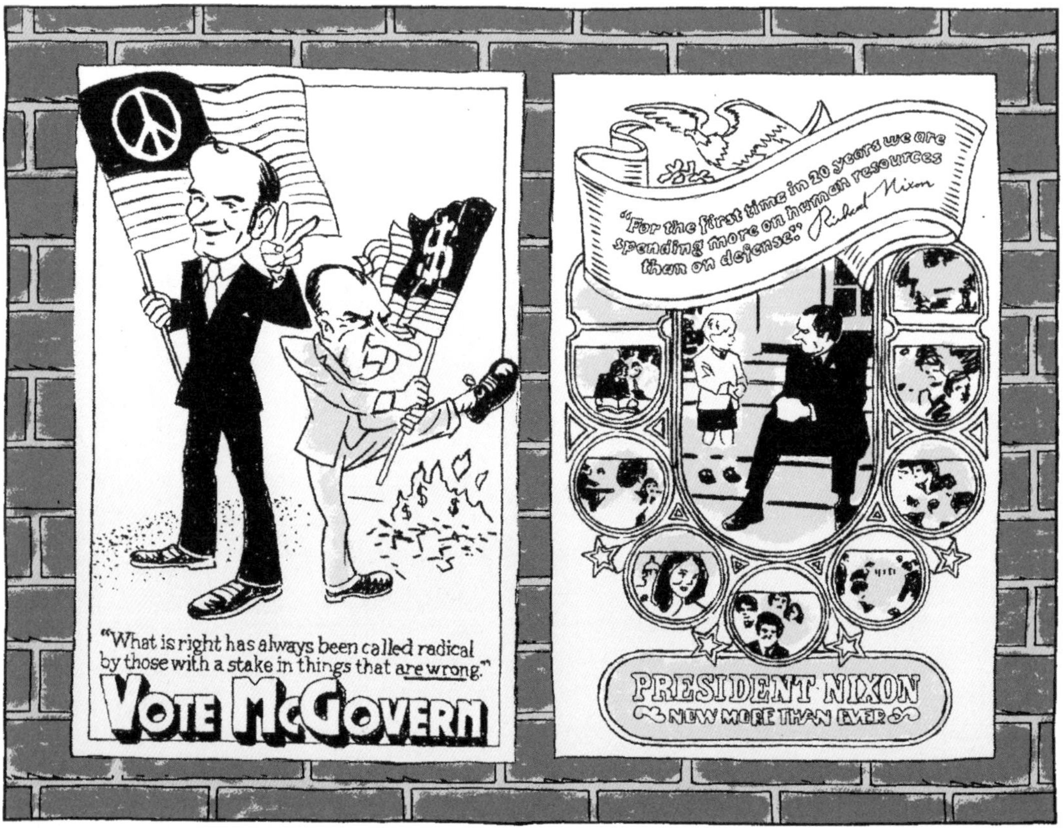
"What is right has always been called radical by those with a stake in things that are wrong."
VOTE McGOVERN
"For the first time in 20 years we are spending more on human resources than on defense." Richard Nixon
PRESIDENT NIXON
NOW MORE THAN EVER

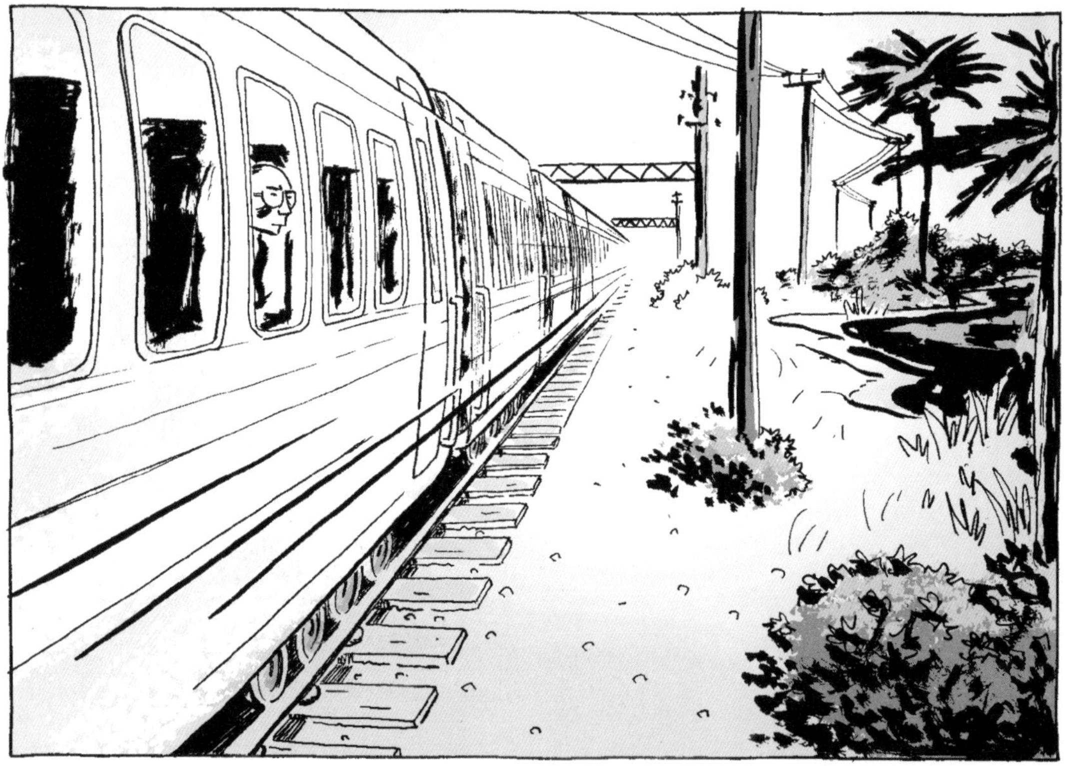

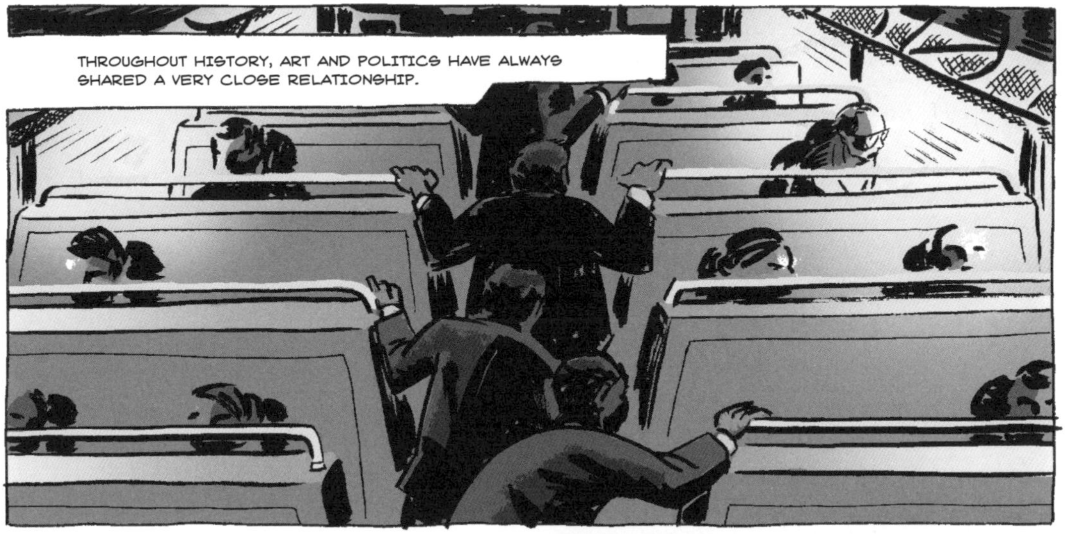
THROUGHOUT HISTORY, ART AND POLITICS HAVE ALWAYS SHARED A VERY CLOSE RELATIONSHIP.

THIS IS BECAUSE ART DESCRIBES A NATION IN A WAY THAT PURE POLITICS CANNOT.

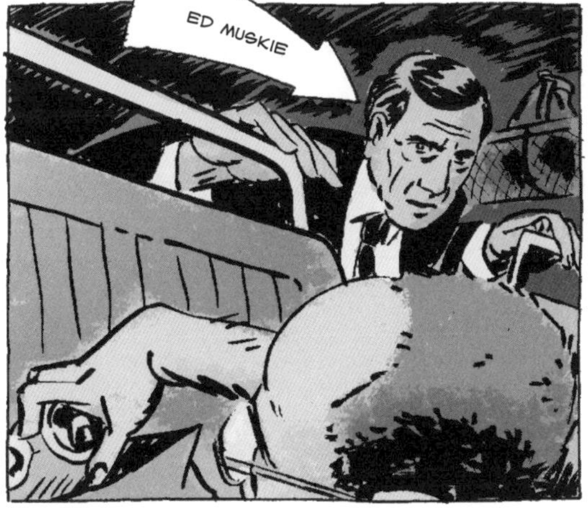
ED MUSKIE

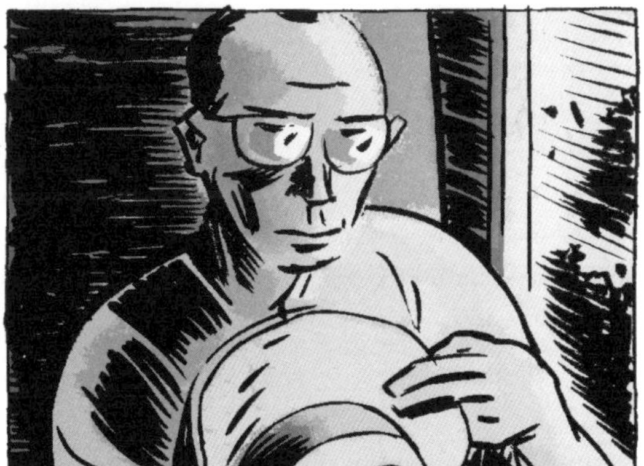

ARTWORKS, FOLK TALES, SONGS, WHATEVER... CREATE A COMMON LANGUAGE, THE NEIGHBORHOOD IF YOU LIKE – THE CULTURAL FRAMEWORK OF A NATION.

INSIDE WHICH EVERYTHING, ALL NATIONAL EVENTS AND ALL POLITICS, OCCUR.

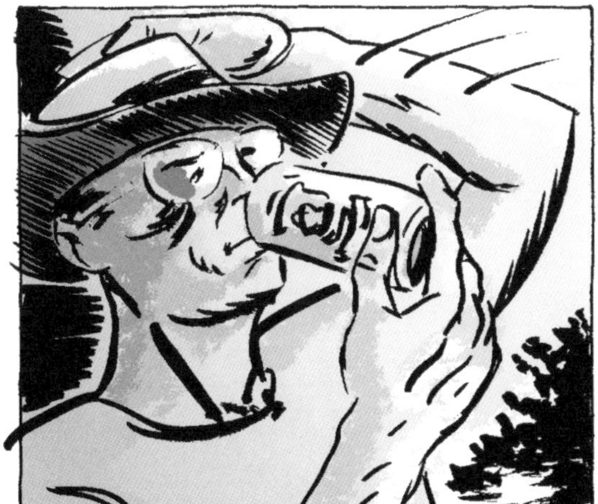

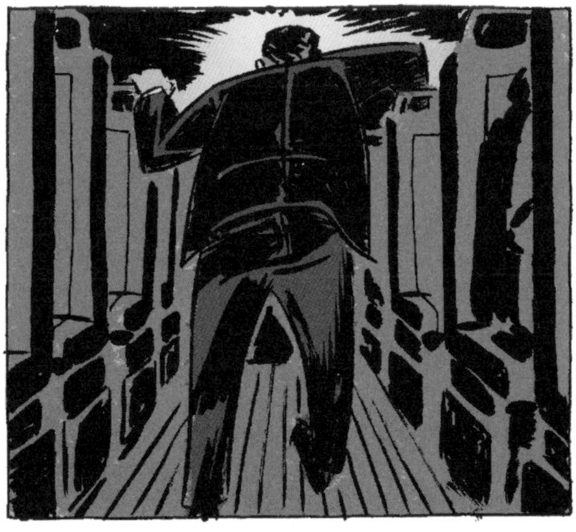

THIS WAS THE POLITICAL REALITY OF THE '60s AND THE '70s.

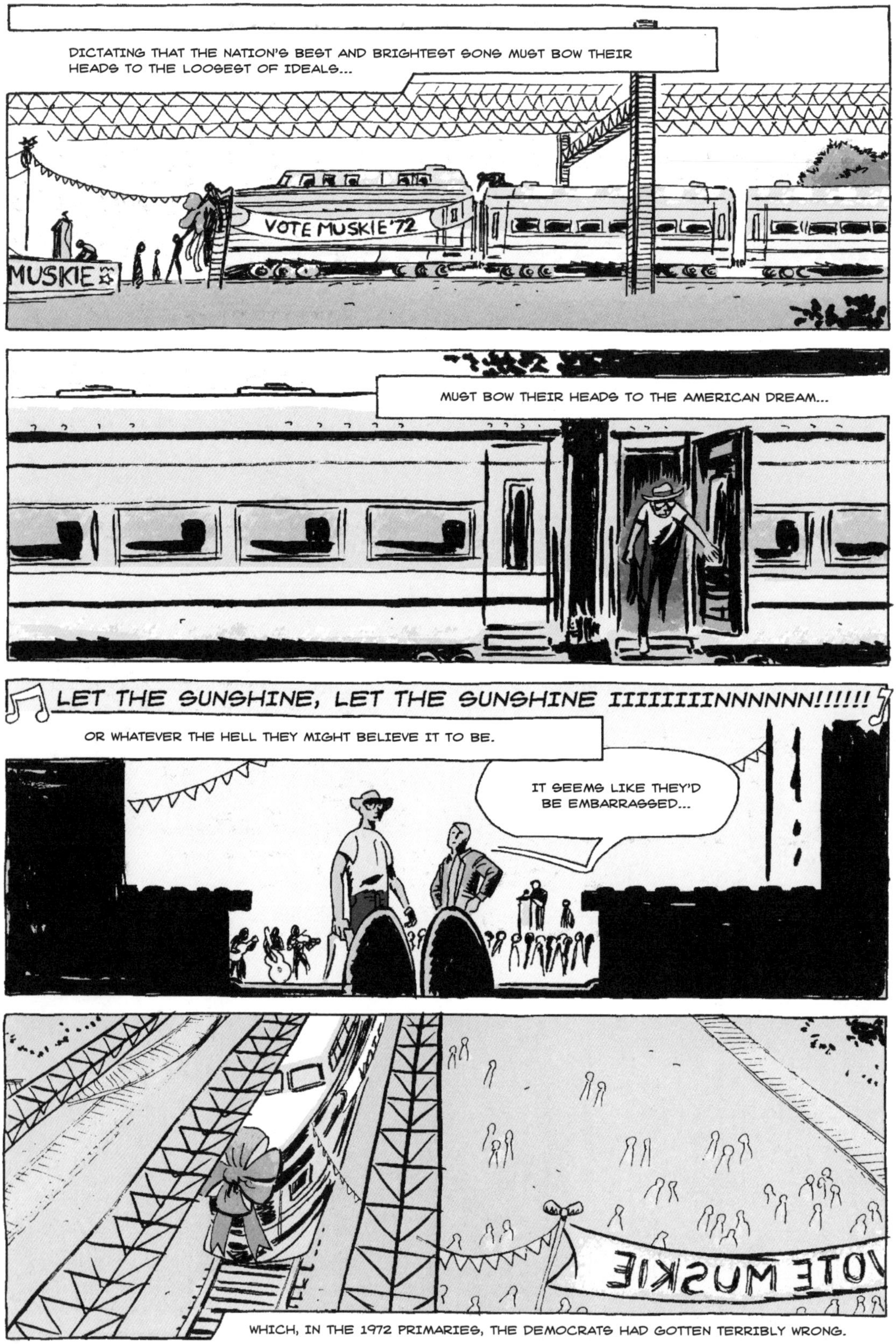
DICTATING THAT THE NATION'S BEST AND BRIGHTEST SONS MUST BOW THEIR HEADS TO THE LOOSEST OF IDEALS...
VOTE MUSKIE '72
MUSKIE
MUST BOW THEIR HEADS TO THE AMERICAN DREAM...
LET THE SUNSHINE, LET THE SUNSHINE IIIIIIIINNNNNN!!!!!!
OR WHATEVER THE HELL THEY MIGHT BELIEVE IT TO BE.
IT SEEMS LIKE THEY'D BE EMBARRASSED...
VOTE MUSKIE
WHICH, IN THE 1972 PRIMARIES, THE DEMOCRATS HAD GOTTEN TERRIBLY WRONG.

THE REPUBLICANS, BY WHICH I MOSTLY MEAN NIXON, WERE FARING A GREAT DEAL BETTER.

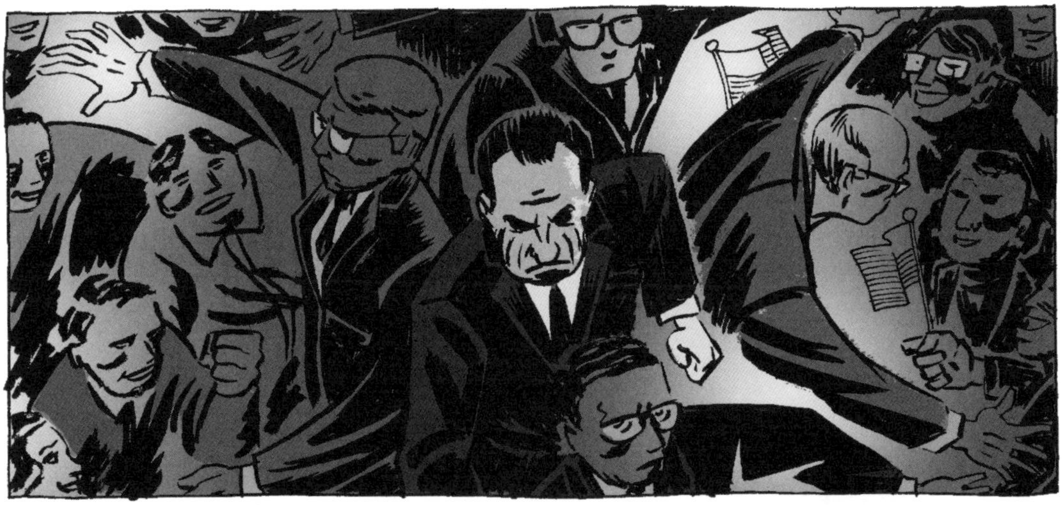

MAYBE PEOPLE PREFERRED HIS VERSION OF SAID DREAM...

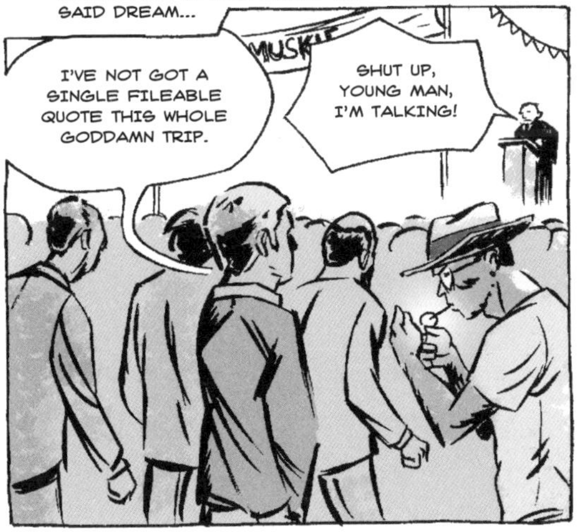

I'VE NOT GOT A SINGLE FILEABLE QUOTE THIS WHOLE GODDAMN TRIP.
SHUT UP, YOUNG MAN, I'M TALKING!

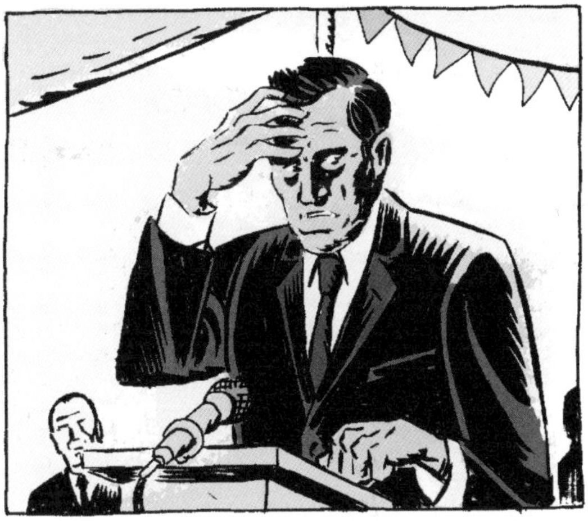

BEING CHEERLEADERS AND TICKER-TAPE PARADES, AND FAX MACHINES AND JET AIRPLANES....

AND SKYSCRAPERS AND WAR, AND ZERO ACCOUNTABILITY AND BIG TITS, AND MONEY.

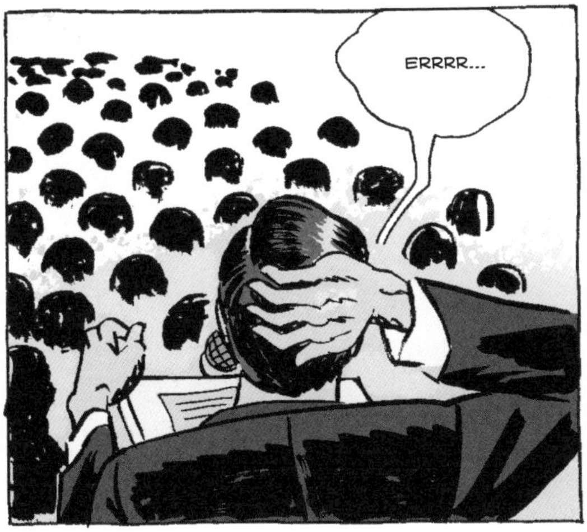

ERRRR...

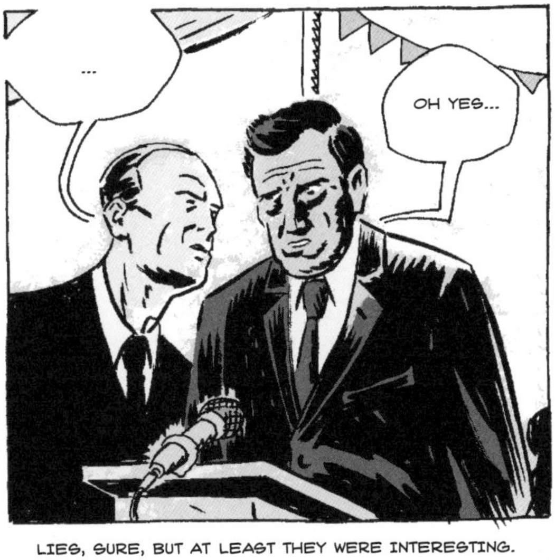

...
OH YES...

LIES, SURE, BUT AT LEAST THEY WERE INTERESTING.

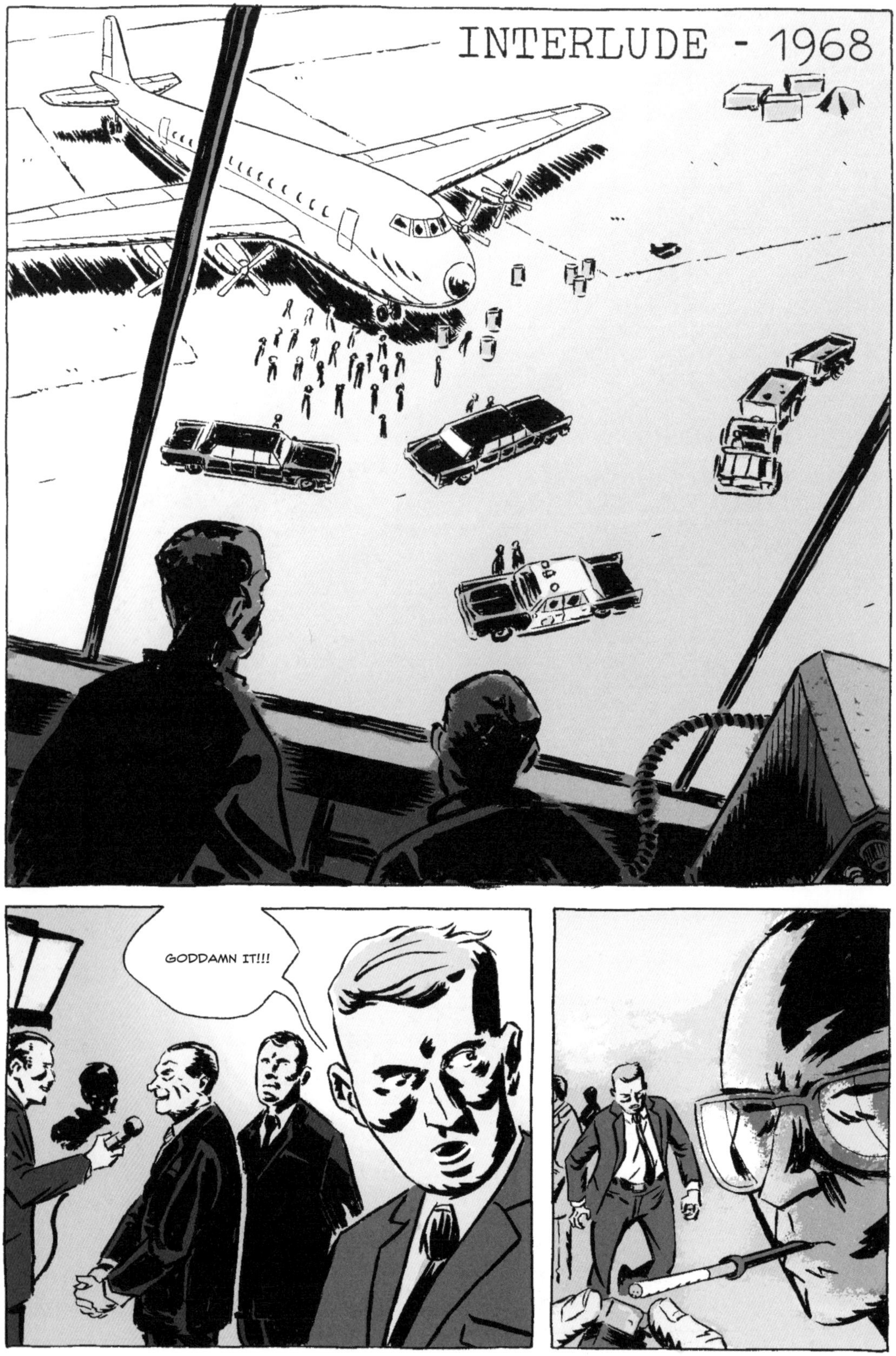
INTERLUDE - 1968
GODDAMN IT!!!

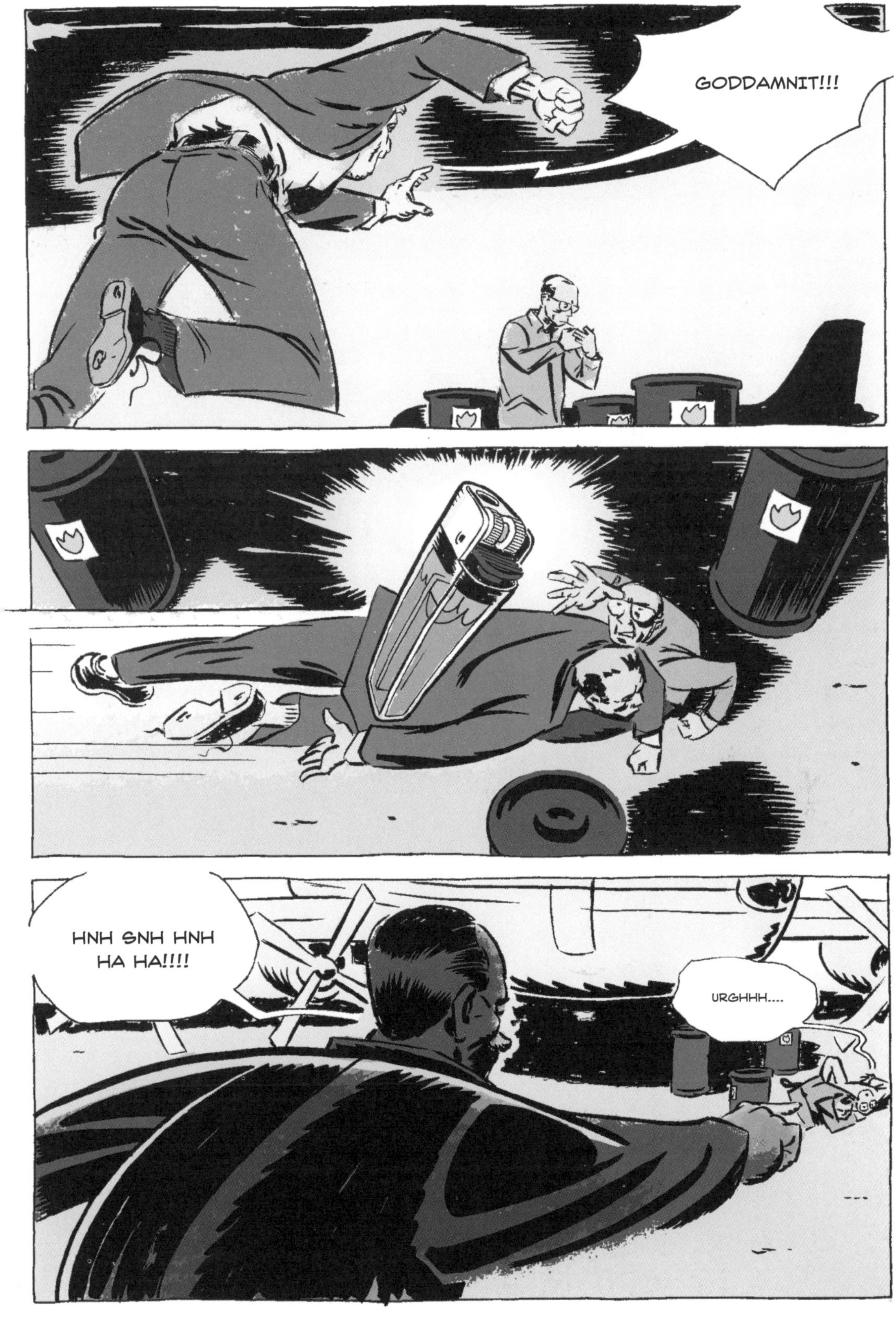
GODDAMNIT!!!
HNH SNH HNH HA HA!!!!
URGHHH....

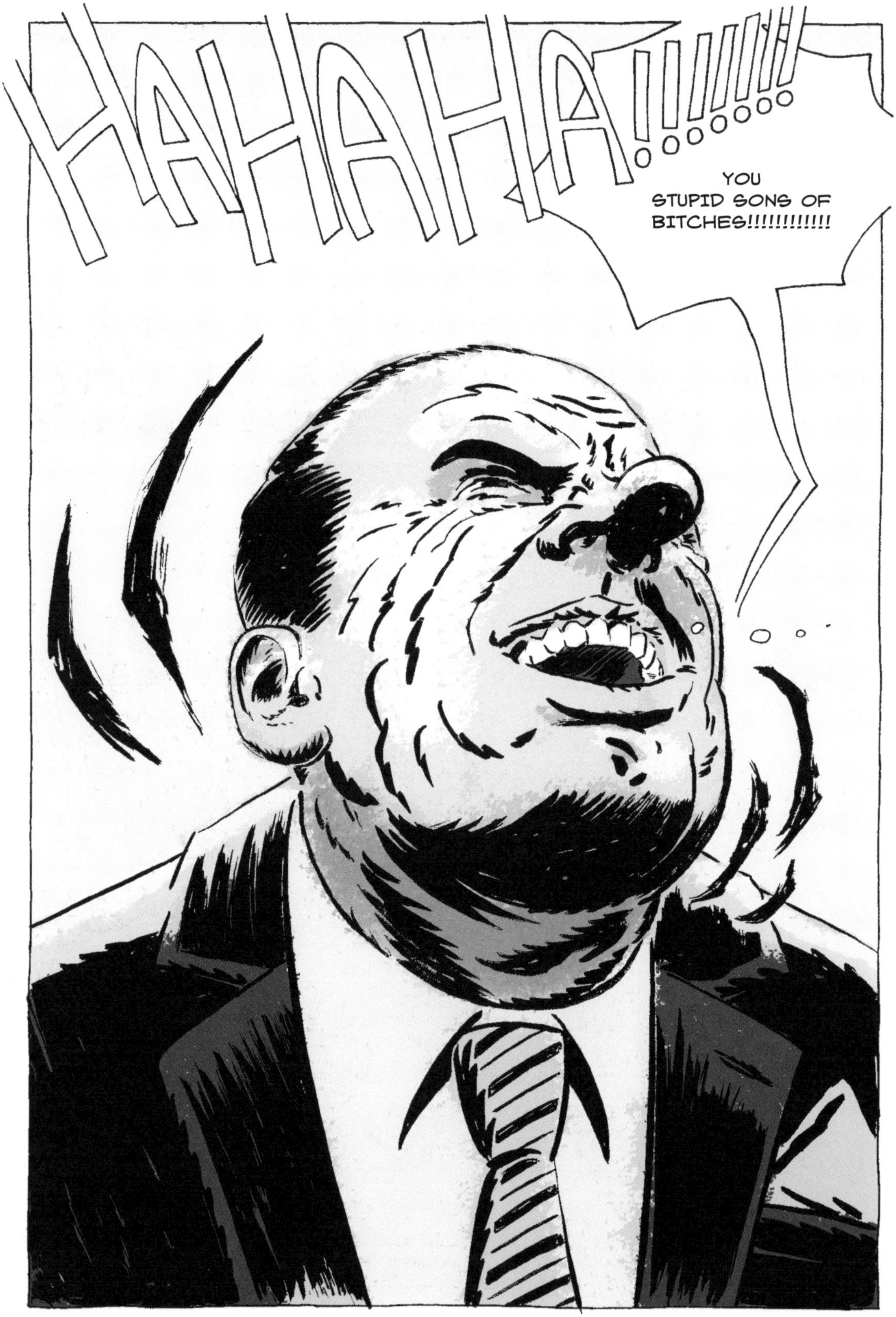
HAHAHAHA!!!!!!!!
YOU STUPID SONS OF BITCHES!!!!!!!!!!!!!

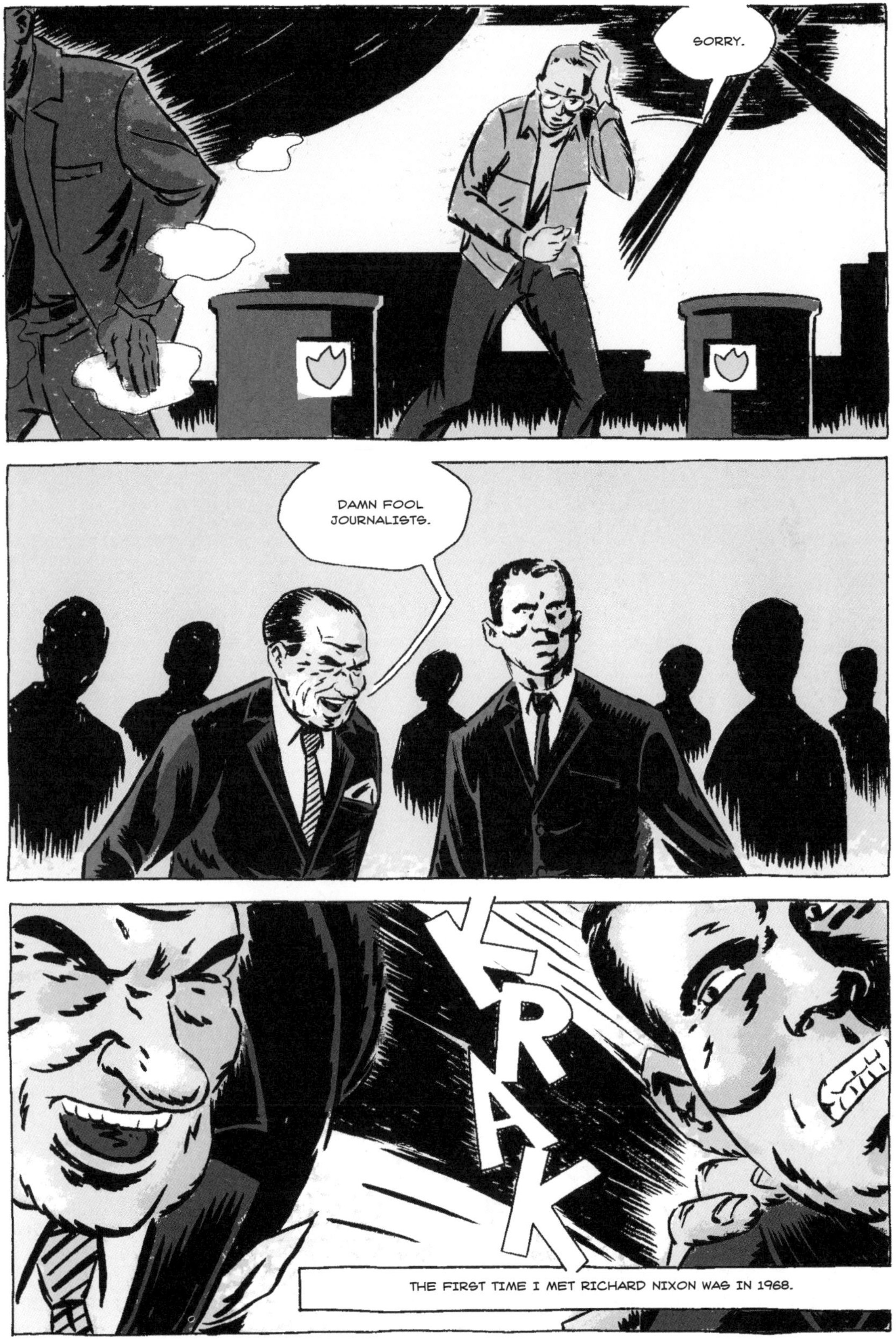
SORRY.
DAMN FOOL JOURNALISTS.
THE FIRST TIME I MET RICHARD NIXON WAS IN 1968.

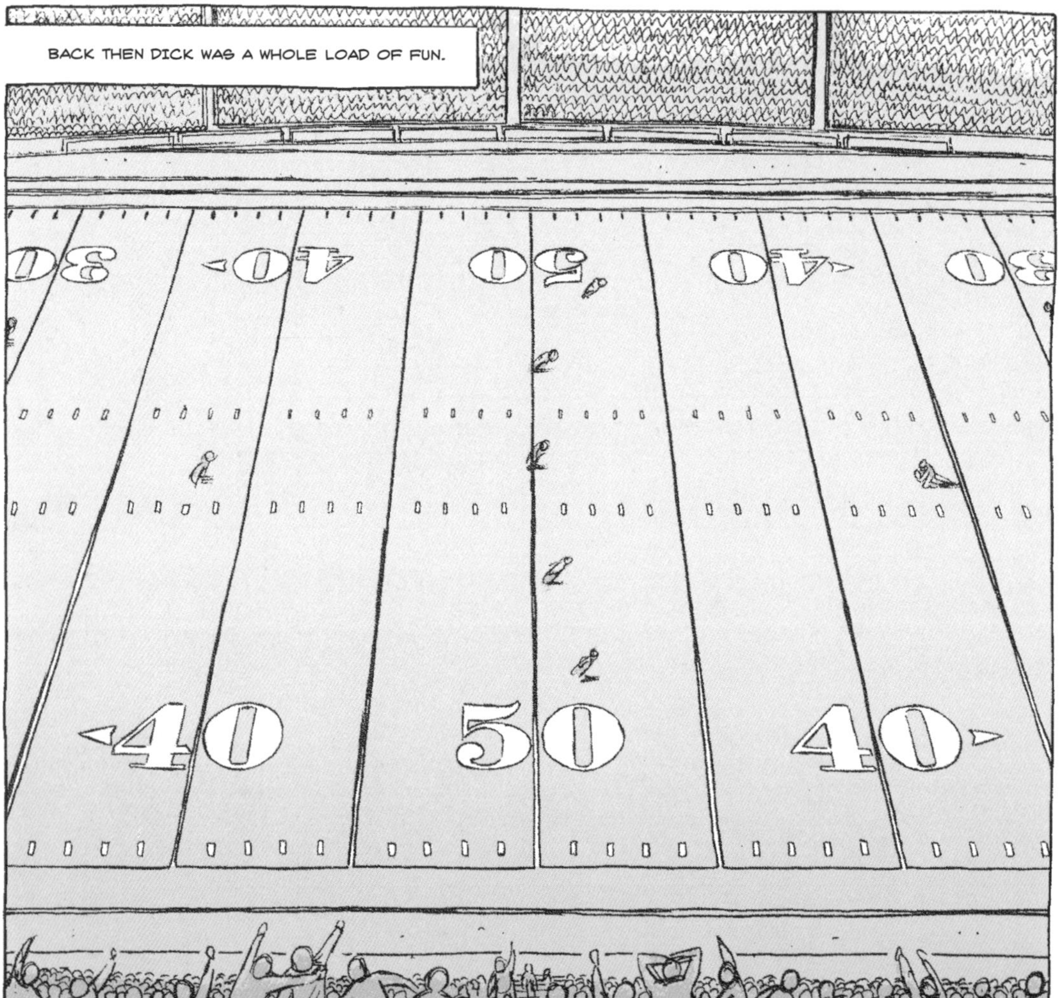
BACK THEN DICK WAS A WHOLE LOAD OF FUN.
40
50
40
30

THEN AGAIN, SATAN'D BE A LOT OF FUN TOO.

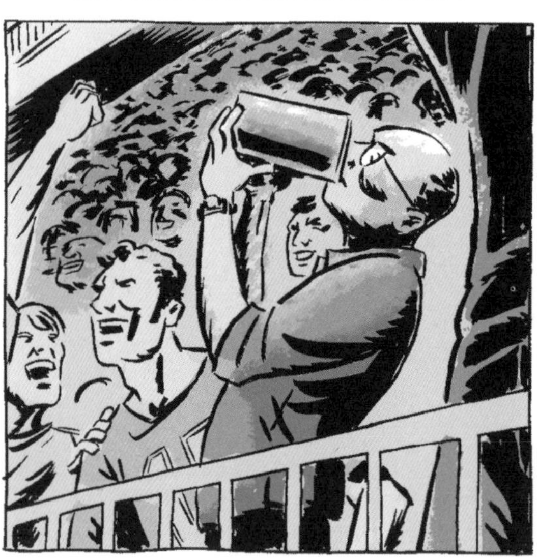

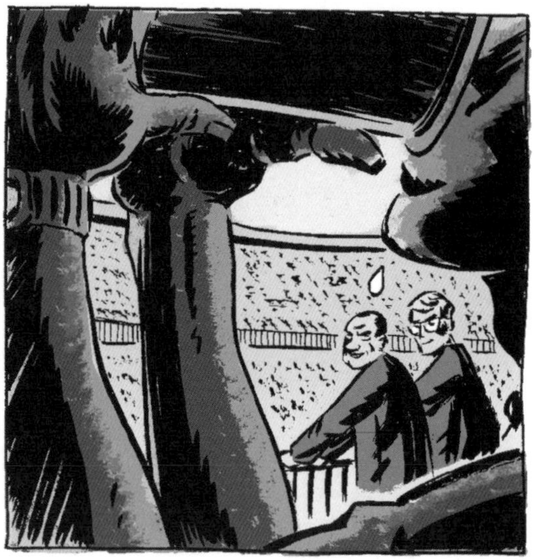

IF HE WAS INTO PRO FOOTBALL.

THE SECOND TIME WE MET WAS 1972.

QUESTIONS?

DAMN STRAIGHT!

HE DIDN'T LIKE ME SO MUCH BY THEN.

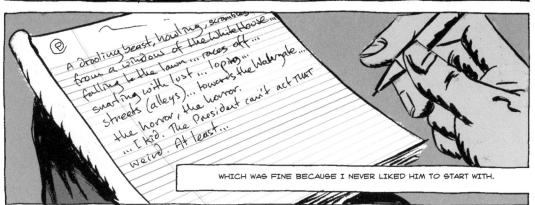

A drooling beast, howling, scrambling from a window of the White House ... falling to the lawn ... races off ... snarling with lust ... loping ... streets (alleys) ... towards the Watergate ... the horror, the horror. ... [kid. The President can't act THAT weird. At least ...

WHICH WAS FINE BECAUSE I NEVER LIKED HIM TO START WITH.

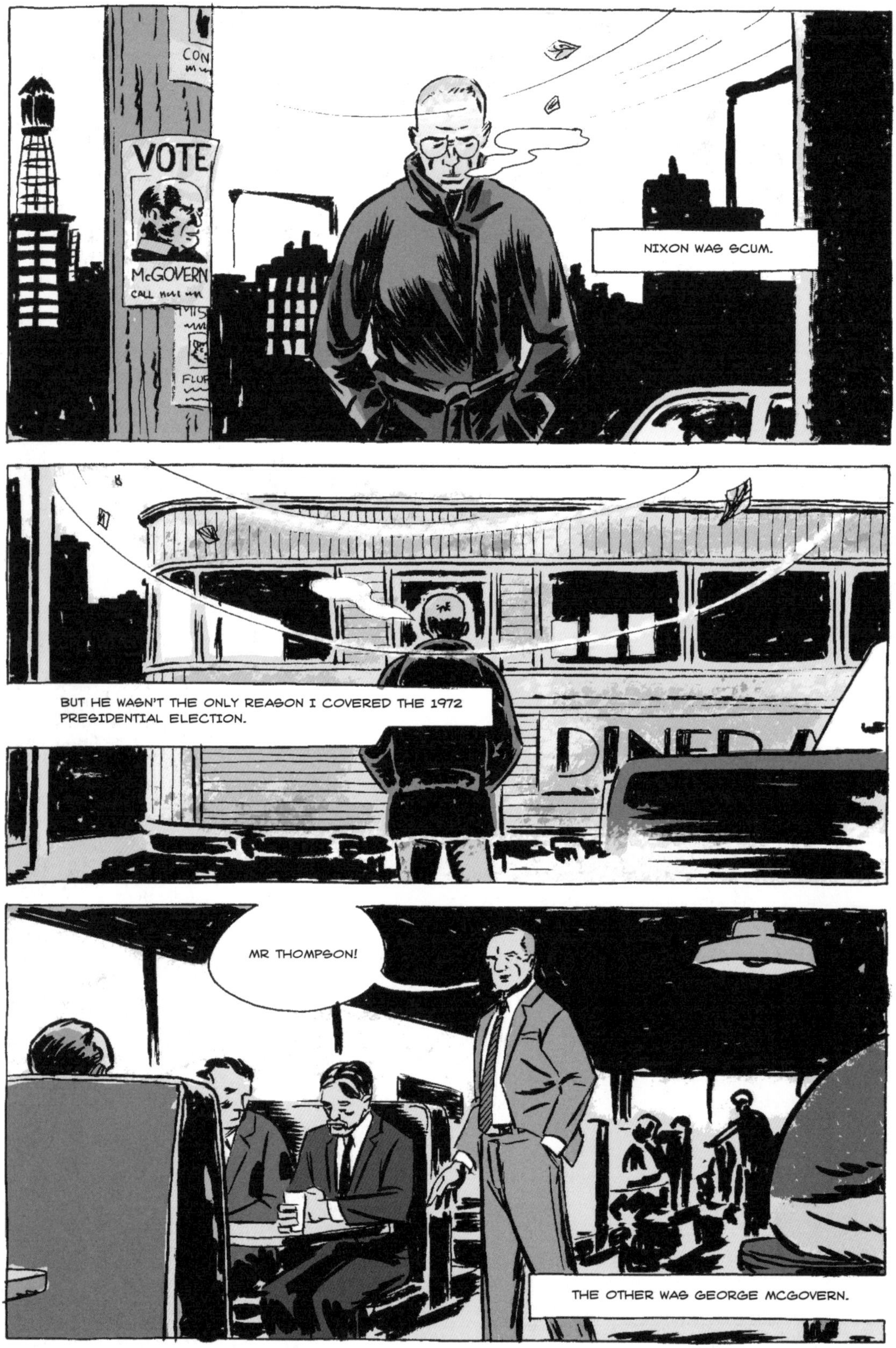
VOTE
McGOVERN
NIXON WAS SCUM.
BUT HE WASN'T THE ONLY REASON I COVERED THE 1972 PRESIDENTIAL ELECTION.
MR THOMPSON!
THE OTHER WAS GEORGE MCGOVERN.

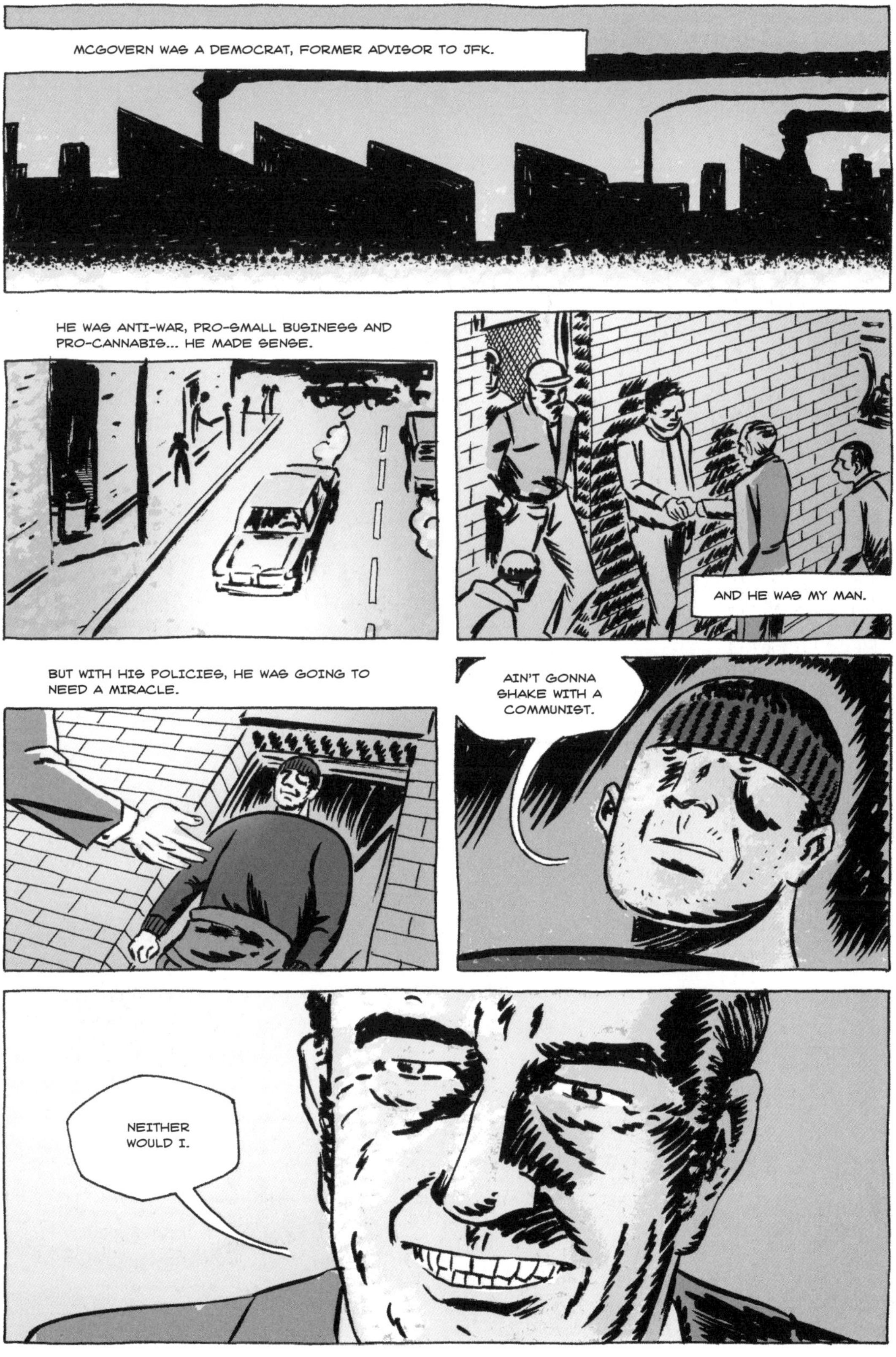
MCGOVERN WAS A DEMOCRAT, FORMER ADVISOR TO JFK.
HE WAS ANTI-WAR, PRO-SMALL BUSINESS AND PRO-CANNABIS... HE MADE SENSE.
AND HE WAS MY MAN.
BUT WITH HIS POLICIES, HE WAS GOING TO NEED A MIRACLE.
AIN'T GONNA SHAKE WITH A COMMUNIST.
NEITHER WOULD I.

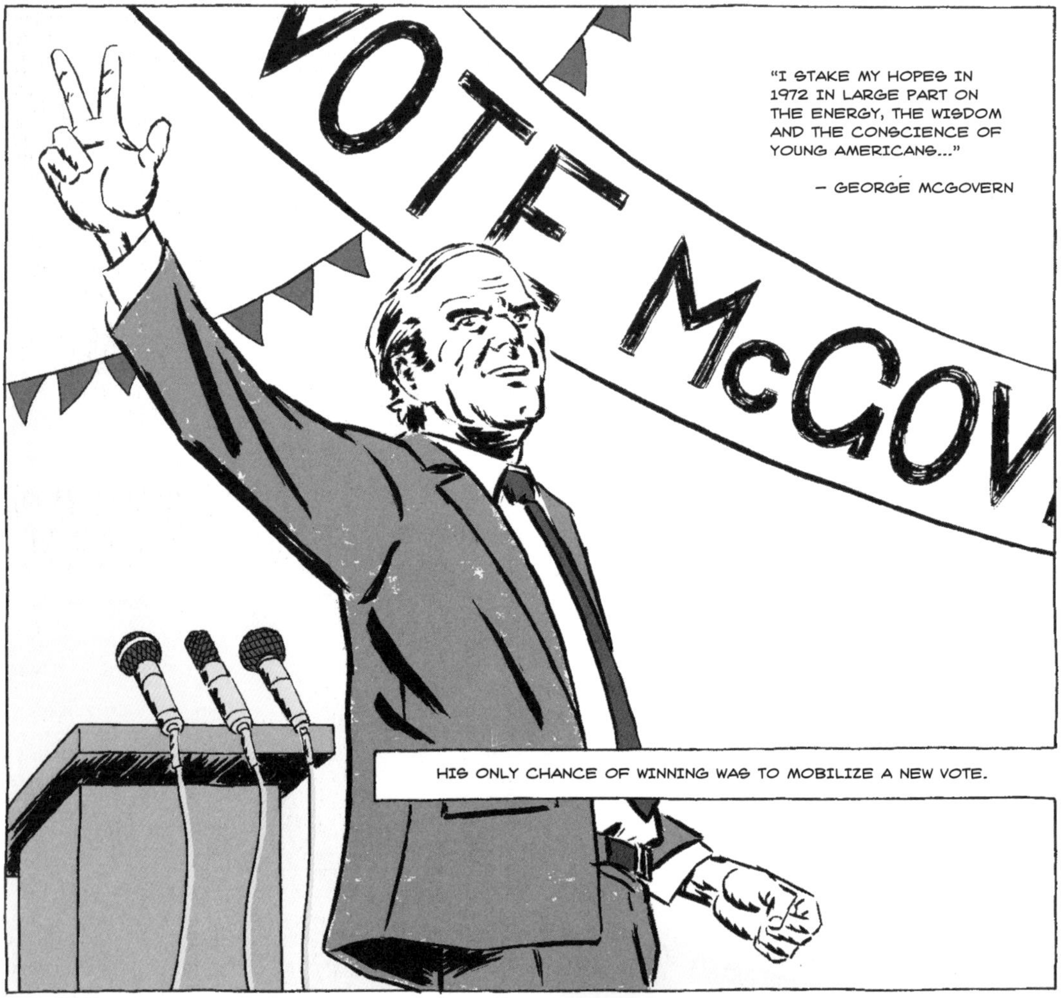
VOTE McGOV
"I STAKE MY HOPES IN 1972 IN LARGE PART ON THE ENERGY, THE WISDOM AND THE CONSCIENCE OF YOUNG AMERICANS..."
– GEORGE MCGOVERN
HIS ONLY CHANCE OF WINNING WAS TO MOBILIZE A NEW VOTE.

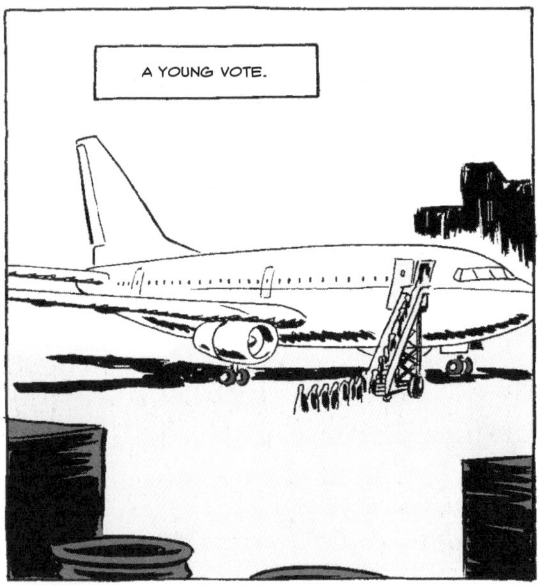
A YOUNG VOTE.

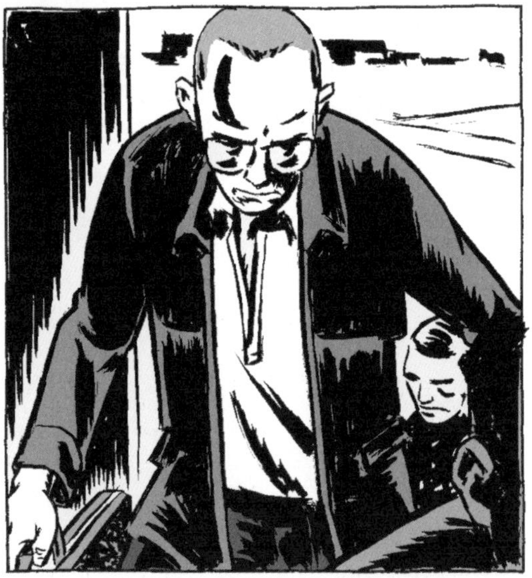
WHICH WAS AN AREA I FELT I COULD HELP HIM WITH.

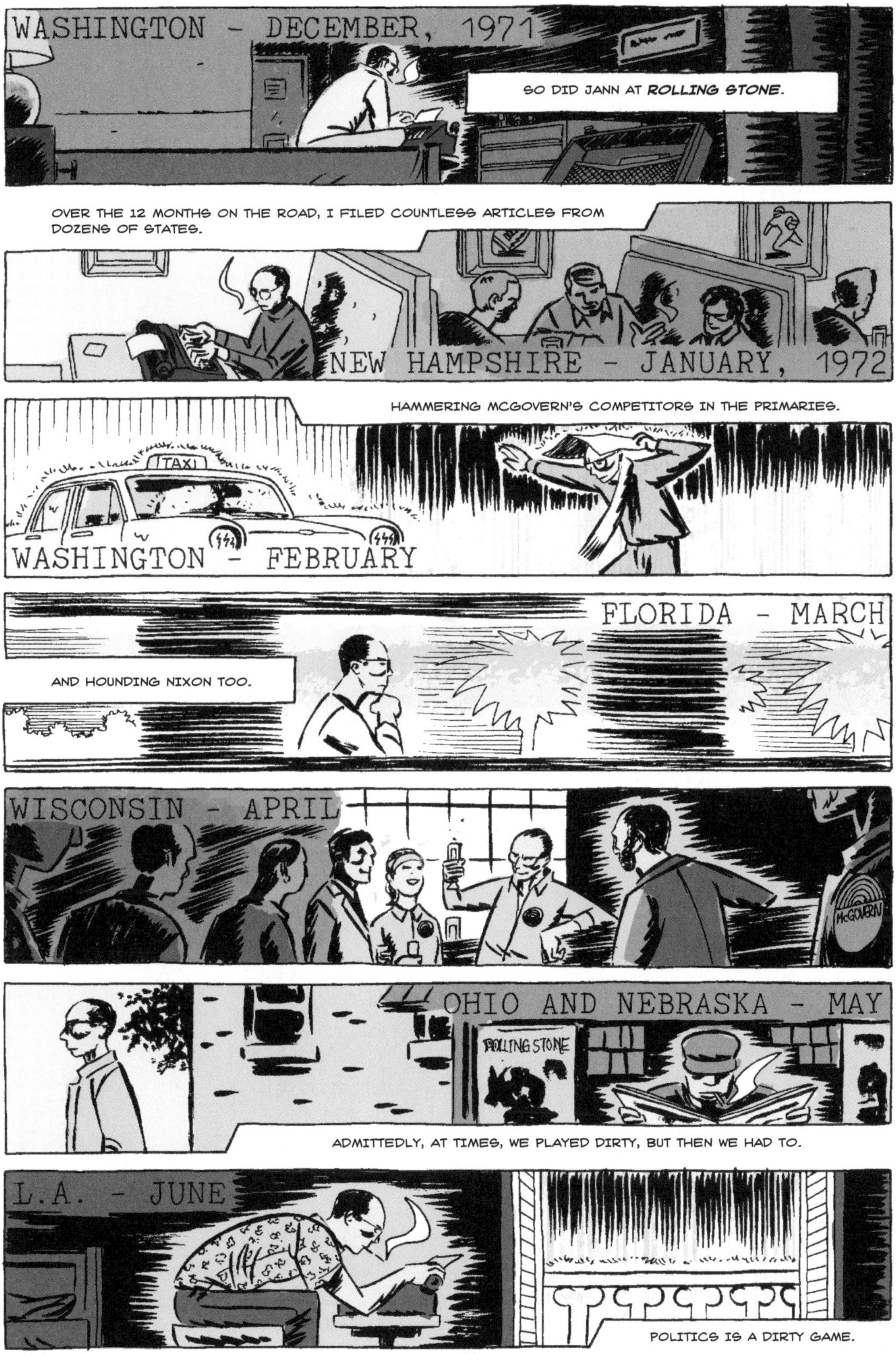
WASHINGTON - DECEMBER, 1971
SO DID JANN AT ROLLING STONE.
OVER THE 12 MONTHS ON THE ROAD, I FILED COUNTLESS ARTICLES FROM DOZENS OF STATES.
NEW HAMPSHIRE - JANUARY, 1972
HAMMERING MCGOVERN'S COMPETITORS IN THE PRIMARIES.
TAXI
WASHINGTON - FEBRUARY
FLORIDA - MARCH
AND HOUNDING NIXON TOO.
WISCONSIN - APRIL
McGOVERN
OHIO AND NEBRASKA - MAY
ROLLING STONE
ADMITTEDLY, AT TIMES, WE PLAYED DIRTY, BUT THEN WE HAD TO.
L.A. - JUNE
POLITICS IS A DIRTY GAME.

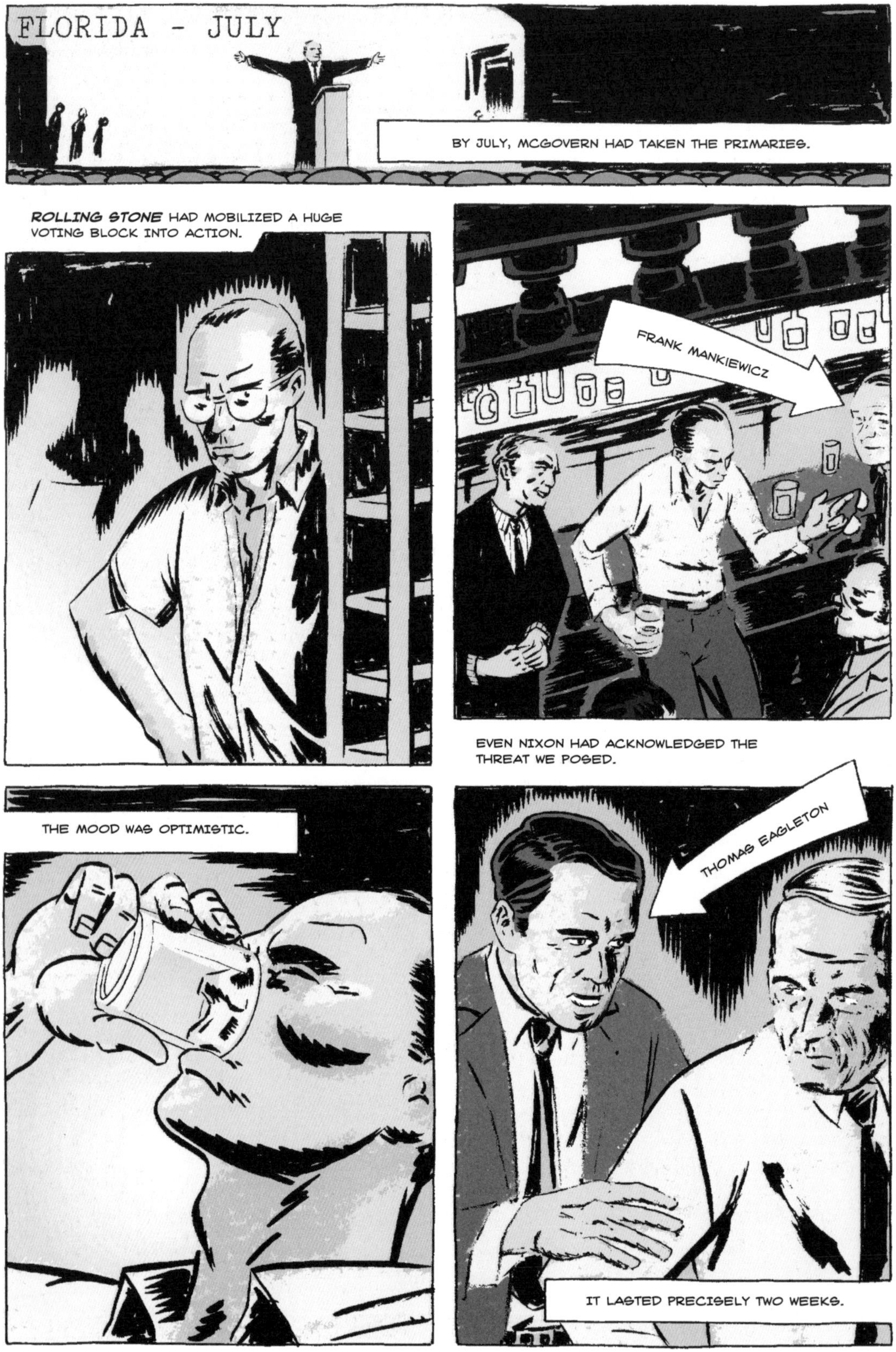
FLORIDA - JULY
BY JULY, MCGOVERN HAD TAKEN THE PRIMARIES.
ROLLING STONE HAD MOBILIZED A HUGE VOTING BLOCK INTO ACTION.
FRANK MANKIEWICZ
EVEN NIXON HAD ACKNOWLEDGED THE THREAT WE POSED.
THE MOOD WAS OPTIMISTIC.
THOMAS EAGLETON
IT LASTED PRECISELY TWO WEEKS.

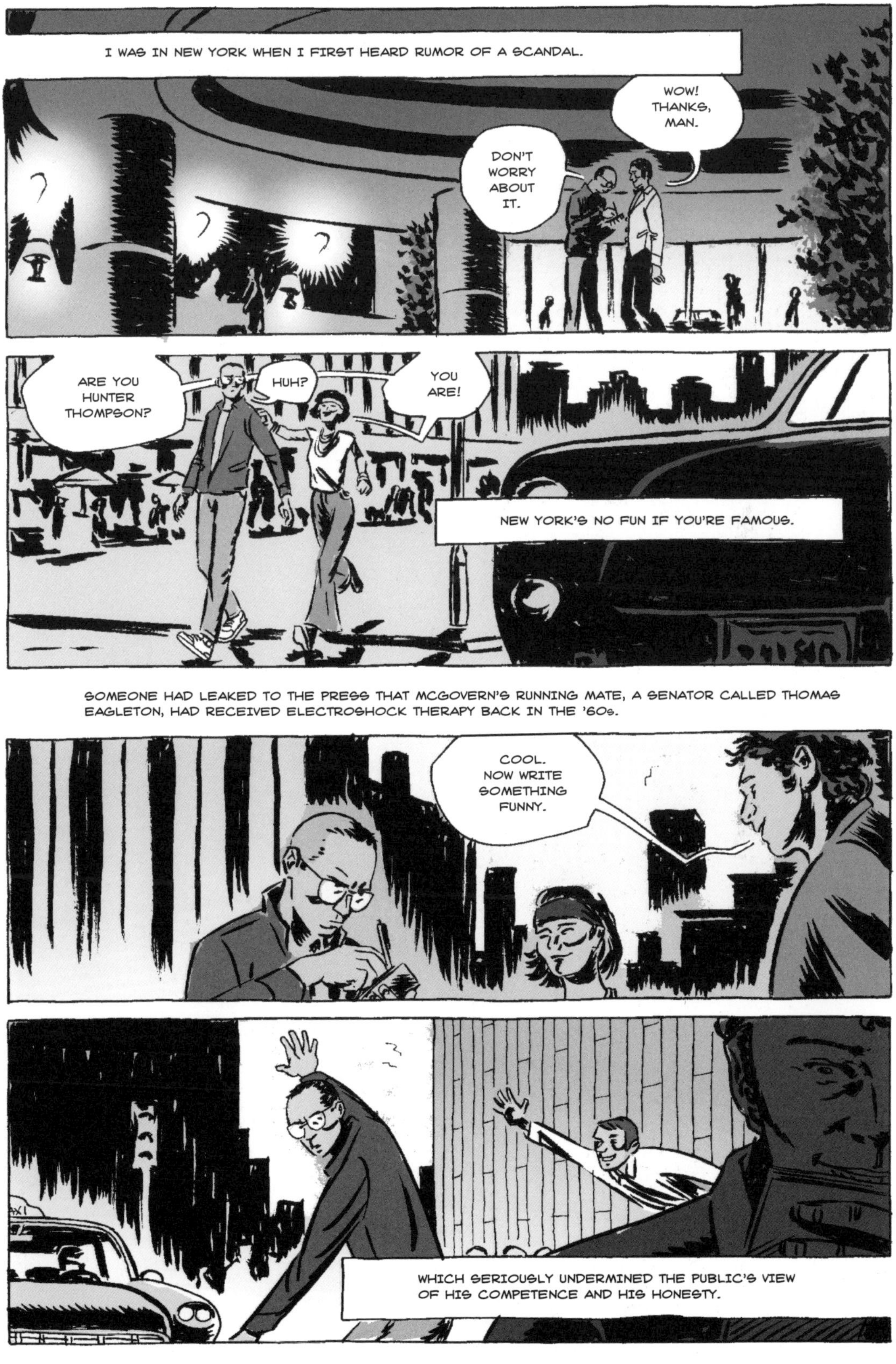
I WAS IN NEW YORK WHEN I FIRST HEARD RUMOR OF A SCANDAL.
DON'T WORRY ABOUT IT.
WOW! THANKS, MAN.
ARE YOU HUNTER THOMPSON?
HUH?
YOU ARE!
NEW YORK'S NO FUN IF YOU'RE FAMOUS.
SOMEONE HAD LEAKED TO THE PRESS THAT MCGOVERN'S RUNNING MATE, A SENATOR CALLED THOMAS EAGLETON, HAD RECEIVED ELECTROSHOCK THERAPY BACK IN THE '60s.
COOL. NOW WRITE SOMETHING FUNNY.
WHICH SERIOUSLY UNDERMINED THE PUBLIC'S VIEW OF HIS COMPETENCE AND HIS HONESTY.

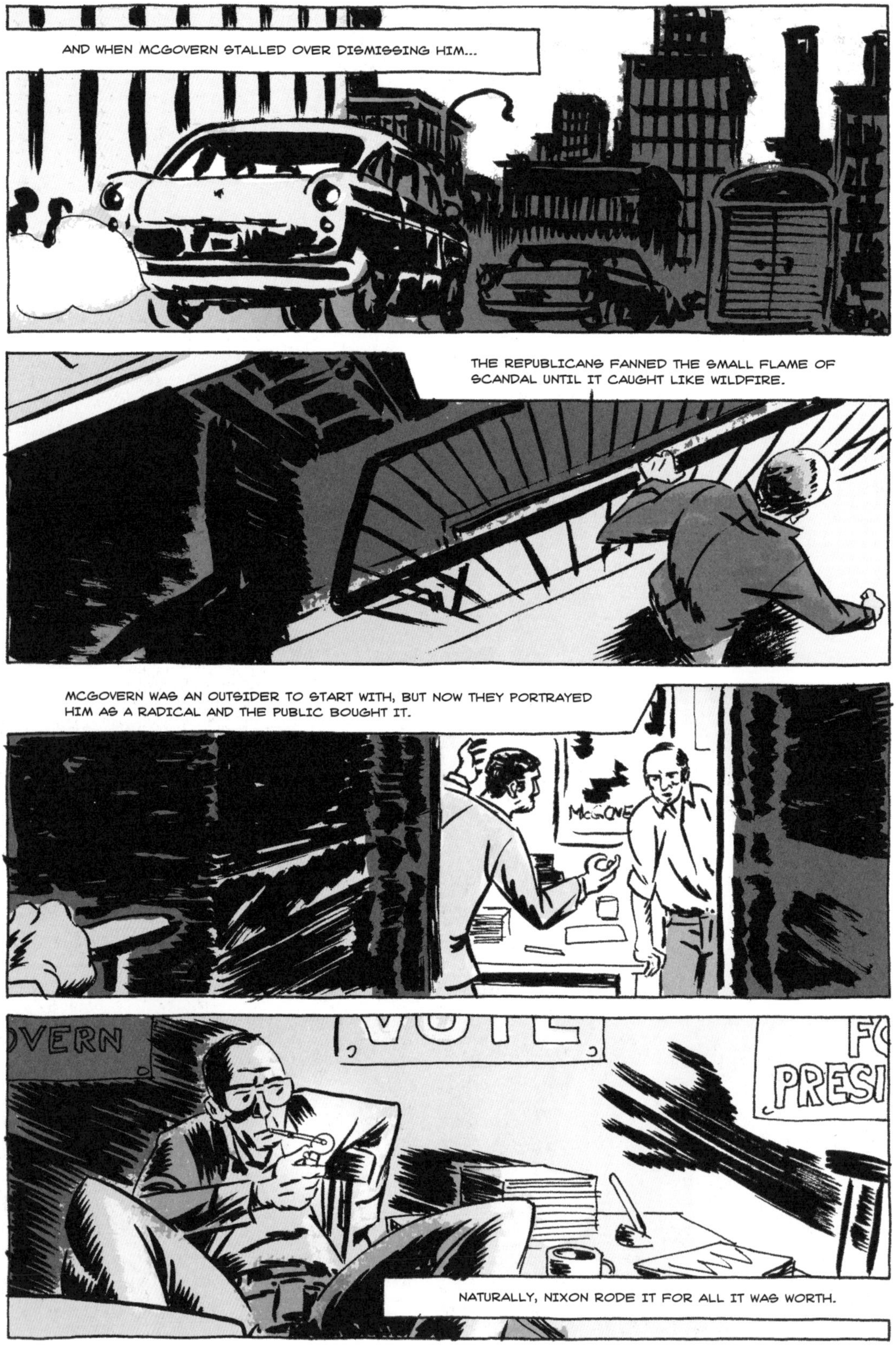
AND WHEN MCGOVERN STALLED OVER DISMISSING HIM...
THE REPUBLICANS FANNED THE SMALL FLAME OF SCANDAL UNTIL IT CAUGHT LIKE WILDFIRE.
MCGOVERN WAS AN OUTSIDER TO START WITH, BUT NOW THEY PORTRAYED HIM AS A RADICAL AND THE PUBLIC BOUGHT IT.
McGOVE
OVERN
VOTE
FO
PRESI
NATURALLY, NIXON RODE IT FOR ALL IT WAS WORTH.

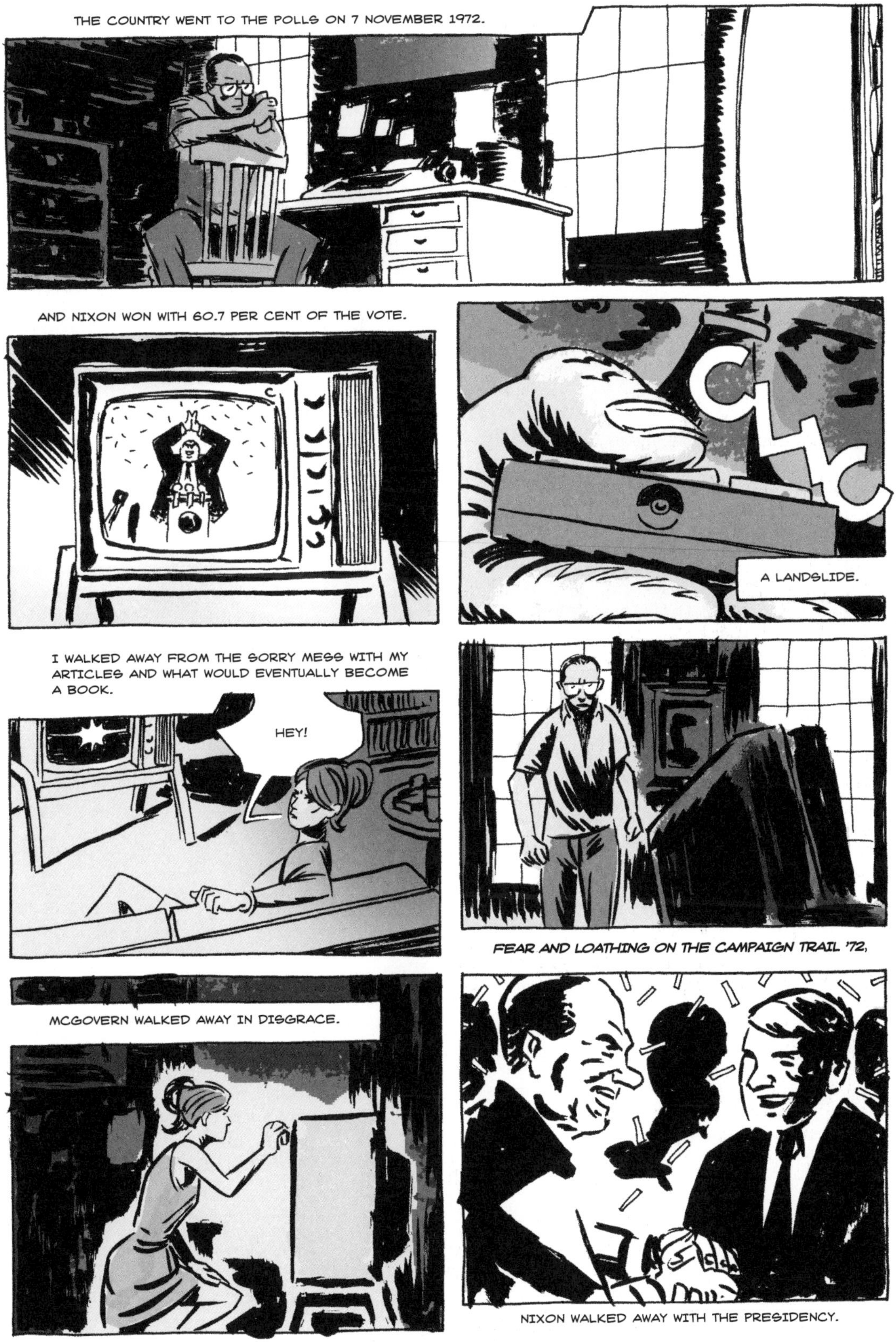
THE COUNTRY WENT TO THE POLLS ON 7 NOVEMBER 1972.
AND NIXON WON WITH 60.7 PER CENT OF THE VOTE.
A LANDSLIDE.
I WALKED AWAY FROM THE SORRY MESS WITH MY ARTICLES AND WHAT WOULD EVENTUALLY BECOME A BOOK.
HEY!
FEAR AND LOATHING ON THE CAMPAIGN TRAIL '72,
MCGOVERN WALKED AWAY IN DISGRACE.
NIXON WALKED AWAY WITH THE PRESIDENCY.

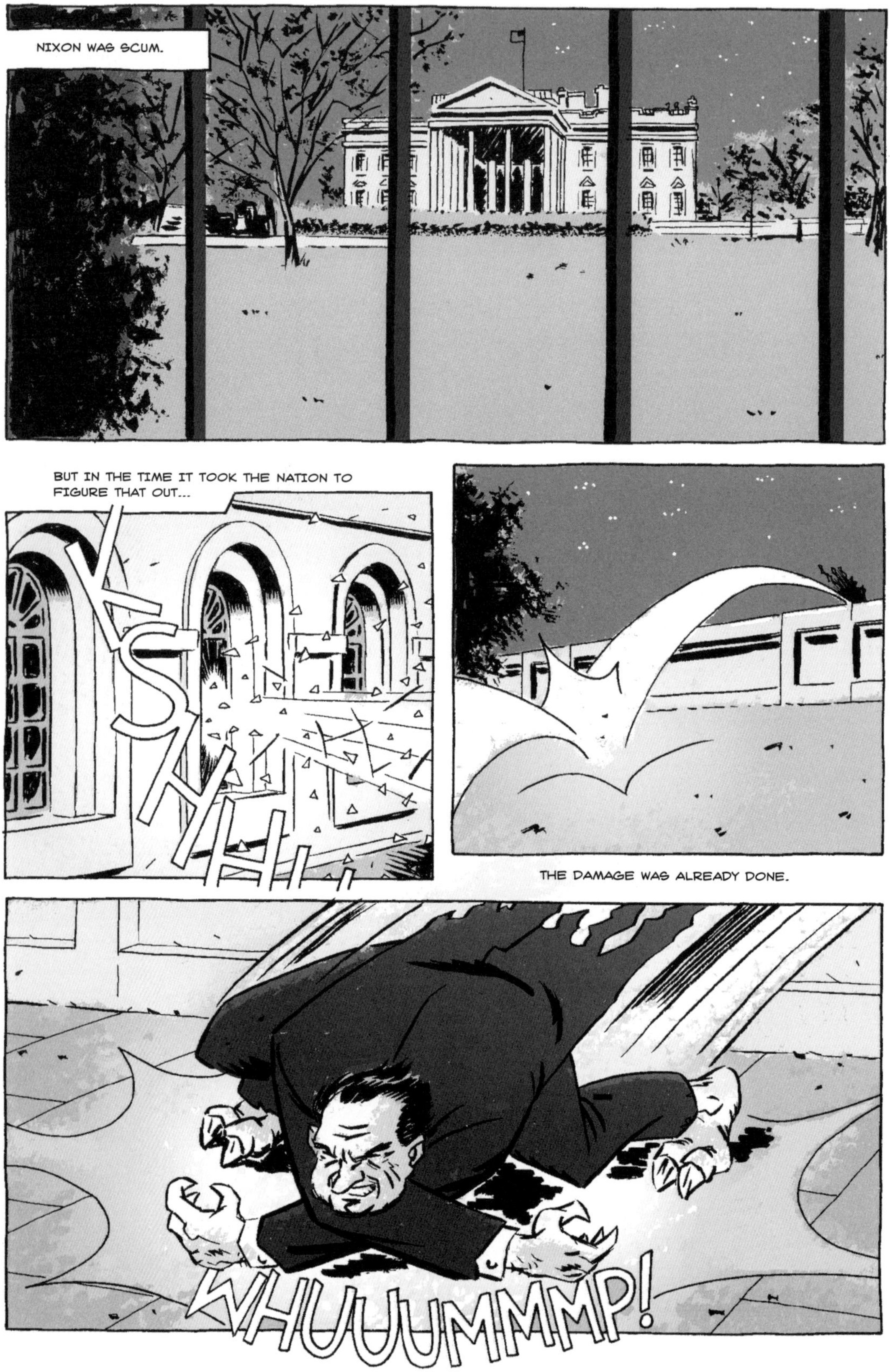
NIXON WAS SCUM.
BUT IN THE TIME IT TOOK THE NATION TO FIGURE THAT OUT...
KSHH!
THE DAMAGE WAS ALREADY DONE.
WHUUUMMMP!

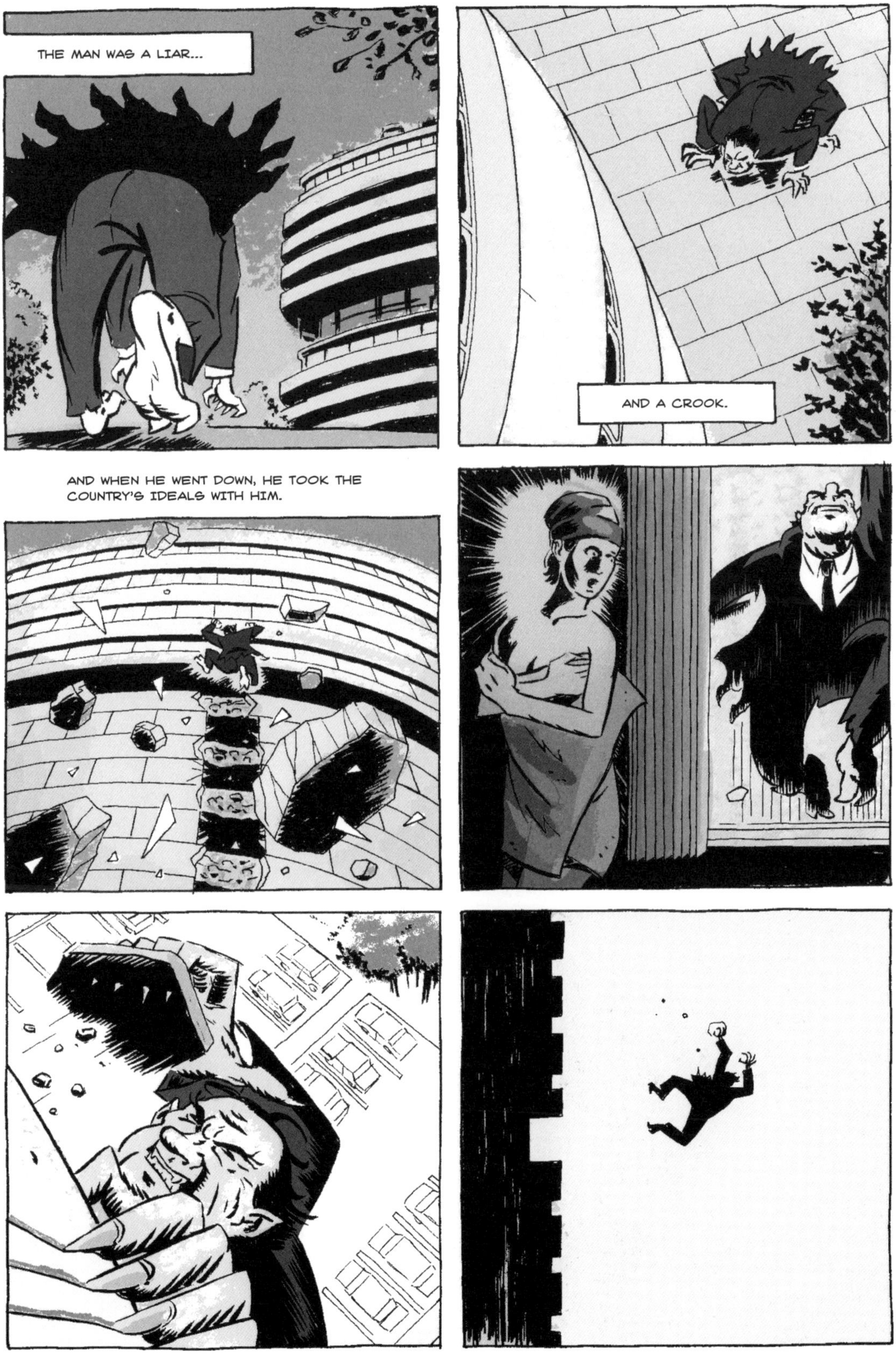
THE MAN WAS A LIAR...
AND A CROOK.
AND WHEN HE WENT DOWN, HE TOOK THE COUNTRY'S IDEALS WITH HIM.

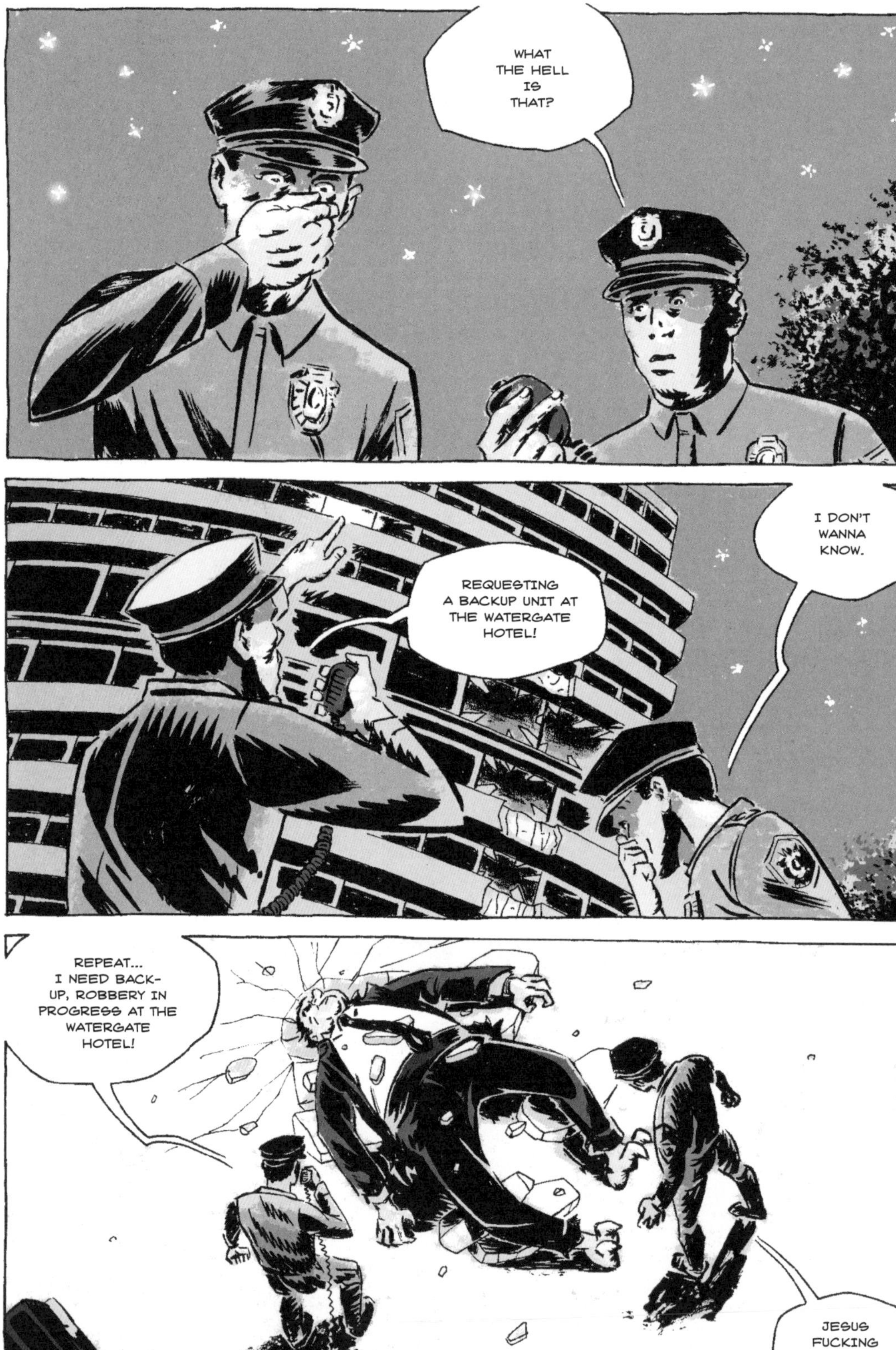
WHAT THE HELL IS THAT?
REQUESTING A BACKUP UNIT AT THE WATERGATE HOTEL!
I DON'T WANNA KNOW.
REPEAT... I NEED BACK-UP, ROBBERY IN PROGRESS AT THE WATERGATE HOTEL!
JESUS FUCKING CHRIST!

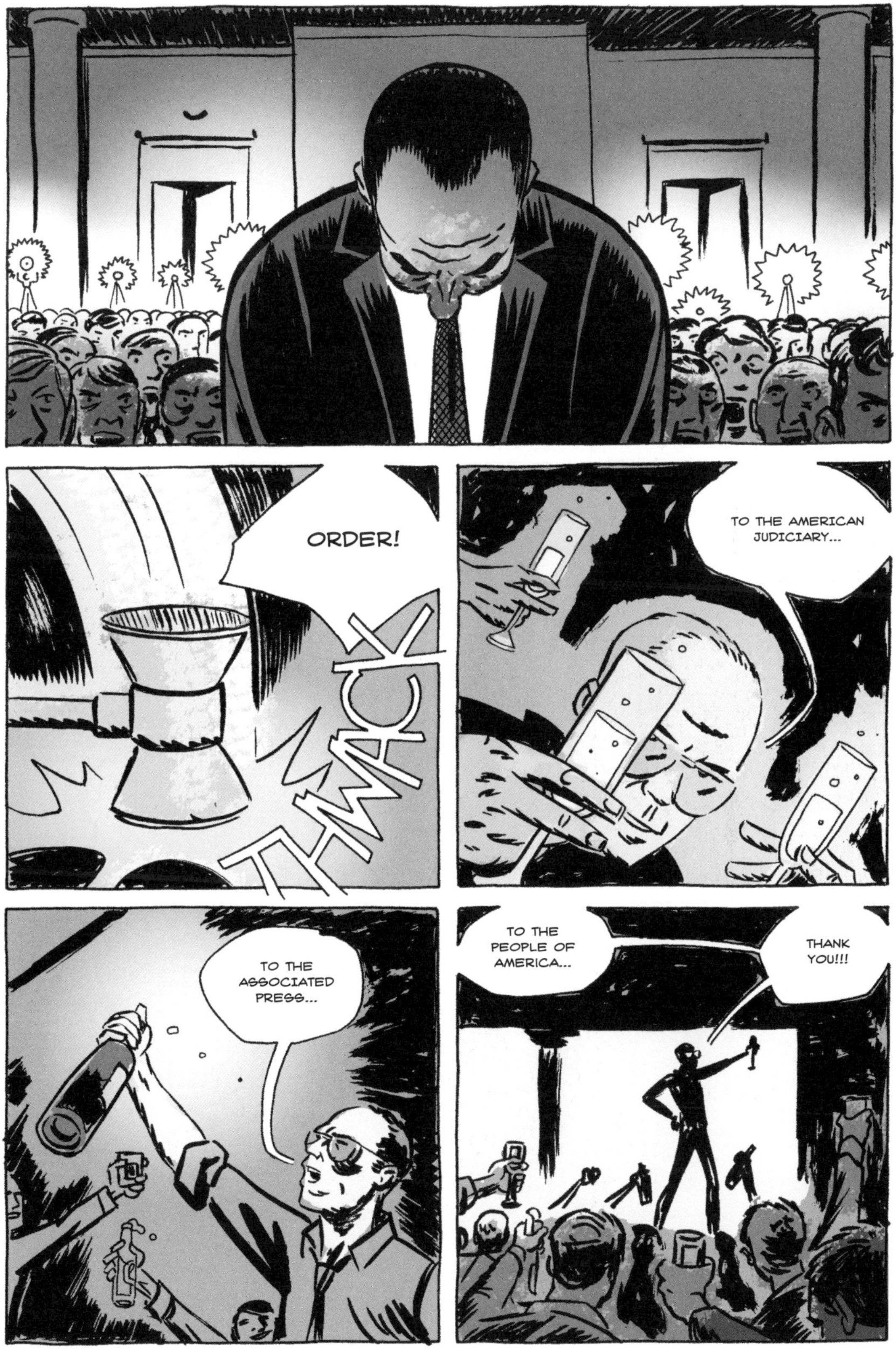
ORDER!
THWACK
TO THE AMERICAN JUDICIARY...
TO THE ASSOCIATED PRESS...
TO THE PEOPLE OF AMERICA...
THANK YOU!!!

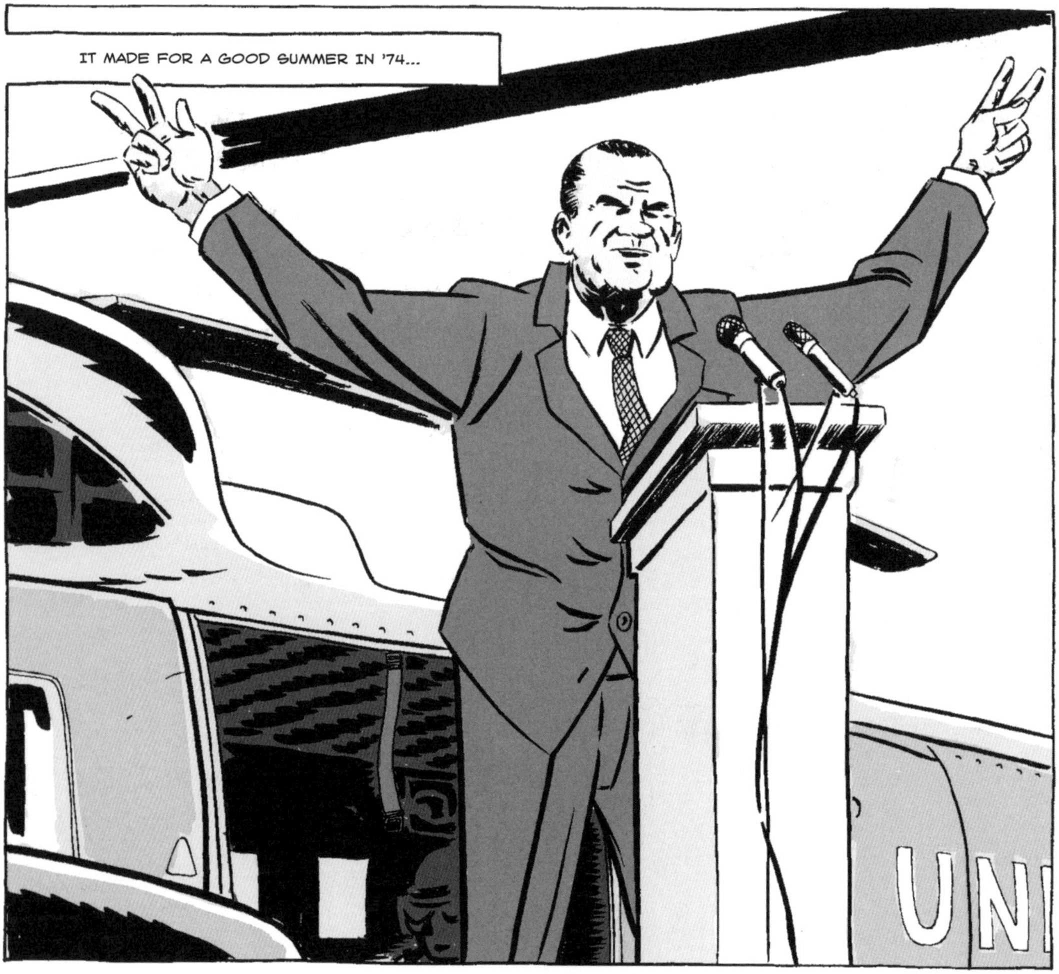
IT MADE FOR A GOOD SUMMER IN '74...

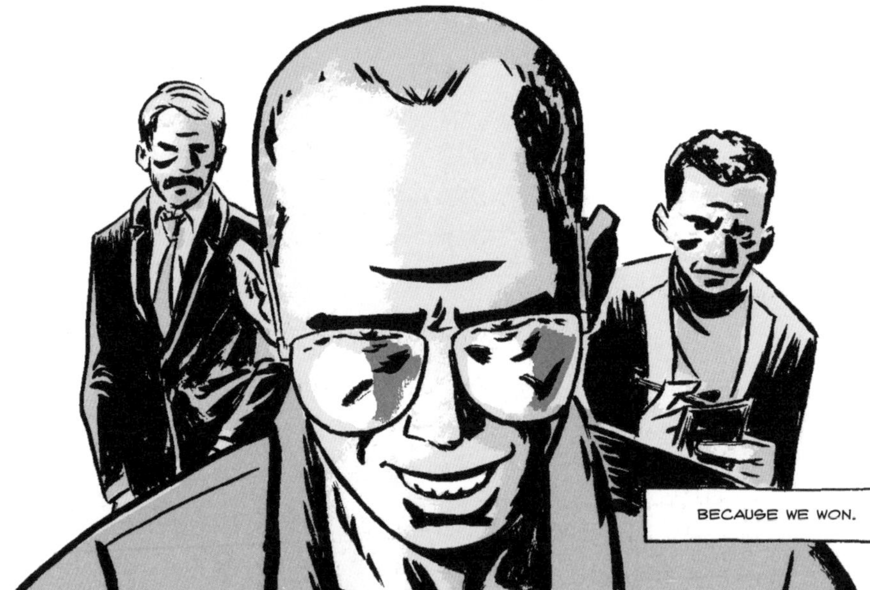
BECAUSE WE WON.

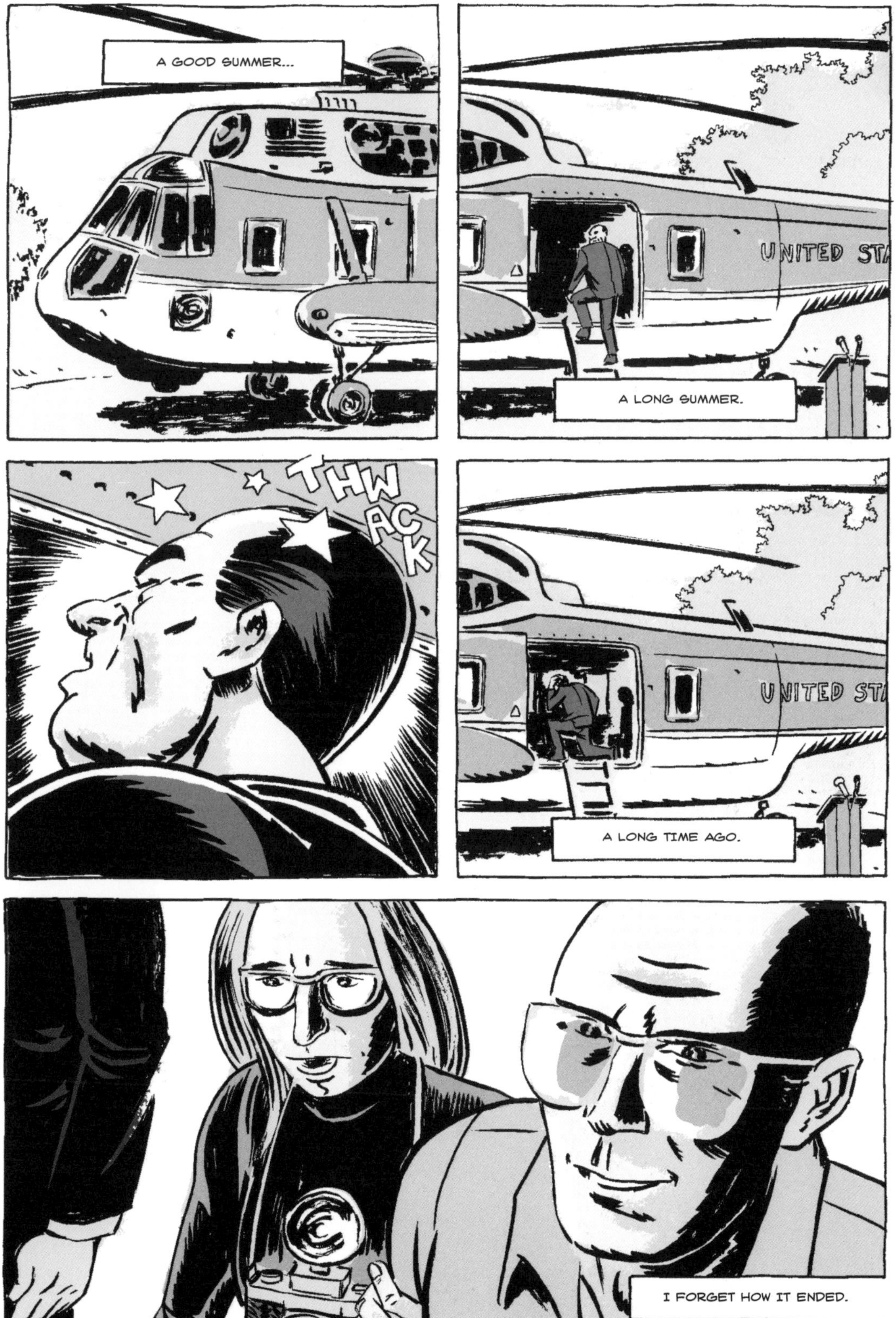
A GOOD SUMMER...
UNITED STA
A LONG SUMMER.
THWACK
UNITED STA
A LONG TIME AGO.
I FORGET HOW IT ENDED.

THE NINETEEN EIGHTIES

SANDY LEFT IN 1980.

SAID SHE COULDN'T LIVE WITH ME ANY MORE.

KHRCH

SHHNNNRRRFEEEEEEEEEEEEEEEEEFFFF

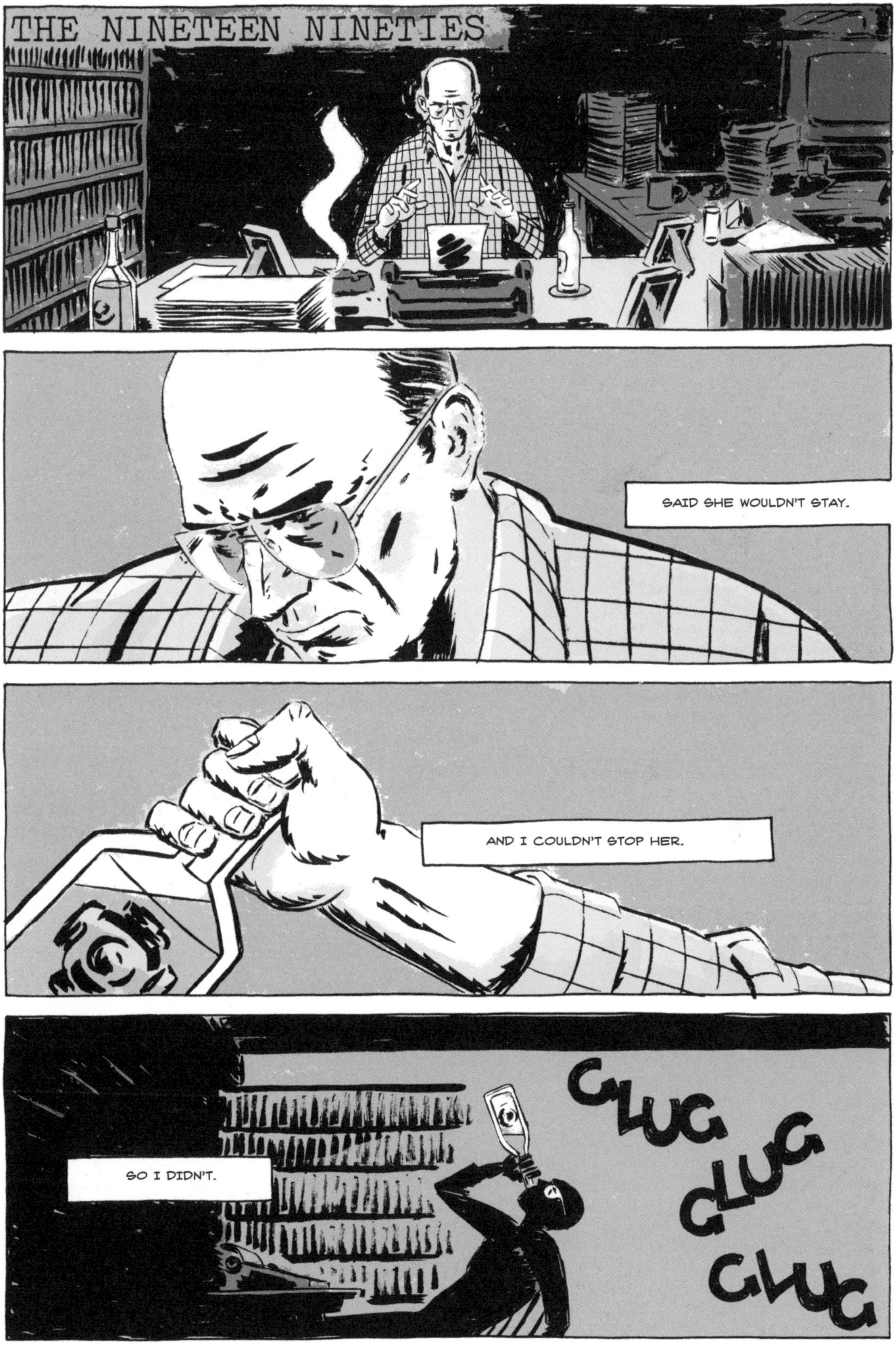
THE NINETEEN NINETIES
SAID SHE WOULDN'T STAY.
AND I COULDN'T STOP HER.
SO I DIDN'T.
GLUG
GLUG
GLUG

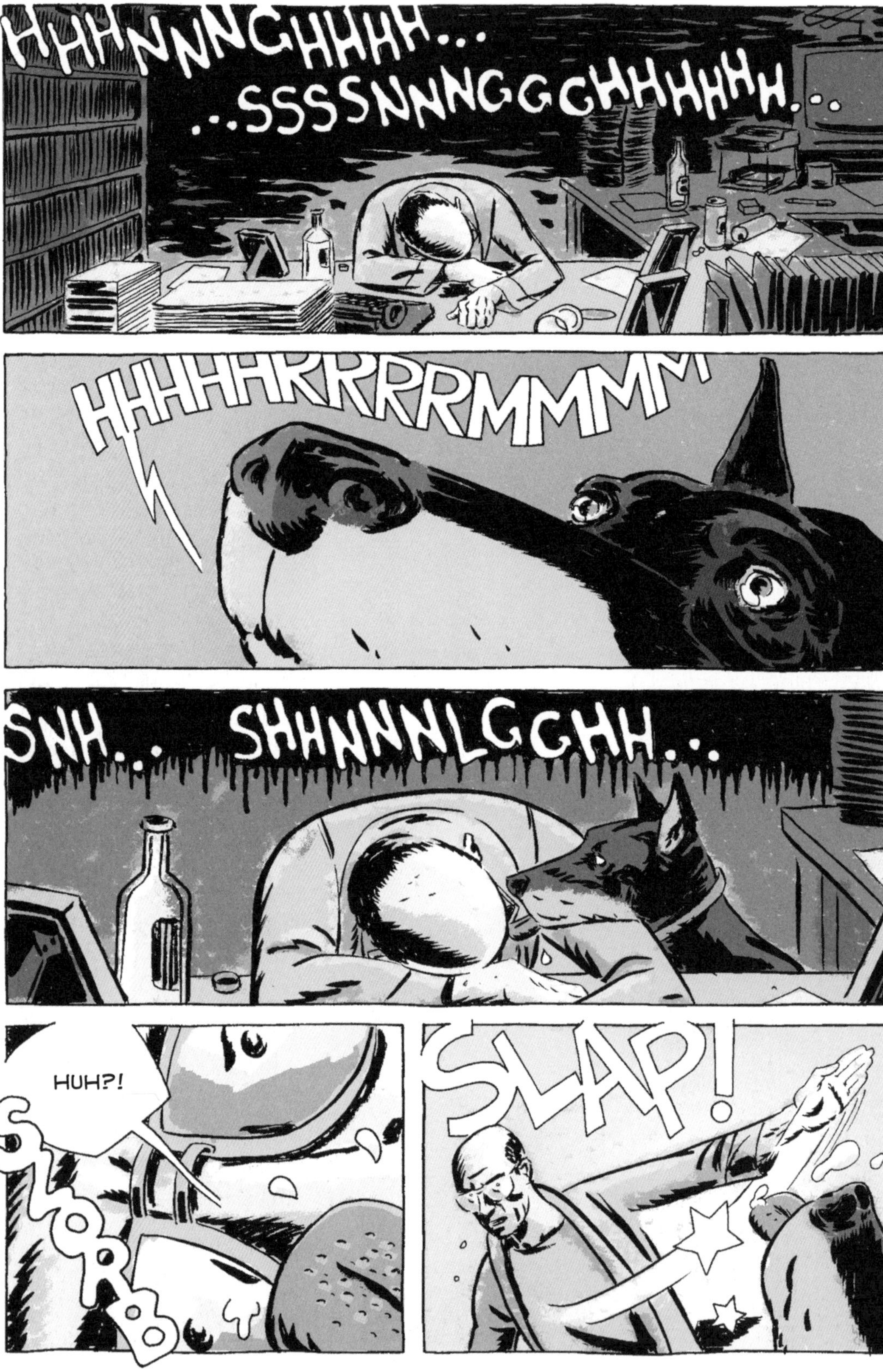
HHHNNNGHHHH...
...SSSSNNNGGGHHHHHH...
HHHHHRRRRMMMM
SNH... SHHNNNLGGHH...
HUH?!
SNORB
SLAP!

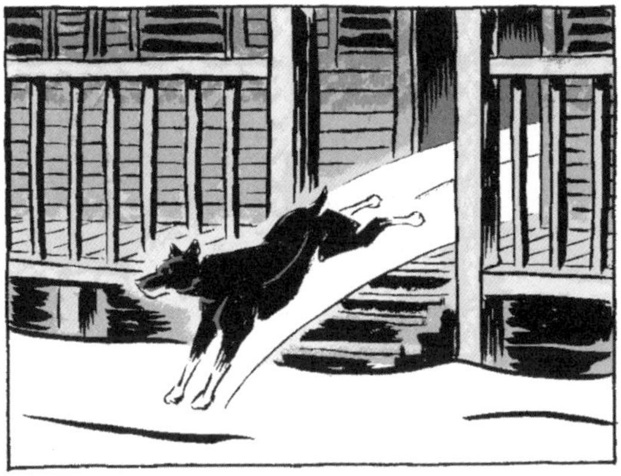

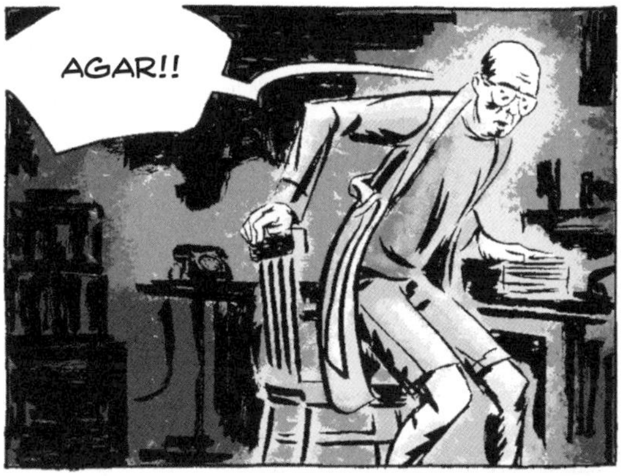
AGAR!!

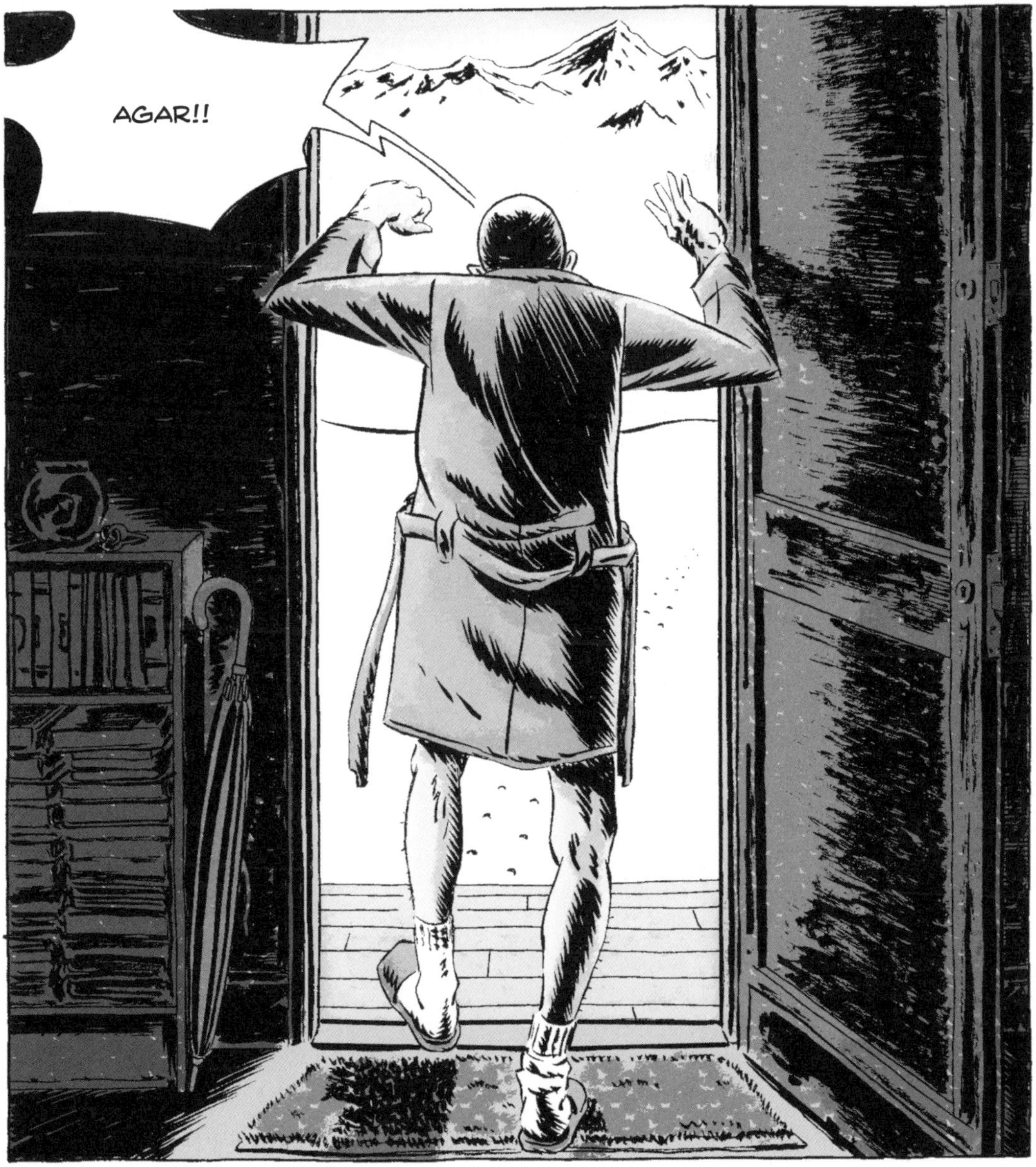
AGAR!!

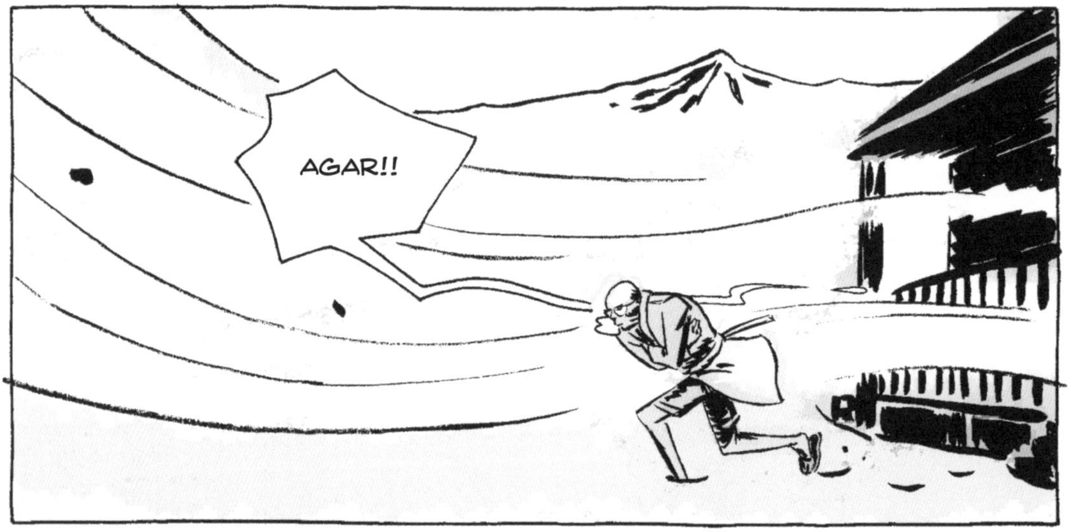
AGAR!!

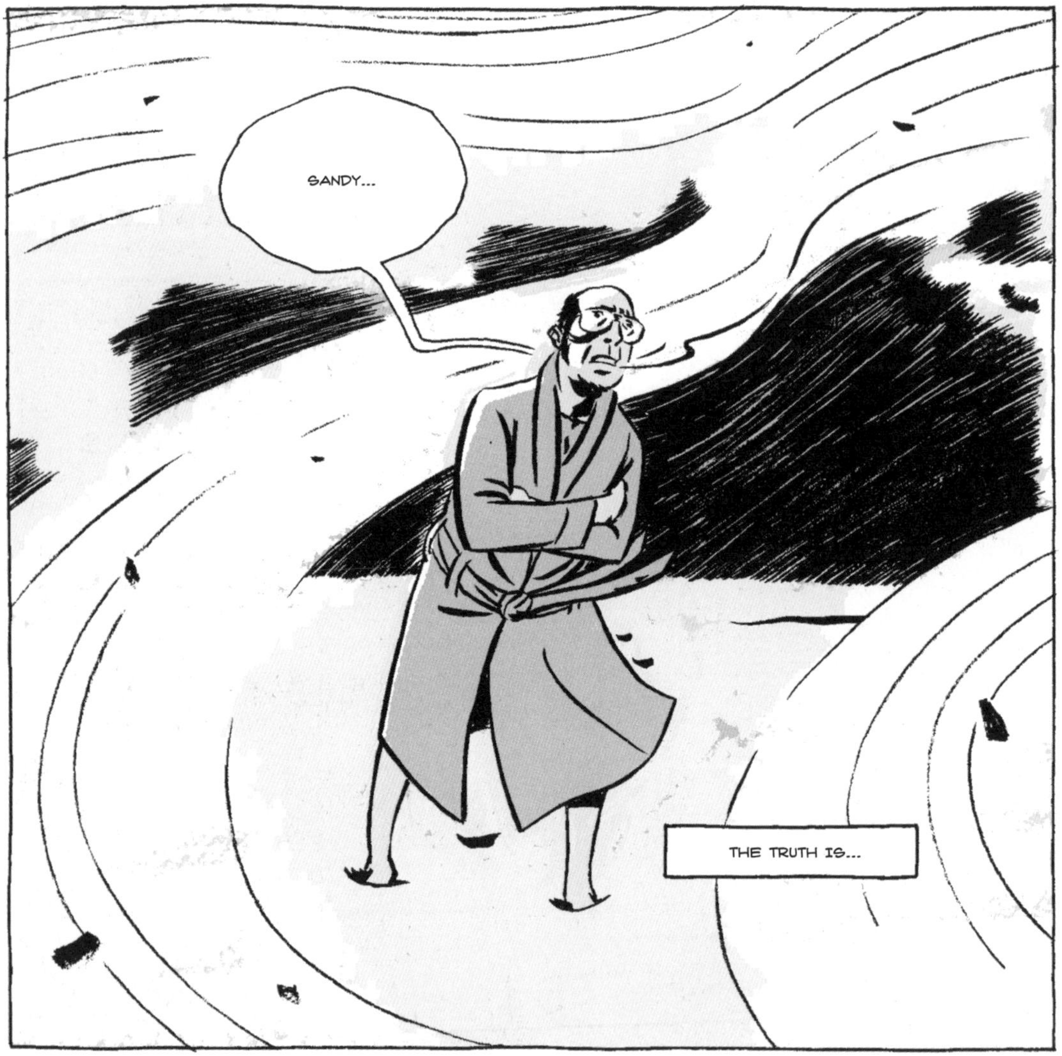
SANDY...
THE TRUTH IS...

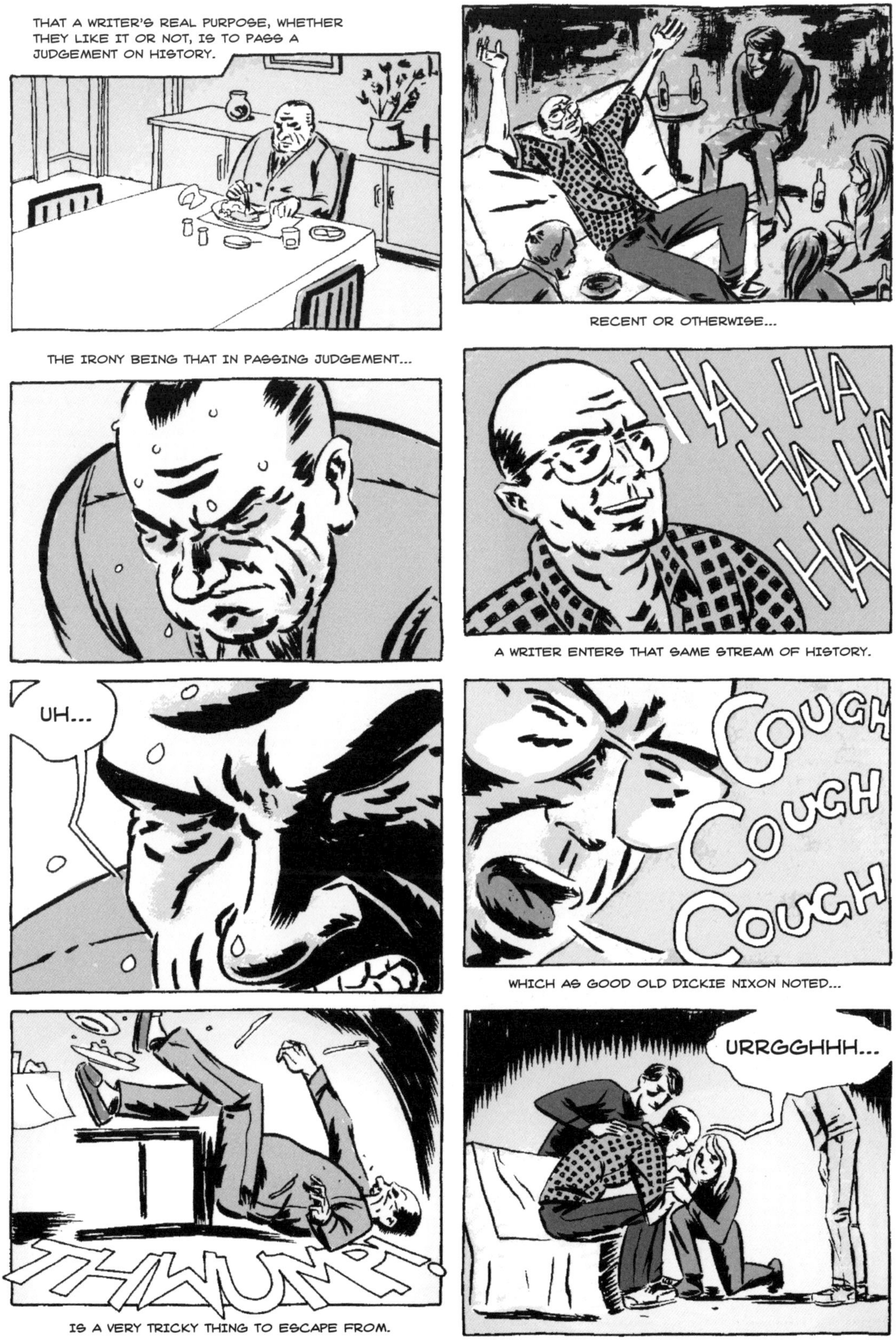
THAT A WRITER'S REAL PURPOSE, WHETHER THEY LIKE IT OR NOT, IS TO PASS A JUDGEMENT ON HISTORY.
RECENT OR OTHERWISE...
THE IRONY BEING THAT IN PASSING JUDGEMENT...
HA HA HA HA HA
A WRITER ENTERS THAT SAME STREAM OF HISTORY.
UH...
COUGH COUGH COUGH
WHICH AS GOOD OLD DICKIE NIXON NOTED...
THWUMP!
IS A VERY TRICKY THING TO ESCAPE FROM.
URRGGHHH...

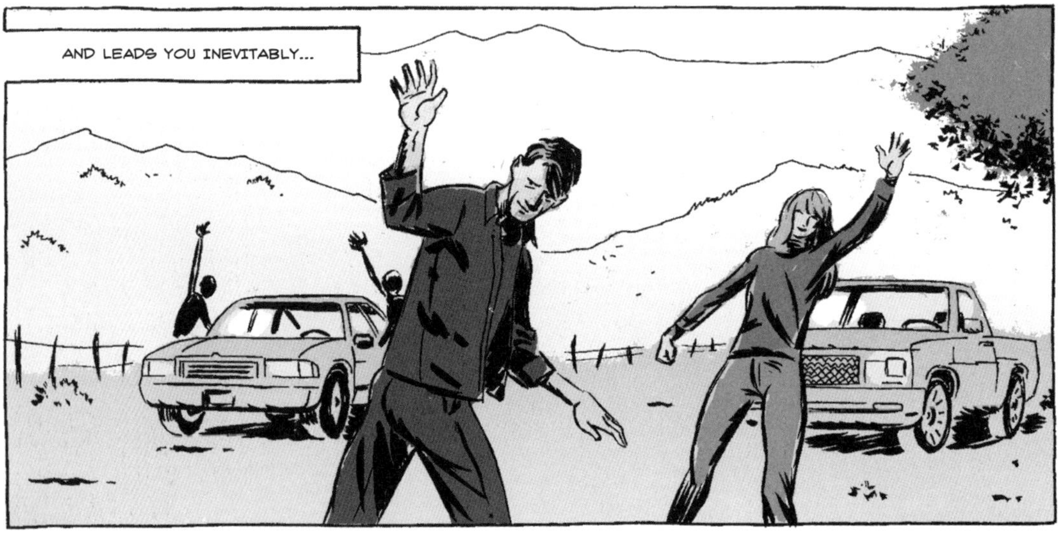
AND LEADS YOU INEVITABLY...

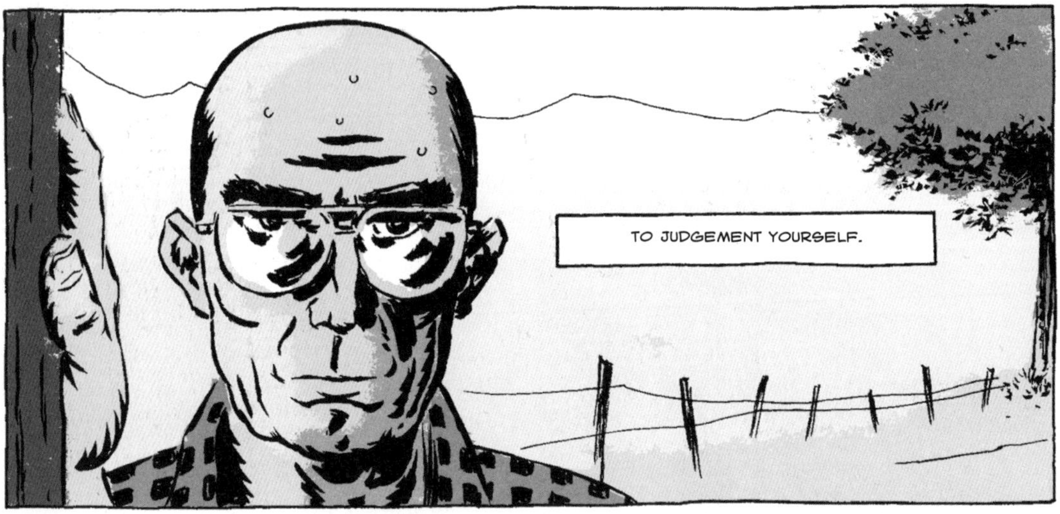
TO JUDGEMENT YOURSELF.

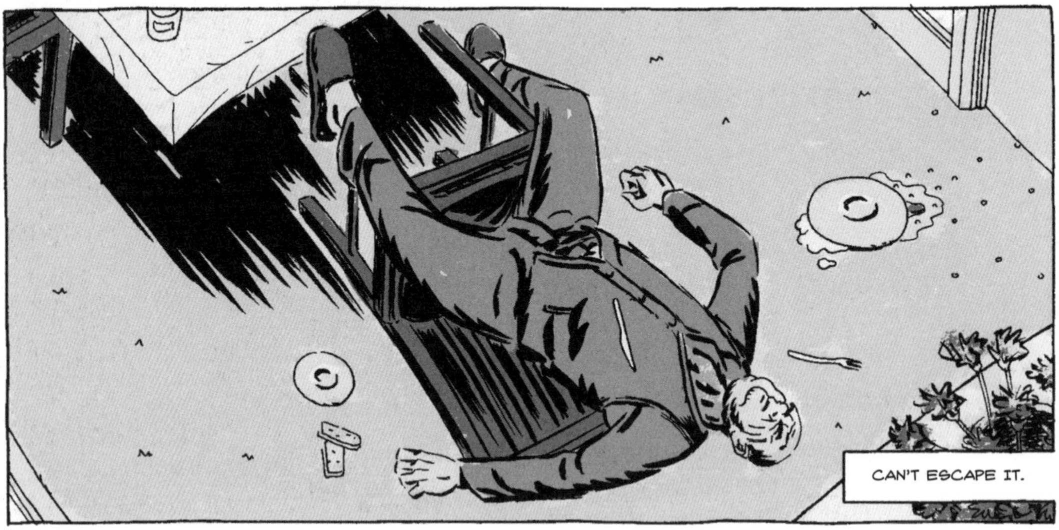
CAN'T ESCAPE IT.

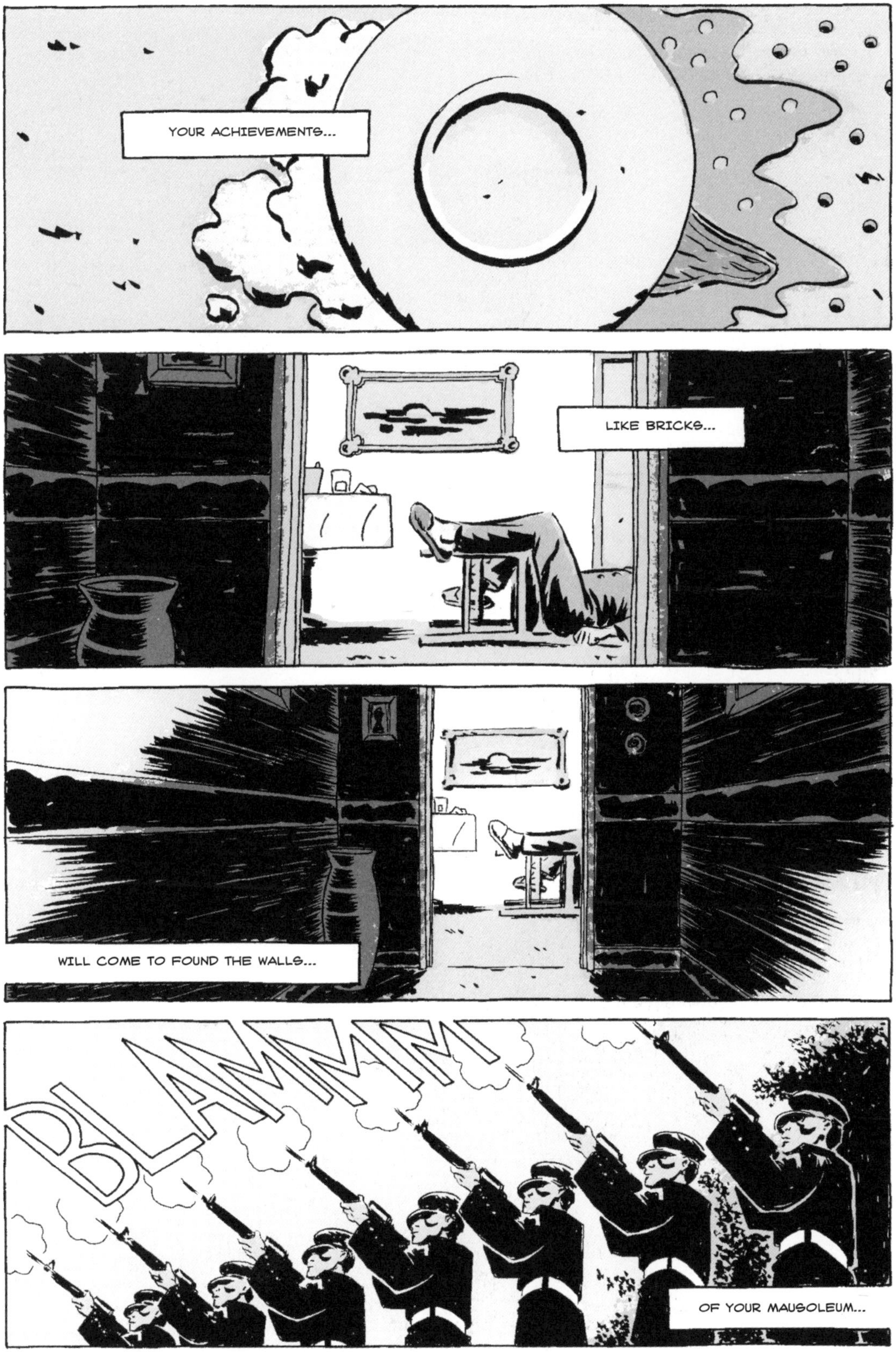
YOUR ACHIEVEMENTS...
LIKE BRICKS...
WILL COME TO FOUND THE WALLS...
BLAMMM
OF YOUR MAUSOLEUM...

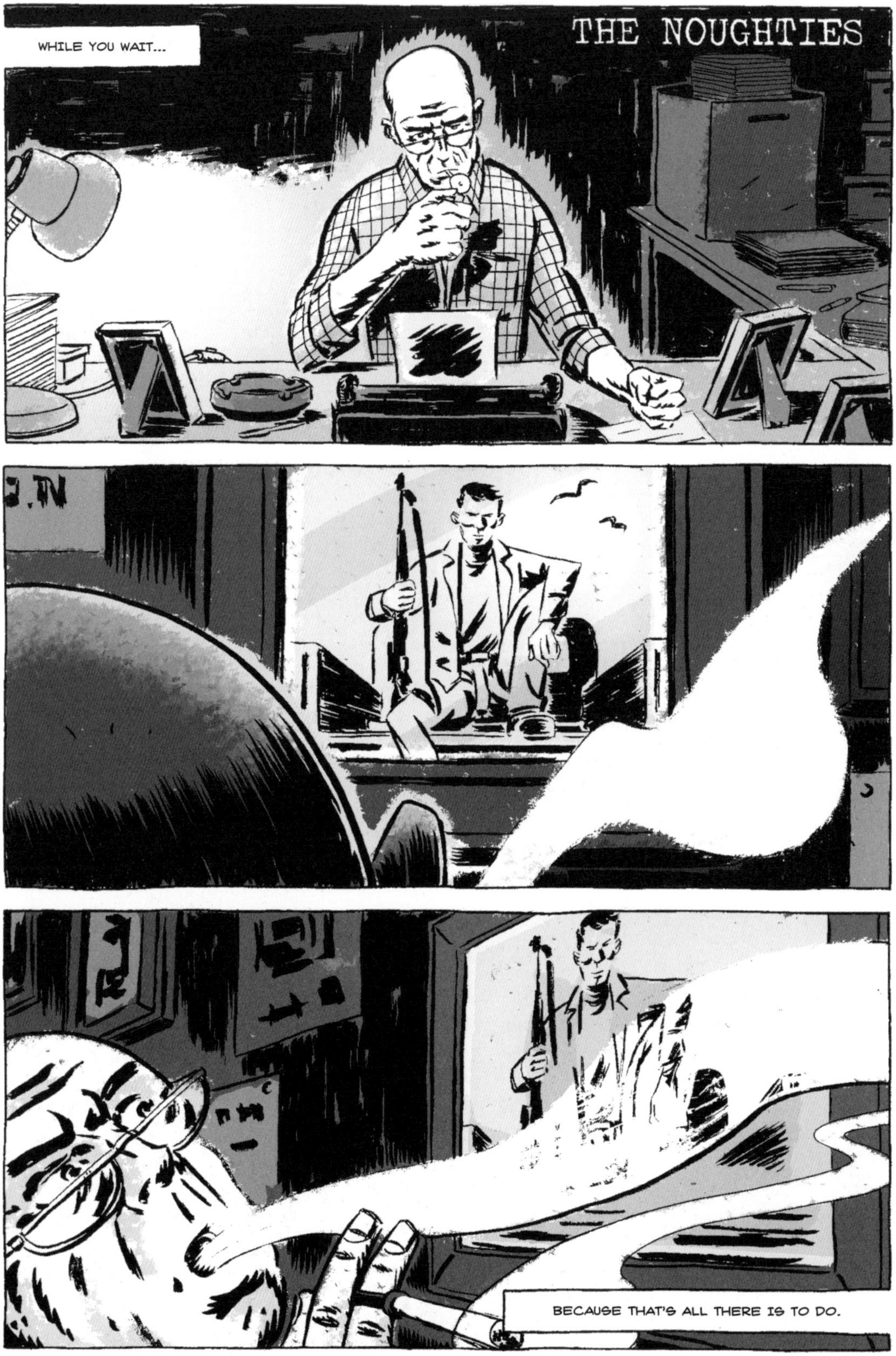
WHILE YOU WAIT...
THE NOUGHTIES
BECAUSE THAT'S ALL THERE IS TO DO.

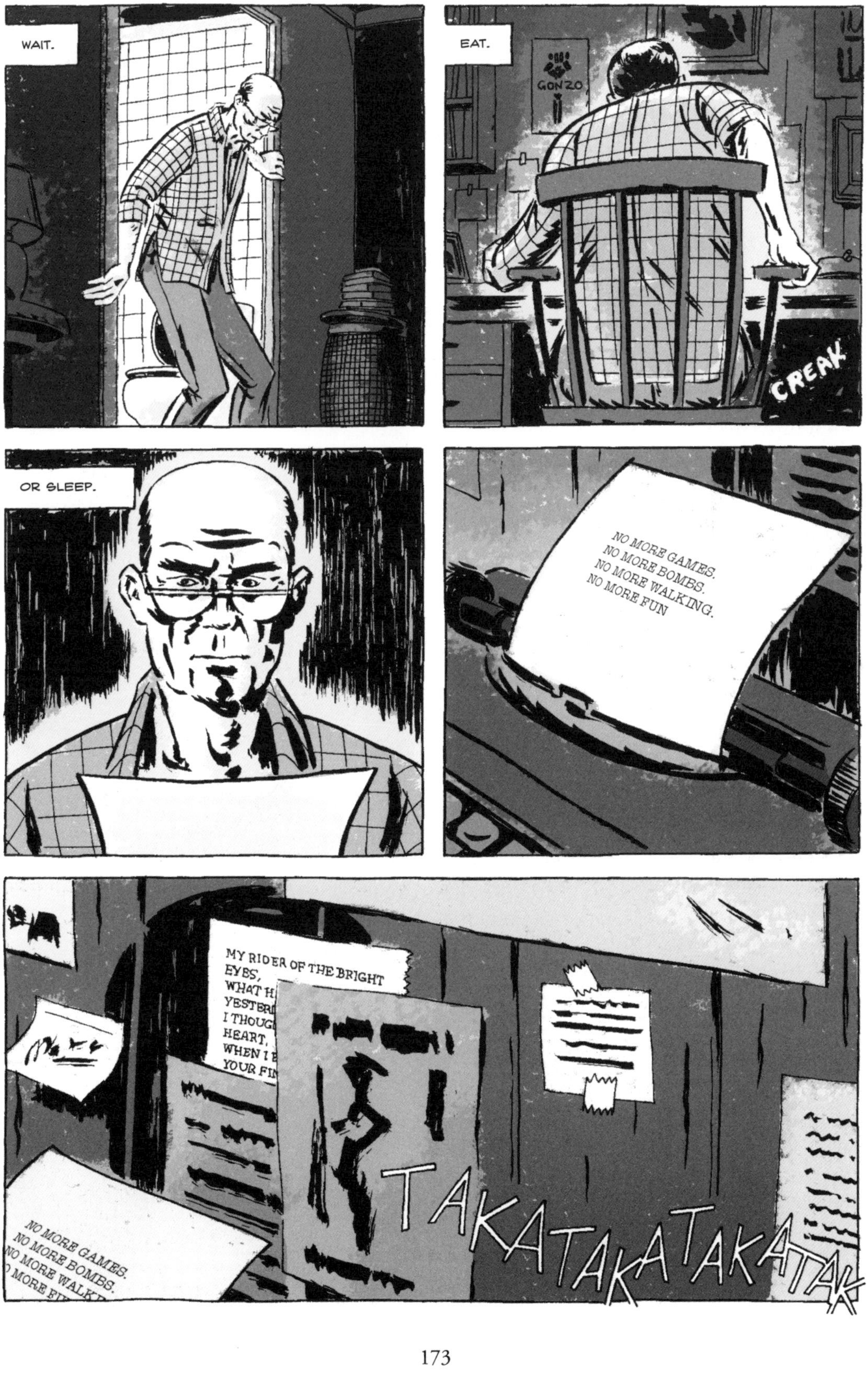
WAIT.
EAT.
GONZO
CREAK
OR SLEEP.
NO MORE GAMES.
NO MORE BOMBS.
NO MORE WALKING.
NO MORE FUN
MY RIDER OF THE BRIGHT
EYES,
HEART,
NO MORE GAMES.
NO MORE BOMBS.
TAKATAKATAKATAK

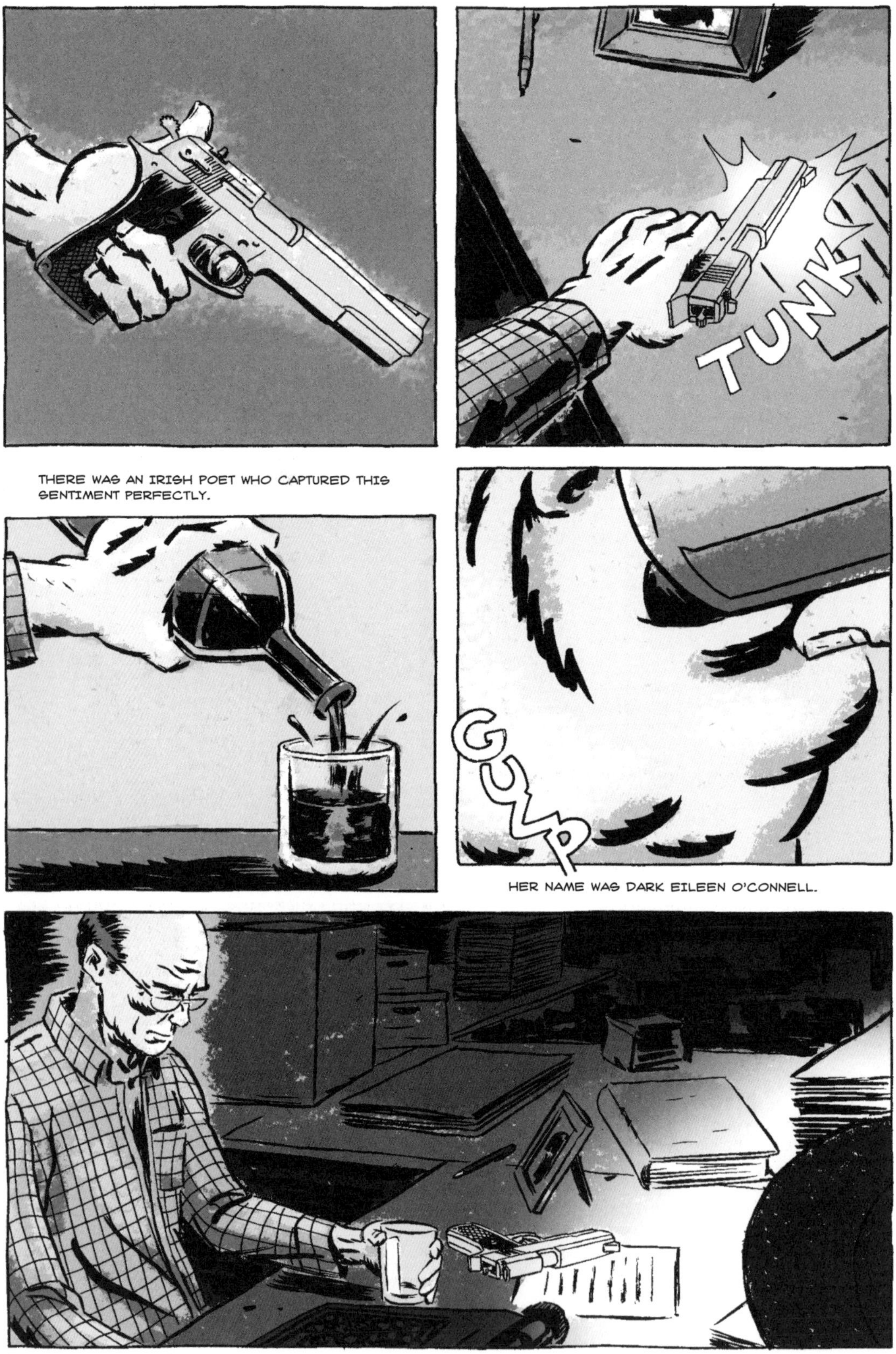
TUNK
THERE WAS AN IRISH POET WHO CAPTURED THIS SENTIMENT PERFECTLY.
GULP
HER NAME WAS DARK EILEEN O'CONNELL.

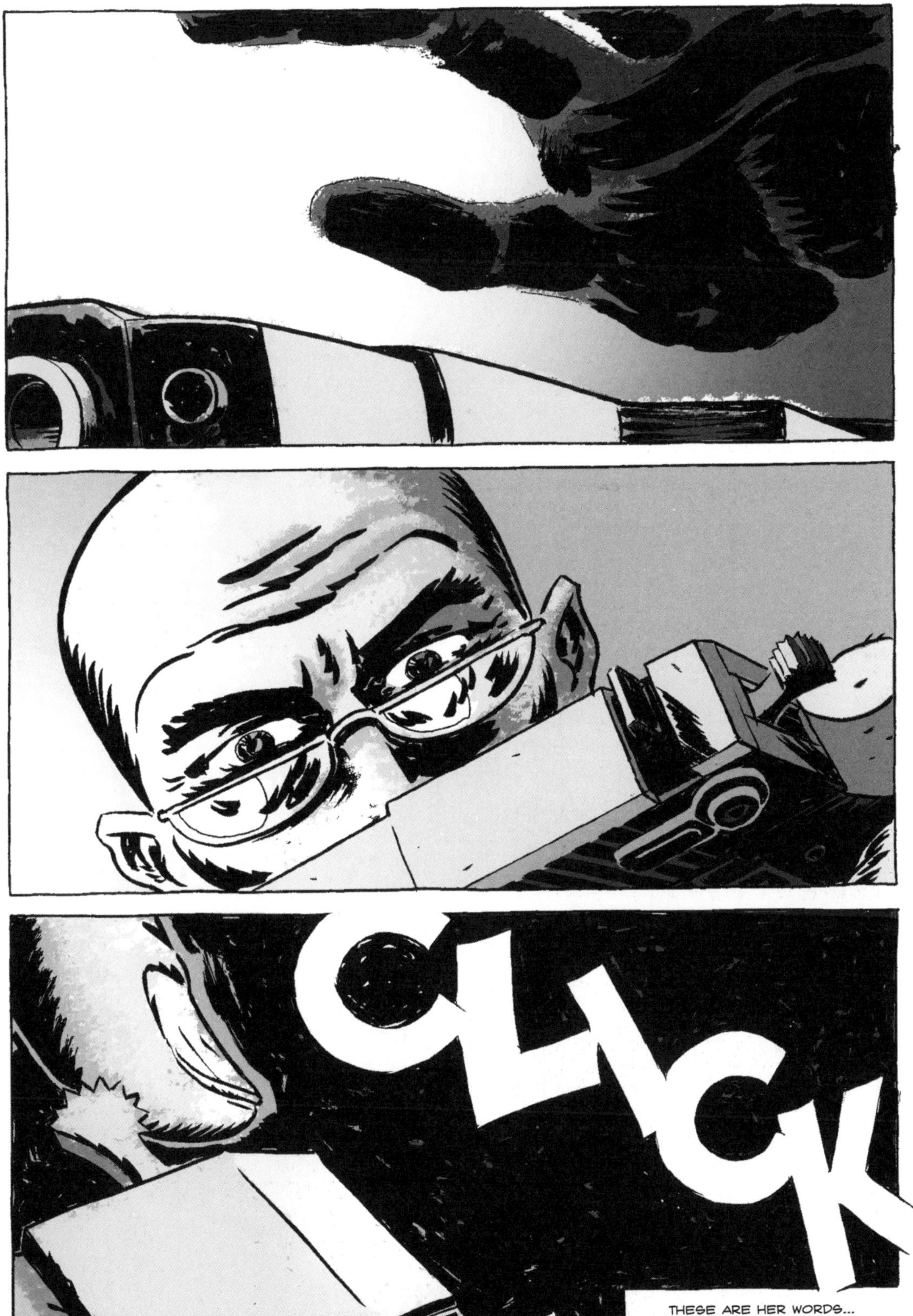
CLICK
THESE ARE HER WORDS...

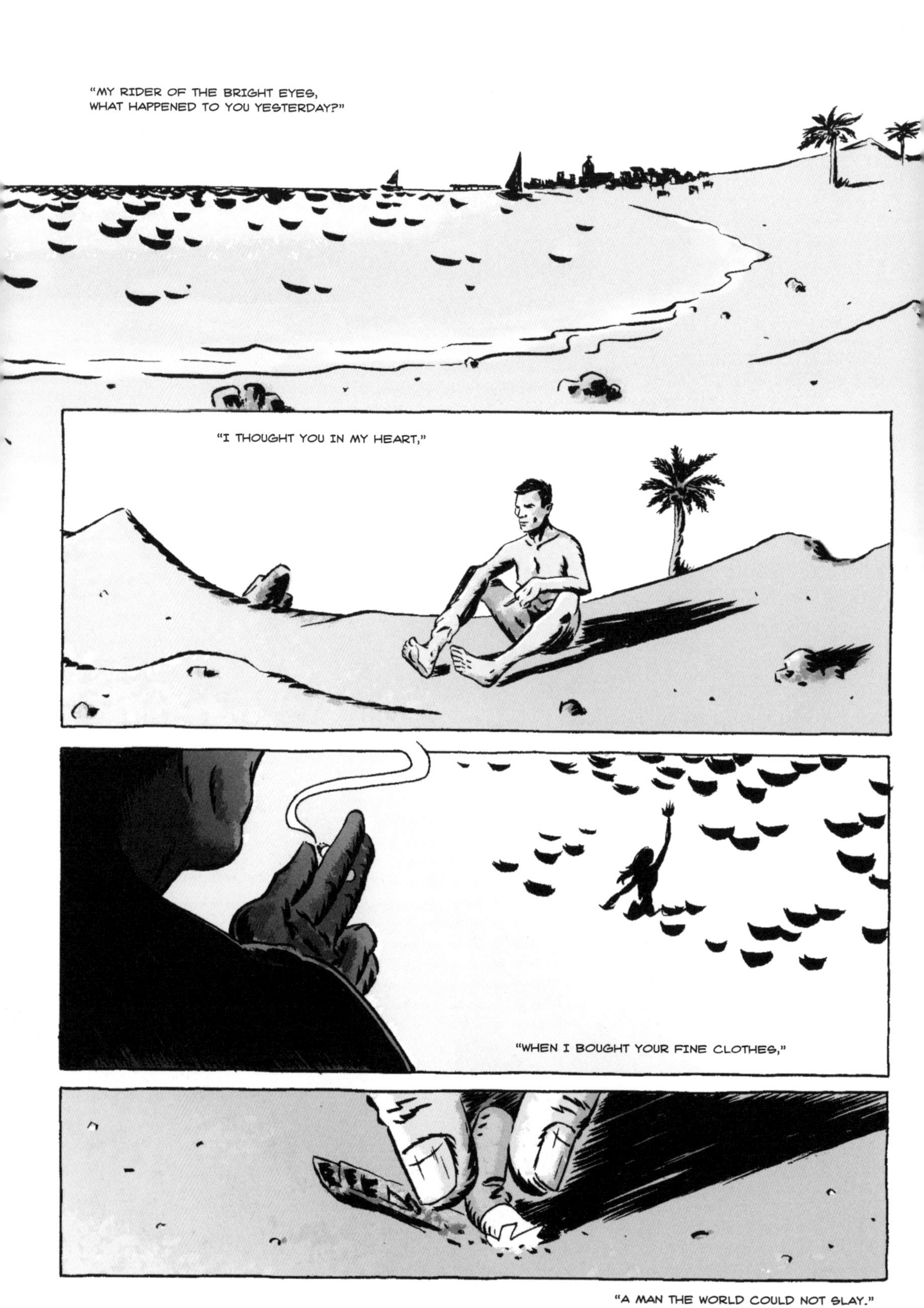
"MY RIDER OF THE BRIGHT EYES,
WHAT HAPPENED TO YOU YESTERDAY?"
"I THOUGHT YOU IN MY HEART,"
"WHEN I BOUGHT YOUR FINE CLOTHES,"
"A MAN THE WORLD COULD NOT SLAY."

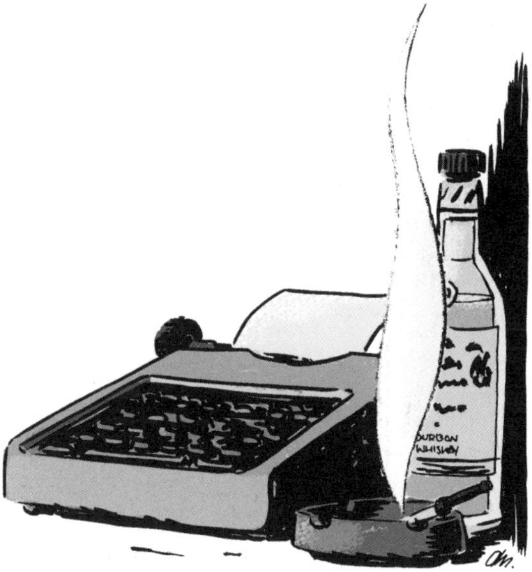
OURBON
WHISKEY

Big Sur: The Tropic of Henry Miller, Hunter S. Thompson (*Rogue Magazine*, 1961)

Hell's Angels: The Strange and Terrible Saga of the Outlaw Motorcycle Gangs,
    Hunter S. Thompson (Random House, 1966)

"The Kentucky Derby is Decadent and Depraved", Hunter S. Thompson, first printed
    Scanlan's Monthly 1970, second printing *The Great Shark Hunt*
    (Picador Books 1979)

Fear and Loathing in Las Vegas: A Savage Journey to the Heart of the American Dream,
    Hunter S. Thompson (Random House, 1971)

Autobiography of a Brown Buffalo, Oscar Zeta Acosta (Straight Arrow Books, 1972)

Fear and Loathing on the Campaign Trail '72, Hunter S. Thompson
    (Straight Arrow Books, 1973)

The Revolt of the Cockroach People, Oscar Zeta Acosta (Vintage Books, 2004)

The Great Shark Hunt: Strange Tales from a Strange Time, Hunter S. Thompson
    (Picador Books, 1979)

The Curse of Lono, Hunter S. Thompson and Ralph Steadman (Bantam Books, 1983)

Generation of Swine: Tales of Shame and Degradation in the '80s, Hunter S. Thompson
    (Picador Books, 1988)

Screwjack, Hunter S. Thompson (Simon and Schuster, 1991)

Songs of the Doomed: More Notes on the Death of the American Dream, Hunter S. Thompson
    (Pocket Books, 1991)

Better Than Sex: Confessions of a Political Junkie, Hunter S. Thompson
    (Ballantine Books, 1994)

Memoirs of Nixon, Richard M. Nixon (Buccaneer Books, 1994)

The Proud Highway: Saga of a Desperate Southern Gentleman 1955-1967,
    Hunter S. Thompson (Villard Books, 1997)

The Rum Diary, Hunter S. Thompson (Bloomsbury, 1998)

Fear and Loathing in America: The Brutal Odyssey of an Outlaw Journalist,
    Hunter S. Thompson (Bloomsbury, 2000)

Kingdom of Fear: Loathsome Secrets of a Star Crossed Child in the Final Days of the American Century, Hunter S. Thompson (Simon and Schuster, 2003)

The Boys on the Bus, Timothy Crouse (Random House, 2003)

Vintage Mencken, H.L. Mencken (Vintage Books, 2004)

Hey Rube: Blood Sport, The Bush Doctrine and the Downward Spiral of Dumbness: Modern History from the Sports Desk, Hunter S. Thompson (Simon and Schuster, 2005)

The Haight-Ashbury: A History, Charles Perry (Wenner, 2005)

Gonzo, Hunter S. Thompson (AMMO books, 2007)

Gonzo: The Life of Hunter S Thompson, Jann S. Wenner and Corey Seymour, (Sphere, 2007)

The Gonzo Way: A Celebration of Hunter S. Thompson, Anita Thompson (Fulcrum Publishing, 2007)

The Joke's Over: Bruised Memories: Gonzo, Hunter S. Thompson and Me, Ralph Steadman (Mariner Books 2007)

Ancient Gonzo Wisdom: Interviews with Hunter S. Thompson, (Picador, 2009)

Gonzo: The Art, Ralph Steadman (Houghton Mifflin Harcourt, 1998)

The Caoineadh, Dark Eileen O'Connell, circa 1773

Permissions

Will Bingley began self publishing comics at the age of 16 in his home county of Cornwall. In 2003 he moved to London, where he embarked on a career in the film industry, working as a scriptwriter and script-editor on several major studio productions, before moving into TV and advertising work.

He is currently a regular arts commentator in the UK press, contributor to several anthologies and journals and is in the process of completing his second graphic novel.

Anthony Hope-Smith studied graphic design and animation and now works as a professional illustrator. He has created visuals for advertising campaigns, videogame box art, book covers, children's book illustration and storyboards for television. His first love has always been comics. This is his first full length graphic novel.

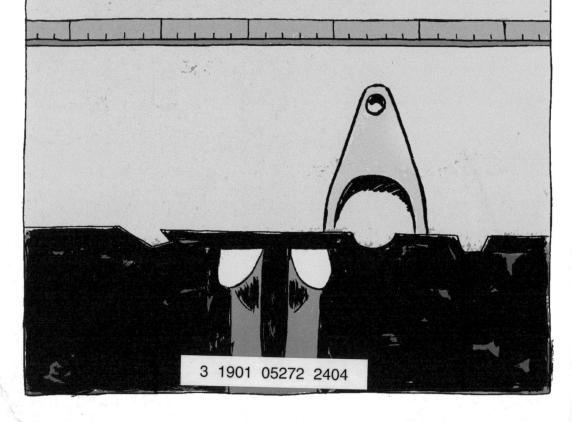